P9-AOD-088

Date Borrowed:

266.009   R1192
Woo   Woodbridge, John D.
             Ambassadors for
             Christ

DEMCO

AMBASSADORS
FOR CHRIST

AMBASSADORS FOR CHRIST

EDITED BY JOHN D. WOODBRIDGE

Immanuel Ref'd. Church
LIBRARY
No. 1192R

MOODY PRESS

CHICAGO

© 1994 by MOODY BIBLE INSTITUTE

All rights reserved. No part of this
book may be reproduced in any form
without permission in writing from
the publisher, except in the case of
brief quotations embodied in critical
articles or reviews.

All Scripture quotations, unless
indicated, are taken from the *Holy
Bible: New International Version*.
NIV. Copyright 1973, 1978, 1984
International Bible Society. Used by
permission of Zondervan Publishing
House. All rights reserved.

**Library of Congress Cataloging in
Publication Data**
Ambassadors for Christ / edited by
John D. Woodbridge.
    416p. 23cm.
    ISBN 0–8024–0939–3 : $24.99.
    1. Missionaries—Biography.
2. Evangelists—Biography.
3. Evangelicalism—Biography.
I. Woodbridge, John D., 1941–
BV3700.A53   1994
266′.0092′2—dc20   94–26560
[B]   CIP

Designed and produced for Moody
Press by Three's Company
12 Flitcroft Street
London WC2H 8DJ

Worldwide co-edition organized and
produced by Angus Hudson Ltd.,
Mill Hill,
London NW7 3SA
Tel + 44 181 959 3668
Fax + 44 181 959 3678

Printed in Singapore

Moody Press, a ministry of the
Moody Bible Institute, is designed for
education, evangelization, and
edification. If we may assist you in
knowing more about Christ and the
Christian life, please write us without
obligation: Moody Press, c/o MLM,
Chicago, Illinois 60610, U.S.A.

1 3 5 7 9 10 8 6 4 2

Immanuel Ref'd. Church
LIBRARY
No. *1192 R*

Contents

Authors

Bendroth, Margaret
Professor, Cambridge,
Massachusetts
Ira Sankey
Mel Trotter

Buss, Siegfried
Educator and missionary,
Tokyo, Japan
David and Joshua Tsutada

Dienert, Ruth Graham
Writer, Fort Lauderdale,
Florida
Ruth Bell Graham

Dorsett, Lyle
Professor, Wheaton, Illinois
Jonathan Goforth

Dretke, James
Professor and missiologist,
Pasadena, California
Samuel Marinus Zwemer

DuRant, Danielle
Writer, Norcross, Georgia
Ravi Zacharias

Erickson, Nancy
Professor, Due West,
South Carolina
David Livingstone

Fisher, David
Writer, Wheaton, Illinois
Peter Deyneka, Sr. and Jr.
Josef Tson

Fuller, Harold
Missionary and writer,
Ontario, Canada
James Hannington
Evangelist Wandaro

Genet, Harry
Writer and publicist,
Wheaton, Illinois
Dieumème Noelliste

Gilbert, Lela
Writer, Dana Point, California
Ted Engstrom

Gill, Ken
Librarian and missiologist,
Wheaton, Illinois
Amanda Smith

Gustavson, E. Brandt
Evangelical executive,
Manassas, Virginia
Paul E. Freed

Hefley, James
Writer and publisher,
Hannibal, Missouri
William Cameron Townsend

Hiebert, Paul
Professor and missiologist,
Deerfield, Illinois
Pandita Ramabai

Hinkson, Jon
Historian, Cambridge,
England
Nelson C. "Bud" Hinkson

Howard, David, Sr.
Missionary and writer,
Elgin, Illinois
Victor Landero

Hykes, Denise
Writer, New York City
Tom Maharias

Jenkins, Jerry
Writer, Zion, Illinois
Joe Gibbs
Sammy Tippit

Johnson, Lin
Writer, Niles, Illinois
Dr. Helen Roseveare

Keylock, Leslie
Professor and writer,
Chicago, Illinois
Ralph Winter

Kim, David
Professor, pastor, and
evangelical executive,
Seoul, Korea
Hyung-Ja Lee

Lam Wing-hung
Professor, Toronto, Canada
Wang Ming-tao

Lewis, Jonathan
Writer, Miami, Florida
Pedro Carrasco

Liefeld, Olive
Writer, Deerfield, Illinois
The Auca Five

Linder, Robert
Professor, Manhattan, Kansas
William Carey

Metzger, Will
Writer and student worker,
Newark, Delaware
Cliffe Knechtle

Millhouse, Martha
Writer, Dallas, Texas
Josh McDowell

Møller, Arvid and Gudveig
Writers, Norway
Sister Annie

Nettles, Thomas
Professor, Deerfield, Illinois
Lottie Moon

Norton, Will, Sr.
Professor and writer,
Charlotte, North Carolina
John and Betty Stam

O'Day, Joseph
Writer and editor,
Chicago, Illinois
The Guinness Family

Phiri, Isaac
Writer, Wheaton, Illinois
Tokunboh Adeyemo

Pierard, Richard
Professor, Terre Haute, Indiana
Karl F. A. Gützlaff

Pluedemann, James and Carol
Evangelical missionary
executive and writer,
Charlotte, North Carolina
Rowland Bingham

Pollock, John
Writer, South Molton, Devon,
England
Billy Graham

Raupp, Werner
Professor, Germany
Ludwig Ingwer Nommensen

Rawley, Phil
Writer, Mesquite, Texas
James Hudson Taylor

Reapsome, James
Writer and editor,
Wheaton, Illinois
The Howard Family

Rhoton, Elaine
Writer, Mosbach, Germany
Peter Beyerhaus
John "Praying" Hyde

Rowdon, Harold
Professor, Lymington, Hants,
England
Frederick W. Baedeker

Russell, Jay
Writer, Great Falls, Montana
Festo Kivengere

Schaeffer, Frank
Writer and film producer,
Salisbury, Massachusetts
Edith Schaeffer

Smith, Harold Ivan
Writer, speaker, consultant,
Kansas City, Missouri
Mary McLeod Bethune

Stewart, David
Pastor and writer,
Auckland, New Zealand
Muri Thompson

Sweeney, Doug
Historian,
Nashville, Tennessee
Peter Cartwright

Taylor, William
Missionary and evangelical
executive, Austin, Texas
Toward 2000

Tucker, Ruth
Professor and writer,
Grand Rapids, Michigan
Adoniram Judson

Vincent, James
Writer and editor,
Chicago, Illinois
Opportunity International

Weerts, Christine
Writer,
Mendenhall, Mississippi
John Perkins

Wells, John and Steve
Writers, West Chicago, Illinois
George Fisk

Whalin, Terry
Writer and editor,
Eden Prairie, Minnesota
Rómulo Sauñe

Wilkins, Rob
Writer, Zanesfield, Ohio
Guy Gardner
Bill Hybels

Woodbridge, John
Carl F. H. Henry

Wyrtzen, Don
Composer and writer,
Nashville, Tennessee
Steve Green

FOREWORD
Ambassadors for Christ

In ancient times the pomp and ceremony attendant to the daily life of a despotic king could be dazzling: the court decked out in rich tapestries and exotic ornaments from far-off regions of the world; an entourage of servants whisking about, attempting to satisfy the king's every wish and whim; ministers scurrying in and out, bearing news and gossip from the corners of the kingdom and abroad. The king would bark orders and expect action. Disobedience could mean death. Moreover, the king could demand booty and monies from peoples his armies had conquered in battle.

The king's ambassadors who represented him to other royal courts would often portray their master as powerful and shrewd— a major player with whom to reckon, either in the field of international relations or in any future war. The ambassadors themselves were officials of considerable wealth and worldly prestige. They often had ready access to the king's treasury from whence they could draw suitable bribes. After all, was it not true that gold coins dropped into the right hands could buy compliance with the king's wishes more easily than unleashing royal armies? Thus, to be an ambassador of a powerful king was to have clout and general access to this world's "pleasures."

When Jesus Christ walked the dusty hills and valleys of Palestine, He taught the crowds and His disciples about another kind of kingdom, His own. But what huge differences existed between His kingdom and those of despotic kings, the earlier kings of Israel, or Rome's client kings! This may explain why Christ's contemporaries often failed to understand His teaching about the nature of His kingdom. Some assumed that He was a political agitator and was planning militarily to overthrow the yoke of Roman domination in Israel. They thought He

really did want to become a political king, the "King of the Jews."

But how, then, could Christ's listeners interpret His assertion that His kingdom was not of this world? Would a hard-fisted political revolutionary say something like that? Also, Christ admonished those who would follow Him to love their enemies and to do good to them—an utterly outrageous thing for a king in antiquity to say. And what about that teaching concerning the meek inheriting the earth?

Even Christ's immediate disciples struggled to understand the nature of their master's kingdom. Even as late as His ascension into heaven, they were still asking, "Lord, are you at this time going to restore the kingdom to Israel?" (Acts 1:6).

Jesus' response must have struck them like a thunderbolt on a clear day. Rather than once again patiently explaining that His was not wholly a political kingdom, He proceeded to commission the disciples to be witnesses throughout the world. They were to be His "ambassadors" and represent a much more important kingdom than Israel or any other political state, including the Roman Empire.

No, they would not have a king's treasury to fund their campaign. No, they might not have resplendent clothes to symbolize that their king was wealthy and powerful. They might not enjoy worldly clout and pleasures. Yet the disciples undoubtedly sensed that their mission was more significant than any ever assigned to an ambassador for an earthly king. They were "sent ones," representing the very Son of God.

Theirs was a divine mission of enormous importance. They were to announce to all peoples throughout the world that Jesus Christ is Lord and the Savior of the world. He is the King of kings. What higher commission could a human being have than to be Christ's ambassador, His personal representative?

Amazingly enough, that is the very mission to which each one of us as a Christian has been called: to be an ambassador for Christ. We are all on an awesome assignment in this life.

The cost of being an ambassador

The mission of serving as Christ's ambassador is not necessarily an easy one. It certainly was not for the disciples, a number of whom, at least according to tradition, were martyred. For the apostle Paul, it led to a foul prison cell. But even in these dire circumstances Paul was determined to be a faithful ambassador for Christ: "Give yourselves wholly to prayer and entreaty; pray on every occasion in the power of the Spirit. To this end keep watch and persevere, always interceding for all God's people; and pray for me, that I may be granted the right words when I open my mouth, and may boldly and freely make known his hidden purpose, for which I am an ambassador—in chains." (Ephesians 6:18–20a; *New English Bible*).

No prestige or political clout were associated with Paul's mission station behind bars. But no discouragement was, either. Paul was planning to be a bold ambassador for Christ, even if physically bound by chains. Later, he too was apparently martyred.

Serving as an ambassador for Christ, then, can be very costly. But as Paul noted, he was counting on the prayers of his brothers and sisters in Christ to sustain him and give him boldness as he proclaimed the gospel.

In a similar fashion we should remember to pray for our own brothers and sisters in Christ, wherever they may be in the world, as they seek to pursue their mission as ambassadors for Christ. We should pray specifically that the Holy Spirit will be their strength.

The apostle Paul, then, was aware that he was an ambassador for Christ. He also reminded the Christians at Corinth about this role: "We . . . are Christ's ambassadors, as though God were making his appeal through us" (2 Corinthians 5:20). He represented Christ to them, and he anticipated

Ambassador to Nineveh: a relief from ancient Nineveh.

that they would represent Christ to others.

Paul was especially pleased with the Christians in Thessalonica, because it appeared that they understood well their mission as Christ's ambassadors. Paul rejoiced that the gospel had come to them, not in word only, "but also with power, with the Holy Spirit and with deep conviction" (1 Thessalonians 1:5). "In spite of severe suffering," they had received the Word "with the joy given by the Holy Spirit" (verse 6). Then the Thessalonians became models for Christian believers in Macedonia and Achaia. And finally, they sounded out the Word of the Lord, "not only in Macedonia and Achaia," but "everywhere" (verse 8). The Thessalonians had truly become Great Commission people.

From Western faith to global faith

Throughout the history of the church there have been many "Thessalonian" Christians, those who have proclaimed the Word of the Lord as ambassadors for Christ. This book tells some of their fascinating and inspiring stories. It focuses especially upon those Christians from various walks of life who in the nineteenth and twentieth centuries helped turn Christianity into the worldwide faith that it is today. For at the turn of the nineteenth century, Christianity was essentially restricted to the lands of the West.

The introduction, "Winning the World for Christ," sets the scene by describing the condition of the evangelical Christian faith on the eve of the eighteenth century.

Thereafter follow the stories of select men and women who, in the next two hundred years, helped make this period a time of stunning Christian growth throughout the world.

Finally, a concluding discussion furnishes a perspective on trends both positive and less encouraging within worldwide evangelical Christianity at the dawn of the third millennium. It emphasizes the dramatic and wonderful changes taking place, particularly in the last twenty years, as non-Westerners begin to play an even more significant role in the fulfillment of the Great Commission. Christianity has truly become a transcultural, global faith.

A well-kept secret

For many of us, it will be encouraging news to learn that, as the third millennium approaches, evangelical Christianity is spreading with surprising speed in certain quarters of the world. Those who live in the West might have surmised that the wearing effects of secularism, which are only too evident in our societies, meant the lagging growth of the Christian faith throughout the world. This simply is not so. By God's grace the growth of Christianity is nothing less than staggering. The statistics found in the conclusion confirm this otherwise hard-to-believe affirmation.

But statistics can be impersonal and sometimes misleading. Perhaps even more encouraging, the stories of the ambassadors for Christ described in this volume will provide us with specific illustrations of how God, the Holy Spirit, has worked and is working in our world today. These stories are of flesh-and-blood men and women, people not much different from ourselves. In fact, they faced some of the very same problems we confront on a daily basis. But even with their weaknesses, the Lord used them in outstanding ways, just as He can use *us* as we depend upon the Holy Spirit's power. Their stories of faith are inspiring.

A rich mix

How did we select the particular individuals whose stories grace these pages? Initially, Tim Dowley of Three's Company in London, England, proposed a list of candidates from the nineteenth and twentieth centuries. Then I met with staff members of Moody Press, and names were added and subtracted. As the sifting process continued, Galen Hiestand, the North American representative of World Evangelical Fellowship graciously proposed the names of some non-Western Christians who he thought deserved our careful consideration. A number of these were added to our list. Various colleagues from different colleges and divinity schools also made suggestions. Slowly the list was firmed up and became what you see in this volume.

We know that there are thousands upon thousands of individuals whose stories deserve to be told just as much as some of the stories found within the covers of this book. The church of Jesus Christ has many wonderful and faithful ambassadors for Christ.

We sought to include persons like Billy and Ruth Graham who would be well-known to an evangelical public. But we also wanted to introduce less well-known persons from other quarters of the globe. Thus, the stories of a good number of non-Western Christians appear within the pages of this book.

Moreover, some of these individuals come from walks of life other than that of pastor or missionary. We are all ambassadors for Christ, whether student, housewife, engineer, auto mechanic, painter, day laborer, musician, nurse, teacher, or preacher, whether retired or still working.

Words of thanks

I would be remiss if I did not thank most sincerely a number of people who made this project possible. Whatever merit this book might possess is due to the accomplished authors who so graciously and skillfully crafted the stories that make up its contents. Almost without exception, the writers submitted essays I found both instructive and inspiring. It was a genuine delight to be a colaborer with each of these fine authors from various corners of the world.

John Fea and Don Anderson deserve a

special word of thanks for their work in editing texts and sorting through many of the details associated with the realization of this project. Galen Hiestand and William Taylor, both of World Evangelical Fellowship, and David Howard, Sr., formerly of InterVarsity and the World Evangelical Fellowship, graciously and patiently educated me regarding recent developments within world Christianity. Without their counsel, this book would not have taken on its obvious world Christian perspective. Their commitment to the spread of the gospel worldwide is so attractive, so infectious, so worthy of imitation. Also, I want to express a word of thanks to Dr. Kenneth Gill and the staff of the Billy Graham Center at Wheaton College for their help in locating photos and graphics.

To all of these and many others, I express deep gratitude.

A final word

When I began working on this project, I did not understand fully where it would take me. It is difficult to explain personal sentiments when they are deeply felt. But after watching David Tsutada pray for his family while in a prison cell during World War II, after observing Ruth Graham calmly but firmly give her Christian testimony to the rulers of Communist China, after sensing the Christian compassion of Pandita Ramabai for the homeless widows of India, after trekking with Samuel Zwemer on camelback through the hot deserts of Saudi Arabia, after witnessing the outpouring of the Holy Spirit in the Solomon Islands during the preaching of Muri Thompson, after sensing tremendous loss when John and Betty Stam were slain by Communists but great joy that their little baby survived, after observing the remarkable boldness of Jonathan Goforth, I came to a better understanding of what the power of the gospel has accomplished in the lives of these Christians. But they represent millions of others, for their lives give further testimony that the gospel is the power of God unto salvation. These Christians, empowered by the Holy Spirit, faithfully served at their assigned posts.

I hope that you, the reader, will also experience the same kind of encouragement in your Christian walk as you learn more about these men and women who have faithfully served the King of kings. For if you have committed your life to Christ as Lord and Savior, you also are an "ambassador for Christ."

John D. Woodbridge

Winning the World for Christ
STILL A DAUNTING TASK IN A.D. 1800

Just before His ascension into heaven, Jesus Christ commissioned His disciples to be His witnesses in Jerusalem, in all Judea, and in Samaria and unto the uttermost parts of the earth (Acts 1:8). But Christ did not furnish them with many details about their mission. He did not tell them how vast the world was. He did not mention how many peoples and tribes were scattered throughout the various continents. He did not indicate how much time might elapse before His commission would be fulfilled. All the disciples knew was that they were commissioned to be witnesses and that they were going to be endowed with power from the Holy Spirit. Each disciple had received his high calling of service—to be an ambassador for Christ.

The disciples and other early Christians took Christ's marvelous charge to engage in world evangelization seriously. With great compassion, and often at immense personal sacrifice, they presented the gospel to their neighbors and friends and headed off for distant lands. Thomas may have even reached India with the Christian faith.

And yet by 1800, nearly eighteen centuries later, the fulfillment of Christ's Great Commission still remained hugely daunting for contemporary Christians. Despite colonial and missionary settlements in the "New World" and in Africa, India, China, and Japan, Christianity remained mostly bottled up in the West. And even in the West, many believers were reeling before an anti-Christian tide.

A bleak future

From several points of view, the future of Christianity looked uncertain in the 1790s, not only on the continent of Europe but in Great Britain and in her former colony, the fledgling United States. The French had let loose anti-Christian furies in Europe during the Revolution of 1789. The English were preoccupied by their deadly struggle with the French.

Believers in the United States were troubled by the spiritually deadening presence of radical strains of their own "Enlightenment." For example, at Yale College in the early 1790s, few students were proclaimed to be Christians. Lyman Beecher, who entered the school in 1793, recalled that the college "was in a most ungodly state. . . . Boys that dressed flax in the barn, as I used to, read Tom Paine and believed him; I read, and fought him all the way. Never had any propensity to infidelity. But most of the class before me were infidels, and called each other Voltaire, Rousseau, D'Alembert. . . ." Moreover, a number of Protestants on the east coast were much more worried about trying to "save the West" in the United States from deism, superstition, and Roman Catholicism than about sending missionaries to far-off foreign shores.

Then again, there was the enormity of the task of reaching the non-Christian world with the gospel. Put simply, beyond the Western nations, the world was overwhelmingly non-Christian. Patrick Johnstone informs us that in the year 1800, Europe, North America, Australia, and New Zealand together accounted for 99 percent of Christians within the world (defining the term "Christian" broadly), whereas the vast regions of Asia, Latin America, Africa, most of the South Pacific, the Caribbean, and the Middle East could only account for 1 percent of the world's Christians. What an incredibly difficult task faced those in the West who hoped to reach the non-Western world for Christ.

Despite overseas efforts carried on by Pietist missionaries from Halle, Germany, in

Lyman Beecher (1775–1863).

Use Means for the Conversion of the Heathen (1792), William Carey proposed that Christ's commission to preach the gospel throughout the world remained an obligation for all Christians. Carey also advocated the formation of voluntary societies of laypersons and pastors to support missionary endeavors.

Admittedly, those who promoted an interest in missions sometimes engaged in activities that could not be easily distinguished from the larger designs of Western governments to explore, conquer, and economically exploit portions of the non-Western world. Western missionaries on occasion worked all too intimately with their own national colonizing governments. This sowed understandable suspicions among some indigenous peoples that the missionaries' real motivations were more colonial and economic than evangelistic.

But to explain the vast Protestant missionary movement of the nineteenth century in terms of European tactics for colonization, or improved communications, or the weakening power of Islam and Hinduism, or the faltering condition of Roman Catholic missionary efforts after the French Revolution, is to overlook the repeated testimony of many of the missionaries themselves. Often they declared unequivocally that their chief desire was to bring the "heathen" to a saving knowledge of Jesus Christ. Some Americans had been influenced by postmillennial eschatology and believed that their efforts might help usher in Christ's kingdom on earth. Or they may have been personally touched by Evangelical awakenings in their countries. These spiritual awakenings and revivals in particular go a long way in explaining why a growing number of men and women were willing to risk their very lives as ambassadors for Christ in far-off and sometimes dangerous lands. Kenneth Scott Latourette makes this point very well in *Christianity in a Revolutionary Age* (1958–62):

The striking improvements in communication and the rapid growth of the commerce and the empires of Western peoples were important factors. The breakdown of non-European cultures under the impact of Western peoples weakened the resistance to Christianity. All of these, however, would have been of no avail had they not been

the late seventeenth century, or by the Society for the Propagation of the Gospel founded in 1701, or by Moravian Brethren missionaries from Herrenhut, Germany, in the 1730s, there were relatively few Protestant missionaries trying to reach vast areas of the world with their huge non-Christian populations. When the new nineteenth century dawned, not many more than one hundred evangelical foreign missionaries, generally from Britain and the United States, were scattered throughout the world. Little wonder, then, that the distinguished historian of missions, Stephen Neill wrote: "In 1800 it was still by no means certain that Christianity would be successful in turning itself into a world religion."

Renewed glimmers of Christian hope

And yet in the last decade of the eighteenth century and in the early decades of the nineteenth a burgeoning interest in spreading the gospel to the ends of the earth simultaneously began to manifest itself more clearly among Evangelicals in Britain. In *An Enquiry into the Obligation of Christians to*

paralleled by the burst of new life within Christianity itself. It was this surge of vitality which was the primary cause of the daring vision, the comprehensive plans, the offering of life and money which sent missionaries to all quarters of the globe.

Indeed, the awakenings generated interest in prayer and sparked calls for world evangelization.

For example, in the United States, revival fires once again were burning strongly in the 1790s in the Connecticut Valley. Even Yale College, where radical "Enlightenment" thought seemed so prevalent, was touched by the Spirit of God. In 1795 Timothy Dwight, the grandson of Jonathan Edwards, assumed the presidency of Yale College. He promptly challenged antagonistic students to a debate concerning the question, "Is the Bible the Word of God?" With Dwight's decisive victory in the debate, "infidelity" fled Yale, or so said a contemporary account. In 1802, seventy-five students out of a student body of 225 were converted to Christ. During the next decades a series of awakenings graced other colleges and prompted coteries of young persons to consider Christian ministries. In 1806 at the famous Haystack Prayer Meeting near Williams College, Massachusetts, Samuel Mills (1793–1818) and his colleagues determined to become missionaries. Other awakenings stimulated a number of young men to dedicate their lives to foreign missionary service. The "heavenly fire" of revival was also burning rapidly in Kentucky and Tennessee. Soon the fire spread to other states.

The Second Great Awakening was ablaze, largely fueled in its Western phase by Baptist and Presbyterian preachers and Methodist circuit riders, and in the Eastern cities by evangelist Charles Finney. The Awakening would last until the 1840s. It helped provide a spiritual impetus to many of the personnel of the new voluntary missionary societies, whether these societies focused on "Home Missions" or foreign missions.

On the continent of Europe, various Evangelical awakenings took place in Germany, Switzerland, and France and had a similar effect in stirring the hearts of young men and women to consider overseas missionary work. For example, in 1810 Robert Haldane led an awakening in Switzerland. In the British Isles, Christmas Evans

> We too are commissioned to be "ambassadors for Christ."

and John Elias were instrumental in awakenings in Wales. Earlier, in the late eighteenth century, John Wesley, one of the principal leaders of the British evangelical awakening, had sent Methodist missionaries Francis Asbury and Thomas Coke to North America.

The "Great Century"

By the 1820s a first wave of recruits of the modern missionary movement had already arrived on foreign shores. In 1793, William Carey (1761–1834) and his family had sailed for India and ultimately settled in the Danish territory of Serampore. Carey represented the Particular Baptist Society for the Propagating of the Gospel among the Heathen. In 1807, Robert Morrison (1782–1834), representing the London Misionary

By the 1820s a host of voluntary missionary societies had come into existence:

1792 The Particular Baptist Society for Propagating the Gospel Among the Heathen

1795 The London Missionary Society

1796 The Scottish Missionary Society and Glasgow Missionary Society

1797 The Netherlands Missionary Society

1799 Church Missionary Society for Africa and the East

1804 British and Foreign Bible Society

1809 London Society for Promoting Christianity Amongst the Jews

1810 American Board of Commissioners for Foreign Missions

1814 Baptist General Convention for Missions

1818 The Methodist Missionary Society

1822 Paris Evangelical Missionary Society

1825 Bombay Missionary Union

Robert Morrison, the first Protestant missionary to China.

Society, sailed for Canton, China, becoming the first Protestant missionary to that vast land. Even after determined efforts, he witnessed only ten baptisms before his death in 1834. The American Adoniram Judson (1788–1850) and his wife Ann began their ministry first in Calcutta, India, and a year later in Burma. Judson would be arrested and languish in prison for a number of years. And in 1817, Robert Moffatt (1795–1883) commenced his work with the Tswana tribe in southern Africa. In 1822, Lott Cary (ca. 1780–1828), a freed American slave from Virginia, planted a Baptist church in Monrovia, Liberia, thereby becoming the first American missionary to Africa.

By the 1820s a host of voluntary missionary societies had come into existence. These voluntary societies often sought monies and recruits across denominational lines.

As increasing numbers of Western Christians tackled the daunting task of winning the world for Christ, the "Great Century" of Protestant world missions was born. It would stretch from 1815 (the end of the Napoleonic Wars) to 1914 (the beginning of World War I).

It is one thing to describe in general terms this movement of Western ambassadors for Christ who threw themselves into the work of proclaiming the matchless gospel to the ends of the world; it is quite another to sense what these people actually experienced. Many of the missionaries encountered enormous hardships ranging from lack of financial and prayer support by Christians at home, the death of a dear spouse or precious little children on the mission field, agonizing feelings of loneliness, invasive life-threatening diseases, to genuine hostility manifested by the very peoples whom they were trying to reach with the gospel. If we are to identify in some sense with the personal sacrifice and the struggles of these Christians, as well as with their faith and joy in the Lord, we would be well served to read the stories of a number of the men and women who were ambassadors for Christ.

Interestingly enough, some of the most effective ambassadors for Christ were not traditional Western "missionaries." A number were non-Western converts who became witnesses for Christ themselves. Several came from walks of life other than the pastoral ministry and brought their skills from their professions to the work of world evangelization. Once again, it becomes clear that all believers, whatever their ethnic background and social background, are in fact ambassadors for Christ.

During the nineteenth century Western Christians with indigenous converts laid a solid foundation for world evangelization. Today Westerners continue to be joined by thousands upon thousands of non-Western co-laborers in the common quest to fulfill the Great Commission. Particularly, within the last twenty years, these non-Western missionaries have advanced the cause of Christ dramatically in regions of the world where Westerners have had little access or success.

Christianity a global faith

On the eve of the third millennium Christianity has become a global faith. Probably more people are coming to Christ today than in any other period in the history of the church. Once again, Christianity is surging forward as one of the fastest growing religions upon planet earth. Undaunted by obstacles and willing to risk life itself, many ambassadors for Christ from all corners of the globe are proclaiming the wonderful news: "Jesus Christ is the Way, the Truth, and the Life." He alone is the Savior of our sin-sick world. He alone is Lord and worthy of worship.

From a human point of view Christ's commission for world evangelization still remains daunting. But the possibility that it may be fulfilled seems much closer today than it did in 1800. The following inspiring stories of flesh-and-blood persons from the nineteenth and twentieth centuries will help us to understand better why this is the case.

Moreover, these stories should encourage each one of us to reflect more seriously about what our own role might be in the wonderful task of world evangelization. For if we name the name of Christ, our Lord's commission to his disciples is also our own. We too are commissioned to be "ambassadors for Christ."

John D. Woodbridge

Missionary Pioneers

GOD'S EXTRAORDINARY PLODDER

William Carey

1761–1834

The story of William Carey's extraordinary accomplishments began in 1775 in the most ordinary of circumstances—in a shoemaker's modest residence in the obscure village of Piddington in the English Midlands. The fourteen-year-old Carey had been apprenticed to Clarke Nichols to learn the cobbler's trade, a craft that would provide his basic income until he was twenty-eight years old. Nichols's other apprentice at the time was another teenager named John Warr, and the two boys soon became close friends.

Like many teenage boys of that era, Carey and Warr frequently talked about their trade, their future, young women, sports, and religion. However, their discussions of religion sometimes strained their friendship because Warr was a fervent Christian who attended a nearby Dissenters Chapel, and he frequently witnessed to Carey concerning his need to repent of his sins and accept Christ as his Savior. Carey, who had been baptized in the Church of England, protested vigorously that he was already a church member and, therefore, had no need to repent. However, he later confessed: "Of real experimental religion, I scarcely heard anything till I was fourteen years of age."

In any case, after months of hot shoe shop debates in which Carey nearly always had the last—but never the final—word, he experienced a crisis of faith in which he at last faced the gravity of his sinfulness and his inability to save himself. After much hesitation and excuse making, Carey yielded his life to Jesus Christ. Consequently, he abandoned lying, cheating, swearing, and what he called "unchaste conversation," and dedicated his life to God. He soon began to accompany his friend John Warr to the little Dissenters meeting house in nearby Hackelton. Little did the Christians of Hac-

> *After months of hot debates Carey experienced a crisis of faith.*

kelton Chapel realize that the young man they welcomed into their midst would one day become the leader in establishing a movement that would literally transform church structures and innumerable lives and cultures.

Young William Carey
Today, William Carey's general significance in the history of missions is universally acknowledged. Noted historian Kenneth Scott Latourette, for example, declared that Carey's career was "one of the most notable in the entire history of the expansion of Christianity." But how did this obscure, plodding young man from the hinterland of England become known as "the Founder of Modern Missions" and perhaps the most famous Christian missionary in the history of the world?

Carey was born on August 17, 1761, in the village of Paulerspury, in Northamptonshire, in central England. At the time, the First British Empire was at its height but was soon to lose most of its valuable North American colonies. It was the century of the First Great Awakening and Jonathan Edwards in America and of the Wesleyan Revival in Britain. It was also the Age of Reason, as the period of the Enlightenment in Europe is often called. And in the offing, within a generation of Carey's birth, were the unsettling French Revolution of 1789 and the consequent Napoleonic Wars that would involve the Great Powers of Europe. Carey's life would be affected by all of these developments.

William Carey (1761–1834).

William Carey is almost universally acknowledged by church historians as "the Founder of the Modern Missionary Movement" and one of the most important Christian missionaries in world history. From poverty, obscure beginnings, and a disadvantaged background in rural eighteenth-century England, Carey emerged as the driving force in the establishment of the modern missionary movement.

Beginning in the late 1780s, young Pastor Carey began to agitate within his denomination for an organized and sustained effort to spread the gospel overseas. After publishing his powerful and now famous [An] Enquiry into the Obligations of Christians to Use Means for the Conversion of the Heathen and the preaching of his equally powerful and famous sermon "Expect Great Things— Attempt Great Things," both in 1792, Carey and his family became part of the first wave of missionaries sent out by the newly formed Baptist Missionary Society. In the end, he left behind a vigorous indigenous Indian Christian community, translations of the Bible in all the major languages of the Indian subcontinent, and an inspiring example of Christian courage and dedication that moved thousands of others to follow in his steps.

A self-described "plodder," Carey was more than that. It was his dogged determination and inspired leadership that marked the beginning of a movement that would literally transform church structures and innumerable lives and cultures. In this, Carey the obscure young preacher who came from a remote part of England representing a small and insignificant religious group, would become "God's extraordinary plodder" who changed the course of history.

Eighteenth-century England was a time of affluence, leisure, and literary pleasures for most aristocrats, merchants, and professional people. But for the common folk, it was a period of hardship and frequent injustice. In a still overwhelmingly rural society, the ordinary citizen had few rights and many obligations and restrictions. Harsh treatment of criminals (including "transportation" to Georgia before 1775 and to Australia after 1788), inhumane treatment of the mentally ill, cruel game laws, significant poverty, widespread illiteracy, and legal discrimination against Nonconformists (non-Anglican Protestants) and Roman Catholics were all commonplace during Carey's youth.

Carey's father was a weaver, schoolteacher, and parish clerk of the village Church of England. This meant that he was a somewhat learned but poor villager who led a simple and uncomplicated rural existence. Young William's childhood was fairly routine except that he had problems with allergies that prevented him from pursuing his urge to become a gardener, and he was,

The Life of William Carey

1761	Born at Paulerspury, Northamptonshire, England
1775	Apprenticed to a shoemaker in Piddington, England, where a fellow cobbler, John Warr, leads him to faith in Christ
1781	Marries Dorothy Plackett at Piddington
1789	Begins ministry as pastor of the Baptist church in Harvey Lane, Leicester
1792	Publishes *An Enquiry into the Obligations of Christians to Use Means for the Conversion of the Heathen*
	Preaches "Expect Great Things—Attempt Great Things"
	Present in Kettering at the founding of the Particular Baptist Society for Propagating the Gospel Among the Heathen
1793	Commissioned as a missionary to India
1794	After five-month voyage, disembarks near Calcutta
	Five-year-old son Peter dies from fever
1797	Completes first draft of the Bengali New Testament
1800	Baptizes Krishna Pal, first native Indian converted to Christ through his ministry
1801	First Bengali New Testament printed by the Serampore Press
1807	Publishes Sanskrit New Testament; granted the doctor of divinity degree by Brown University
1807	Dorothy Carey dies
1808	Marries Charlotte Rumohr
1812	Serampore printing presses and manuscripts destroyed by great fire
1818	Serampore College established
1820	Organizes the Agricultural Society of India
1821	Charlotte Carey dies
1822	Marries Grace Hughes
1828	Serampore Mission severs ties with the BMS
1834	Dies at Serampore and buried there

BANGLADESH

INDIA • Calcutta

by all accounts, precocious. Limited in formal education, he nevertheless quickly mastered not only English but also Latin, Greek, Hebrew, Dutch, and French. He also loved history and geography and enjoyed studying what today would be called botany and horticulture.

However, as was the custom of the day, his impoverished parents tried to find young Carey a suitable trade as soon as possible. Thus, he was apprenticed at age fourteen to shoemaker Nichols, and continued in that vocation for another fourteen years. During that same period, he also took on the additional jobs of schoolteaching and preaching—not unusual for that day when needs were great and monetary rewards for such professions were minimal. In the years following his conversion to Christ, Carey devoted himself to Bible study and lay ministries. Eventually, he became convinced of the necessity of believer's baptism by immersion and on October 5, 1783, at the age of twenty-three, duly arranged for the ordinance at the hands of a Baptist minister.

Baptist pastor

During this period of rapid spiritual growth and change, Carey married Dorothy Plackett, the illiterate daughter of a poor farmer with a large family. When they exchanged vows on June 10, 1781, in Piddington, Dorothy was twenty-five and Carey not yet quite twenty. Dorothy became a minister's wife when Carey accepted the pastorate of the Moulton Baptist Chapel in 1785. At the same time, Carey taught school and continued his work as a cobbler in order to support a growing family amid grinding poverty. Two years later, William Carey was ordained a Baptist minister. The stage was set for Carey's historical call to missions.

Despite economic hardships, Carey did not cease his study of the larger world, which included reading Captain James Cook's account of his journey to the South Seas. Carey also read Jonathan Edwards and followed closely the work of John Eliot and David Brainerd among the American Indians. In addition, he made and hung a huge world map on the wall of his Moulton cottage on which he indicated the latest religious and political statistics of the different countries as he was able to obtain them. Thus, he began to develop a biblical

perspective on missions and soon became convinced that foreign evangelism was a central responsibility of the church.

Carey's ideas were revolutionary. Many eighteenth-century English church leaders were convinced Calvinists who believed that the Great Commission was given only to the apostles, and the conversion of the overseas world of their day was none of their concern. Most simply had not given the matter much serious thought. In this context, Carey raised the question: Should not the gospel be taken to all the people of the world? Captivated by this vision, Carey talked incessantly about what might be done. He raised the question among his ministerial colleagues of the Northamptonshire Baptist Association, only to be rebuffed by the otherwise kindly old Calvinist Baptist minister John Collett Ryland, who, according to a probably somewhat embellished story, told Carey, "Young man, sit down. When God pleases to convert the heathen, he will do it without your aid or mine!"

Carey refused to be silenced. Instead, he combined the fact that he was a child of the Wesleyan revival with the fact that he was also a child of the Enlightenment and worked out his response. Convinced that Christianity and reason were completely compatible, Carey used his mind to make connections.

As historian Kenneth Manley has pointed out, "Carey conducted an *Enquiry*. He gathered facts, and drew conclusions." All of Carey's Baptist contemporaries knew the Scriptures and many knew about Cook's journeys. But it was Carey who saw the interdependence of the gospel message and Cook's voyages, and the obligations of the missionary enterprise. He insisted on the relevance of this interdependence for Christian practice. The result was a book that has become a classic presentation of the case for missionary work: *An Enquiry into the Obligations of Christians to Use Means for the Conversion of the Heathen*, published in Leicester in the spring of 1792. Carey's volume was a clear statement of a rationale for

William Carey shows his world map to villagers of Moulton.

> *He made and hung a huge world map on the wall of his cottage.*

> ## The impact of the sermon was direct and immediate.

missions that opened the eyes of many Christians to the worldwide dimension of missions and provided a new model for missionary organization. His overpowering conclusion was that Christian missions is not an *option* but a *duty*.

Shortly after the publication of his book, Carey preached at an Association meeting at Nottingham—again hammering away at his theme of taking the gospel to all the people of the world. The sermon has not survived, but his text was Isaiah 54:2: "Enlarge the place of thy tent, stretch thy tent curtains wide, do not hold back; lengthen thy cords, strengthen thy stakes." It was a stirring missionary appeal with two points: (1) expect great things, and (2) attempt great things. (The familiar form of these points, which adds "from God" and "for God," while entirely consistent with Carey's spirit and theology, seems to have been a later addition.)

The impact of the sermon was direct and immediate, and few sermon headings have been so frequently cited. The sermon and Carey's persistent lobbying finally won over Andrew Fuller, one of the most prominent Baptist ministers of the era. By the close of this associational meeting the next day, those in attendance voted to establish a foreign missions organization. It was a serious undertaking for most of those present who, like Carey, lived on meager incomes. Involvement in foreign missions would mean tremendous financial sacrifices for both them and their congregations.

At the following Association meeting at Kettering on October 2, 1792, the gathered Baptists made the momentous decision to form the Particular Baptist Society for the Propagation of the Gospel—later simply the Baptist Missionary Society (BMS). Twelve ministers, one theological student, and one layperson subscribed 13 pounds, 1 shilling, and 6 pence to begin the organization. Andrew Fuller was named the society's first home secretary.

The BMS's first appointee was the erratic visionary John Thomas, a Baptist layman who had gone to India as a medical doctor with the Royal Navy and stayed on as a free-

lance evangelist. Now, back in England, he wanted to return to India to minister. Carey offered himself to the new society as a suitable companion to Thomas and was immediately accepted. At first Carey had thought in terms of going to Tahiti, but Thomas now persuaded him to think rather of India as the best place to begin.

In many ways, Carey was unsuited to answer his own call for missionary volunteers. He was, after all, thirty-two years old, married, with three young sons under age nine, and a pregnant almost illiterate wife (Carey had taught her the rudiments of reading and writing) who understandably did not want to leave family, town, and neighbors to go to someplace thousands of miles away called India. Of course, Carey did go and never returned to England. But the cost in terms of his wife's mental and physical health and the welfare of his children was extremely high. Only a deep commitment to his Christian duty and unswerving perseverance sustained him. As he later confessed: "I never could say—no. I began to preach at Moulton because I could not say—no. I went to Leicester because I could not say—no. I became a missionary because I could not say—no." For better or for worse, for Carey, going to India was a matter of obedience to the Great Commission.

India: the early years
At first, Dorothy Carey declined to join her husband in India. Instead, it was agreed that Carey and his oldest son Felix should go, along with Dr. Thomas and wife and child, and Dorothy and the other children would join Carey later. However, difficulties with the British East India Company, which controlled the city of Calcutta to which they planned to go, made it necessary to delay their voyage. Unable to obtain places on an East India Company ship because the company opposed missionary work, the Carey party boarded a Danish vessel that agreed to let them off near Calcutta. The passage of time allowed Dorothy to deliver a fourth son, Jabez, and be persuaded to join the missionary expedition by Thomas.

Five months later, after an unusually

> ## "I became a missionary because I could not say—no."

difficult passage marked by numerous heavy storms and much human misery, the Carey and Thomas families entered British India illegally on November 11, 1793. What, asks church historian Timothy George, were Carey's credentials upon landing?: "education, minimal; degrees, none; savings, depleted; political influence, nil; references, a band of country preachers half a world away." And what were his resources?: "a weapon, love; a desire, to bring the light of God into the darkness; a strategy, to proclaim by life, lips, and letters the unsearchable riches of Christ." So began a ministry that would last for more than forty years.

Carey's early years in India were incredibly difficult. On the positive side of the ledger, Carey was able to study the Bengali language and culture and began to learn Sanskrit. The negative side was much more substantial. Thomas proved enthusiastic but unreliable, especially in the handling of money, and periodically lapsed into insanity. The challenges facing the group were immense. Initial funds were soon depleted and Carey, in keeping with his philosophy of bivocational ministry, took on secular employment so that his family could survive. Communications from England were few and far between. Cultural adjustment was difficult, and the misbehavior of the European traders made it hard for the missionaries to explain the gospel to native Indians. They were harassed by the East India Company, and dysentery and various fevers afflicted Carey and his family.

After moving from place to place, the Careys finally settled at Mudnabatty in the summer of 1794 and remained there for six years. However, almost immediately after they arrived, five-year-old Peter Carey contracted a virulent fever and passed away. Peter's death permanently broke Dorothy Carey's mental health and she never recovered. She spent the remainder of her days ranting and raving at Carey, often in the next room as he worked to translate the Bible into Bengali. With a body racked by pain and increasingly psychotic in her behavior, Dorothy Carey lived with her various delusions until she died thirteen years later at age fifty-one.

Moreover, after six years of grueling apprenticeship, Carey could not claim even one native Indian convert to Christ. He requested reinforcements from England, and they finally arrived in 1800. In order to avoid further confrontations with the East India Company, Carey decided to move to the Danish territory of Serampore near

William Carey's Bible, on display in Calcutta.

Opposite:
William Carey
with his
Brahmin
pundit.

Calcutta. He and his family arrived there on January 10, 1800, and were later joined by the newly arrived missionaries, chief among whom were printer William Ward and school-teachers Joshua and Hannah Marshman.

The Serampore years

The Carey family and their new friends agreed to live together communally, like the early Christians in the book of Acts and the Moravian missionaries of their own day. All of the proceeds from their labors would be funneled back into the common treasury, save for the bare essentials required by each family. All profits would be used for the furtherance of their mission work. During Carey's lifetime, it is estimated that some 90,000 pounds were contributed to the cause in this way. Ward summarized the rules of the community in his journal:

All preach and pray in turn; one superintends the affairs of the family for a month, and then another; brother Carey is treasurer, and has the regulation of the medicine chest; brother John Fountain is librarian. Saturday evening is devoted to adjusting differences, and pledging ourselves to love one another. One of our resolutions is that no one of us do engage in private trade; but that all be done for the benefit of the mission.

For as long as Carey lived, this arrangement worked. It supported the base of the operation of Carey, Ward, and Joshua Marshman, who became known as "The Serampore Trio," perhaps the most successful missions team in history. As for Carey, this communal arrangement was never meant to be an end in itself but rather a means toward the extension of their primary work of sharing Jesus Christ with the people of India.

Insightful into the work of Serampore is Carey's description, from a letter to John Ryland, of a typical day of his life in 1806:

I rose this day at a quarter before six, read a chapter in the Hebrew Bible, and spent the time till seven in private addresses to God and then attended family prayer with the servants in Bengali. While tea was pouring out, I read a little in Persian with a Moonshi who was waiting when I left my bedroom. Read also before breakfast a portion of the Scriptures in Hindustani. The moment breakfast was over sat down to the transla-

> ## Perhaps the most successful missions team in history.

tion of the Ramayuna from Sanskrit, with a pundit, continued this translation till ten o'clock, at which time I went to the College of Fort William, and attended the duties there teaching Bengali, Sanskrit, and Marathi till between one and two o'clock. When I returned home I examined a proof sheet of the Bengali translation of Jeremiah, which took till dinner time. After dinner translated with the assistance of the chief pundit of the college, greatest part of the 8th chapter of Matthew, into Sanskrit. This employed me till six o'clock. After six sat down with a Telugu pundit to learn that language. Mr. Thomas [son of the Rev. Thomas Thomas of London] called in the evening. I began to collect a few previous thoughts into the form of a sermon at seven o'clock, and preached in English at half past seven, the congregation gone by nine o'clock. I then sat down to write to you, after this I concluded the evening by reading a chapter of the Greek Testament, and commending myself to God. I have nevermore time in a day than this, though the exercises vary.

Carey and the Serampore Mission adopted certain principles that served as models for missionaries who followed in their steps. For instance, they agreed that non-Christian peoples must be approached in their own languages. Moreover, they affirmed that missionaries needed to spend time acquainting themselves with the history and culture of the people among whom they lived. They also were in accord that their preaching should center on a positive proclamation of Christ. Further, the Serampore missionaries were convinced that the centrality of the Bible was itself the chief instrument in the conversion of non-Christians. In addition, they strongly indicated that the church in India must represent indigenous Indian Christianity and be a truly Indian church. Finally, they believed in the value of education, not as a substitute for evangelism nor as an act of social benevolence, but as a long-term benefit for Christians and non-Christians alike.

The Serampore years were spent in putting these principles into action. That is why

Carey, for example, prepared grammars for Bengali, Sanskrit, and Marathi and why he accepted the post of professor at secular Fort William College in Calcutta in 1801, thereby influencing many future leaders of the country. It is also why Carey translated into English three volumes of the great Indian epics, and why Ward prepared his four-volume *Account of the Writings, Religion, and Manners of the Hindoos,* long an accepted authority on that subject. It is why Carey increasingly avoided confrontation with Hindu and Muslim leaders and instead concentrated on "preaching Jesus Christ and him crucified." By the time Carey died in 1834, the Serampore Baptists had established nineteen preaching stations in such places as Bengal, Assam, the Northwest Provinces, and Delhi.

The Serampore Trio gave themselves over to translating and printing the Bible in as many Asian languages and dialects as possible. Consequently, Carey translated the entire Bible into six different languages. The New Testament was translated and printed in twenty-three others, whereas portions of the Bible were translated and distributed in many dialects. More than 213,000 copies of the Scriptures in forty different languages and dialects issued from the Serampore presses during Carey's lifetime.

Breaking caste
That is why when Krishna Pal, the first native Indian converted to Christ, was baptized on December 29, 1800, the missionaries discussed at great length what this meant in terms of breaking caste. Breaking caste caused many problems for converts since it meant that they were rejected by Hindu society and treated as outcasts. This could, and sometimes did, create an unhealthy dependence upon the missionaries for employment and support. This led Carey, in a strongly worded statement in 1805, to advise Indian Christians to form their own churches, choose their own pastors and deacons from among themselves, and see that the Word of God was preached in each church by a native minister.

That is why Carey and the Marshmans worked to establish a network of native free schools. By 1818, these schools numbered ninety-two, with more than ten thousand students. It is also why, in 1818, they

> *Carey patiently collected the evidence.*

founded Serampore College for purposes of education at higher levels. Carey served as professor of divinity and as lecturer in botany and zoology at the college from 1818 until his death in 1834.

Sati
In addition to the implementation of the foregoing principles, Carey also attempted to improve life in his adopted country. In this, the evangelical social conscience was alive and well. For example, Carey worked tirelessly to end the practice of *sati,* that is, the burning of widows on their husbands' funeral pyres. Carey patiently collected from the pundits the evidence of the Sastras, the ancient Hindu writings, and in this way confirmed the belief of the missionaries that *sati* though countenanced by Hindu law was in no way commanded by it. Carey's scholarly researches in this matter anticipated by fourteen years the same conclusion by Hindu scholars. He also vigorously opposed slavery and rejoiced when the slave trade was abolished within the British Empire shortly before his death.

In 1820, Carey organized the Agricultural and Horticultural Society of India. Today, an herb and two trees found in India bear his name. His achievements as a botanist are extraordinary.

Thus, the broad pattern of Western missionary effort was clearly illustrated in the world of Carey and his colleagues: personal evangelism, church planting, Bible translation, the publication of religious works, study of the culture, education, agriculture, medical work, attempts to alleviate human suffering and social conditions. It is all there in this pioneering story.

The later years produced a series of grievous trials. Most notable among them was the disastrous Serampore fire in March 1812, which destroyed the mission's precious printing presses and many priceless manuscripts. There was also in 1815 the schism between the older Serampore missionaries and the younger BMS men, as well as the sad break in 1826 with the home BMS committee. On the other hand, there were the many triumphs mentioned above.

Following the death of Dorothy, Carey enjoyed a happy thirteen-year marriage to Charlotte Rumohr from 1808 to 1821 and another pleasant relationship with widow Grace Hughes, whom he married in 1823 and who outlived him by a year.

Conclusions

When he died on June 9, 1834, Carey was mourned by an indigenous Indian Christian community numbering in the thousands, and by tens of thousands of other Indians who appreciated his contributions to the land where he had spent most of his life. Carey and his Serampore associates had baptized more than 1,500 new Christians, and thousands more attended classes and services. Moreover, by the year of his death fifty missionaries were serving eighteen mission stations throughout India.

He also left behind two missionary sons and a missionary nephew, as well as his massive linguistic accomplishments, his educational institutions, and, most of all, the inspiration of his bravery, perseverance, and determination. He had inspired the organization of the London Missionary Society (Congregationalists) in 1795, the Church Missionary Society (Church of England) in 1799, the American Board of Commissioners for Foreign Missions (Congregationalists) in 1810, and the General Convention of the Baptist Denomination in the USA for Foreign Missions in 1814. Further, he had inspired the British Methodists and British General Baptists to launch their own missionary efforts in 1816. He inspired Charles Simeon and Henry Martyn and Adoniram Judson. By 1834, fourteen missionary societies in England alone, as well as several others in America and Europe, were devoted to the missionary cause—all owing their existence to the inspirational example of William Carey.

His was an extraordinary life by anyone's standards. But he did not see himself as an exceptional person. To the contrary, Carey was embarrassed by fame. In 1813, when he was told that his work had been commended on the floor of the House of Commons, he responded, "I wish people would let me die before they praise me."

In reality, he saw himself as a plodder. He once remarked to his nephew Eustace Carey, who became his first biographer, "If, after my removal, anyone should think it worth his while to write my life, I will give you a criterion by which you may judge of its correctness. If he gives me credit for being a plodder, he will describe me justly. Anything beyond this will be too much. I can plod. I can persevere in any definite pursuit. To this I owe everything." Yes, William Carey was a plodder. But this brilliant, resourceful, and persistent man was "God's extraordinary plodder"—and by his fruit we have known him.

Robert Linder

Further Reading

James R. Beck. *Dorothy Carey: The Tragic and Untold Story of Mrs. William Carey.* Grand Rapids: Baker, 1992.

Eustace Carey. *Memoir of William Carey.* Hartford: Robins & Smith, 1836.

S. Pearce Carey. *William Carey, D.D., Fellow of Linnaean Society.* New York: Coran & Co., 1923.

Timothy George. *Faithful Witness: The Life and Mission of William Carey.* Birmingham, Ala.: New Hope, 1991.

John Clark Marshman. *The Life and Times of Carey, Marshman, and Ward: Embracing the History of the Serampore Mission,* 2 vols. London: Longman, Brown, Green, Longmans, & Roberts, 1859.

Stephen Neill. *A History of Christianity in India, 1707-1858.* Cambridge: Cambridge Univ., 1985.

E. D. Potts. *British Baptist Missionaries in India, 1793–1837.* Cambridge: Cambridge Univ., 1967.

George Smith. *The Life of William Carey: Shoemaker and Missionary.* London: John Murray, 1887.

Brian Stanley. *The History of the Baptist Missionary Society.* Edinburgh: T. & T. Clark, 1992.

Ruth A. Tucker. *From Jerusalem to Irian Jaya: A Biographical History of Christian Missions.* Grand Rapids: Zondervan, 1983.

FIRST GREAT U.S. MISSIONARY HERO

Adoniram Judson

1788–1850

Adoniram Judson grew up in a parsonage, the son of Abigail and Adoniram Judson, Sr. In many respects the story of his parents is as fascinating as his own. Adoniram, Sr., graduated from Yale amidst the revolutionary ferment of 1776, but it was not until 1787 that he was ordained and settled into a parish. The stumbling block was his own vow not to accept a call that was less than unanimous. After more than ten years and four calls that were less than unanimous, he lowered his standard, and accepted a call to First Congregational Church in Malden, Massachusetts—a church that was deeply divided before he entered the picture and more so after he became their pastor. In fact, his ordination was delayed because a vocal minority strongly objected to his traditional Calvinist beliefs that reminded them of Jonathan Edwards and their Puritan forebears. But at thirty-six, he could not be choosy, and he was eager to settle down in a church that would provide a home for his new bride.

The senior Judson was determined that any unconscious desire for popularity would not soften his preaching, so Sunday after Sunday he forcefully preached the wrath of God to a shrinking congregation. It was a difficult time—particularly for the young bride, and it was in these circumstances that baby Adoniram was born in 1788.

An unpopular father

Despite the turmoil in his parents' lives, Adoniram knew nothing but security behind walls of the spacious parsonage at Malden. But before he reached his third birthday things began to change. In April 1791, his father was served his "Dismission," and a year elapsed before he was called to a church in Wenham that appreciated his opposition to the new breed of ministers and theologians who were more lax on issues of church discipline.

Young Adoniram spent his next seven years in Wenham—always as conscious of the wrath of his father as the wrath of God. As he grew older he became more aware of his father's inflexibility and the resulting troubles—particularly in 1799 when the town council repeatedly refused to grant a desperately needed raise in salary. Later that year the family moved to a location south of Boston, where the elder Judson served as a missionary of the Massachusetts Home Missionary Society for two years, and from there they moved on to another pastorate in Plymouth. During those years the sixteen-year-old Adoniram left home and entered Brown University.

Although his father hoped that this school, unlike nearby Harvard, would be a safe haven for his son, at Brown Adoniram's beliefs were first tested. His best friend, Jacob Eames, was described as being "amiable, talented, witty, extremely agreeable in person and manners, but a confirmed Deist." Soon Adoniram, too, was dabbling in deism.

Detour into darkness

After three years in the college classroom, the brilliant nineteen year old graduated from the four-year program as valedictorian of his class. He returned home to Plymouth to live with his family and start a school of his own and to write. Within a year, he published a grammar and a math book, but life was too slow in the little country town. And he hated living a life of deceit, pretending that he still believed what his father

Soon Adoniram was dabbling in deism.

> *He was determined to see the big city and pursue his dream of becoming a playwright.*

preached from the pulpit.

So, in the summer of 1808, at age twenty, Adoniram set out for New York City. His mother was deeply hurt and his father was outraged, but he was determined to see the big city and pursue his dream of becoming a playwright. But success in New York proved to be elusive. He joined a group of street actors, but when that venture fizzled they began living "a reckless, vagabond life, finding lodgings where we could, and bilking the landlord where we found opportunity."

But Adoniram soon felt depressed and unfulfilled. One night he left New York without even bidding farewell to his friends. He set out for his uncle's home in Sheffield, not knowing where his life was headed. On the way, he stopped at an inn where he spent a restless night interrupted by the cries and groans of a sick man in the room next to his. When he inquired about the well-being of the man the next morning he was shocked to learn that he had died during the night. Even more astonishing was the disclosure that the man's name was none other than Jacob Eames.

For the somber twenty-year-old Adoniram this was a time of deep soul-searching. He trudged on home under a cloud of depression and uncertainty, only to find an air of excitement at the parsonage in Plymouth. His father and some other ministers, disenchanted by the state of higher education, were forming their own seminary at Andover. They encouraged him to enroll, and with nothing to lose, he agreed—registering as a special student, making no profession of faith.

The call to missions

At Andover, Adoniram's life quickly turned around, and within a matter of months he made "a solemn dedication" of himself to God. This commitment was followed by a pledge to serve God as a missionary—to be America's first foreign missionary. The only problem facing him was that there were no

Adoniram Judson is America's first great missionary hero. The modern missionary movement began in 1793, when William Carey set sail from England to India. Other British missionaries followed in his footsteps—some joining him in India, others going to the South Seas, Africa, and China. But it was not until nearly two decades later that Americans joined in the action.

The first team of missionaries was commissioned in 1812, and among them were Adoniram and his wife Ann, who would quickly capture the hearts of their fellow Americans. Theirs was a story of inspiration and sacrifice and suffering, and through Ann's letters and journals ordinary Americans vicariously became a part of their mission venture in the quaint and distant land of Burma. Supporters rejoiced with the Judsons when they baptized their first convert and organized their first little Burmese church; and they grieved with them when the Judsons lost little children to tropical diseases and when Adoniram languished in prison.

The story of the Judsons became the most widely read missionary lore of the nineteenth century. When Adoniram returned home in 1845 for his first and only furlough, he was a venerated saint. A Brown University professor described his reception:

Hundreds were gazing for the first time upon one, the story of whose labors and sorrows and sufferings had been familiar to them from childhood, and whose name they had been accustomed to utter with reverence and affection as that of the pioneer and father of American missions to the heathen. They recalled the scenes of toil and privation through which he had passed, they remembered the loved ones with whom he had been connected, and their bosoms swelled with irrepressible emotions of gratitude and delight.

The Life of Adoniram Judson

1788	Born in Malden, Massachusetts
1807	Graduates from Brown University
1808	Enrolls at Andover Seminary
1812	Marries Ann Hasseltine; leaves Boston Harbor for India
1813	Arrives in Burma
1819	First convert; Burmese church organized
1824	Arrested and imprisoned
1826	Ann dies
1834	Marries Sarah Boardman
1845	Sarah dies; furlough
1846	Marries Emily Chubbock
1850	Adoniram dies

INDIA   BURMA (MYANMAR)

> *As soon as they arrived in India both were baptized again.*

North American mission societies capable of funding such a venture. He sailed to Britain in search of financial backing, but was called home by the American Board of Commissioners for Foreign Missions when they were awarded money from a sizable inheritance.

With funds in hand, Adoniram had one final matter to settle before he sailed for his destination of India. Prior to his trip to Britain he had "commenced an acquaintance" with Ann Hasseltine, and he was convinced that she was the very partner he needed in this ground-breaking venture.

Ann had come to faith during a time of revival in her home town of Bradford, Massachusetts. She studied at Bradford Academy and then taught school, but she longed to be a missionary. In fact, when she later testified of her commitment to foreign missions she insisted that she was not influenced by her desire to marry Adoniram— "an attachment to an earthly object"—but was rather prompted by an "obligation to God . . . with a full conviction of its being a call." In February 1812 they were married, and thirteen days later they sailed for India with six other newly commissioned missionaries.

Baptists by conviction

The long sea voyage gave the Judsons time to get to know each other and also time for reflection on the Bible and on doctrinal issues—particularly baptism. Adoniram finally concluded that he could no longer endorse infant baptism. Ann resisted, insisting that she could not so easily become a Baptist. But after considerable discussion and study, she too rejected infant baptism in favor of believer's baptism by immersion, and as soon as they arrived in India both were baptized again by a Baptist missionary—one of William Carey's colleagues.

Not surprisingly, the folks back home— mission executives, friends, and relatives— were shocked by the news that their most prized missionaries had defected to the Baptists. But the Baptists in America were only too eager to step in and make up for the lost support from the Congregationalists.

The Judsons, like missionaries before

them, did not find a warm welcome in India. The East India Company controlled immigration and wanted nothing to do with missionaries—or anyone else who might potentially interfere with the company's profit making. Soon they were on board ship again sailing for the Isle of France off the coast of East Africa, and then back to the Malay Peninsula, but to no avail. No one wanted the sea-weary missionaries. Finally, with few options left, they sailed for Burma, where hostility to foreigners was a known fact. Whether they would be able to stay on and conduct missionary work was certainly not an assumption they could make. There was no resident European community, thus making theirs a truly pioneer venture.

Finally . . . Burma

Complicating their trials was Ann's poor health. She had given birth to a stillborn baby on their voyage and was so ill she had to be carried off the ship. Rangoon, the capital, was anything but an inviting city. Poverty and oppression hung over the city like a dense smog. But they were permitted to stay, and that was their most pressing need. Finally, two years after leaving Boston Harbor, they were able to settle down in missionary work and establish a home of their own.

For Adoniram, the most pressing concern was learning the difficult Burmese language—studying twelve hours a day so that he would be able to write tracts and translate the Bible into the tongue of the people. Ann concentrated her efforts on getting to know her household servants and neighbors, learning to communicate by sheer necessity. But despite their best efforts, the progress of evangelism was slow.

In order to communicate more effectively with the people, the Judsons decided to construct a Christian *zayat*—a shelter where people met to talk over the day's events or be instructed by a Buddhist teacher. Their prime location, on a well-traveled road near their mission house, opened the way for the gospel among the Burmese people. In May 1819, five years after they began their minis-

> *Despite their best efforts, the progress of evangelism was slow.*

Adoniram Judson—the first great U.S. missionary.

try, they reported their first convert, and by the summer of 1820, they were ministering to a little church with a nucleus of ten baptized members.

Brutal imprisonment

There was indeed cause for rejoicing, but the joy was tempered by the harsh realities of life. Ann became so ill that she had to return to the United States. While she was away, Adoniram completed his translation of the New Testament, but was forced to move several days' journey north to the capital at Ava while political turmoil swirled around him. Hostilities between Burma and Britain were heating up, and by 1824, the two nations were at war. Ann returned from medical leave and joined him in Ava, but their reunion was short-lived. He was accused of spying for Britain and was taken into custody and confined to a vermin-infested "death" prison with common criminals.

At night his ankles were tied together and

Adoniram Judson on the forced march to a new prison.

fastened to a pole suspended several feet above the floor so that only his head and shoulders touched the ground. He and the other prisoners were so stiff and numb in the mornings that they could barely walk. During the day, they were confined in tight quarters under the watchful eyes of the brutal guards. Ann managed to smuggle food to her husband by bribing the guards, but her efforts were curtailed when she gave birth to their first child, Maria. During this time, Adoniram was transferred to another location. He and the other prisoners, weak and frail due to their confinement, were forced to make the grueling trek on the sharp gravel road barefoot in the scorching sun. Some died along the road, and Adoniram himself was tempted for a fleeting moment to end his misery—to jump to his death when he crossed a bridge over a dry river bed. The pain seemed unbearable, but he continued on, vowing to live if only for Ann and the baby.

For Ann, who was so ill she had to find

> *Ann died—little Maria following soon after.*

village women to suckle her baby, it was a time of sheer desperation. She learned that her husband was no longer in the nearby prison, but she was not told where he was or if he were dead or alive.

The burden of grief

Finally late in 1825, after nearly a year and a half of confinement, Adoniram was released in order to serve as an interpreter for the peace negotiations. He, Ann, and baby Maria had a short and delightfully happy time together as a family before he was called back to hammer out the treaty. But that would be their last time together. During the time of separation, Ann's health continued to deteriorate and before they could be reunited she died—little Maria following soon after.

In an effort to assuage his grief, Adoniram poured himself into his translation work. But after a time, the pain of his loss and the festering unresolved guilt he felt for not having been with Ann when she was dying totally consumed him. As time passed, his output slowed to a stop, and the second anniversary of Ann's death found him out in the jungle living as a recluse beside an open grave thinking nothing but morbid thoughts of Ann's decaying body.

For forty days he continued his vigil, turning his back on the other missionaries and on God. It was a time of despondency and unbelief, as he disclosed in a letter to his in-laws: "God to me is the great unknown. I believe in him, but I find him not."

Through the prayer and support of fellow missionaries, Adoniram managed to pull himself out of his paralyzing depression and continue his ministry. And as he did, he encountered a response like nothing he had seen before. He was amazed by what he described as a spiritual awakening "through the whole length and breadth of the land." God had allowed him to experience the very depths of despair, only to refine and use him in a greater capacity than ever before: "I sometimes feel alarmed, like a person who sees a mighty engine beginning to move, over which he knows he has no control."

In the years that followed, Judson completed his translation of the Old Testament and the Burmese church continued to grow. In 1834, eight years after Ann died, he married Sarah Boardman, a widowed missionary. She, like Ann, was a true partner in ministry, but bearing eight children in less than ten years took its toll. She died in 1845. The following year while on furlough in the United States, Adoniram met and married Emily Chubbock, a talented young author who was less than half his age—and worse yet, she wrote "secular" books. In some people's eyes, their hero had stumbled. But Emily rose to the occasion and served effectively alongside her husband and delighted readers back home with her fascinating descriptions of primitive missionary work.

In 1850, four decades after he committed his life to foreign mission outreach, Adoniram Judson died. He left behind a wife and three little children in Burma and other children back in America. But he also left behind a Burmese translation of the Bible and a growing Burmese church that continues on today, despite very difficult times.

Ruth Tucker

Further Reading

Anderson, Courtney. *To the Golden Shore: The Life of Adoniram Judson.* Grand Rapids: Zondervan, 1972.

Brumberg, Joan Jacobs. *Mission for Life: The Story of the Family of Adoniram Judson.* New York: The Free Press, 1980.

Knowles, James D. *Memoirs of Mrs. Ann H. Judson.* Boston: Lincoln & Edmands, 1829.

PIONEER MISSIONARY TO CHINA

Karl F. A. Gützlaff

1803–1851

One day in 1820 King Frederick William III of Prussia visited Stettin to review the troops stationed there. A seventeen-year-old boy wrote an emotional poem of homage to the sovereign that was passed to him. Its words so deeply moved the king that he ordered the boy be found. When he questioned the precocious youth, he learned that the boy had left school and now worked in a shop that manufactured women's clothing. The king thereupon decreed that he should receive a scholarship to continue his education. In such an unlikely fashion the career of Karl Gützlaff, one of the most important Protestant missionaries in China, was launched.

Karl Friedrich August Gützlaff was born on July 8, 1803, in Pyritz, a provincial town southeast of Stettin in Pomerania, Germany. His father was a tailor who had attended the Francke school in Halle, the center of German pietism, and the boy was raised in a Christian atmosphere. The loss of his mother and his father's remarriage caused him to become a loner. At age seven he entered the local grammar school and received a modest classical education, but his youthful faith was undermined by a rationalistic teacher.

In 1813, he dropped out of school and was apprenticed to a girdlemaker in Stettin. There he came into contact with the growing interest in foreign missions and came to feel that this was his calling. However, he lacked the means for further study until his fortuitous encounter with the Prussian king. At first Gützlaff would go to Halle, but he changed his mind after receiving a letter from the German missionary Karl Rhenius, who served under a British society in India, telling him about the mission seminary operated by Pastor Johannes Jänicke in his Berlin church.

Studies

This school was a product of the German revival movement (the "Awakening"), and many of its graduates served under Dutch and British mission societies. Gützlaff entered in April 1821 and spent two years there. He was an ambitious student with broad intellectual interests. This disturbed both the director and other students who saw his lack of spiritual depth. Finally, in June, he experienced a crisis conversion. But he retained a strong belief in the power of personal effort and an enthusiasm for knowledge. At the school he was influenced by Moravian (Herrnhut) piety with its strong christocentric, individualistic, and nonconfessional emphasis. From contemporary evangelicalism and German romanticism Gützlaff also acquired an indifference to church dogma and organization, an interest in philanthropic and social endeavors, and a tendency toward enthusiasm, feeling, and adventurism.

Missionary service in Asia

After completing his studies in 1823, he received a call from the Dutch Missionary

He spent all his time among Chinese residents and arranged to take a Chinese name and be adopted into a clan.

The Life of Karl F. A. Gützlaff

1803	Born July 8
1820	Prussian King visits Stettin; gives scholarship to Gützlaff
1821	Conversion
1826	Ordained; sails for Indonesia
1828	Works among Chinese in Siam
1829	Goes to Malacca and Singapore
1830	Marries Mary Newell and returns to Siam
1831	Mary dies
1833	Founds *Chinese Magazine*
1834	Marries Mary Wanstall
1835	Founds Society for the Diffusion of Useful Knowledge
1839–42	First Anglo-Chinese (Opium) War
1844	Founds the Chinese Union
1847	First Germans arrive in response to his appeal
1849	Makes trip to Europe; Mary dies
1850	London group formed; sends out Hudson Taylor in 1853; marries Dorothy Gabriel
1851	Returns to China to find Chinese Union in disarray; dies August 9 in Hong Kong, where he was buried

INDIA

SIAM (THAILAND)

Society and went to Rotterdam for further preparation. Following a visit to London in 1825, where he met some important figures in Asian missions, he became convinced that his work lay in the East. He was ordained in September 1826 and sailed for Indonesia. Upon arriving in Java, he was slated to work in north Sumatra, but a conflict raging there forced a reassignment to the island of Bintang. While in Java he met Walter Medhurst, a British missionary who was ministering among the overseas Chinese in preparation for the day he could enter China proper. He took Gützlaff along as he preached among the Chinese and Malays, and the young German began studying Chinese as well. From Medhurst he also obtained the ideas of itinerant missionary work, literary distribution, and the use of indigenous workers.

Gützlaff spent the next year in Bintang and here made the crucial decision to redirect his efforts. He learned classical Chinese as well as various dialects, spent all his time among Chinese residents, and arranged to take a Chinese name and be adopted into a clan from the province of Fukien. In July 1828, he went to Siam (Thailand), taking with him a large number of Chinese Bibles and tracts that had been published in Malacca. In this Malayan city was the headquarters of the mission to the overseas Chinese and its printing press and school, as China proper was closed to Christian work. By relocating to Siam, Gützlaff severed his relationship with Dutch society, but they remained on good terms and occasionally he even received money from it.

Since he had now learned the rudiments of medical treatment and could cure some cases of opium addiction and eye disease, he gained a measure of popularity. However, opposition from Roman Catholic and Buddhist circles forced him to leave a year later, and he went to Malacca to arrange for the printing of a Bible translation. While there he renewed his acquaintance with Mary Newell, whom he had earlier met in London and was now running a mission school for girls. They were married in early 1830 and went back to Siam. They worked as a team in translating Scriptures, writing tracts, and ministering to the people. But in February 1831 tragedy struck; Mary died in childbirth.

> *In all ways he tried to identify with the Chinese.*

China

Although he had gained considerable respect, Gützlaff decided to leave the promising field to go to China. This action was heavily criticized back in Europe, because, as a lone world missionary, he had not sought the counsel of those in the visible church who had called him to this ministry, and his goal was not to establish congregations but to distribute Bibles and tracts. Before leaving, however, he appealed to the American Congregationalists and Baptists to send laborers to continue the mission in Siam.

In June he left on a commercial vessel (a junk) in Chinese dress and went as far as Tientsin. After disembarking in Macao, he sought to persuade the British East India Company to establish regular commerce in other seaports. In 1832 he made a second coastal voyage in a company ship as far as Korea, which put him on the fateful path of combining mission work with political and economic interests. The Chinese authorities suspected the motives of the missionaries, a problem that was accentuated when he made a third trip in 1833 on a British opium smuggling ship. It reflected how an individual operating on his own without the guidance of others could make unwise moves. One could falsely estimate God's leading when left to one's own resources.

"All things to all men"

Nonetheless, by this time he claimed Chinese nationality, had mastered the language, and lived the lifestyle, even wearing indigenous clothing—a purple garment with a blue sash. As one observer put it, he had the ability to blend so much of what appeared natural to the Chinese with what was new, that they could hail him as "the child of the Western ocean." They even recognized him as a descendant of one of their countrymen who had gone abroad in the emigrations. In all ways he tried to identify with the Chinese, or, as Paul put it, he had become all things to all men so that he might win some (1 Corinthians 9:20–22).

Gützlaff now began making regular journeys into the interior (actually a few miles from the coast), giving out literature and medicine. He insisted that the opportunities for spreading the gospel were enormous through Bible translations, tract publication, and founding of schools. Moreover, the dissemination of the divine Word would open the door for useful arts and sciences, and commercial relations would be beneficial for both Chinese and Westerners. To inform people about Western culture and help open China to trade and Christianity, in 1833 he founded a Chinese language journal (known in English as the *Chinese Magazine*), and in 1835 he founded the Society for the Diffusion of Useful Knowledge in China. He also sent appeals to Britain and America for workers. Among the respondents were David Livingstone, who applied to the London Missionary Society for service in China. War in China caused Livingstone to go to Africa instead, but he had the same pioneer spirit and idealism as Gützlaff.

In 1834 while in Malacca to secure more literary material for distribution, Gützlaff met and married Mary Wanstall, a British missionary teacher. Then Robert Morrison, the first Protestant missionary in China, died. He had lived in Canton where the East India Company employed him as Chinese secretary and translator. In December 1834 Gützlaff succeeded him.

With a regular salary, Gützlaff was financially secure. But this was more harmful than he realized. Now tied down, he could not travel as much as he wished. His job also had the practical effect of linking missions and trade interests, since Chinese officials saw his travels as preparation for future European incursions. His close involvement with the British authorities during the first Anglo-Chinese, or "Opium," War in 1839–1842 and appointment as a colonial official at Hong Kong in 1843 further compromised his position.

The Chinese Union

The war had destroyed his earlier ventures, but China was now somewhat more open to Christianity. Although foreigners were limited to five port cities, Chinese could

> *He trained the preachers and colporteurs and sent them out almost like a missionary order.*

Karl Friedrich
August Gützlaff
(1803–1851).

study and practice the faith. In 1844 Gützlaff launched a new effort, the Chinese Union, in which Chinese workers would spread the gospel through the interior and evangelize the kingdom in a generation. He trained the preachers and colporteurs (literature distributors) and sent them out almost like a missionary order. At the same time he revised his earlier Bible translations and produced numerous literary works in Chinese and English. He appealed for funds and missionaries to help out, and the Basel and Rhenish Missionary Societies commissioned the first German workers in 1847. "China Associations" (Gützlaff societies) to further the work sprang up in many European cities, and, after the death of his wife, he returned home to promote the venture during the years 1849 and 1850. While in Britain he married Dorothy Gabriel.

Criticism

Soon stories trickled back that the Chinese Union was a failure. The glowing reports hid the reality that Gützlaff had been deceived by workers who started out with bags full of Bibles and traveling money and returned with journals of travels never made and lists of converts never baptized. Some even sold their Bibles to his printer who then resold them to him. He returned to Hong Kong in January 1851 to rebuild the tottering Chinese Union and combat his many critics. But on August 9, 1851, he died a broken man of rheumatic gout and dropsy.

The Gützlaff legacy

New missionaries came, but the Chinese Union soon died out. Its real fulfillment came through the London group, which in 1853 sent out a young missionary named J. Hudson Taylor. Although he soon came home due to health problems, in 1865 he formed the China Island Mission (CIM) and returned with new vigor. He modeled his enterprise after Gützlaff's—living and dressing as a Chinese, emphasizing itinerant evangelism and literature distribution in the interior, downplaying confessional differences, and depending upon faith for support.

The one province in which CIM did not labor was Kwangtung, because here Gützlaff had operated. In Taylor's view the right method was already in practice there. In later years Taylor called Gützlaff "the father" of CIM's work. Certainly Gützlaff's pioneering labors for Christ had not been in vain. A king's scholarship for a German boy had been handsomely repaid for a much more glorious kind of kingdom.

Richard Pierard

Further Reading

Gützlaff, Karl. *Missionary Travels in China to Distribute Bibles.* Bristol: Wright & Albright, 1841.

Barnett, Suzanne W. "Practical Evangelism: Protestant Missions and the Introduction of Western Civilization into China, 1820–1850." Ph.D. diss., Harvard Univ., 1973.

Barnett, Suzanne W., and John King Fairbank, eds. *Christianity in China: Early Protestant Missionary Writings.* Cambridge: Harvard Univ., 1985.

Latourette, Kenneth Scott. *A History of Christian Missions in China.* New York: Macmillan, 1929.

CHRISTIANITY, COMMERCE, AND COLONIZATION: THE MISSION OF

David Livingstone

1813–1873

Following the Napoleonic wars a spirit of reform was evident in Europe, particularly in Britain. Industrialization seemed to herald unlimited possibilities for the future, and even those in positions of poverty and inequality could aspire to social and economic advancement. The Livingstone family was typical of the new urban work force. Two generations had been employed at the cotton mill at Blantyre, Scotland, before David was born in 1813. David's father, Neil Livingstone, left the mill to become a tea peddler, a job which allowed him to travel and circulate religious tracts to his customers. The family of seven lived in a ten-foot by fourteen-foot room owned by Blantyre Mills.

The priority of education
The Livingstones placed great value on education, but Neil earned so little that he was forced to put his sons to work in the mill. At age ten, David became a piecer. He worked from 6 A.M. to 8 P.M. six days a week, yet persevered through long evening hours to learn Latin, science, mathematics, and astronomy. He was a voracious reader, and free time was spent reading or roaming the countryside around Blantyre, studying rocks and plants. He also became a capable astronomer and could locate his position anywhere on the globe.

Long hours of work and study robbed David of his childhood. There was never time to play. He was different and this was resented. Being the frequent subject of ridicule, he became remote and was considered unsociable. One Blantyre resident

Hard work and deprivation prepared him well for later life.

For centuries Africa was a mystery to Europeans. Deserts, waterfalls, diseases, intense heat, and alternating droughts and torrential rains had made the land so inhospitable that one thousand years had seen little advance in knowledge of the interior. What interest there was in the area derived from the slave trade. This situation changed as nineteenth-century abolition movements spurred development in Christian missions which, in turn, fostered a curiosity about geography.

The task of penetrating this unknown land fell to a young Scottish Christian, David Livingstone. Combining his interests in science, religion, travel, and exploration, Livingstone entered the relatively new field of medical missions—his assignment, South Africa. In spite of his enthusiasm Livingstone experienced great difficulty in converting natives to Christianity. He finally concluded that saving souls would have to be preceded by exposing Africans to "superior" European civilization. This meant opening the interior to trade, communication, and settlement. Convinced of God's will, exploration became Livingstone's controlling passion, taking priority over regular missionary work, health, comfort, and family. By the time of his death in 1873, Livingstone had opened a continent and established the opportunity for what he viewed as Britain's "civilizing mission."

The Life of David Livingstone

1813	Born in Blantyre, Scotland, March 19
1823	Becomes piecer at cotton mill
1836	Enters Anderson's College, Glasgow, to begin study of medicine
1839	Accepted as probationer by London Missionary Society
1840	Completes medical study; ordained; sails on *George* for South Africa
1845	Marries Mary Moffatt
1847	Founds mission at Kolobeng
1854	Makes journey to Luanda, Angola
1856	Makes first visit to London since leaving for Africa
1857	Publishes *Missionary Travels and Researches in South Africa*
1858	Resigns from the London Missionary Society and accepts government position as head of expedition to the Zambesi
1858–64	Explores the Zambesi, the Shire, and Lakes Malawi and Shirwa
1861	Mary dies
1864–65	Makes last visit home and to London
1865	Publishes *Narrative of an Expedition to the Zambesi and Its Tributaries*
1866–69	Journeys inland to Lakes Malawi, Tanganyika, Bangweulu
1871	Meets Henry M. Stanley
1873	Dies near Lake Bangweulu, May 1
1874	Entombed in Westminster Abbey, April 18

AFRICA

River Zambesi

ZAMBIA

described him as "sulky" and "feckless." Unable to tolerate anyone of lesser ability or strength of will, David never learned to get along with other people. However, hard work and deprivation prepared him well for later life.

Neil Livingstone was very religious and demanded much of his children. He once thrashed David for reading a travel book after he had suggested Wilberforce's *Practical Christianity*. Having been raised a strict Calvinist, David was terrified of the possibility of damnation, and his fears were increased by his father's insistence that his love for science was ungodly. He could find no peace, and he shed many private tears over his sinfulness and the expected divine punishment.

Liberalism and missions

When David was nearly twenty he came upon a volume by Thomas Dick titled *The Philosophy of a Future State*. Dick, an astronomer, gave assurance that science could be reconciled with Christianity. About the same time, a traveling Canadian evangelist, Henry Wilkes, preached near Blantyre. David attended the services with his father. Wilkes attacked the established church and orthodox Calvinism. Both Livingstones soon converted to a more liberal congregationalism, and David was particularly proud to be in the vanguard of what he saw as a newer truth.

Around the same time Britain was being evangelized by liberal Protestantism, slavery was abolished throughout the British Empire. Abolition inspired an interest in missions, and missionary societies began to make their appearance. In the meantime David Livingstone was evaluating his own career possibilities. He had become a spinner at the mill and received a somewhat larger wage, but he was much attracted by appeals for medical missionaries for China. This was a new idea for Livingstone, and he convinced his father that he should prepare for such a career. With this goal in mind he entered Andersons College in Glasgow to study medicine.

With his medical training underway Livingstone applied to the London Missionary Society. He was accepted as a probationer and began classes in Hebrew, Greek, and Latin, subjects he found completely

David
Livingstone
expounds the
Bible to African
villagers.

worthless when he reached the mission field. His practice preaching during this time was a disaster. His voice was heavy and dull and his presentation terrible. Members of one congregation threatened they would never return if they knew he was to preach.

A new destination: Africa

In 1840 Livingstone completed his medical studies and was ordained at Albion Chapel, in Finsbury. By this time the Opium War between Britain and China had begun, and the London Missionary Society decided that no more missionaries would be sent to China until the war was over. A quick change of plans found Livingstone boarding the *George* in December to sail for South Africa. The voyage was not an easy one. A storm forced a detour to Rio de Janeiro for repair of the ship's masts. Drunken sailors dominated the waterfront, and Livingstone was found in one instance endangering his life by handing out temperance tracts. Three months later he arrived in Cape Town.

Livingstone began learning the Setswana language and soon left the Cape to search for an appropriate place to begin a mission of his own. He traveled north to Kuruman

> *Livingstone himself was taken as a god.*

and the Tswana territory. Robert Moffatt, the founder of Kuruman, had spent twenty years building his mission. On his arrival, Livingstone expected to find a thriving town with a large population and numerous converts. He was disappointed on all counts. The land was almost a desert, plagued by drought and covered with scrub. The villagers had to move frequently to find enough food for their cattle, making it almost impossible to maintain any coherent educational effort. Many tribal practices, such as polygamy, conflicted with Christian principles.

There was total confusion in religion. Livingstone found that many natives believed that Christianity was something to be eaten and drunk. He himself was taken as a god. Europeans were a strange sight to the isolated tribes, and preachers were believed to have supernatural powers. They often frightened the people just by their presence. To get people to understand that his God was not visible, Livingstone prayed with his head lowered. This brought gales of laughter from the assumption that his God was underground.

Less than ideal family life

Livingstone tried unsuccessfully to establish missions at Mabotsa and Chonuane. He finally settled at Kolobeng. By this time he had married Robert Moffatt's daughter, Mary. The courtship was not romantic. Livingstone decided that he needed a wife, and Moffatt's daughters were the only possibilities. Mary was not attractive; Livingstone described her as "dark" and "thick," but she was literate and would not be wanting to return to Britain. Mary's married life would be most unhappy. Livingstone completely dominated the relationship and never showed much concern for Mary's comfort or that of the five children that resulted from the marriage. They would have frequent separations, and there was very little communication between the two.

Life in Africa was extremely hard. Transportation was difficult. There were dangers from wild animals. Insects, parasites, and diseases took their toll and added to the mis-

> *The lion completely crushed his upper arm.*

> *Livingstone's life was dominated by the one obsession of opening Africa to Christian missions.*

ery. Cleanliness was almost impossible. Rooms in the houses had to be smeared with cow dung to lay the dust and discourage fleas. Livingstone wrote to a sister of his great desire for a bath, the fleas making existence nearly intolerable.

Once when he responded to a native's pleas for help against a lion attack, Livingstone foolishly carried only one gun. He wounded the lion, but it was still able to attack him and completely crush his upper arm in addition to leaving severe gashes with its teeth. He was forced to set the arm himself with nothing to reduce the pain. He was ill for weeks but made light of the incident in his letters, not wanting to let on about his carelessness.

A new obsession

Having only one convert to show for twelve years of labor, David Livingstone became more and more disillusioned with regular missionary work. He perceptively realized that the continent of Africa must be opened so that Europeans could travel and settle with ease. Africans could then learn firsthand that European ways were superior and would be more willing to give up their customs for a Western faith. He now viewed "Christianity, Commerce, and Civilization" as inseparable. Livingstone put his family on a ship to Britain, having made no direct arrangements for their care once they should arrive, and set out to explore the upper Zambesi River in Angola. The Zambesi (now spelled Zambezi) has its source in modern-day Zambia, flows through eastern Angola, then meanders in a southeasterly direction back through Zambia and Mozambique to the southeastern coast of Africa. He was certain that God had a highway across Africa, and it was his personal calling to find it.

From this point on, Livingstone's life was dominated by the one obsession of opening Africa to Christian missions. In four years he traveled four thousand miles through

unexplored territory. He was almost constantly ill, having acquired malaria on his first excursion north of the Zambesi, but his force of will prevented him from succumbing to diseases or discomforts that carried off many of his companions. He was so determined to get more of his countrymen to come to Africa that he often did not reveal the true difficulties and dangers of the situation. He wrote of the beauties of the country and downplayed the diseases, making malaria seem no more of a problem than a common cold. Two mission groups sent at his request were wiped out by fever. He could not sympathize with their suffering and blamed the disasters on their personal failures rather than his own misinformation.

After spending four years crossing the continent Livingstone returned home to a hero's welcome. His numerous honors included a doctorate in civil law from Oxford. He rapidly wrote *Missionary Travels and Researches in South Africa* (1857), which became a bestseller, increasing both his personal wealth and his fame. His schedule permitted him very little time for his wife and children, and he seemed unresponsive to the sufferings they had endured during his four-year absence. Mary could not get along with her in-laws, had to move several times, and experienced great difficulty providing for her family. During this period she developed a serious drinking problem, which would contribute to her early death.

The Zambesi Expedition

During his stay in England, Livingstone negotiated with the Royal Geographic Society and the government to receive backing for his exploration of the Zambesi, which he believed was navigable by steamboat as far as the confluence of the Kafue River on the border of modern-day Zambia and Zimbabwe. When support was forthcoming he resigned from the London Missionary Society and once again set sail, this time as leader of the Zambesi Expedition. Mary, who was pregnant, was left at the Cape, and the rest of the group proceeded north.

Difficulties in travel and arguments with

Livingstone is wounded by a lion while helping an African.

> "There are many regrets
> that will follow me
> to my dying day."

Dr. David Livingstone's helpers carry his body to the coast.

Opposite: Dr. David Livingstone (1813–1873).

his companions had already taken their toll on Livingstone by the time the group approached the river's Kebrabasa gorge. Here they found a fifty-foot-wide channel, which continued for thirty miles. It was filled with boulders and unscalable walls. Everything Livingstone had planned depended on being able to navigate this area, and for once in his life he felt that God had deserted him. However, it was not long before he decided that "God's boulders" were directing him north up the Shire River to Lake Malawi and Lake Shirwa. In spite of the failure to achieve its immediate objective, the Zambesi Expedition did map out central Africa, identified the natural resources of the area, such as coal and copper, and showed that the symptoms of malaria were diminished by the use of quinine.

In 1861 Mary joined the expedition and died a few months later. Livingstone showed real grief at her death and wrote home that

"there are many regrets that will follow me to my dying day." He admitted that "for the first time in my life I feel willing to die." With Mary's death he became closer to his children and began to show them some fatherly attention for the first time.

Livingstone made his last trip home in 1864. He was not received as cordially as he had been on the previous visit. During his expedition he made frequent attacks on the Portuguese. He was furious at their continuation of the slave trade and with their claims to have already explored areas where he insisted he arrived first. This was causing foreign policy problems for Britain. With help from friends Livingstone spent 1865 writing the 600-page *Narrative of an Expedition to the Zambesi and Its Tributaries.* During this visit Livingstone's mother died, and he learned that his eldest son, Robert, was fighting on the Union side in the American Civil War. Robert, who had changed his name to keep from disgracing his famous father, later died in a Confederate prison camp.

In darkest Africa

In 1866 David Livingstone returned to Africa determined to end the Eastern slave trade and establish a trading post. The British wanted him to find the source of the Nile. With these as his goals he began his last journey inland. Accompanying him were sixty porters and numerous donkeys and camels. The area ultimately explored included Lakes Malawi, Tanganyika, and Bangweulu, as well as the Luangwa and Chambeshi rivers. Livingstone was seriously ill during much of the expedition, suffering from fever, nausea, ulcers, and bleeding. He frequently had to be carried for days at a time.

Around 1870 word reached England that Livingstone had been killed. Several expeditions were sent out to try to locate him. A young journalist, Henry Morton Stanley, was finally successful. Stanley was able to provide Livingstone with supplies and other comforts that temporarily improved his physical condition. Livingstone planned a trip around Lake Bangweulu, still trying to locate the source of the Nile, and after this he expected to return to London. His health continued to deteriorate and on May 1, 1873, two servants, Susi and Chuma, found

> *"If God has accepted my service, then my life is charmed till my work is done."*

him on his knees near his bed. He had already been dead for several hours.

At Susi's insistence the body was carefully prepared, carried to the coast, and sent back to England. It took five months to reach the coast, and ten men died on the trip. On April 18, 1874, Livingstone was buried in Westminster Abbey.

David Livingstone was a complex individual. He never lost the Calvinist conviction that God controls human affairs. He was convinced of the divine plan for his life and pursued it with a single-mindedness that allowed him to transcend intense pain and discomfort. He once said, "If God has accepted my service, then my life is charmed till my work is done." This devotion to duty enhanced his greatness, yet took its toll on family and companions. He could not sympathize with human failings in "God's instruments." Yet he had a sincere compassion for the African and showed anguish over his behavior. At the end of his life however, he regretted not having spent more time with his wife and children. Nonetheless, he still pushed himself to his death, obsessed with attaining his goals.

Livingstone knew that he would not always witness the results of his labors, and he stressed that God's plan is greater than the span of a man's life. He also concluded that his primary calling was to pave the way for others. His belief that Britain had a "divine mission" in Africa, inspired, as he had hoped, both generations of missionaries and imperialism. But he would have been sorely disappointed to find that "Commerce" and "Civilization" were not necessarily joined with "Christianity," and Britain's influence did not make Africa a "Christian Continent."

Nancy Erickson

Further Reading

Holmes, Timothy, ed. *David Livingstone: Letters and Documents, 1841–1872.* London: James Curry, 1990.

Jeal, Tim. *Livingstone.* New York: G. P. Putnam's Sons, 1973.

Ransford, Oliver. *David Livingstone: The Dark Interior.* New York: St. Martin's, 1978.

Stanley, Henry M. *How I Found Livingstone.* New York: Scribners, 1872.

North America

MUSCULAR CHRISTIANITY ON THE WILD FRONTIER

Peter Cartwright

1785–1872

Peter Cartwright's conversion marked a major turning point in his life. Though only a teenager at the time, Cartwright's young life had been filled with the rough and tumble worldliness of the American frontier. Born in 1785 to a poor, irreligious veteran of the Revolutionary War and a once-widowed, devout Methodist mother, Cartwright migrated with his family to the Kentucky frontier about 1790. The move was a very dangerous trek. Two hundred families banded together for the journey. One hundred of the younger men, well armed, led the way. Despite these precautions, at one point seven families lagged behind and perished at the hands of the Indians.

By 1793 the Cartwrights had settled a mile north of what is today the Tennessee border, in Logan County, Kentucky. The region was referred to in those days as "Rogue's Harbor" due to the large number of escaped convicts and other outlaws who lived there. Needless to say, young Peter's childhood influences were not always positive. When he was not working to help his family survive the severe conditions of frontier life, he found himself involved in such "worldly" activities as horse racing, card playing, and social dancing. Religion played a relatively minor role in his childhood development—until his sixteenth year, that is.

Conviction of sin

In 1801, Cartwright attended an ecumenical revival held at a Presbyterian church about three miles north of his home. His heart had felt heavy with the conviction of sin for some time. The powerful aftershocks from the recent Cane Ridge revival were reverberating throughout Kentucky. As Cartwright recalled many years later, he went forward at one of the services and

> "Unspeakable joy sprung up in my soul."

prayed for mercy. What happened next jolted him: "In the midst of a solemn struggle of soul, an impression was made on my mind, as though a voice said to me, 'Thy sins are all forgiven thee.' Divine light flashed all around me, unspeakable joy sprung up in my soul. I rose to my feet, opened my eyes, and it really seemed as if I was in heaven. . . . [T]hough I have been since then, in many instances, unfaithful, yet I have never, for one moment, doubted that the Lord did, then and there, forgive my sins and give me religion."

The itinerant preacher

Cartwright joined the Methodist church immediately and began speaking in local services. The following year (1802) he was granted an exhorter's license. Before long he hit the roads and trails working as an itinerant Methodist preacher. He preached in Kentucky, Tennessee, Indiana, and Ohio, becoming quite successful and gaining renown throughout his territory as "the Kentucky boy." His salary was a mere $80 per year for his labor. He was fond of pointing out that even this paltry sum was difficult to collect.

His job was often lonely and always hard. "A Methodist preacher in those days," wrote Cartwright, "went through storms of wind, hail, snow, and rain; climbed hills and mountains, traversed valleys, plunged through swamps, swam swollen streams, lay out all night, wet, weary, and hungry, held his horse by the bridle all night, or tied him to a limb, slept with his saddle blanket for a bed, his saddle or saddle bags for a pillow, and his old big coat or blanket, if he had any, for a covering." The frontier ministry required hardy preachers. In many ways, Cartwright epitomized the rugged individualism so highly esteemed in the nineteenth-century American West.

In 1806, Cartwright was ordained a deacon by the first Methodist bishop ordained in the United States, Francis Asbury. Asbury had been influential in founding the Methodist Episcopal Church in the United States in 1784. He had enlisted thousands of young itinerant preachers, heralding the values of self-discipline and self-sacrifice among those who would preach the gospel. Asbury believed that the clergy had become too comfortable in the posh churches of the Eastern cities. He challenged many of his recruits to work among those who would otherwise go without institutional religion. Though often deemed an autocratic leader by his associates, Asbury never asked his ministers to suffer hardships that he himself did not endure as well. Asbury preached daily, and his own travels averaged five thousand miles per year (on horseback), often taking him through extremely rough terrain. Cartwright's ministry represented the very selfless commitment that Asbury was looking for.

A recognized leader

Cartwright ascended the ranks of the Methodist hierarchy quite rapidly. In 1808 he was ordained an elder by William McKendree, another early and influential Methodist bishop who had tutored Cartwright in English grammar and other subjects. In 1812 Bishop Asbury made him a presiding elder, and by 1816 he was appointed as a delegate to the Methodist General Conference. Cartwright would cherish his role as presiding elder throughout his career.

A position equivalent to that of district superintendent in today's Methodist church, the presiding elder assisted the bishops by supervising all the churches and circuit preachers in his district. Presiding elders visited the Methodist quarterly meetings, where they preached and administered the sacraments. They examined and licensed

> He enlisted thousands of young itinerant preachers.

Frontier life in nineteenth-century America was not for the faint-hearted. It required strength, ingenuity, and perseverance. Even though land seemed plentiful and the horizon endless, pioneers fought constantly against adverse conditions. They lacked most of the amenities that had made life comfortable back East. Settlements were relatively few and far between. The Indians, whose lands they occupied and whose livelihood they threatened, often repaid violence with violence. Times were hard and Christian values were often overlooked or forgotten altogether in the rude struggle for survival. If the gospel were to go forth in such conditions, preachers would need to be found who were hardy souls—equal to the daunting tasks of frontier living.

Peter Cartwright was such a preacher. The son of a Revolutionary War veteran, Cartwright moved to the Kentucky frontier with his family when still a young boy. He was converted at a revival meeting and became a Methodist exhorter at the tender age of sixteen. Soon Cartwright, often referred to as "the Kentucky boy," would become the most famous Methodist itinerant on the frontier, preaching widely in Kentucky, Tennessee, Indiana, Ohio, and Illinois.

His Autobiography, first published in 1856, chronicles Cartwright's many fascinating experiences as a preacher, denominational official, politician, social reformer, and farmer. In many ways, he personified what many have called the "Age of Methodism." Whereas Presbyterians, Episcopalians, and others found it difficult to establish parishes on the wild and sparsely settled frontier, the Methodist church grew rapidly as itinerants like Cartwright took the gospel to the people, riding horseback from settlement to settlement and offering periodic, large-scale "camp meetings" for spiritual revival, sacramental renewal, and Christian fellowship.

Opposite:
Revd. Peter
Cartwright and
his wife.

The Life of Peter Cartwright

1785	Born in Amherst County, Virginia, September 1
1793	Cartwright family settles in Logan County, Kentucky
1801	Converted during a revival at the Lane Bridge camp meeting in Russellville, Kentucky
1802	Given an exhorter's license in the Methodist Episcopal church
1803	Becomes an itinerant preacher in Kentucky, Tennessee, Indiana, and Ohio
1806	Ordained a deacon in the Methodist Episcopal church by Bishop Francis Asbury
1808	Ordained an elder in the Methodist Episcopal church by Bishop William McKendree
1808	Marries Frances Gaines
1812	Named presiding elder by Bishop Francis Asbury at the Tennessee Conference
1816	Appointed delegate to the Methodist General Conference
1824	Moves to Pleasant Plains, Illinois
1824	Elected a representative (Sangamon district) to the Illinois state legislature
1832	Reelected over Abraham Lincoln to the Illinois state legislature
1846	Defeated by Abraham Lincoln in an election for a seat in the U.S. House of Representatives
1872	Dies in Pleasant Plains, Illinois, September 25

ILLINOIS
• Pleasant Plains
USA

> *The Methodist church grew from 72,784 to 1,756,000 members.*

new preachers, acclimated recent converts, oversaw the educational and charitable work of the churches, and governed the administrative procedures of their districts. Cartwright served as a presiding elder for more than fifty years, during which time the Methodist church grew from 72,784 to 1,756,000 members. His *Fifty Years As a Presiding Elder* (1871), published just a year before his death, records his activities in that office.

In 1808, "after mature deliberation and prayer," Cartwright decided it was his "duty" to get married. Thus on August 18 of that year, his new wife's nineteenth birthday, he married Frances Gaines. Peter and Frances had nine children, eight of whom survived to adulthood. At his death in 1872, Cartwright had fifty grandchildren, thirty-seven great-grandchildren, and seven great-great-grandchildren. Frances was said to have been a strong and independent woman, characteristics that proved essential to the wife of an itinerant frontier minister. Their family life was not as difficult as one might imagine, though, and together Frances and Peter created a warm and hospitable home.

In quest of a future home

In 1823, Peter Cartwright decided he wanted to move away from Kentucky. He noted four reasons for this decision. "First, I would get entirely clear of the evil of slavery. Second, I could raise my children to work where work was not thought a degradation. Third, I believed I could better my temporal circumstances, and procure lands for my children as they grew up. And fourth, I could carry the gospel to destitute souls that had, by their removal into some new country, been deprived of the means of 'grace.'" He consulted with Frances "and found her of the same mind," and then set out with two companions "to explore Illinois in quest of a future home." The Cartwright family settled in Pleasant Plains, Illinois, on November 15, 1824, never to move again. Cartwright transferred to the Illinois Methodist Conference, received an appointment to preach the Sangamon Circuit, and

would supervise other Illinois circuits as a presiding elder for the rest of his life.

The slavery issue
Although Cartwright was adamant in his opposition to slavery, he proved an equally strident opponent of radical abolitionism. He criticized both Northern and Southern "ultraisms," calling for an end to slavery by means of peaceful, evangelistic persuasion. He supported the colonization of African-Americans back in Africa and worked hard to prevent the schism between Northern and Southern Methodists in 1844. He argued that the issue of slavery had never been and should never be a test of membership in the Methodist church. He labeled his stance "conservative" and attempted to occupy "the middle ground" between Northern and Southern "extremes."

Politics and education
Cartwright also enjoyed a stint in the Illinois state legislature, entering the political fray primarily to protest the effort to legalize slavery in Illinois. He was elected in 1824 to represent his Sangamon district in the lower house of the Illinois General Assembly. He was re-elected over Abraham Lincoln in 1832. Cartwright served his state as a committed social reformer and as chairman of its standing committee on education. He was the first to introduce a bill for the establishment of a state university in Illinois and he played a key role in the development of several Illinois colleges, including Illinois Wesleyan University, McKendree College, Jacksonville Female Academy (now Mac-Murray College), and Garrett Biblical Institute (now Garrett Theological Seminary).

His final political campaign in 1846 resulted in a loss to Abraham Lincoln in a race for the United States House of Representatives. Cartwright, the Democratic candidate, campaigned against what he called Lincoln's "infidelism." Though Lincoln, the Whig candidate and Cartwright's junior by twenty-four years, was indeed a religious anomaly in 1846, he managed to overcome his reputation as an infidel and carry the election with 6,340 votes to Cartwright's 4,829.

Cartwright's support of higher education in Illinois is quite significant given his own meager educational background and his

> *Cartwright favored a simple gospel for simple people.*

opposition to advanced theological training for ministers. Cartwright was representative of many frontier ministers who opposed theological seminaries while encouraging and supporting other educational ventures. Ironically, though he often lambasted "velvet-mouthed and downy D.D.'s for their intellectual arrogance and impractical, deliberative approach to Christian ministry," Cartwright himself accepted a D.D. (Doctor of Divinity) degree in 1842 and saw a great deal of value in education. His main objection to ministerial education was that it gentrified the clergy and removed them from the grass-roots needs of the churches. Moreover, it undermined the Methodist tradition of ministerial itinerancy and led to a more localized, urban, and comfortable kind of evangelism. Cartwright called the American "experiment" in seminary education "a perfect failure" and castigated fellow Methodists for their increasingly secular eagerness for book learning and academic credentials.

Like Asbury before him, Cartwright favored a simple gospel for simple people. He had little use for preachers who could not "mount a stump, a block, or old log, or stand in the bed of a wagon, and without note or manuscript, quote, expound, and apply the Word of God to the hearts and consciences of the people." It was true, he admitted, that many of the old-time itinerants could not "conjugate a verb or parse a sentence, and murdered the king's English almost every lick. But there was a divine unction attended to the Word preached, and thousands fell under the mighty power of God."

Muscular Christianity
Referred to affectionately as "Uncle Pete" in his later years, Cartwright remained faithful to his calling to preach the gospel wherever the need arose. While maintaining his travels in the service of his denomination and its ministries, he kept a farm to support his family and remained active in community service and social reform. He wrote an *Autobiography* in 1856, recalling his many

> *Cartwright had to confront drunken mobs and other toughs using his fists.*

years of gospel labor. This book has made a lasting impression on thousands of people since its publication and has been consulted frequently by those seeking to understand the nature of Christian life and ministry on the nineteenth-century American frontier. Its readers get a close-up view, warts and all, of the muscular Christianity preferred by Cartwright and other pioneer preachers in the wild West.

Cartwright's life as an itinerant preacher and camp-meeting revivalist often proved lonely and physically grueling. Not only did the heavy work load and the thousands of miles on horseback test the mettle of even the toughest itinerants, but there were times when, in order to maintain order at revivals, Cartwright had to confront drunken mobs and other toughs using his fists. For Cartwright, this was all in a day's work. He did not have time to worry about the obstacles and hardships he faced. He had committed himself from the beginning to itinerant preaching as "the best and most scriptural mode of successfully spreading the gospel of Jesus Christ." Likewise, he based his commitment to camp-meeting revivals on the fact that "there the Word of God has reached the hearts of thousands that otherwise, in all probability, never would have been reached by the ordinary means of grace." As Peter Cartwright realized early on, the spread of the gospel on the American frontier required preachers who were not afraid of its conditions. While foxes have holes and birds of the air have nests, the Son of Man's most fervent frontier disciples often have had no place to lay their heads.

Doug Sweeney

Further Reading

Cartwright, Peter. *Autobiography of Peter Cartwright*. Edited by Charles L. Wallis. Nashville: Abingdon, 1956; 1856.

——. *Fifty Years As a Presiding Elder.* Edited by W. S. Hooper. Cincinnati: Hitchcock and Walden; New York: Nelson and Phillips, 1871.

Grant, Helen Hardie. *Peter Cartwright: Pioneer.* New York: Abingdon, 1931.

Greenbie, Sydney, and Marjorie Barstow Greenbie. *Hoof Beats to Heaven: A True Chronicle of the Life and Wild Times of Peter Cartwright, Circuit Rider.* Penobscot, Maine: Traversity, 1955.

——. *Hoof Beats to Cane Ridge: Being the Second Volume in the True Chronicle of the Life and Wild Times of Peter Cartwright, Circuit Rider.* Penobscot, Maine: Traversity, 1962.

Watters, Phillip M. *Peter Cartwright.* New York: Eaton & Mains, 1910.

MOODY'S GOSPEL SINGER

Ira Sankey

1840–1908

The convention hall was filled to overflowing with a throng of curious, expectant men and women, lured by the renown of the great Dwight L. Moody's preaching. Like any revival crowd, they were a diverse lot, some seeking religious thrills, others eager for reasons to scoff, and not a few hoping for an experience of salvation. The noise of the crowd died to an excited buzz as Moody and his entourage mounted the platform. Then all voices stilled as a short, portly man stepped forward and began to sing.

Ira Sankey's voice was rich and clear, and its pure emotion filled the packed convention hall. Under its sway the crowd's restlessness stilled and, throughout the auditorium, men and women relaxed in their seats, and opened their hearts to listen. His song over, Sankey resumed his seat and Moody began to preach.

By many accounts Ira Sankey was a conventional man, known for his muttonchop whiskers, silk vests, high hats, and a penchant for "patting small boys on the head," as one description ran. But the power of his musical gift made him one of the most famous figures of the late nineteenth century. The hymns he sang, wrote, and compiled earned him a reputation on both sides of the Atlantic Ocean and a permanent place in the history of American revivalism. Ira Sankey "sang the gospel" in a way his listeners never forgot.

In 1870 Ira Sankey was a solid, respectable civil servant, earning a quiet living as a federal revenue collector in Newcastle, Pennsylvania. A Civil War veteran and Methodist family man with a local reputation for musical talent, he was a leading member of the local Young Men's Christian Association (YMCA), in those days an organization largely devoted to evangelizing men and boys.

His decision that year to attend the national YMCA convention in Indianapolis changed his conventional life in ways he could not have foreseen—or perhaps not even willingly chosen. Never a man to seek adventure, he found it suddenly thrust upon him.

A surprise solo

On the opening day of the convention, Sankey rushed in late to a morning meeting, eager to catch a glimpse of the famous evangelist, Dwight L. Moody, who was scheduled to preach. But as he quickly saw, the service was off to a rocky start. A well-intentioned songleader was flogging the congregation through a long, slow hymn, rendering it in the best foot-dragging style. Sankey's seatmate, a close friend who was well aware of his musical abilities, nudged him aside with a whisper: "When that man who is praying gets through, I wish you would start up something."

And Ira Sankey did. As the hymn closed, without embarrassment or affectation he came forward and began to sing: "There is a fountain filled with blood, drawn from Immanuel's veins, and sinners plunged

> *A solid, respectable civil servant, earning a quiet living as a federal revenue collector.*

The Life of Ira Sankey

1840	Born in Lawrence County, Pennsylvania, August 28
1870	First meets with D. L. Moody
1873–75	Evangelistic tour of Great Britain
1875–81	Evangelistic meetings in Chicago, Boston, San Francisco, Baltimore, St. Louis
1875–91	Six best-selling editions of Gospel Hymns, with royalties going to Moody's Northfield Schools
1908	Dies in Brooklyn, N.Y., August 13

USA

●Chicago
ILLINOIS

D. L. Moody's gospel singer, Ira Sankey.

beneath that flood, lose all their guilty stains." His voice was pleasant, his face sincere, and the total effect deeply moving; the men assembled were so transfixed that they forgot to join in on the chorus, and Sankey finished his famous rendition as a solo.

Prayed out of business

As soon as the morning service ended, the great Moody himself pressed forward and began peppering Sankey with questions. "Where are you from? Are you married? What business are you with?" Nonplussed, Sankey replied to the interrogation in some bewilderment. He then fell speechless when Moody looked at him and, with all the straightforwardness of the evangelist's nature, informed him that "you will have to give that up; I have been looking for you for eight years."

Needless to say, the proposition came as a shock to the dignified, thirty-year-old civil servant. He promised Moody to put the matter to prayer, but as he later recalled, "I presume I prayed one way and he prayed another; however, it took him only six months to pray me out of business."

International evangelism

Within three years the partnership between Moody and Sankey was an internationally famous one. Ira Sankey abandoned his government career for the uncertain life of an itinerant evangelist. In the American revivalist tradition, musicians like Sankey had always played an important, though normally secondary, role to the evangelistic preacher; under his influence and example the gospel soloist moved toward center stage.

> *They quickly became
> the center of a
> religious revival not seen since
> John Wesley's day.*

In 1873 Moody and Sankey set off for an evangelistic tour of the British Isles that lasted until the summer of 1875. Though the two were virtually unknown when they arrived in Great Britain, they quickly became the center of a religious revival not seen since John Wesley's day. Millions flocked to hear Moody's simple but moving sermons and Sankey's stirring gospel songs. Through the deft use of publicity and the hard toil of a grinding schedule, the two evangelists became a national sensation, holding as many as thirty-four meetings in one week.

Sankey's sweet baritone was a major ingredient in their success. "Mr. Sankey sings with the conviction that souls are receiving Jesus between one note and the next," one eyewitness testified. "The stillness is overawing; some of the lines are more spoken than sung." Sankey's favorite hymn, "The Ninety and Nine," with its pas-

toral imagery and gentle, pleading tone, earned him the lasting affection of his audiences. His fame proved especially durable among conservative Scots Covenanters, initially skeptical about his use of popular tunes and the portable organ which served as his only accompaniment.

A tour of major American cities and a second trip to the British Isles followed. Huge audiences filled each auditorium Moody and Sankey visited, all eager to hear the most famous preacher of their age, and his equally famous musical partner.

On both sides of the Atlantic, Sankey's gospel song collections became bestsellers and a permanent part of sacred music's repertoire. Through his "story hymns" ("Jesus of Nazareth Passeth By" and "The Ninety and Nine") Sankey would, in his own words, "sing the gospel" while Moody preached it. As one admirer commented, "He had the power to send his voice into the soul. . . . He reveals, as none other can, the sentiment of his hymn, and, enunciating

> *Sankey would
> "sing the gospel"
> while Moody preached it.*

Ira Sankey's final appearance at the Metropolitan Tabernacle, the famous London church, in 1901.

every word and syllable with remarkable distinctness, makes himself heard with ease in the remotest parts of the very largest audience-chamber."

Disarming style

Despite his clear instincts as a showman, Ira Sankey retained the basic simplicity of his nature. He donated all the considerable proceeds from his hymnals to Dwight L. Moody's missionary training schools in Northfield, Massachusetts. Moreover, his vocal ability remained a natural talent, never highly trained or polished. As he himself admitted, he improvised the tune for his famous hymn, "The Ninety and Nine," during a service, using the words from a poem he had read only moments before.

Sankey's lack of affectation aptly complemented Moody's straightforward preaching style. "Mr. Moody startles us and arouses us," one observer wrote, "while Mr. Sankey soothes and comforts." His style also reflected the unabashedly sentimental piety of his age. Moody knew instinctively, as one historian has noted, that "the American-born, middle-class urbanite of his day was still a villager under his skin." Moody's sermons and Sankey's simple melodies, with words evoking the pieties of the Christian home and a tender, loving Christ, had tremendous power to move skeptics and admirers alike.

Modern listeners, accustomed to hard-driving television commercials and the cynicism of popular entertainment, might not immediately appreciate the emotional appeal of Ira Sankey's hymns, so popular in his own day. His approach was simple, and deeply emotional, fitting perhaps to the Victorian audiences he routinely thrilled, but often difficult to translate into a late twentieth-century idiom.

But as the pages of any church hymnal easily attest, the songs have endured. Lines to a chorus or scraps of a tune are part of the "mental furniture" of believers across a wide variety of traditions. They are an eloquent testimony to the piety of an earlier age and of a simplicity we have perhaps lost, but that we may still remember and must always long for.

Margaret Bendroth

A sketch of D. L. Moody at the time he met Sankey.

Further Reading

Chapman, J. Wilbur. *The Life and Work of Dwight L. Moody*. Boston: United Society of Christian Endeavor, 1900.

Nason, Elias. *The American Evangelists, Dwight L. Moody and Ira D. Sankey*. Boston: Lathrop & Co.,1877.

Sankey, Ira. *My Life and the Story of the Gospel Hymns*. Chicago: P. W. Ziegler, 1907.

———. *Sankey's Story of the Gospel Hymns*. Philadelphia: Sunday School Times, 1906.

Sizer, Sandra. *Gospel Hymns and Social Religion: The Rhetoric of Nineteenth-Century Revivalism*. Philadelphia: Temple Univ., 1978.

Weisberger, Bernard. *They Gathered at the River: The Story of the Great Revivalists and Their Impact upon Religion in America*. Chicago: Quadrangle Books, 1958.

FROM SLAVE TO EVANGELIST
Amanda Smith
1837–1915

Amanda Smith, born in slavery, became a well-known and respected evangelist in the United States and overseas. She was a determined woman who followed the Lord's call to evangelistic work in spite of recurrent feelings of inadequacy and unworthiness. Enduring racist and sexist slights, she followed the Lord's leading to enjoy an effective ministry that extended to four continents.

No cost was too great for Amanda as she proclaimed the kingdom of God in its fullness. Like the apostle Paul, she often worked to pay for her expenses and suffered many hardships along the way. The banners of temperance and holiness accompanied her evangelistic message, and her heart went out to help the poor. Truly she was an ambassador following in her Master's footsteps.

Amanda Smith was born in 1837 in slavery to Christian parents, Samuel and Mariam Berry, in the state of Maryland. Through hard work her father managed to buy his freedom. Her mother's mistress had experienced a dramatic conversion at a Methodist camp meeting and a short time later contracted typhoid fever. As she lay dying, her last request was for Mariam and her children to be given their freedom. Free from the bondage of slavery, the family moved to Pennsylvania where its home became one of the main stations of the Underground Railroad.

At the young age of seventeen, Amanda married a man named C. Devine. He turned out to be a heavy drinker, and their home life was filled with strife. The marriage ended after only a few years when Devine was killed in the Civil War. Two daughters had resulted from that union. One died in infancy, and the second, Mazie, died in her twenties. During her first marriage Amanda became aware that, although she attended church meetings most of her life, she had never had a conversion experience.

Strong-willed and full of pride, Amanda tried to dictate the terms of her conversion to the Lord. However, one evening in 1856 she was drawn to a Baptist revival meeting by the beautiful singing. Before the meeting ended, Amanda joined the crowd at the altar pleading with God to have mercy on her. Days of incessant prayer were followed by fasting and Bible study. Amanda was caught in a struggle between God and the devil. Finally she surrendered to the Spirit of God and received the assurance that she was a new person in Jesus Christ.

Her life was now committed to Christ, yet she still had setbacks. One of these was her second marriage in 1863 to James Smith, a promising young preacher in the African Methodist Episcopal Church. Amanda looked forward to a life of ministry with her new husband. It soon became evident, however, that this was not to be. His desire to serve the Lord dwindled as hers accelerated. He left the ministry and moved the family to New York, where life was hard. Amanda had to work long hours washing and ironing to help cover their expenses. Three more children were born, all of whom died in infancy.

Amanda was caught in a struggle between God and the devil.

She was seeking a spiritual confirmation from God known as sanctification.

Seeking God's blessing

One Sunday in September 1868 the Lord led Amanda to attend Green Street Church, Philadelphia, pastored by John Inskip. She was seeking a spiritual confirmation from God known as sanctification. Even then she felt Satan taunting her that she was not good enough to receive a special blessing from God. The Lord touched her in a special way that morning, and she came away convinced that the Lord had taken control of her life for good.

Amanda threw herself into evangelistic work. It became second nature for her to share the gospel with people she met in her daily life. She rarely left home without a handful of tracts to give away, and there were many reports of people saved through her ministry. Attending revival meetings was her passion, and her preaching and inspired singing were a blessing to all.

The year 1869 marked a turning point in Amanda's life. She had always been active in her church and had taken part in the services of other churches near her home. However, in 1869 she heard a call from the Lord to go to Salem, New Jersey, to minister in meetings there. She obeyed the call, closed up her New York apartment, and left on her first evangelistic trip, which lasted seven months. In 1870 she began a full-time evangelistic ministry.

Invitations came regularly to speak and sing at camp meetings and churches around the country. Donations for her support came in less regularly, and Amanda had to do domestic work on occasion to carry on her ministry. She preached the doctrine of entire sanctification along with an evangelistic message.

The role of a "tent-making" evangelist was acceptable to Amanda, and she thrived in the work. However, in July 1870, while attending her first national holiness camp meeting, in Oakington, Maryland, she felt a call to the mission field. She heard a missionary describe the Zenana work in India and felt that she must go to India to save those people. A similar experience occurred in

Amanda Smith, the African-American evangelist.

July 1872. While attending the Sea Cliff Camp Meeting, she began to sense a call from God to go to Africa. She attended a commissioning meeting for new missionaries and was convinced that she had a part to play in the conversion of Africa. Many years passed before she was able to fulfill this conviction. The opportunity came in a roundabout way.

Welcomed in England

In 1878 friends persuaded Amanda to take a trip to England. She embarked on a three-month trip, which turned into two years. Perhaps to help overcome feelings of inadequacy, the Lord began her English ministry aboard ship. When the ship's captain learned that Amanda was a preacher, he insisted that she lead the Sunday service. Although some passengers found a female preacher objectionable, she was gradually

Her preaching and inspired singing were a blessing to all.

The Life of Amanda Smith

1837	Born in Long Green, Maryland, January 23, one of the five children born in slavery to Samuel and Mariam Berry
1854	First marriage, to C. Devine, in September
1856	Assured of conversion
1863	Second marriage, to James Smith
1869	Called by God to evangelistic work
1870–78	Preaches in camp meetings in northeastern United States
1878–79	Ministers in England
1879–81	Ministers in India
1882–90	Ministers in Africa
1892	Moves to Chicago, Illinois
1899	Opens Amanda Smith Orphans Home
1915	Dies in Sebring, Florida, February 15

● Chicago

USA   MARYLAND

Long Green ●

well-received, and her English tour was off to a good start. Besides preaching at church services, Amanda attended the Keswick Convention and numerous other revival meetings around the British Isles.

Amanda was impressed by the respect she received in Britain. In her autobiography racial slights are mentioned regularly as she ministered in the American Christian community. She was sometimes excluded from meetings or unable to find adequate housing because of her race. In Britain Amanda was treated quite differently. Sometimes she felt like a spectacle as people, especially children, constantly stared at her. She understood, however, that these people had never seen a black person before and were simply in awe.

Another form of rejection came from within her own African-American denomination, the African Methodist Episcopal Church. Many men were against the ordination of women and resented her as a female evangelist. There were attempts to discourage her from attending denominational conventions and, to do so, she had to manage on her own. It was only when a prominent minister publicly commended her that she was welcomed to preach as she did in other circles.

In Britain, Amanda found herself in the middle of the highest society. No one shunned her; rather it became fashionable to entertain her. The contrast made a lasting impression, which found its way into her autobiography as a subtle condemnation of racial injustice within the American church.

On to India and Africa

An English acquaintance convinced Amanda to join her on a missionary trip to India. She also helped, through British friends, to raise Amanda's support for the expedition. In November 1879 they arrived in Bombay, and Amanda was unprepared for the sights that greeted her. Even as a slave she had never seen the poverty she found among the Indian poor. She became especially concerned with the plight of women, who seemed to have no rights and whose very

> *The physical needs of the people must be a concern of the Christian community.*

existence seemed dependent on the whims of their fathers and husbands.

A high point of Amanda's stay in India was her work at an orphanage in Colar. She began to understand that preaching the gospel needed to be supplemented in the Indian context. The physical needs of the people must be a concern of the Christian community.

In 1882 Amanda realized her dream to go to Africa. Again supported by her British friends, she arrived in Monrovia, Liberia, in January. In Africa her ministry expanded to include many new denominational circles. She also became very active in temperance work and helped to organize the Gospel Temperance Band in Africa.

During her eight years in Africa, Amanda was able to travel to several countries. She sang and preached and encouraged those caring for the needs of the African people. This short period of her ministry took a heavy toll on her health. Like so many others working in Africa, she experienced regular bouts of fever and other illnesses.

Return to the United States

In 1890, suffering from severe illness, Amanda retired from her work as a missionary and returned to the United States to pursue a less rigorous lifestyle. Not one to remain idle, however, Amanda continued the same pattern of work she had followed in the past. She preached at church services and camp meetings in the eastern United States.

Through the invitation of a friend, Amanda moved to Chicago, Illinois, in

> *She is remembered affectionately as "Amanda Smith, the colored evangelist."*

1892. She lived in a temperance community, which became the suburb of Harvey. There she wrote her memoirs, and, drawing on her experience in India, worked to assist black orphans in the Chicago area.

In 1899 she opened the Amanda Smith Orphans Home in Harvey. Located at 147th and Halsted, this was the first orphanage for black children in the state of Illinois.

Amanda dedicated the remainder of her life to the orphanage. It was granted a state charter as the Amanda Smith Industrial School for Girls in 1912. That same year Amanda retired to Sebring, Florida, in a home provided by George Sebring, a wealthy real estate investor. She went to be with the Lord on February 15, 1915; her body was transported back to Illinois and buried near Harvey in the Memorial Garden Cemetery in Homewood.

After a hard but rewarding life, Amanda has taken her place among the prominent American evangelists. She is remembered affectionately as "Amanda Smith, the colored evangelist."

Ken Gill

Further Reading

Smith, Amanda. *Amanda Smith: An Autobiography.* London: Hodder & Stoughton, 1894.

RESCUED FROM ALCOHOLISM

Mel Trotter

1870–1940

In the biting cold of a Chicago night in January 1897, a homeless man staggered down an icy street toward Lake Michigan. He wore no coat or hat and had sold his own shoes to buy one last drink of whiskey. But the wind and snow hardly troubled him, for he had a single, desperate purpose: to throw himself into the freezing waters of the lake and end his ruined life.

But as he stumbled down Van Buren Street, a young man standing outside the Pacific Garden Mission stepped forward to break his fall. Tom Mackey gently helped the ragged, dirty stranger to his feet, brought him inside, and helped him gently into a chair in a meeting room where Harry Monroe, the mission's superintendent, was preaching to a group of derelict men.

At the sight of the bedraggled newcomer, Monroe was moved with sorrow and pity. "Oh God, save that poor, poor boy," he instantly prayed aloud. In simple words he gave an account of God's love in his own troubled life, a story that gave sudden hope and purpose to a man without reason to live.

At the close of his message, Harry Monroe gave an altar call and the young man, Mel Trotter, walked forward and gave his life to Christ. It was the most simple act of faith imaginable, but it was the beginning of a new life and a new career. Mel Trotter was on his way to becoming an evangelist.

Born in Orangeville, Illinois, in 1870, Melvin Ernest Trotter spent most of his early years fighting—and always losing—a battle with alcohol. One of seven children born to William and Emily Trotter, he grew up in rural Illinois as the son of an alcoholic bartender. Like his two elder brothers, Mel learned to tend the saloon when his father was incapacitated by drink, and soon decided that he would find his way in life by his own wit rather than through the discipline of schooling.

At first the plan seemed to work. At age seventeen he took up barbering, left home, and began to make a good living. But the money was gone as quickly as he earned it, spent in heavy drinking and frantic gambling. Soon he was unemployed.

Undismayed, Trotter moved on, this time to Pearl City, Iowa, where he found more work and fell in love. In 1891 he married Lottie Fisher, and his life began to look more stable.

But disappointments and bitter tragedy soon followed. Lottie discovered that her bridegroom was not only undependable, but deeply addicted to alcohol. He lost his job again, and the newly married couple was forced to move on in search of work.

In the well of despair

Trotter spent the next six years in a cycle of drunken binges and sober resolves, spinning further into a well of self-hatred and powerless remorse. Once he remained sober for eleven agonizing weeks, only to return to his lifelong habit when his resolution failed.

The birth of a son only intensified the grip of Trotter's alcoholism. Unable to keep his repeated promises to straighten out his life, he began to desert his family regularly, sometimes resorting to burglary to finance his ruinous habit. Once hospitalized and

> *He sold his shoes for one last drink.*

treated for alcoholism, he sold his medication for three drinks of whiskey, fifteen minutes after he returned to the streets.

Not even the death of Trotter's two-year-old son could break his addiction. One day, returning home after a ten-day binge, he found his only child lifeless in its mother's arms. Lottie, who had never once left the child's side, was broken and distraught with grief. Swearing never to drink again, Trotter left the funeral—only to drown his sorrows in the nearest saloon. He was very close to reaching bottom.

He hopped a freight train to Chicago, where he landed penniless and hopeless on the bitter cold night of January 19, 1897. Without friends, family, or any reason to continue living he sold his shoes for one last drink and set out for Lake Michigan where he planned to commit suicide.

Detoured from suicide

But here, at the end of his earnest and empty resolutions to live a better life, Mel Trotter met the one power greater than his need for alcohol. The forgiving and healing Christ stopped him in his path, in the person of Tom Mackey, a young rescue mission worker looking for lost souls in the bone-chilling cold of a Chicago blizzard.

Trotter met Christ Himself that night as he came forward to pray in the Pacific Garden Mission. "Jesus loves you," Harry Monroe, the mission superintendent, told him, "and so do I. He wants to save you tonight. Put up your hand for prayer. Let God know you want to make room for Him." In simple response, Trotter did; at twenty-seven years of age his battle with alcohol was over.

But Mel Trotter's new life never took him far beyond the struggles of his early years. Until his death in 1940 he worked as a rescue worker, mission superintendent, and evangelist, devoting his energy to redeeming the lives of men and women who fought the same demons he once knew all too well.

Soon after his conversion, Trotter sent for his wife and went back to barbering. Living frugally, he earned enough to pay back $1,800 of past debts, despite the fact that his

The Life of Mel Trotter

1870	Born in Orangeville, Illinois
1897	Converted at Pacific Garden Rescue Mission, Chicago
1900–40	Becomes supervisor of Mel Trotter Rescue Mission, Grand Rapids, Michigan
1905	Ordained by Presbytery of Grand Rapids
1912–18	Serves as interim manager of Pacific Garden Rescue Mission
1900–31	Yearly speaker at Northfield Bible Conference, Northfield, Massachusetts
1921–40	Leads evangelistic crusades in United States and Great Britain
1940	Dies in Holland, Michigan

Mel Trotter
(1870–1940)

> *Trotter himself helped supervise sixty-eight rescue missions.*

hands still shook from drinking and his haircuts often drew blood from his customers.

But every evening Trotter went back to the Pacific Garden Mission, leading services and singing. On the skid rows of his Chicago neighborhood he became known as "the man who raved about Jesus." His new vocation was becoming clear.

Multiplying the missions

In 1900 Mel Trotter became superintendent of a new rescue mission in Grand Rapids, Michigan, a position he kept for the next four decades. From an initial fund of $1,100 the Mel Trotter Rescue Mission, as it came to be called, eventually took over a popular burlesque theater across the street from the original site. In this spacious new location, the mission housed a Sunday school with up to six hundred students, as well as "mothers meetings," Bible studies, and regular evangelistic services, which brought in hundreds of converts.

The mission gradually transformed its skid row neighborhood of saloons and houses of prostitution. The drinking establishment next door soon closed for lack of business and was bought by the rescue mission. Dedicating the new site to God, workers poured the remaining liquor down the sewers.

From there the mission continued to expand. Rescue workers fanned out into local hospitals and prisons; the mission sponsored curbside evangelistic meetings and a radio broadcast. Converts from the mission also established new outposts in cities around the United States. Trotter himself helped supervise sixty-eight rescue missions, many of them founded by former alcoholics who had found new life and hope through the work in Grand Rapids. In countless ways the Mel Trotter Rescue Mission—with Mel Trotter as the foremost example—lived up to its motto: "Everlastingly At It."

A simple message

Trotter was also well-known as an evangelist. A protégé of the famous Billy Sunday, he often stayed behind to establish missions for new converts in towns the revivalist had visited. But Trotter was equally famous in his own right. His style was energetic and positive, full of humor and the wisdom of experience. "As he speaks," one account ran, "you realize that he has not only looked into the Book, but into human hearts, hungry or self-satisfied, proud or stricken, broken, despairing. Every week he has come to close grips with human need."

Mel Trotter's life was far from easy, even after his conversion. His marriage did not survive the rigors of his schedule; in 1919 he and his wife were separated. He faced constant temptations of money and status, inevitable accompaniments of the traveling evangelist's lifestyle.

But Trotter remained a simple person, for the great lesson of his life was a simple one: God loves you in the midst of the deepest failure and despair, and His love has the power to change even the most ruined life. Nothing Mel Trotter did, before or after that profound discovery, could ever change or improve upon that simple truth.

Margaret Bendroth

Further Reading

Henry, Carl F. H. *The Pacific Garden Mission.* Grand Rapids: Zondervan, 1942.

Reese, Ed. *The Life and Ministry of Mel Trotter.* Glenwood, Ill.: Fundamental Publications, 1975.

Trotter, Mel. *These Forty Years.* Grand Rapids: Zondervan, 1939.

Zarfas, Fred. *Mel Trotter: A Biography.* Grand Rapids: Zondervan, 1950.

A HEART FOR THE WORLD

Ruth Bell Graham

1920–

I cannot recall what my earliest memory of my mother is but I am quite certain it is associated with joy. I now understand that her joy did not stem from perfect or ideal circumstances but from a deep, abiding love affair with the Lord Jesus.

Mother was born in China during the time of warlords and bandits. She grew up hearing gunfire in the distance at night. Then the Japanese invaded China. She can recall seeing the bombs in their berths as the planes swooped low over their compound. She doesn't remember fear being part of her childhood. She lost a brother to dysentery when he was eighteen months old but remembers no lingering shadow of sorrow. Her mother frequently suffered debilitating migraine headaches and would have to go to bed in a darkened room. But my mother's overwhelming memory was the effort her own mother made to keep their home running smoothly and to create a happy environment for the family.

Role model parents

Her mother, Virginia Bell, was very talented and creative in her homemaking skills. She was a single-mindedly supportive wife for Nelson Bell. After they left China to return to the States he set up private medical practice in Asheville, North Carolina. When he was called to an emergency in the night, she too, would get up, ride the thirty minutes to the hospital and wait in the car until he was through, just to keep him company. Her philosophy of child rearing was simple: her job was "not to make them happy but to

> *Her life's commitment was to serve Jesus Christ, her husband and her family.*

How does she live with one of the world's greatest men? Is there a special trait she needs to have? Training? How does she live in his shadow without feeling left out? Do she and her husband have difficult times? What is she really like? Ruth Bell Graham is known to many, and much has been written about her, but no one in her immediate family has written, to any extent, about her—until now.

How do I think of my mother? How do I see her in my mind? How would I characterize her to someone who had never heard anything about her? One overarching trait she has is joy. She has benefited from the living water that "will be in him [her] a spring of water welling up to eternal life" (John 4:14). Her joy is all the more notable because her life has not been easy. She has experienced her own stress and hurt and has also daily confronted the needs of others from around the world. She has a heart for the world. She has said countless times what a privilege it has been for her to be in the position to serve her Lord. She wished she could do more. Early on she made Christ her vision.

make them good." She succeeded in doing both well. Her life's commitment was to serve Jesus Christ, her husband, and her family.

My mother's father, Nelson Bell, a busy surgeon who became chief of staff of one of the world's largest Presbyterian hospitals at the time, created a secure, loving home filled with music, quality family experience, and humor. In turn, he adored his wife who had been his childhood sweetheart. His fidelity to Christ and His service never wavered. It was his life's purpose. His perspective was to serve the whole person, not just see a person "saved." At times, in China, he would give his own blood to save a patient. But he knew eventually all his patients would die, and he was very concerned with the condition of their souls. He was staunch in his belief in the Bible as the infallible Word of God, which "is useful for teaching, rebuking, correcting, and training in righteousness" (2 Timothy 3:16). In spite of his responsibilities and schedule, he was never too busy for interruptions or impromptu visits with those who came to his back door. He made weekly visits to comfort those confined in the hospital. During his last year of life, he was the moderator of the Southern Presbyterian Church. It was a tumultuous year of struggle over the decision to join with the northern church. Despite strong debates, he never held a grudge; he would fight tooth and nail for his position and never compromise. But he never took things personally. He was always a friend.

These were Mother's role models. Her parents exercised a profound effect upon the development of her character and laid the foundations for who she is. I observe traits in her now that I know were formed long ago by these two godly people who were sold out to Christ and committed to their family. A quote of T. T. Carter applies to Mother: her "true response is the result of a habit formed through countless, nameless acts of conscientious obedience, which by use have become the bright and cheerful exercise of the one purpose of giving its best and purest to One most fully loved."

> Her parents exercised a profound effect upon the development of her character.

Ruth Bell Graham.

Preparation for aloneness

One of the deep sorrows of my mother's life occurred when she had to leave the shelter of her home, that secure compound, and go away to northern Korea to high school. She has often said that God was then preparing her for a lifetime of good-byes. But, to a young thirteen-year-old girl whose heart was breaking with homesickness, she had no idea what God's purposes would be and therefore turned to the One she knew she could trust above all others, her heavenly Father. Early in her life she made Christ her home.

What she witnessed in her family home, she now practiced for herself—dependence on God in every circumstance, love for His Word, concern for others above self, and an indomitable spirit displayed with a smile. Self-sacrifice was a way of life. Horatia K. F.

Self-sacrifice was a way of life.

Eden once described a Mrs. Ewing in a way that aptly described Mother: "I never knew her to fail to find happiness wherever she was placed and good in whomever she came across. Whatever the circumstances might be, they always yielded to her causes for thankfulness and work to be done with a ready and hopeful heart."

When I left home at age thirteen and was torn by homesickness, her well-worn advice was for me to look around to find someone who was more homesick than I and cheer her up. Mother's weekly letters to me were full of news and always encouraging. She never failed to close a letter by telling me she loved me and was praying for me.

An interest in China
Although Mother left China at age eighteen to go to Wheaton College and did not return until 1980, she never forgot China or its people—the land and people of her happy childhood. She read, studied, and interviewed those who might afford any clue about her homeland and how the Christian church was faring under intense persecution. She also corresponded with a variety of people who shared her interest. China was in her blood. It became a passion that bore fruit—from individual Chinese friends whom she was able to get released from China through her contacts, to being present as my father sat with the leadership of China to explain to them what he believed about Jesus Christ, to eventually seeing her youngest son start a ministry (Eastgates Ministry) to the Chinese church. She has seen the doors to China open dramatically to the West and particularly to the gospel, which is her life's one passion.

In 1989, my two sisters and I were privileged to accompany our mother back to China to visit her hometown, Huaiyin. As we toured the grounds of what used to be the Love and Mercy Hospital, Chinese officials told us about their plans for the new hospital they were building. When it was Mother's chance to reply, she gave the gospel plainly and clearly. She has the heart of an evangelist. And though often her gift is overshadowed by that of my father's, her gift is exercised effectively in behalf of individuals. At her

The Life of Ruth Bell Graham

1920	Ruth McCue Bell born in Tsingkiang, China, June 10 (in the Chinese year of the monkey, in which are spawned multi-talented, adventuresome, and witty people!)
1943	Graduates from Wheaton College Marries William Franklin Graham in Montreat, North Carolina, August 13
1945	Virginia (Gigi) Leftwich is born
1948	Anne is born
1950	Ruth (Bunny) Bell is born William Franklin III is born
1958	Nelson (Ned) Edman is born, January 12
1973	Nelson Bell, Ruth's father, dies on August 1
1974	Virginia Bell, Ruth's mother, dies on November 8
1980	Visits China

•Chicago
ILLINOIS
USA

deepest core is the desire for individuals to know Christ in a personal and intimate way. My father preaches to the masses, reaching thousands; my mother talks to individuals, loving them one by one, showing her love and concern for them as people. Early in life spreading the gospel of Christ became her purpose.

A loving, loyal spirit

One word that does not apply to mother in any form is *condemnation*. She has a marvelous capacity to accept people where and as they are. As someone has written of another, it also applies to Mother: "She did not try to set others right; she only listened to and loved and understood her fellow-creatures." However, she does have difficulty with those who attack the ones she loves. She is fiercely loyal. She stays in touch with an assortment of friends—from a London waif she has tried to nurture along, to those of royal blood, to the mountain men who helped build our house, to early childhood friends.

Mother has a strong sense of family and holds to traditions passed through the generations—like oyster stew for Christmas breakfast, although no one likes it except my father and her! She is happiest when in her home in the mountains of North Carolina surrounded by her children, grandchildren, and her well-worn books. (Her grandchildren—all nineteen of them—adore her.) Living, as I did, in Virginia under the shadow of the mountains that nurtured her parents, I understand her feelings for being rooted. Recently she was visiting me, and we drove to her parents' hometown of Waynesboro. Although I lived in the area, she gave me directions and could remember the location of the house where my great-grandmother lived when Mother returned with her family from China.

Antiques and books

Mother has never been tempted by the need for status or acquiring "things." She is now surprised to be told that the things she has enjoyed collecting have grown to be valuable—like her primitive mountain antiques that she brought, because they were less expensive, to furnish the old log house she built out of salvage. Old things have always appealed to her and make her feel at home.

She has a strong distaste for the new. With love for old things also came an eye for detail. When I returned with her to China, I began to understand the source of her preferences. Obviously, Chinese culture is ancient, and until the Cultural Revolution, old things and elderly people were revered. Mother absorbed this appreciation, along with her artistic sensitivity.

She is a collector of books and through the years has stumbled across some rare or unusual ones that she personally enjoys. She has never understood why people collect books just to decorate a room. Her books are her friends. They show where she has read by their markings, marginal comments, and notations. Her bedside is crowded with books, from the latest bestseller, to something on China, to poetry, to biography, and always, nearby, her beloved Bible. When someone once told her he felt guilty if he started one book before finishing the first, she told him she did not. "After all," she said, "you don't finish all the pickles before you open the olives." Her view is that there are times for different things. One day you may need to read something funny, the next day need a mystery, and yet that night you may want a devotional book for comfort. Her reading reflects her interests and needs.

Collector of quotations

She is also a collector of quotations. There are few situations where she cannot come up with a choice quote from someone she has read. Her favorites are John Trapp (a sixteenth-century biblical scholar), C. S. Lewis, and George MacDonald. One of her favorites is, "No one is useless, he can always serve as a bad example." When asked if she and my father ever argue, she has often said, "When two people agree on everything one of them is unnecessary." One of her favorite quotes is by C. S. Lewis, speaking of George MacDonald, "He seems to have been a playful man, deeply appreciative of all the really beautiful and delicious things that money can buy but no less content to do without them." Often she quotes George MacDonald saying of himself, "Let me, if I may, be ever welcomed to my room in winter by a glowing hearth, in the summer by a vase of

A Graham family group. Left–right: Gigi Tchividjian, Anne Lotz, Ruth Graham Dienert, Ruth Bell Graham, Billy Graham, Franklin Graham, Ned Graham.

flowers; if I may not, let me think how nice they would be and bury myself in my work." These quotations that she loves are a window to her own attitude and perspective on life.

Mother sprinkles all her conversations with humor and understanding. In consequence they are never dull though sometimes a touch outlandish due to her marvelous sense of the ridiculous. She doesn't take herself so seriously that she cannot laugh at herself. Several years ago she drove up to stay with me for a few days. Having never driven to my home before, she was unsure of the cutoff. But she noticed a little red car with Virginia license tags so she just followed it. By the time she got to Winston-Salem she realized that the little red car was not going to Virginia! She had gone one and a half hours out of her way. Some would get uptight and frustrated. Not my mother. She was chuckling when she arrived safely—but late—at my home.

> *She doesn't take herself so seriously that she cannot laugh at herself.*

Conviction and purpose

Life has not been easy for Mother. With five children to raise, a home to run, a husband rarely at home and usually far away, and the world watching for any flaws and expecting her to be perfect, she has experienced her share of sorrows, burdens, injustice, confusion, pressure, and hurt. However, I would not say I have ever seen Mother display anger or doubt. As a single parent, I am now viewing my mother with new eyes. With the heavy responsibility of family, a home to run, bills to pay, not enough money to meet the demands, being expected to act and dress appropriately although she was never "trained" for her position, a husband who was married to his ministry and often preoccupied, she maintained her perspective. How did she do it? Early on she made Christ her center.

Mother feels deeply and has strong opinions on most things. She has always been a private person, and because of her position does not have the privilege of "spouting off." My older sister, Gigi, says Mother would be in better health now if she had "kicked a few shins." Instead, she has written

> *Her suffering has been the seed for the blossoming of rich, thoughtful poetry.*

her views. In the preface to her first book of poetry she wrote, "I wrote because I had to. It was write or develop an ulcer—or forget. I chose to write. At times I wrote for the sheer fun." And the world is richer for it. Her suffering has been the seed for the blossoming of ˙ rich, thoughtful poetry, personal accounts of the worldwide ministry of my father, humorous insights, and always a record of her pilgrimage with the Lord. Some of her writing has been published. Some will remain just hers—expressions of her emotions to her best friend, the Lord Jesus. Early on she made Christ her confidant.

Clipped wings

In recent years Mother has suffered greatly from degenerative arthritis and is in constant pain. She never utters a word of complaint and always asks me what she can do for me. It has been sad for me to see her in such pain, knowing how she stayed home to rear the children so my father could travel, only to have her wings clipped now that she is free to go. However, this does not stop her from wearing us all out with her ideas and projects. Her mind is not arthritic! You can tell from the way she walks that she is in pain, and as you look at her eyes it is revealed. But she rarely admits it, even to the doctor. She is stubborn. We would have her no other way.

How does one live with one of the world's most famous men? God began training my mother for this position years ago in China. It was far from easy. But she had a tender and yielded heart. Her happiness and fulfillment did not depend on her circumstances. She is the lovely, beautiful and wise woman she is today because early in life, she made Christ her home, her purpose, her center, her confidant, and her vision.

I associate joy with my mother, and now I understand that "the joy of the Lord is her strength."

Ruth Graham Dienert

Further reading

Cornwell, Patricia Daniels. *A Time for Remembering: The Story of Ruth Bell Graham.* San Francisco: Harper & Row, 1983.

Graham, Ruth Bell. *It's My Turn.* Old Tappan, N.J.: Revell, 1982.

——. *Sitting by My Laughing Fire.* Waco, Tex.: Word, 1977.

Martin, William C. *A Prophet with Honor: The Billy Graham Story.* New York: W. Morrow, 1991.

LEADER OF AMERICAN EVANGELICALISM

Carl F. H. Henry

1913–

What makes Carl F. H. Henry the man that he is? The seriousness of his commitment to Christ explains much about his values and aspirations. Those who know Henry, the man behind the public persona, understand very well that he prizes more than anything else his walk with the Lord. Any heralded achievement and any garnered accolade has the worth of a mere tawdry trinket compared to the resplendent riches he finds in Christ Jesus.

Born in New York City in 1913, Henry does not remember a Bible in his home or grace offered at the table or hearing more than one prayer by his mother. Henry's father struggled with a drinking problem and during Prohibition ran a small distillery out of the family kitchen. Recalling the young Carl Henry, before he was converted at age twenty, he said, "I lived my life in sensuality and obeyed the prompting of my own instincts and notions. Yet by God's grace I chose the road less traveled. I became a biblical theist, a follower of Jesus of Nazareth." In a 1987 interview he declared, "Christ has been real to me in a vital way ever since June 1933. It was a blinding experience. I know he is real. He's alive. He is the Risen One. I've never, even in the most serious crises of life, doubted that."

Henry wants others to share in that vital knowledge of Christ. In his own way he has been an evangelist, tirelessly looking for appropriate occasions to say or write a word for his Savior. Henry's belief that Christian conversion supernaturally changes lives has served as a working premise of his ministry.

Henry's personal interests could have taken him down paths far distant from the one that led to his leadership role in the evangelical movement. For a time he was interested in a career in politics, and journalism's

The TV lights swept across the platform. There he was, a tall figure with a kindly face, slowly ambling up to the microphone. Dr. Carl F. H. Henry had just been introduced to a crowd of some five hundred seminary professors and students as one of the principal spokespersons for American evangelicalism since World War II. With his inimitable voice wavering here and there, Henry began to pull back the curtain on his perception of key turning points in the history of evangelicalism. His perspective was worth hearing, for he had participated in many of the events he was describing.

There he was in 1991, edging toward his eightieth birthday, still charting cultural trends and probing strengths and deficiencies of theological positions. There he was, still defending the great truths of the Christian faith after having delivered literally hundreds of addresses and having granted scores of interviews in the United States and abroad and after having penned hundreds of thousands of words about topics ranging from politics and society to the authority of the Bible.

Decades earlier, members of the media had already recognized Henry as a major player in the resurgence of American evangelicalism, dubbing him "the thinking man's Billy Graham." Indeed, to review the history of the evangelical movement during the last half-century almost inevitably draws one to assess Henry's place in that history.

> ## *Henry wants others to share in that vital knowledge of Christ.*

siren call beckoned strongly as a potential career option. As a young newspaperman he wrote for a number of great dailies, including the *New York Herald-Tribune,* the *New York Times,* and the *New York Daily News.* Henry was a wordsmith who could inundate his editor with a torrent of words or turn out a finely chiseled single phrase with almost embarrassing ease.

But Henry became a theologian who has written thirty-five books and who has helped spark a renewed interest among evangelicals to engage their neighbors with the claims of Christ upon their minds, souls, and bodies. Rather than retreating from the field of battle, Henry has called Christians to join him in the ongoing "culture war," which, if anything, he believes has intensified within recent years.

Fundamentalism and evangelicalism
Perhaps Henry's most famous book of cultural analysis is *The Uneasy Conscience of Modern Fundamentalism,* published in 1947. Henry was concerned that nonevangelicals had criticized American fundamentalism for having "no social program calling for a practical attack on acknowledged world evils." According to Henry, many fundamentalist pastors during the thirties and forties had become "increasingly less vocal about social evils." He said, "Whereas once the Gospel was a world-changing message, now it was narrowed to a world-resisting message."

That Henry could criticize fundamentalism while upholding its central doctrines reflects his discomfort with aspects of the movement. In the 1940s the word *evangelical* was "in the air," but it was not especially associated with any specific movement. But with the advent of the National Association of Evangelicals in 1942, formed to rival the political ambitions of aggressive Catholicism and to give a voice to the millions of unheard Christians not represented by the

> ## *Henry has called Christians to join him in the ongoing "culture war."*

The Life of Carl F. H. Henry

1913	Born in New York City on January 22
1933	Converted to Christ in June
1938	Earns his B.A. from Wheaton College
1940	Marries Helga Bender
1941	Receives M.A. from Wheaton and is ordained; begins teaching at Northern Baptist Theological Seminary
1942	Receives Th.D. from Northern Baptist
1947	*The Uneasy Conscience of Modern Fundamentalism* published
1947–55	Teaches at the new Fuller Theological Seminary
1949	Receives Th.D. in philosophy from Boston University; helps found the Evangelical Theological Society
1956–58	Serves as editor of *Christianity Today*
1966	Serves as chairperson of the World Congress on Evangelism
1969–74	Teaches at Eastern Baptist Theological Seminary
1974–86	Serves as lecturer-at-large for World Vision
1979	Serves as president of the American Theological Society
1989	Serves as cochairperson of the Evangelical Affirmations conference

New York City •

USA

> *He enjoined members of the evangelical community to desist from infighting and to close ranks around essentials.*

Carl F. H. Henry during his period as editor of *Christianity Today*.

Federal Council of Churches, a specifically "evangelical" movement began to break away from fundamentalism. These "new evangelicals" believed that the "Christ against culture" motif of fundamentalism cut off conservative Christians from opportunities for spiritual witness and social service.

Fuller Theological Seminary
In May 1947, John Ockenga invited Henry to join the faculty of a fledgling school. In its very first year of existence, Henry became acting dean of Fuller Theological Seminary in Pasadena, California. He threw himself into varied activities ranging from teaching duties and writing to organizing large public meetings such as the annual Rose Bowl East Sunrise Service (1949) and the Mid-Century Rose Bowl Rally (June 1950)—the largest evangelical gathering in southern California—at which Billy Graham spoke to a crowd of fifty thousand. In 1949 Henry played a pivotal role in the founding of the Evangelical Theological Society.

By 1955 he was approached about assuming the editorship of a new magazine, *Christianity Today*. That year he wrote to Billy Graham: "I have no personal reputation for bitterness; my friends have included men in all theological brackets. But in an evangelistic and missionary thrust, I have but one uncompromisable zeal—that Christ be known in his total claim upon life."

***Christianity Today* and the World Congress on Evangelism**
Despite early struggles, the magazine met with spectacular success, its paid readership (150,000 in 1967) far surpassing that of *The Christian Century*. It became a powerful thought magazine recognized as a major voice for American evangelicalism. Moreover, by some accounts it was now the nation's most frequently quoted religious magazine.

As editor for *Christianity Today*, Henry interviewed theologians such as Emil Brun-

ner, Karl Barth, Rudolf Bultmann, and Helmut Thielicke. He received numerous invitations to speak throughout the world. His opinions were sought out by both secular and evangelical publications.

A high point in his ministry occurred when, as its tenth anniversary project, *Christianity Today* sponsored the World Congress on Evangelism in 1966 in West Berlin. Twelve hundred evangelists and evangelism directors from more than one hundred countries attended. Billy Graham served as honorary chairperson, Henry as chairperson.

The Congress represented a major breakthrough for world evangelism because it brought together Christians from diverse social, economic, and ethnic backgrounds to think through the task of the Great Commission in the context of theology and social concern. The members of the Congress defined evangelism only in terms of the proclamation of the gospel: they distanced themselves from "all theology and criticism that refuses to bring itself under the divine

Twenty-seven years after the World Congress on Evangelism in Berlin, where they were chairman and honorary chairman, Carl Henry and Billy Graham reminisce, while the president of Southern Baptist Theological Seminary, Dr. R. Albert Mohler, looks on.

authority of Holy Scripture, and all traditionalism which weakens that authority by adding to the Word of God." The Congress helped Christians work together more effectively, and it prepared the way for later Lausanne conferences.

But difficulties surfaced back at Henry's Washington base. In 1968 he was impelled to leave his position as editor of *Christianity Today* under less than pleasant circumstances. The executive committee's motivations for this decision are difficult to untangle, but J. Howard Pew reportedly wanted more fiery criticism of the economic and political policies of the National Council of Churches. When the full board later reversed this hasty action by the executive committee and asked Henry for a lifelong commitment to the editorship, he declined on the grounds that it would be difficult to recover his prior relationship to the executive committee and that he should not be precluded from a vocational alternative in the future.

In later years Henry commented about his departure with sadness and with less than totally concealed pain. He was particularly perturbed that *Christianity Today* began to lose its nonevangelical readership and its commitment to scholarly theological reflec-

tion. In his view the magazine began to shy away from a head-on tackling of social and political problems and adopted a more popular format in quest of a "mass market readership." He believed that the magazine was no longer serving as an "indispensable theological guide" for clergy and laypeople.

Later years

During the seventies and eighties, Henry's teaching stints at schools such as Eastern Baptist and Trinity Evangelical Divinity School, and his global role as lecturer-at-large for World Vision International and, more recently, for Chuck Colson's Prison Fellowship filled his days with innumerable opportunities for speaking and writing.

In 1976 in his book *Evangelicals in Search of Identity*, Henry raised questions about a crumbling unity within the evangelical movement. Like a theological seismologist, he registered before many in the general public knew of its existence the unsettling rumbling that "all was not well" among conservative Protestant Christians. They were dividing over a bevy of issues ranging from definitions of biblical authority to women's ordination, and this despite the fact that some "evangelicals" were basking in the national limelight and their future appeared bright. Jimmy Carter's candidacy for the presidency as a "born-again" politician had helped convert 1976 into the "year of the evangelical."

During these years Henry struggled to find a way to bolster what appeared to him to be a faltering evangelical movement now possessing a wing known by the 1980s as the progressive, or "open," evangelicals. These open evangelicals defended a form of biblical infallibility limited to matters of "faith and practice" (not including history and science), claimed that their stance was the "central tradition of the church," and portrayed the doctrine of biblical inerrancy as a fundamentalist doctrinal innovation.

Henry roundly disagreed with this analysis regarding the nature and history of biblical authority. He personally affirmed the doctrine of biblical inerrancy: "The doctrine of inerrancy is to me not a dispensable doctrine, and the Church has nothing to gain by evading the issue." He nonetheless lamented that the debate over the meaning and significance of inerrancy had turned acrid and divided the ranks of evangelicals. But he did not have at his disposal the editorship of a magazine such as *Christianity Today* with which he could enjoin members of the evangelical community to desist from infighting and to close ranks around essentials.

Henry also realized that the "new evangelical" appeal of the late 1940s for Christians to penetrate society had sadly been accompanied by an unfortunate development: an uncomfortable number of evangelicals had been impacted by the secular values of the culture they were trying to reach for Christ. Henry put it this way: "While evangelicals seek to penetrate the culture, the culture simultaneously makes disconcerting inroads into evangelical life. . . . A disturbing number of church members cling to the idols of money and material things, sex and status, that bewitch the Western world."

Carl Henry does not take any ultimate credit for his many accomplishments. If some of them happened to have enduring value, they were, in fact, God's doing. "I have . . . done what I was convinced to do in behalf of a cause that we believe matters more than all others, in the hope that this fallible effort has in our lifetime helped to hold high the flag of biblical faith. At the very least, I have helped to dispute the view that to be evangelical is to be theologically illiterate and have nurtured the view that what lies beyond the sunset is more rewarding than a pluralistic smorgasbord."

Henry still is not wavering in his desire to serve Christ, whom he came to love and confess as Savior and Lord sixty years ago. Henry and his wife, Helga, are still looking forward to what more they can do with the Holy Spirit's strength for Christ's church. The evangelical movement is deeply indebted to these very humane and winsome Christians.

John D. Woodbridge

[This chapter is taken from D. A. Carson and John D. Woodbridge, eds., God and Culture: Essays in Honor of Carl F. H. Henry (Grand Rapids: Eerdmans, 1993).]

Further Reading

D. A. Carson and John D. Woodbridge, eds. *God and Culture: Essays in Honor of Carl F. H. Henry.* Grand Rapids: Eerdmans, 1993.

Carl F. H. Henry. *Confessions of a Theologian: An Autobiography.* Waco, Tex.: Word, 1986.

JESUS' TRANSFORMING POWER

John Perkins

1930–

After reading the story of John Perkins in his book With Justice for All, *a couple living in suburban Chicago decided to attend a seminar on Christian Community Development led by Perkins at his Voice of Calvary Ministries (VOC). There in Jackson, Mississippi, the two suburbanites became uncomfortable, for Pastor Perkins didn't talk; he preached. His words made the couple uneasy— perhaps like the rich man to whom Jesus said, "Go sell all your possessions. . . . come, follow Me."*

The couple met Melvin Anderson who grew up under Perkins's ministry in rural Mississippi and now is president of VOC. They met Freddy and Helen Johnson, attending their fourth seminar, who left BMWs and affluent suburban Raleigh, North Carolina, to move near a housing project and talk to kids about Jesus, help with homework, take them to camp. VOC presents the gospel and meets physical needs as it tells inner-city kids about Jesus, builds houses, and provides free medical help through doctors and nurses.

That's what John Perkins is about. He reaches people—black, white, rich, poor—and says, "Jesus died and rose for you, to reconcile you to God and others. Now, what are you going to do about it?"

The couple sold their home, left their retirement plans and frequent flyer miles, and moved to Mississippi. When God said "Go," the couple could follow Him, because John Perkins did in 1957, and cleared the way for others. My husband and I are that couple.

During the 1930s in the rural South, sharecroppers spoke of "farming on halves." That meant that their share of the harvest for the white plantation owner was half, whereas their share of the farming—clearing, cultivating, planting, and harvesting—was whole. The landowner dictated everything sharecroppers did: even the supplies they needed had to be bought from his store where they were charged 30 to 45 percent interest. Often they were in debt at the end of the year.

"The half-world"

John Perkins, born in rural Mississippi in 1930, grew up in a family of sharecroppers. He lived in a world that said to be black was to be less than whole; maybe about half.

If he doubted it, there were many painful reminders. His mother suffered from pellagra, a painful disease caused by a lack of protein. She died when he was seven months old. There was the hard labor in the fields, endless debt to the white landowner, ill-equipped schools open only three months a year, a separate waiting room in the doctor's office—where you'd wait until he'd seen all his white patients, if he saw you at all.

When John was sixteen, his older brother, Clyde, a decorated soldier in World War II, was shot and killed by a deputy marshall on the streets of his hometown, New Hebron, Mississippi. It was just another reminder of the half-world in which he lived.

California

Perkins's worried family sent him to California for safety. There, in 1957, after he had established the start of a successful life, God showed him how to be truly whole: through the gospel of Jesus Christ with its power to transform people. It was there God told him to go and share this love with

> *He lived in a world that said*
> *to be black was to be*
> *less than whole;*
> *maybe about half.*

The Life of John Perkins

1930	Born in Mississippi
1957	Comes to a strong faith in Christ while in California
1960	Moves back to Mississippi
1970	Beaten in a Brandon jail, Mississippi
1975	Starts Voice of Calvary Ministries
1980	Named Mississippi's outstanding religious leader of the year
1982	Founds Harambee Christian Family Center in Pasadena, California
1987	Helps form the Christian Community Development Association

USA

MISSISSIPPI
• Jackson

his people in Mississippi.

"An inner battle raged for the next two years," Perkins said. He now held a management position in industry and owned a big, twelve-room house. "On the one hand, I had a growing hunger to go back to Mississippi and share this newfound love of God with my people. On the other hand I was afraid. We were just beginning to make it."

His was an against-the-odds success. When he arrived in California at age sixteen, he had three dollars in his pocket and one change of clothes. He got a good job with Union Pacific Foundry and was chosen as a union steward. After marrying Vera Mae, also from Mississippi, he served in the Korean War, then returned to his job in California, rising from janitor to leadership. He saved money, bought stock in the company, and saw the stock divide twice.

In spite of Perkins's financial and professional successes, God continued to press on him the call to return. "God took the power of Paul's love for His people and shot it through me."

Return to Mississippi

In June 1960, the Perkinses loaded their U-Haul and migrated back to the South. It was not a great time for a black man to live in Mississippi. But this first faithful step was the start of a ministry to the poor that the Perkinses have lived out for the past thirty-three years.

They have begun ministries in three communities and helped found a nationwide movement called Christian Community Development. Perkins practiced, then put into words, a ministry to the poor using "Three Rs": Relocation to a community in need, Reconciliation between the races, and Redistribution of the economic base.

When they first returned to Mississippi, the Perkins and their five children moved into a small, three-bedroom house in New Hebron with Vera Mae's grandmother. Christian friends in California had pledged to send $75 a month, but that wouldn't feed a family of seven, so right away Perkins started to work, cutting wood and picking cotton.

"Though I didn't realize it at the time, those experiences were building the foundation for our ministry. The people were seeing that I really was one of them. I was not an outsider. I was not a 'have' giving handouts to the 'have nots.' I was choosing to become a 'have not' in order to take my people the gospel. I was once again becoming one of them. Their needs became our needs."

> *Relocation*
> *to a community in need,*
> *Reconciliation*
> *between the races, and*
> *Redistribution*
> *of the economic base.*

> "When I think of John Perkins, I think of a person who is totally dedicated to spreading the gospel."

Spiritual need

One need was the spiritual enrichment of his people. While the center of the black community was the church, it was too often based on emotions, not the Word, "My people had a zeal for God but not according to knowledge," Perkins wrote in his autobiography, echoing the apostle Paul (Romans 10:2).

He and Vera Mae fed local residents knowledge that the Perkinses had gained in their three years in California working with child evangelism, prison ministry, and intensive Bible studies. The first summer they offered Bible classes and vacation Bible schools in rural communities throughout the area where they had grown up.

That fall, they gave chapel services in the public schools in five counties, reaching more than fifteen thousand youth each month with the saving gospel of Jesus Christ. Eula Camper Newsome, who works for the Community Law Office in Mendenhall, Mississippi, was in fifth grade at New Hymn School in Pinola, when Perkins came to her school.

"When I think of John Perkins, I think of a person who is totally dedicated to spreading the gospel. I thank God he came to my school and showed me what I was lacking in my life. Because of him I am a Christian today."

Perkins was chaplain at Prentiss Institute, a black junior college, and that is where the then sixteen-year-old Artis Fletcher met him.

"I rededicated my life to Christ under his preaching and I was discipled by him," said Fletcher, who now serves as pastor of Mendenhall Bible Church. "He made himself available to get to know and spend time with you and he used that as an opportunity to teach you."

Mendenhall

The Perkinses moved to Mendenhall, the county seat of Simpson County, in 1961, as a central point for work throughout the area. They invited youth to their home for Bible studies and included them in family devotions and meals.

They bought five lots and laid the foundation for building the offices of the ministries, a gym, and a church. In his home, Perkins helped train future leaders of the ministries, youth he brought to Christ. Dolphus Weary, head of Mendenhall Ministries, and Melvin Anderson, of Voice of Calvary in Jackson, were part of the generation of blacks to take over the ministries he started.

"I was always drawn to John and Vera Mae Perkins," said Anderson, who lived with his grandmother in nearby D'Lo. "There was something special about the way I was treated in their home; I felt a sense of being loved, but more important than that, I felt needed. I felt my presence was really important to them."

The Perkinses continued responding to needs. Through Bible classes, they learned that many of the students couldn't read, so they began remedial reading classes and later a tutoring program and adult education.

As Vera Mae looked for people to help her care for her children, she saw a need for child care for preschoolers. She began a day-care center that now is the Simpson County Head Start Program.

Seeing so many people living in dilapidated homes, Perkins formed a housing cooperative that built ten brick duplexes in which families still live today.

"As we adopted Jesus' strategy of addressing people's felt needs," Perkins wrote, "we had the chance to point to their deeper needs. The natural man is more aware of his natural needs, not his spiritual needs, so that is where we had to meet him."

Over the years, other needs were met through the ministries, including Genesis One Preschool, a thrift store, a health center, and a farm.

Evangelicals and justice

The South in the mid-sixties was raising up issues of rights for blacks. Perkins was caught in a struggle. "I felt torn between my commitment to justice and my commitment to the church. Almost all the evangelicals I knew opposed the movement. The church

> "We adopted Jesus' strategy of addressing people's felt needs."

seemed to have no room for social justice."

In Simpson County there were only fifty registered black voters. In 1965–67, Perkins helped to register 2,300 blacks in the county. At the same time, many white evangelical churches withdrew their support.

"My heart was torn between my evangelical friends and my commitment to the suffering and agony of my people."

In December 1969, a black man in Mendenhall was arrested, beaten, and jailed for allegedly making phone calls to a white woman. When another black man was arrested, the black community feared he would be beaten too. Seventeen children and adults left Christmas choir rehearsal to go to the jail to protest. Angered, the officer put all seventeen in jail.

The children were released, but Perkins remained locked up. A crowd, angry and fearing brutality, gathered outside the jail. From his cell, Perkins called for them to put aside their anger and work for change— beginning with a boycott of Mendenhall stores.

Perkins posted bond on Christmas Eve, and his community left their Christmas layaways unclaimed. They continued the boycott through February. They asked for jobs for blacks in downtown businesses, paved streets, and integrated schools, and they marched in downtown Mendenhall each Saturday, seeking justice.

While they marched, store owners, many of them members of the Ku Klux Klan and deacons at First Baptist Church, stood on the sidewalk and insulted marchers. They were under police surveillance. A black man leading protests against the white establishment raised bitter feelings and anger. On February 7, 1970, it exploded.

That day, as students from Tougaloo College, a black school, were on their way back to Jackson after the march, they were stopped by the highway patrol just as they crossed the county line. All were jailed. One frightened student called Perkins, who left Mendenhall to help them. At a jail in Brandon John Perkins came face to face with centuries of racial hatred and bigotry.

Brutality

Before he entered the building, police started beating him. Inside the nightmare got worse.

John Perkins, founder of Voice of Calvary Ministries.

"Five deputy sheriffs and seven to twelve highway patrolmen went to work on us. They kept on beating and stomping me, kicking me in the head, the ribs, the groin." He was beaten with a blackjack by five officers repeatedly, kicked, stomped on by law enforcement officers.

"One of the officers took a fork with the two inner tines bent down and he brought that fork up to me and he said, 'Have you seen this,' and he took that fork and put that fork into my nose, then he took that fork and pushed it down my throat, and then they took me over and beat me to the ground. They were like savages—like some horror out of the night. And I can't forget their faces, so twisted with hate."

Looking into those faces, Perkins found that he couldn't hate back. "When I saw what hate had done to them, I couldn't hate back. I could only pity them. I didn't ever want hate to do to me what it had already done to them."

His friends bailed him out, and Perkins went back to his ministry. He recovered from the attack. But it was a slow and painful process to heal the decades of anguish he had suffered from whites.

"For someone to think that he can forget the brutality and injustice of a system because of some light revival and worship is self deception. It will take more than that.

"I know, because for repentance and forgiveness to work in my life, God had to see me through months of agony and pain after being beaten almost to death. The Lord had to lead me through a great time of soul-searching.

"And it wasn't until I could look at a Mississippi highway patrolman, fully uniformed and ready for service, and look at him without feeling a sense of bitterness, that I could really begin to relate my faith in a creative way to the task of reconciliation and evangelism."

Heart attack
Five months after the beating, Perkins suffered a heart attack and was hospitalized in Mound Bayou, a small black community in the Delta where he had helped organize some co-ops. After a partial recovery, he was hospitalized again with ulcers; two-thirds of his stomach was removed.

Lying in bed, broken, bleeding, beaten, Perkins experienced another healing that led to a call for racial reconciliation.

"The Spirit of God worked on me as I lay in that bed. An image formed in my mind. The image of the cross—Christ on the cross. It blotted out everything else in my mind. The Spirit of God kept working on me and in me until I could say with Jesus, 'I forgive them, too.' I promised Him that I would 'return good for evil,' not evil for evil. And He gave me the love I knew I would need to fulfill His command to me of 'love your enemy.'

"The Spirit of God helped me to really believe what I had so often professed, that only in the love of Christ is there any hope for me, or for those I had once worked so hard for. It's a profound and mysterious truth—Jesus' concept of love overpowering hate. I may not see its victory in my lifetime, but I know it's true. Because it happened to me."

Perkins moved to Jackson for his safety and a chance to heal, and began organizing a church and ministry under his call to reconciliation and his belief that, "True justice could come only as people's hearts were made right with God and God's love motivated them to be reconciled to each other."

The call gave birth to Voice of Calvary Ministries in 1975, based on an interracial church and a ministry of a health center, thrift store, and a housing ministry. And he helped open a health center in New Hebron, where his mother had died from malnutrition.

Recognition
Ten years later to the day after being beaten in a Brandon jail, on February 7, 1980, Perkins was honored by the governor of Mississippi as the state's outstanding religious leader of the year. Later that year, Wheaton College awarded him an honorary doctor of law degree in recognition of his work.

In 1982, Perkins felt called back to California, and moved with Vera Mae into a high crime and drug area in Pasadena. There they developed Harambee Christian Family Center, which reaches children with the gospel, creates a sense of family, and builds leaders.

In 1987 he met with fifty Christian leaders to form the Christian Community Development Association (CCD), which today involves more than 150 CCD ministries across the country. "The hope we offer must be more than a proclamation, it must be demonstrated in tangible ways and trustworthy because of our physical presences in the community," he said.

In 1991, he began publishing *Urban Family*, a magazine focusing on positive models of African-Americans and others applying solutions to urban problems.

And John Perkins continues the call for making real Jesus' sermon in Luke 4:18. "Unless the church fulfills its responsibility to proclaim by word and deed the Good News to the poor, the poor have no true hope. We, the church, bear the only true gospel of hope. Only through us can the power of Christ's love save and deliver them."

Christine Weerts

Further Reading
Aeschiliman, Gordon D. *John Perkins: Land Where My Father Died.* Ventura, Calif.: Regal, 1987.

Perkins, John. *With Justice for All.* Ventura, Calif.: Regal, 1982.

GOD'S FOOTBALL COACH

Joe Gibbs

1940–

One of the most vivid memories of Joe Gibbs's childhood in North Carolina in the 1940s is that he was often in church. He was nine when he went forward to acknowledge that he believed in God.

"Even at that age and in that day, I had heard all the stuff about life being accidental. I didn't buy it. A couple of things fused in a puddle of water millions of years ago, and we wind up with men and women and the ability to love each other in a world like this? In church I learned that God made us, and He made us special."

Gibbs believed that God created the world, and not just because that made him feel better than the other theory. To him it simply made sense. Even as a child he was fascinated by nature, and there was no way he could believe that all the beauty and harmony and order in the universe just happened. "That was my first big decision in life, and I never wavered from the basics of it: I decided that people, this earth, the Bible, all of it was done on purpose by Someone who knew what He was doing. It was as simple as that. I went forward and prayed, 'God, I know You're there. I know You made me.' I chose to believe that, and I always have."

Joe Gibbs also believed that the Bible itself was proof of the existence of God. "It was written by more than thirty-five authors over 1,500 years, and still it's perfect. When I think of how one simple football play gets distorted when it goes from a coach to a player and then to the quarterback, I'm amazed that anything in the Bible fits together. Yet it all does."

Gibbs came to learn over the years that the Bible—even the Old Testament—applied to him today. "I'll be going through some crisis, wondering what in the world

> When the Washington Redskins won the 1992 National Football League Super Bowl, 37–24, over the Buffalo Bills, Joe Gibbs became one of the winningest coaches in NFL playoff history. Gibbs began his coaching career in 1964 as an assistant coach at San Diego State University where he had previously played under Coach Don Coryell. He later held coaching positions at Florida State, the University of Southern California, and Arkansas before entering the pro ranks as offensive backfield coach for the St. Louis Cardinals, 1973–77.
>
> After a season with the Tampa Bay Buccaneers, Gibbs joined the San Diego Chargers as offensive coordinator in 1979. In 1981 he became head coach of the Washington Redskins—his first head coaching job at any level.
>
> After dedicating his life to Christ while coaching at Arkansas, he became one of the most evangelistic spokesmen in professional sports, especially during his dozen years as coach of the Redskins.
>
> Originally from North Carolina, Gibbs lives outside Washington, D.C., with his wife, Pat. They have two grown sons, J.D. and Coy.

God would say about it, and I'll find not just a word or a verse about it but lots of passages I can study and think about."

Formula for success

One of his favorite verses is Joshua 1:8: "Do not let this Book of the Law depart from your mouth; meditate on it day and night, so that you may be careful to do everything

Opposite:
Coach Joe
Gibbs.

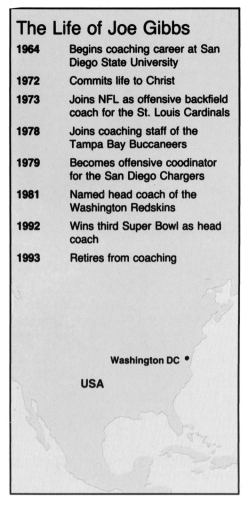

The Life of Joe Gibbs

1964	Begins coaching career at San Diego State University
1972	Commits life to Christ
1973	Joins NFL as offensive backfield coach for the St. Louis Cardinals
1978	Joins coaching staff of the Tampa Bay Buccaneers
1979	Becomes offensive coodinator for the San Diego Chargers
1981	Named head coach of the Washington Redskins
1992	Wins third Super Bowl as head coach
1993	Retires from coaching

Washington DC •

USA

> *"I wanted my own way, and I didn't have much time for people who disagreed with me."*

surgery, and recovery became a slow, torturous process, yet that period remains a major source of bonding in their marriage.

After Joe became head coach of the Redskins he found himself drawn into an investment scheme that went bad, and he wound up owing more money than he had ever made. Only close friends standing by and new friends stepping forward helped him succeed in paying back every creditor.

But the biggest crisis in Gibbs's life had come during his tenure with the Arkansas Razorbacks in 1972. In his quest to keep climbing the rungs on the ladder to coaching success, he had set aside any spiritual priorities. He and Pat attended church, but his life revolved around football and setting himself up for the future. "I have to admit it," he said, "I was an egotist. I was rigid. I wanted my own way, and I didn't have much time for people who disagreed with me."

A parade of witnesses
That year he was impressed by his Sunday school teacher, an older man named George Tharel. He was also impressed by Raymond Berry, a Hall of Fame NFL receiver who joined the coaching staff at Arkansas and would go on to coach in the pros. Berry was a Christian who had a peace about him that commanded respect. "He was soft spoken," Gibbs said, "and his players listened to every word. He was self-effacing and gentle. I didn't let it show, but his life was working on me."

Another coach seemed to have become a different person. "His language was clean. His relationship with his family was special. He had a fresh outlook on everything. I finally asked him, 'What is it with you?' He said he had given his life to Christ and that he'd totally changed."

That made Gibbs think. He considered himself a believer. "But that was the extent of my faith." Meanwhile, Pat had gone forward in an evening service and received Christ as her Savior. She was serious in her commitment.

written in it. Then you will be prosperous and successful."

Gibbs says that if he had learned the truth of that verse as early as he learned that God created him, he might not have had to learn so many of life's lessons the hard way.

Those lessons include enduring his wife's high-risk surgery and seeing her left with facial disfigurement, the frustration of seeking a head coaching job most of his adult life, and having trouble handling the financial rewards when that job finally came along.

Strength for trials
Gibbs feels God was his source of strength during the difficult time when his wife had a tumor removed from behind her ear in the acoustic canal. Complications arose in the

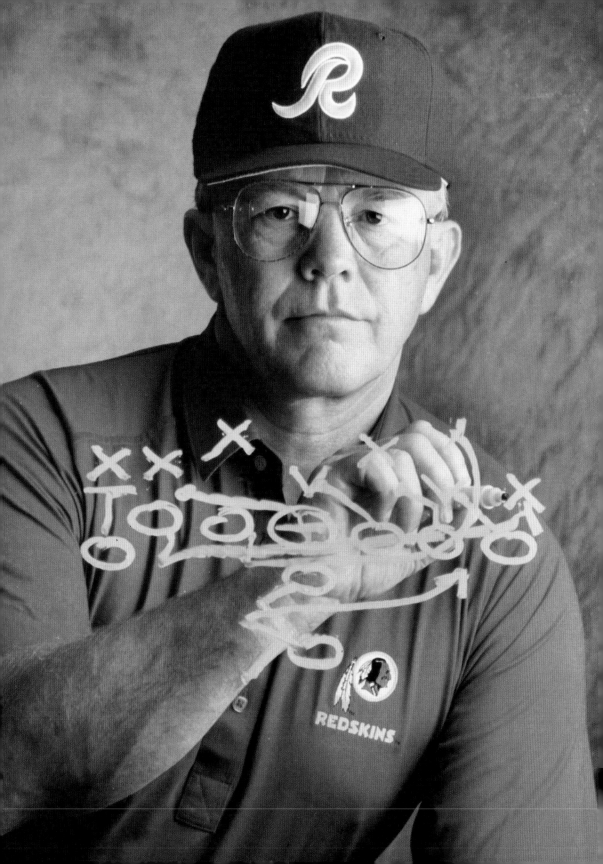

The Christian family of a high school recruit impressed Gibbs. So did the family life of another assistant coach at Arkansas. "Somehow God put these people in my path as a mirror. I saw it was not reflecting me. They had what I wanted, but I was not what they were. I believed in God, but I was not committed to Jesus Christ. I was living by the world's standards, and except for not having yet landed the job I wanted and thought I deserved, I was measuring up. The problem was that I was not succeeding on God's scale. My success was empty, and I was not happy."

Finally, in church one night Joe prayed silently, telling God he was ready to commit himself to Christ. "Then I went forward to make a public statement that I meant business with God. I felt a great weight lift from my shoulders when I rededicated my life, but no one told me life would get easier."

And it didn't. But through all the turmoil and trials he has faced in the two-plus decades since then, Gibbs relied upon God and saw his former Sunday school teacher, George Tharel, as his spiritual father until Tharel died a few years ago. He also read his Bible daily and decided to give his testimony and share his faith in Christ every time he got a chance to speak publicly.

Washington Redskins

When Joe Gibbs was finally selected for his first head coaching job with the Washington Redskins, his team lost its first five games. But after that, no Redskin team lost more than two regular season games in a row until 1988. The Skins would go on to appear in four—and win three—Super Bowls under Gibbs before his retirement in 1993. He became one of the most successful coaches in the history of the NFL.

He also founded Joe Gibbs Charities, focusing upon a young people's home and school called Youth For Tomorrow, which helps wayward teens finish high school and introduces them to Christ.

Now involved in a variety of commercial enterprises, including owning a stock car racing team, Gibbs continues to speak out for Christ. Regardless where he is asked to say a few words, he not only tells of his own faith, but also tells people how to receive Christ and gives them the opportunity to do so.

A faithful witness

Typically he'll say, "A life spent chasing society's myths will end in frustration. If you've ever tried to attain success and happiness on your own—without involving the One who made you and loves you—you'll find out sooner or later that I'm right. No matter how much you accomplish, how much money you make, how many houses and cars you own, or even how many people you entertain, life isn't complete.

"People are looking for something only God can give them. He created us with a void that can be filled only with a personal relationship with Him. When we try to fill that void with the things of the world, our bottomless well gets only deeper.

"Not only will true success elude you when you seek happiness on your own, but you will also have no resources when trouble comes. I shudder to think how I would have coped with Pat's surgery, with disastrous seasons, with financial ruin if I hadn't placed my faith in Christ.

"Run from the myth that material success will bring you happiness. And ignore its counterpart, the lie that the world loves you. They love you only as long as you deliver for them.

"The last myth that needs to be trashed is the one that says life is all there is. You only go around once, so grab all the gusto you can. Would a personal God who made you special and who loves you unconditionally leave you to a life of frustration and unhappiness?

"What is the alternative to all this struggling for success and happiness and things? The answer lies in a personal relationship with Christ. God sent Him to live a perfect life and die for our sins. He came back to life and through Him we have the path to God. All you have to do is believe in Him and receive Him into your life. The decision is yours."

Jerry Jenkins

Further Reading

Gibbs, Joe, with Jerry Jenkins. *Fourth and One: Living and Learning the True Meaning of Success*. Nashville: Nelson, 1992.

THE TEACHER WHO TAMED THE KLAN

Mary McLeod Bethune

1875–1955

Put that book down!" the girls taunted. "You can't read!" they sneered.

"Well, I'm going to learn," Mary responded, biting her lower lip to stop the tears threatening to spill from her ebony eyes.

Their mocking laughter burned in Mary's ears with scorching humiliation. Her white playmates were right, she *couldn't* read— not yet, anyway. But she could learn, couldn't she?

Mary McLeod was born the fifteenth of seventeen children to Sam and Patsy McLeod, ex-slaves who farmed and provided domestic services in nearby Mayesville, South Carolina. Because the McLeods were too poor to own work animals, the children pulled the plows. Educational opportunities for black children were nonexistent in those days until Emma Wilson opened a mission school in their area. Papa McLeod could afford to send only one of his children to Miss Wilson's school. He prayed God would show him which one. Mary was chosen.

By the time Mary had completed her studies at the mission school, she showed such promise that Mary Crissman, a dressmaker in Denver, sponsored her to attend Scotia Seminary. While at Scotia, Mary learned a lesson that would become the pivotal point of her life. She learned that the "whosoever" in John 3:16 meant that, to God, a Negro girl had as much chance as anybody else.

Mary graduated from Scotia in 1894 and

> *When James Gamble first visited "Hell Hole" he demanded, "Where is this school?"*
>
> *"In my mind and my soul," Mary answered. "And that is where it will always be unless you help me."*
>
> *When Thomas White called on the school, he spotted a broken-down Singer sewing machine (his major competitor). Shortly after that, he returned with a new White sewing machine along with carpenters and plumbers he had personally hired to work on building the campus.*
>
> *Once John Rockefeller complimented Mary on doing a great job and told her to stick with it. Her reply was, "All I need is the glue with which to stick." Rockefeller supplied some "glue" in the form of a cash donation.*
>
> *Once she had demonstrated her entrepreneurial skills, Mary persuaded numerous wealthy Northerners to serve on her school board.*

Mary McLeod Bethune.

> *"At Moody we learned to look upon a man as a man, not as a Caucasian or Negro."*

prepared to begin a teaching career. But those plans changed when she was awarded a scholarship to Moody Bible Institute. So Mary moved to Chicago, where she soon became a vital part of the inner-city ministry teams. Years later she remarked, "At Moody we learned to look upon a man as a man, not as a Caucasian or Negro. A love for the whole human family entered my soul and remains with me, thank God, to this day."

No openings
While studying at Moody, Mary felt a clear call to mission service in Africa, but that dream was to be shattered. Ironically, she could not find a mission board to sponsor a black woman to Africa. Her letter of rejection read, "There are no openings in Africa for black missionaries." And the implication that there never would be an opening became her greatest disappointment in life.

So Mary taught for a while in Georgia and then returned to Sumter, South Carolina, where she met and married fellow educator Albertus Bethune. In 1899 they moved to Palatka, Florida, where they opened a mission school, and where Mary gave birth to their son. For the next few years she spent her days caring for her small family, teaching in the mission school, and visiting prisoners.

In 1904 Mary met a traveling Methodist minister who told her of the horrible conditions for black laborers who had migrated to Daytona to work on the railroads. "Conditions down there are dreadful," he warned her. "Appalling squalor. Are you ready for that?"

Mary answered an emphatic "Yes."

The conditions in Daytona were as bad as the worst days of slavery. Supplies were limited at best, so Mary practiced resourcefulness. She collected pieces of discarded matting, carpet, and a bed or two, made benches out of dry goods boxes, and ink out of elderberries. On October 4, 1904, Mary rang the bell to open the new school—that same bell given to her by the Methodist minister who commissioned her to "Go ring yourself up a school."

Head, hand, and heart
Five girls and her son formed the first student body. They recited the Twenty-third Psalm, sang "Leaning on the Everlasting Arms," and prayed for guidance. From this small beginning, a new kind of school was launched. Students "will be trained in head, hand, and heart: their heads to think, their hands to work, and their hearts to have faith." All over the school Mary posted signs with a one-word message that read: "THINK!"

The Life of Mary McLeod Bethune

1875	Born in Mayesville, South Carolina
1887	Attends Scotia Seminary
1894	Attends Moody Bible Institute
1904	Opens mission school in Daytona
1920	Confronts Ku Klux Klan
1923	School merges with Cookman Institute to become Bethune-Cookman College
1935	Appointed first black woman to head a federal agency
1936	Forms "The Black Cabinet"
1944	Retires from public life to devote her energies to Bethune-Cookman College and the National Council of Negro Women
1955	Dies and is buried at Bethune-Cookman College

•Chicago
ILLINOIS

USA

Daytona
•
FLORIDA

For five dollars down and five dollars a month Mary bought an abandoned garbage dump known as "Hell Hole." It would become the permanent site for the Daytona Beach Literary and Industrial School for Negro Girls. Within two years, despite strong white opposition, she had 250 students enrolled. Civic leaders demanded to know why black children, especially girls, needed an education. Mary's answer was always, "Because they are God's children."

To finance their education her students often fished early in the morning, filleted and fried their catch, and made sandwiches to sell to railroad workers. Mary personally baked and sold thousands of sweet potato pies to pay the school's bills. Many days they did not know where their next meal would come from, but she always trusted in God's provision.

It was in these lean years that Mary developed extraordinary fundraising skills. During the winter months Daytona attracted hundreds of wealthy vacationers. Mary's musical groups were popular entertainment for these part-time residents. Through contacts made at their concerts, Mary was able to solicit benefactors for the school—people such as James Gamble of Proctor and Gamble, sewing machine manufacturer Thomas H. White, and oil magnate John D. Rockefeller.

Of all the challenges Mary faced, though, her greatest threat came from the Ku Klux Klan. As the school grew, the Klan could no longer ignore Mary. With the ratification of the Nineteenth Amendment to the Constitution, women gained the right to vote, and in 1920 Mary led a spirited voter registration drive that prompted Klan harassment.

Quit running!
Faith and courage, patience and fortitude became her motto. "Social change cannot happen quickly," Mary advised her students, "but it can happen. Use your minds, but keep your lips closed. Don't be afraid of the Klan!" she preached. "Quit running! Hold your heads up high. Look every man straight in the eye and make no apology to anyone because of . . . color."

The stage was set for a showdown between Mary and the Klan on the night before the mayoral election of 1920. The Klan had arranged to cut the electrical

> *All over the school Mary posted signs with a one-word message that read: "THINK!"*

power to the surrounding neighborhood, plunging it into darkness. The sound of horns and galloping horses alerted Mary and her students to the Klan's approach. She quickly assessed the scene: 100 white-robed figures were marching menacingly toward the center of the campus. Inside the dorms several hundred young girls froze in terror as the Klansmen paraded onto the plaza. Suddenly, a teenage girl screamed, and hysteria swept through the school.

But Mary had anticipated the Klan's visit and knew well their tactics of intimidation. Since the campus had its own electrical system, she ordered, "Lights out . . . so they'll know we're home!" Within moments both the campus and surrounding neighborhood were pitch black. Now, it was the *Klansmen* who were surrounded in darkness and being watched. Mary waited a few moments, then ordered the spotlights on top of the dorms to be snapped on, bathing the Klan in bright light and causing their horses to scurry.

In the midst of this pandemonium came the calm, steady voice of one young student who began singing, "Be not dismayed whate'er betide, God will take care of you." One by one, frightened young women began to join in. At first nervously, then confidently, their voices joined in unison, "Beneath His wings of love abide, God will take care of you." Surprised and confused, the Klansmen retreated—and in a far less orderly manner than they had arrived.

Early election day Mary arrived at the polls to discover yet another challenge—two voting lines. One line was for white voters, the other for blacks. Blacks could not vote until all whites had voted. That could take until nightfall.

Mary spent the day walking the line, passing out cold lemonade, reassuring black voters—especially women voting for the first time—and encouraging all to stay in line. Finally, the black citizens of Daytona voted. Mary rejoiced, "They kept us waiting all day, but WE VOTED!" And as a result, the Klan-endorsed candidate for mayor was defeated. Word spread across the nation of Mary Bethune's courage, and she became known as "the teacher who tamed the Klan."

The school continued to grow, and with the growth of public education for blacks (though segregated and inferior), Mary transitioned her school into a junior college. In 1923 it merged with the Cookman Institute and came under the sponsorship of the Methodist Church. By 1929 the school had been renamed Bethune-Cookman College.

Civic groups

When the college became fully accredited, Mary turned her attention to organizing black women's civic groups, such as the National Council of Negro Women, to confront issues of segregation and discrimination. Through this work she became friends with First Lady Eleanor Roosevelt, who encouraged the president to use Mary in his administration. In August of 1935 Mary Bethune became the first black woman to head a federal agency, when she was appointed director of the National Youth Administration's Division of Negro Affairs. In that post Mary worked tirelessly, creating programs to combat discrimination in employment, persuading industry to hire blacks, and funding black students for graduate programs.

One year later she organized the Federal Council on Negro Affairs, which became known as "The Black Cabinet." This informal group worked to enlist black support of New Deal programs, but also promoted nondiscrimination in government facilities, greater opportunities for blacks in government jobs, and prevention of government policies harmful to blacks. Mary also took time to lead protests against Washington establishments that discriminated against blacks.

At 69 years old Mary left government service to devote the last years of her life to the National Council of Negro Women and Bethune-Cookman College. She never went to Africa as a missionary, but several of her students did. Late in life she reaffirmed the passion of her early call to ministry. "The drums of Africa still beat in my heart," she said. "They will not let me rest while there is a single Negro boy or girl without a chance to prove his worth." She once explained her philosophy for life: "I had faith in God, faith in my people and in my friends, and faith in Mary McLeod Bethune."

In 1955 Mary McLeod Bethune died and was buried on her beloved campus.

Thousands of Bethune-Cookman College graduates have recited and lived out her recitation, "Legacy of Love":

I leave you love.
I leave you hope.
I leave you the challenge of developing
confidence in one another.
I leave you a thirst for education.
I leave you a respect for the use of power.
I leave you faith.
I leave you racial dignity.
I leave you a desire to live harmoniously
with your fellow man.
I leave you, finally, a responsibility to our
people.

Harold Ivan Smith

Further Reading

Halusa, Malu. *Mary Bethune: Educator.* New York: Chelsea House, 1989.

Smith, Elaine M. "Mary McLeod Bethune," in *Notable American Women: The Modern Period*, Eds. Barbara Sicherman and Carol Hurd Green. Cambridge, Mass.: Belknap Press of Harvard University, 1989, 76–78.

Weatherford, Doris. *American Women's History.* New York: Prentice-Hall, 1994, 35–37.

ASTRONAUT

Guy Gardner

1948–

G uy Gardner has almost always been a tangle of paradox. The calculated control and the tender, unexpected emotions. He can, with equal commitment, fly an F-4 Phantom bombing mission or cry during *Mary Poppins*.

In temperament and gifts, he is the ultimate technician—the focused, rational, figure-out-what-to-do-and-do-what-it-takes kind of Guy. His heart, on more than one occasion, has run into a God who is unfathomable, uncontrollable, unsolvable, with a love beyond comprehension. The sparks, needless to say, have often flown. By his own admission, Gardner has sometimes confused his success with his own abilities. His humility, in the end, has been more a matter of losing than winning.

And Gardner has always been a winner. Early in his childhood, even before men had flown in space, Gardner wanted to be an astronaut. Perhaps it was the idea of adventure. His father, a man with emphysema so bad that he often had to sit up to sleep, went from one job to the next. Finally he ended up as a clerk in the post office garage, keeping track of and maintaining post office vehicles. His mom was a secretary.

Only the pursuit of God interrupted Gardner from his dream. And then only briefly. He had grown up attending church, but it was only in his junior year of high school that he gave his life completely to Christ. He was serious. He mulled over the possibility of entering the "ministry." Should he be a pastor? There were more than a few problems: he was poor at reading, writing, and speaking in front of others.

> *It was only in his junior year of high school that he gave his life completely to Christ.*

Guy Gardner was 41,000 feet over the earth, flying a T-38. A routine mission. Somewhere over the bayous surrounding New Orleans, the reds and purples of twilight faded into night. From below, the tiny points of light began to puncture the black landscape: blanketing the city in an orange glow, dotting the canals, spacing the oil derricks, and, further on, marking the desolation of the lonely souls spread throughout the delta, a tender sort of marooning.

For a man accustomed to staying in control, the realization hit Gardner with a kind of G-force that took his breath away—millions of people, millions of souls, each with his or her own life, own joys, own problems.

"It really gave me a sense of insignificance," Gardner recalls. "You realize that you are just a tiny speck in this vast universe, this vast humanity. But, at the same time, there came this feeling that our God is so incredible, so awesome. Each and every person is so special."

A few years later, when he orbited the planet in the Atlantis space shuttle, the same feelings hit him. As he cruised at 27,000 kilometers per hour, the earth was drifting under him in dream colors, the sun sliding on the Mediterranean Sea, the Himalayan mountain range casting long blue shadows, a storm was brewing darkly in the Pacific, and tiny volcano peaks were rising from the clouds of the Galapagos Islands. As he drifted toward sleep, he thought again, "So many souls, so great the love of God."

The Life of Guy Gardner

1948	Born in Virginia
1964	Commits his life to Jesus Christ
1969	Earns bachelor's degree from Air Force Academy; marries Linda A. McCabe
1970	Earns master's degree from Purdue University
1970–71	Pilot training, Craig Air Force base and F-4 upgrade, McDill Air Force base
1972	Flies 177 combat missions in Vietnam
1973–74	F-4 instructor pilot, Seymour-Johnson Air Force base
1975	Test pilot school, Edwards Air Force base
1976	Test pilot, Edwards Air Force base
1977–78	Instructor at Test Pilot School, Edwards Air Force Base
1978	First application to NASA rejected
1978–80	Operations officer, Philippines
1980	Accepted by NASA
1984	Recommits life to Jesus Christ
1988	First shuttle space flight, copilot of Atlantis
1990	Second shuttle space flight, copilot of Columbia
1991	Commandant of USAF Test Pilot School, Edwards Air Force base
1992	Head of joint human space flight venture for NASA (Shuttle-Mir program director)

USA

• Edwards Air Force Base

His only real gifts were math, science, and physical coordination. He was a master at calculating cosines or vortexes, but he knew, in an analytical fashion, that these were not the equations for great sermons.

With precision, passion, and honors, he moved quickly toward his renewed dream to be an astronaut. After graduating from the United States Air Force Academy, where he majored in astronautics, mathematics, and engineering sciences, he married Linda McCabe in December 1969 during one of the worst blizzards in New York's history. After receiving his master's degree from Purdue University, he received pilot training at Craig Air Force base in Selma, Alabama, and McDill Air Force base in Tampa, Florida, where he was upgraded to a F-4 pilot.

Vietnam

From January to December of 1972, Gardner served his country in the Vietnam War. While his wife, Linda, nervously watched the evening news broadcasts, Guy coolly and methodically conducted more than 150 combat missions in a F-4 Phantom, including air-to-air combat missions north of Hanoi, one of the most embattled areas of the country.

Gardner showed his mettle. He was, for the most part, a man without fear. He was reasoned. "It would be hard to say which of the missions were the most dangerous, because I didn't feel fear. It was just my job, and I was trying to do the best I could at my job. If you allowed yourself to be fearful, it would interfere with doing your job."

Clearly, Guy Gardner was in control: of his emotions, his career, and his life. His spiritual life, distanced from need, slowly became less relevant. "I always knew the Lord was there if I needed Him," Gardner says, "but He was not a conscious, integral part of my day-to-day thought process."

Transition

Although he was by nature gentle, not arrogant, a secret, slowly acidic form of pride began to enter Guy's heart. He began,

Opposite: Astronaut Guy Gardner.

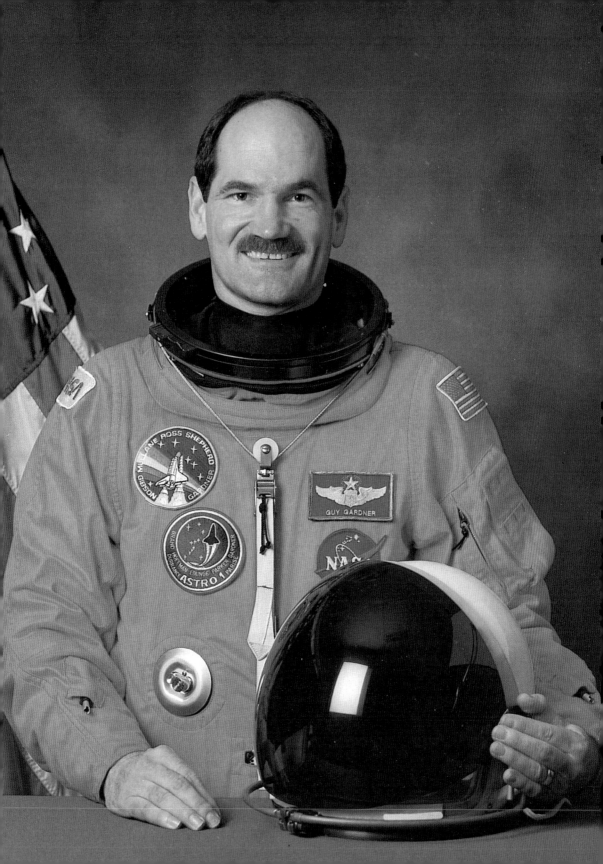

> *There was life, he decided, outside NASA.*

praise by praise, to accept credit for his own success. After his stint in Vietnam, he graduated at the top of his class at the USAF Test Pilot School at Edwards Air Force base. Still in his mid-twenties, Gardner was on the top of the world, soon to be headed "out" of this world—as an astronaut. Or so he hoped.

Slowly, God began to demand his attention. Curiously, those qualities that helped make Gardner a success—commitment, tenacity, cool reason—often plagued his relationship with God. He clung to his independence and prided himself on being able to handle almost any situation. He had been trained for, and was gifted at, handling crises.

Almost nothing shook Gardner. On Christmas Eve 1975, during a cross-country trip to his in-laws in New York, Linda miscarried. Guy, shifting into the cool reason of crisis mode, was able to care for his wife's physical and emotional needs. He took the first exit off the New York turnpike and found the nearest hospital. He comforted himself in the fact that they already had one healthy child.

NASA says no

In 1978, shortly before the birth of their third child, Guy received another blow, perhaps the most severe of his life. His application to become an astronaut was turned down by NASA. Although he had reached the final stage of interviews and many of his friends considered him a "shoo-in," Gardner's dream was crushed. What he had spent a lifetime dreaming about, and working toward, he now had to relinquish. "I really believed that my dream was over," Gardner said.

To make matters worse, the Air Force assigned him to a job in the Philippines instead of an expected and coveted transfer to test the new F-15 fighter plane. The Gardners, now with three children, had to move halfway around the world to what Guy described as a "nothing" job. Suddenly, Gardner was stripped of what he had hung onto all of his life—his dreams and his challenges.

Still, he survived, even prospered. As part of the job, the Gardners were furnished with a live-in housemaid, who helped take care of the children. That, combined with the lack of challenge on the job, freed the Gardners to spend more time together as a family and to slow down. Guy began to rediscover some important priorities in his life, as well as devise career alternatives to becoming an astronaut. There was life, he decided, outside NASA.

Just as he released his dream of becoming an astronaut, he read in a newspaper that NASA was again accepting applications. Freed from the "need" to become an astronaut, Gardner applied. In 1980, he was accepted.

Recommitment

It was then that God really began his humbling work in Guy Gardner. The man who, through fortitude, reason, and cool temperament, had not bowed, now was broken. In their move to Houston, the Gardners bought a "fixer-up" house because it was all they could afford. They also had "fixer-up" cars. Their youngest child has asthma and spent many nights in the emergency room. And the initial stage of being an astronaut, Gardner discovered, was not all that it was cracked up to be: endless briefings, little challenge, no responsibility, and a very long line for a shuttle flight.

Gardner, the unflappable, soon found himself crushed by the weight of home renovation and car repair, as well as by the weightlessness of his initial work. "I just couldn't handle it," Gardner says.

On the crest of realizing his lifelong dream, Gardner was humbled. He realized anew his need for the Lord. He recommitted his life, giving the Lord his dreams, his talents, and his career. Linda became a new believer. Together, they sought to serve the Lord.

Space travel and God

Slowly Gardner began to rely less on his own capabilities and more on God. He began to tell others about God's love for His

> *He recommitted his life, giving the Lord his dreams, his talents, and his career.*

The Gardner family at Edwards Air Force Base after Guy's last flight. Left–right: Sarah, Jennifer, Jason, Guy, Linda, and Worthy, Guy's mother.

special creation, each and every human soul. Because he is naturally introverted and because the successful, professional people he rubbed shoulders with did not care for "Bible thumpers," Gardner first attempted to speak the language of the gospel with his life—to live above reproach, to develop the attractive love of deep Christian community, to care for and serve others, to lead others by serving, to have a heart ringing with laughter. Questions came. Opportunities opened up.

Finally, in December 1988, Guy Gardner experienced a new perspective. Looking out the window of the Atlantis-STS-27 space shuttle, just two flights after the Challenger tragedy, he saw a swirling silver-blue jewel set against an unimaginable infinity of stars. The paradox of human life: so seemingly insignificant, yet so loved by the titanic heart of God.

Gardner has often been asked if he felt closer to God while in space. His answer is always the same: "No, I did not. I enjoyed the new perspective of viewing His creation, and it was more meaningful because of my close relationship with God. But I'm close to Him on earth and in space. You don't have

to go into space to find, or get closer to, God."

In 1991, Gardner retired from NASA to become commandant of the USAF Test Pilot School at Edwards Air Force base. In preparation for his new job, he began to pray for wisdom, James 1 style. What came to Gardner was the importance of the servant-leadership demonstrated by Christ. He sought to serve the needs of his staff, freeing them to do their jobs, as well as be the best people they could be.

Among the staff and the students, Gardner's reputation grew: approachable, genuine, caring, and a man who lives out his beliefs. He gained credibility to share the gospel verbally. That was—and continues to be—important to Gardner, as important as anything else he might do with his life. For he knows that through his words a whole new world opens up—one high above the silver-blue one he saw out his shuttle window—the eternally lovely place where the human heart connects with the grace of God.

Rob Wilkins

"THANKS FOR THAT GOOD QUESTION!"

Cliffe Knechtle

1954–

Outdoor preaching in America? Maybe Jesus Christ and George Whitefield could pull off street preaching in their day, but these are modern times! Street preaching today has a bad reputation, even among those sympathetic to its message. But onto the university campus in 1979 came a young man who would break the stereotype of individuals whose outdoor bombastic rantings to passersby were one-way diatribes against the evils of society. Cliffe Knechtle has successfully revived this type of evangelism and combined it with electrifying question-and-answer sessions in an unlikely place—the university campus.

Picture a lanky, tousled-haired six-foot-er, dressed casually in a sweater and Levis, standing on the patio of the Student Center at one of America's leading universities. It's noon. Classes are changing. Some students are eating their lunch outside. Laughter at a coarse joke ripples through a group of men. Girls, showing off the remnants of their summer tans, scurry to the next class with a diet soda in their hands. Who could capture the attention of these seemingly self-sufficient passersby?

A lanky preacher

The casually dressed man stands on a low wall, and a loud, persistent voice is raised above the din. "I want to talk to you today about Jesus Christ. You have a God-shaped vacuum inside of you." Curious, skeptical, and often hostile eyes glance toward this interferer. Many quickly avert their eyes, chuckle, and pass on. Others with smirking faces comment to their companion, "Who's that nut?" The fellow who told the coarse joke yells, "Go back to your TV station, preacher. We don't have any money for you."

"I'm here to give, not take," Cliffe Knechtle responds in a serious tone. "Why not give me a few minutes of your time? Don't knock something before you've given it a hearing!"

Students in groups of ones and twos pause for an instant. "Maybe we'll have some fun with this guy," thinks a contingent of fraternity men. Here and there a shy individual stands at a distance, listening—but with fur-tive glances lest any of his friends sees him paying attention. Several Christian students, having prayed, begin to stand still and move close to Cliffe. Others, noticing a crowd forming, stop. The Christian students unobtrusively filter to the back of the small crowd, allowing their friends an unobstructed view. The Christians continue to pray and begin to engage individuals in dialogue even as Cliffe begins.

"God made you—and this gives you significance. It accounts for both the noble and

Evangelist Cliffe Knechtle in a characteristically committed stance.

The Life of Cliffe Knechtle

1954	Born on May 20, 1954 in New York City
	Cliffe's parents point him to Christ at an early age, while he is growing up in New Canaan, Connecticut
1976	Attends Davidson College in North Carolina
1979	Attends Gordon-Conwell Theological Seminary
	Joins staff of InterVarsity Christian Fellowship as traveling evangelist in the USA
1980	Ordained by the Southern Baptist Church
1982	Marries Sharon McDonald on June 5 (now has three sons)
1986	Publishes *Give Me an Answer*

New York City ●

USA

the ignoble, the creative and beautiful, the destructive and humble we see in ourselves."

Listening

The brief presentation continues. But soon Cliffe invites questions. You can almost read the thought that comes to their minds. "What's this? Most preachers don't listen. This could be interesting. Think I'll hang around for a few minutes and watch him get shot down." As Cliffe is hit with a number of the "top ten pagan questions" (often expressed with attitudes of hostility and incredulity), he is ready with an arsenal of

> *He will prepare students to recapture a lost audience— modern man.*

scriptural arrows and darts of supporting insight from a bevy of secular thinkers. His lively personal demeanor, coupled with a "no holds barred, ask me any question," begins to intrigue these students whose motto is "Question Authority." Even when their questions are of the smoke screen variety, Cliffe patiently responds. He knows he will win the attention of his listeners as he treats them with dignity.

Almost imperceptibly the mood of the crowd changes. The hostility abates, many pass on, numerous others listen carefully to his insightful comments to each questioner. You can almost hear the students' thoughts: *There's something different about this guy. He listens. It's not a one-way lecture. His answers are powerful. He seems to know what I'm like!*

After forty-five minutes the crowd has pretty well dispersed. The students who now pass by the patio area don't even notice the large number of groups of people now in twos and threes avidly discussing Jesus Christ with a Christian student who has simply asked them, "Well, what do you think about what Cliffe said?" And the lanky young six-footer? He's melted into the campus scene, sitting at one of the tables, continuing to talk to the fellow who yelled at him in the beginning. Now that his friends have left, he's become honest about the vacuum in his life. An audience has been exposed to truth clothed with gracious words. Seekers of truth have become visible (by their questions or just their attention) and can now be engaged in conversation about the Author of life. Soon Cliffe will move on to another campus, invited by students in InterVarsity Christian Fellowship and other evangelical groups. There he will pray with them and prepare these students to recapture a lost audience—modern man.

Boston bars

Cliffe Knechtle got his start in speaking to non-Christians when he began to frequent bars in Boston while a student at Gordon-Conwell Theological Seminary. "I got tired of talking about the gospel only to Chris-

Cliff Knechtle
preaching on
campus.

tians. Leighton Ford challenged me, so I went where the audience was. I would listen to men in the bar curse God. Then I'd say, 'Gentlemen, I demand equal time. I want to say something positive about God!'

"I see a model for what I do in Paul's preaching in the hall of Tyrannus (Acts 19:9) and at the Areopagus (Acts 17:22–23). I try to combine love and truth in what I say. Sometimes I err too much on the truth side. I come off as harsh—too strong. I'm struggling with that. Yet there is also an inherent offense of the gospel. I'm constantly learning about communication. My dad would tell me stories as he put me to bed at night. That's how I learned story telling."

Dialogue preaching

Cliffe's approach is "dialogue preaching." He casts his gospel net widely and then begins to pull it in. His question-and-answer sessions are like the strands of that net, catching certain people who might never be reached by the best-planned, financed,

advertised, and prayed-for evangelistic event. Why? Because many non-Christians will never come to these. Cliffe believes Christians must go where the fish are and catch them in the midst of their activities, drawing alongside them. Although the size of the crowds who pause to listen is often small, Cliffe speaks to a higher percentage of non-Christians than many other evangelists.

Can a person raised in a Christian home in suburban America develop a passion for the lost and an affection for the poor? Yes, and Cliffe is proof. Cliffe is the first to admit that he is nothing apart from the grace of God and the human agents that God used to mold him into a bold witness: his wife, parents, five younger brothers and sisters, and the Leighton Ford family. What obstacles is he now facing?

It's spring break and thousands of college

> *Cliffe speaks to a higher percentage of non-Christians than many other evangelists.*

students are in Florida. Inside a Ft. Lauderdale motel room, Cliff Knechtle paces back and forth as he talks to his wife, Sharon, on the phone—restless, intense, and, in his words, "scared spitless." He's about to go out on the beach, stand up, and call these fun lovers to listen to the words of Jesus. It takes a lot of courage to do this. Cliffe doesn't have it. His wife is a great support and often traveled with him at first. But not since the birth of their second child. "It is a real struggle to have to travel and be away from my family," Cliffe says. But soon he walks to the beach and attracts a crowd to his compelling message.

Another challenge that Cliffe faces in his dialogue preaching is the temptation to respond condescendingly. After all, he is often personally attacked, and his ideas are not dealt with intelligently. What's it like to try to deal seriously with a question he's heard hundreds of times before? "I try to remember this is a real person, loved by God. I ask for patience to listen. Often I help them by rephrasing questions to express their point clearly. I remember that not only are nonbelievers inspecting me, but the Christians are learning from my attitudes. I constantly experience the sovereignty of God in causing certain hecklers to move on, and the serious, personal questions to be asked."

The local church
One big question is, how can his evangelism influence the local church? Cliffe is learning

> *All the other supposed saviors are idols that lead us to destruction.*

about this firsthand as he spends part of each year as an assistant pastor in a local church. Here he tangles with ways to help people share their faith one to one.

Modern men and women are on the run. This target is hard to hit. The gospel continually needs to be forwarded to their new address, both literally (finding people recently moved to an area), and figuratively (noticing the changing felt needs of people). Whether it's Mars Hill in Athens, Greece, or the University of Georgia in Athens, Georgia, Cliffe Knechtle offers the church one distinct way to identify and be bold in the campus and marketplace today. Most people have never heard the gospel stripped of its Christian subculture jargon. Cliffe wants to change that. He hopes others will follow his lead.

Motivation
Why does he do it? "Two reasons. I love Jesus, and I'm convinced He offers quality to life, for I've experienced it. Next, truth is crucial. Jesus is real, and all the other supposed saviors are idols that lead us to destruction. When He comes again I wouldn't want anyone to say to me, 'Cliffe, why didn't you have the guts to tell me?'"

Will Metzger

TRANSFORMED HIPPIE

Tom Maharias

1949–

Anastasios Maharias was born in Thessaloniki in northern Macedonia on September 22, 1949. As a child in Greece, Tasos was independent and adventuresome, qualities that would get him into trouble and later make him the leader that he now is. Once he followed a gypsy and his dancing bear from neighborhood to neighborhood; his parents found their son the next day at the police station.

In 1957 Tasos and his family migrated to New York City. As their boat approached the west side of Manhattan the millions of lights overwhelmed his seven-year-old mind; he thought he was in outer space. That sight still remains vivid. His new dwelling—a sixth-floor walk up on Amsterdam Avenue in the Washington Heights section of Manhattan—was quite different from his one-family house in Greece. During his first few months on the streets of New York, Tom (his American name) had much adjusting to do. His recollections were not too pleasant: Italian, Irish, and Spanish children flattened his bicycle tires and called him "Greece-ball" to instigate fistfights. One boy took out a knife and chased him through the streets; when he caught Tom he stabbed him . . . surprise! It was a trick knife where the blade retracts into the handle. From this and many other experiences Tom began to view others with cynicism and distrust. A crust of toughness developed as a defense mechanism to combat the continual pressures he felt daily.

A doomed lifestyle

Tom's parents were hard workers and had little time to communicate with him. They were unaware of the lifestyle changes introduced to him by other young people on the streets. Mesmerized by the rock-and-roll music of the 1950s, Tom was motivated to

No matter how "messed up" a person is morally, spiritually, physically, emotionally, or mentally the gospel is the power of God for the salvation of everyone who believes. Its transforming power has the same effect on people today as it did with the demoniac that Jesus encountered two thousand years ago. One such man, Tom Maharias, is living proof the gospel is still the power of God unto salvation!

New York's *Daily News Magazine* features Tom Maharias on its cover.

The Life of Tom Maharias

1949	Born Anastasios Maharias in Thessaloniki, Greece, September 22
1957	Migrates to New York
1965	Becomes submerged in the drug culture and the hippie movement
1968	Conversion at Word of Life
1970	Graduates from Institute of Christian Service, Bob Jones University
1971	Marries Victoria Riccardella
1974	Begins Manhattan Bible Church
1977	Begins Spanish ministry
1978	Founds Manhattan Christian Academy
1982	Founds Transformation Life Center
1985	Founds New York Gospel Outreach
1987	Founds Manhattan Love Kitchen
1990	Sabbatical in Boca Raton, Florida
1991	Returns to New York City, establishes infrastructure of Manhattan Bible Church Ministries
1993	MBC Cells: Manhattan Bible Church "divides" to "multiply"

New York City •

USA

> *Two months before graduation he was expelled for having a fistfight with the principal.*

develop his own band, which would play for his junior high graduation at the Trocaderra Nightclub. By his senior year in high school Tom's whole manner of life had crumbled: socialistic ideas, shoulder-length hair, outlandish clothes, an immoral relationship, and drug dealing. But he thought he was doing great, living like a king! Inwardly and outwardly he was a full-fledged rebel; two months before graduation George Washington High School expelled him for having a fistfight with the principal. Humiliated, his parents asked him to leave home.

Congruent with the hippie lifestyle, Tom and his girlfriend Vicky moved into their friends' apartment in Greenwich Village. Considering themselves "seekers of truth" they were willing to try any new idea that presented itself: Krishna, transcendental meditation, Marxism, and Kahlil Gibran. Once while experiencing the effects of LSD they ran through Central Park asking everyone the questions that were plaguing them: "Who are we? Where did we come from? Why are we here? Where are we going?" Soon after this "trip" they rescued one of their friends from jumping from a six-story tenement building. Later that same night Tom began to hallucinate; the room filled with demonic images, and a huge lion and a serpent were coming to get him. In desperation he cried out, "Oh God, please help me! Jesus, please help me!" Such experiences unnerved Vicky, and she returned home to finish school.

Diagnosed as schizophrenic

Tom's parents asked him to see psychiatrists at Lenox Hill Hospital; in order to put off his parents and show them he was OK, he agreed. Diagnosed as schizophrenic he was tied up and given shock treatments for ten days. These were dark days; a spiritual war was raging within for possession of his soul. Through the requests of Vicky and threats from his brother, Jimmy, the doctors released Tom. Once again he found himself by Bethesda Fountain in Central Park, won-

Tom Maharias
plays his guitar
at a peace rally
in the 1960s.

dering what life was all about. He came to one conclusion: he wanted to escape all the sin and pain of New York City. But wherever he went he carried his problems with him. Tom finally made his "escape": he ran to the West Side Highway and hitch-hiked upstate to Lake George.

The war within intensified. One day looking into the sky, he cried out to God, "I am!" Soon after this a young man came up to him and asked if he could speak to him about spiritual things. Tom accused him of being Satan; the young man responded to the accusation by saying, "No, I'm Bruce."

Looking for Jesus

For the next two hours Tom asked questions and Bruce answered them from the Scriptures. Bruce invited Tom to go with him to Word of Life Island. On their trip to the camp Tom (still hallucinating) thought the boat actually came up out of the water into the sky. At the island the first person he met was a happy, white-haired man holding a Bible. Robbie Robertson pointed to the Bible and told Tom he needed to hear the Word of God. Tom thought he had met God.

The next morning Tom went looking for Jesus. Unable to find Him he asked someone on the second day, "Do you know where Jesus is?" The man said he usually met Jesus down by the lake and asked Tom if he wanted to go. Bob sat on a rock with Tom and introduced him to Jesus Christ by reading to him John 3:16. Bowing his head Tom prayed, "Lord, please forgive me for all my ego, self, and pride. I put all of it down and I ask you, Lord Jesus, to come into my heart and change my life. From now on you can have total control of my life. Just tell me what to do and I'll do it."

That was the beginning of a new life for Tom Maharias. At a service that night he let everyone know he had accepted Christ as his Savior. He called his girlfriend and told her he had met Jesus; Vicky came to Word of Life thinking he had found a hippie commune. The next day Tom took her to the same rock by the lake and introduced her to Jesus. After hearing Tom's "testimony" Vicky asked Jesus to be her Savior. This was not only the beginning of a new relationship between them, it was also the beginning of a new evangelistic lifestyle for Tom.

Since that day in 1968, Tom has never stopped sharing that the gospel is the power

> *To evangelize New York City with the gospel of Jesus Christ and to help train leaders for world evangelization.*

of God for the salvation of everyone who believes. As he attended the Institute of Christian Service at Bob Jones University in South Carolina he "hung out" at the Augusta (Georgia) Christian Servicemen's Center sharing his faith with soldier boys; through his personal influence several hundred young men experienced the same transforming power of the gospel. On weekends he traveled across the United States preaching in churches and sharing his conversion story with youth groups. In the summer of 1971, accompanied by an evangelistic team, Tom returned to the streets of New York. He saw the power of God at work again financially and spiritually. Many heard the good news and trusted Christ as their Savior.

A church grows in Manhattan
After graduation Vicky and Tom were married on June 5, 1971. They purposed in their hearts to return to New York City and trust God to plant a church. In 1974 they moved to Washington Heights and started a church in the living room of their apartment. Many of their friends and family heard what God had done for them. It was obvious to all that they were transformed.

The congregation grew and grew! Today, Manhattan Bible Church is located in two buildings at the corner of Ninth Avenue and West 205th Street. Its many ministries have one premise: to evangelize New York City with the gospel of Jesus Christ and to help train leaders for world evangelization. Manhattan Christian Academy (p 3–Grade 12) is a safe haven for children to learn academics and Christian character. As teachers communicate with the families, they have a natural inroad to share the gospel.

The majority of the population of the Washington Heights/Inwood section of Manhattan is Hispanic, providing the need for the Spanish Ministry. Transformation Life Center is a one-year rehabilitation program in upstate New York for men who want to live life from God's point of view.

Its public relations director, Billy Schneider, was Tom's junior partner in crime. Through Tom's persistent witnessing of twenty years, Billy came to trust in the transforming power of Jesus. Knowing that New York City is called the "capital of the world," Pastor Tom founded New York Gospel Outreach to provide a worldwide missions experience in America to the youth of America. It is an intense, one-week project that enables young people not only to share their faith on the streets of New York City but also to "take it home." Overwhelmed with the plight of the homeless, Pastor Tom began to ask God for a practical way to share the gospel with them. In answer to his prayers God provided the finances to open Manhattan Love Kitchen. (Its director, Jewel Jones, a former member of the Eldorados, turned to Jesus Christ through the testimony of Pastor Tom.)

In January 1991, Pastor Tom was given a six-month sabbatical in Boca Raton, Florida. In his extended time of reflection and meditation God showed him that to continue in his quest of sharing the faith he would have to establish an infrastructure of leadership in the church. Upon his return to New York City he chose nine men with leadership potential. This intensive training is now in the process of multiplication. The leadership is presently being trained to conduct small-group Bible studies, much like the one Tom and Vicky started in 1974 in their living room. MBC Cells divides Manhattan Bible Church into thirty different geographical locations for the purpose of multiplication. This opens up yet another avenue for the people to share with friends and family the gospel—the power of God for the salvation of everyone who believes.

Denise Hykes

Further Reading

Power for Living 47 (June–August 1989). Glen Ellyn, Ill.: Scripture Press.

Tucker, Ruth. *Sacred Stories*. Grand Rapids: Zondervan, 1989.

Wyrtzen, David. *Raising Worldly-Wise But Innocent Kids*. Chicago: Moody, 1990.

A BIG VISION

Bill Hybels

In 1976, Bill Hybels and a group of young people went door-to-door, taking a survey. For a few months, they asked the following question: "Do you go to church?" If the person said "Yes," the survey was over. If "No" there was a follow-up question: "Why not?" To summarize the results: The church is irrelevant and hungry for my money. The overriding feeling: "The church is answering questions that I am not asking."

This information was valuable. What was even more important, and certainly unexpected, was the emotional impact. "Day after day," says Hybels, "you stand fourteen inches away from somebody and you ask him questions about God and you see a blank expression. And you realize that you are looking into the eyes of someone who is facing a Christless eternity."

After coming home, Hybels would be completely drained. He remembers saying to his wife, "Honey, if I ever preach an irrelevant sermon, if we build a church that does not flow with life and creativity and risk taking, if we ever bore people with the gospel or with church, we've got to get out because it's killing people."

The church, when it is functioning properly, must be a force to deal with. Empowered by the Holy Spirit, cut loose by hearts centered on the will of God, fired by a vision of eternal importance, the church should penetrate the society around it with the light and love of the gospel of Jesus Christ. Evangelism, for an active New Testament church, should be as natural as breathing.

His earthly father: stretching

In leading Willow Creek Church, Hybels was prepared by his two fathers. First, there was his earthly father. As Bill was growing up, it was an unspoken assumption that he

For Bill Hybels, church is the business of danger.

Danger, that is, in its active sense: the wrench of human pride, the salt of a decaying society, light in a dark world, the impossible movement of life from death. When it comes to defining church, Hybels's verbs are always active, close to the edge of something daring, even unheard of.

To some extent his view of the body of Christ is a reflection. The church he pastors, Willow Creek Community Church, in a suburb northwest of Chicago, is dynamic. More than fourteen thousand people attend each weekend, while more than one hundred ministries are active during the week. Many who attend and serve were formerly unsaved or unchurched. But mostly his perspective of the church is shaped by a vision: the vision of Jesus Christ. Through his ministry at Willow Creek, thousands upon thousands have come to share the same vision of the Savior.

was to carry on the family business—a successful produce company in Kalamazoo, Michigan. It was a goal that young Bill willingly embraced. Certainly, there was the appeal of the boats, planes, and fast cars: money, he knew, wasn't completely worthless. More than that, there was the action and, from an early age, he had been caught up with the idea of risk, adventure, and winning. But mostly, there was the love of his father. It was a deep love.

> *Evangelism should be as natural as breathing.*

The Life of Bill Hybels

1951	Born in Kalamazoo, Illinois, December 12
1969	Converted, August
1973	Joins staff of South Park Church in Park Ridge, Illinois
1974	Marries Lynne
1975	Opening of Willow Creek Community Church in Palatine, Illinois
1978	First book published
1979	Nearly two thousand people attend Willow Creek
1979	Willow Creek splits
1979–81	Hybels and Willow Creek survive greatest crises
1990	Willow Creek becomes second largest church in America, with more than 14,000 people

USA   •Chicago   ILLINOIS

*"If this is real,
this is the greatest thing
on the face of the earth."*

his father's forty-five-foot sailboat for a solo trip across Lake Michigan. When he was fifteen, he traveled through Africa and Europe by himself: one time he ran out of cash in Nigeria, and his dad wired him some money. Eventually.

For some, his father's actions would have been cruel. For Bill, they were stretching. From his father, Bill learned self-esteem, survival skills, not to be afraid of the unknown, and to have a love for challenge and risk.

His heavenly Father: saving
Then, there was his heavenly Father. He also was preparing the young Hybels. At age seventeen, at Awana camp, Bill began a real relationship with God through Jesus Christ. He had just memorized Titus 3:5—"Not by works of righteousness which we have done, but according to His mercy He saved us"— and suddenly the scales fell from his eyes.

"It was an awareness of the free gift of salvation out of love that stopped me dead in my tracks," Hybels says. "I thought my heart was going to explode—I couldn't imagine that kind of love. I remember just standing there saying, 'You've got to be kidding. This is too good to be true. If this is real, this is the greatest thing on the face of the earth.'"

Later that same year came the struggle over career. Should he pursue his father's business? Or ministry? The director of a youth association pulled him aside and asked a question that changed the direction of his life: "Bill, what are you going to do with your life that lasts for eternity?" The question startled Hybels: he began to see how much he was focused on the "here and now"—the money, the things and, above all, the compelling, nearly obsessive idea of "just winning."

Hybels went to college, still planning to go into business. He left school after two years because he was "bored silly." He decided to leave his father's business to pursue ministry. "It was very hard on him," Hybels says of the reaction of his father, who was a Christian. "In my subculture, fathers pass on business to their sons. That's

"He really believed in me," says Hybels, "and he thought there was virtually no end to what I could accomplish with my life." His father was an entrepreneur and risk taker, a man who could, with equal dexterity, direct a company and sail across the Atlantic Ocean.

So Harold Hybels, in his unorthodox and sometimes distant manner, prepared his son. By the time he was in first grade, the younger Hybels could drive the company pickup truck. When he was in fifth grade, his father sent him off on a train for a skiing vacation in Aspen, Colorado. He forgot to tell his son, however, that the train did not stop in Aspen, but in a town twenty-five miles away. In seventh grade, Bill took out the name of the game." Graciously, Harold let his son leave.

Hybels moved to Chicago, rented "a dive" with three of his camp Awana buddies, and began his first battle on the "spiritual front lines"—a minimum wage job in the shipping department of the Awana Youth Association, assigned to a team of two middle-aged women who were stuffing plastic awards into cellophane packages. He felt like he was on an adventure of a lifetime.

The plunge into ministry

In 1973, Hybels left the shipping department. He had been invited by a close friend to come on staff of the South Park Church in Park Ridge, Illinois, a suburb of Chicago. His friend, Dave Holmbo, worked with youth and music and had started Son Company, a singing group formed from the kids in the high school ministry.

Soon, Hybels was asked to lead a Bible study after the Son Company rehearsal. More precisely, he would take a passage of Scripture and lead a discussion on its relevance to real life. With no particular plan or vision in mind, Son Company grew from about thirty to eighty. Most of those came by invitation and were not necessarily interested in music. Soon the group met at a separate time, and a whole evening was set aside. The meeting was designed to reach kids and their "seeking" friends with the gospel. Such was the birth of the Son City Spectacular.

At the first Son City, more than 150 to 200 teenagers showed up. Holmbo and Hybels were stunned. Within six months, the attendance grew to about 300. By 1975, the group had split into two nights and between 1,000 and 1,200 students attended. In 1972, when Son Company started, the annual budget for the entire youth ministry was $300. Three years later, it was $80,000. The large numbers, however, were not what was really important. It was more the sense of God being unleashed in dramatic ways in individual lives.

From the beginning, God's sovereignty was clearly evident. The right people with the right gifts were gathered at the right time and the right place. The coupling of Holmbo and Hybels as leaders was critical, both for how they differed from one another, and for

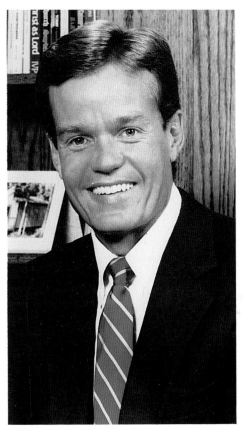

Bill Hybels, pastor of the phenomenal Willow Creek Community Church, in suburban Chicago.

what they shared. They played off one another. Dave provided the artistic direction: music, drama, and programming. Bill provided the spiritual leadership and the businessman's feel for the nuts and bolts. They both shared a "big" vision for the church that moved past their early frustration. "They shared a mutual frustration with how it (church) had been done in their past and a mutual yearning to do it another way," says Bill's wife, Lynne.

Youth offered a unique "soil" for the planting of an entirely different kind of ministry: endless energy, teachable minds and hearts, unlimited idealism, an ability to comprehend the word *impossible*, extraordinary passion, and a nearly complete abandonment to the cause. "We were on a roll," Hybels says.

> *Seeker-friendly services . . . create a "safe place to hear an unsafe message."*

Starting a church

In 1975, in the middle of the explosive movement of the South Park youth group, Hybels got another call. This one was even more bizarre. It was, from just about any perspective one would care to choose, illogical, threatening, risky, and doomed to fail. Maybe even downright stupid. It was this leading from the Holy Spirit: Bill Hybels, at twenty-three, was to start a church. And not just any church, but one capable of taking on the world.

Explains Hybels, "I just felt that if we were ever going to reach a city or a state or a country or the world, as Jesus asked us to, then we were going to do it through whole families, not just youth."

From a worldly perspective, it was not a coherent vision. He had no money, no members, no structure, no facility, no precedent, no influence, no way to support himself and his wife, no seminary degree, no elders, and not even a hint of logic. What he had was this: the unmistakable, unrelenting leading of the Holy Spirit.

Hybels and Holmbo, who was initially reluctant, quit their jobs at South Park. Holmbo would live on his wife's salary and do some music teaching on the side. The Hybelses would take in two boarders, and Lynne, whom Bill married in 1974, would teach flute lessons. They felt like pioneers.

Despite the long odds, they had powerful memories. From their experience with the youth group, they had learned some valuable lessons. Without really knowing why or how, they had stumbled onto some critical strategies for church life, most of which empowered Willow Creek Community Church. Says one former pastor, "The vast majority of our philosophy (today at Willow Creek) was developed during the Son City days. All we have done since then is put handles on what we did by instinct then." Among those strategies are the following.

The concept of "ownership." Ministry is not just what the leaders do, but is shared by all people. The key to involvement and ownership is the use of spiritual gifts. "Kids were learning that they could play a part in the ministry," Hybels says. "Some could sing; others could do art; others could do sound and lighting; others could counsel and help others. We were beginning to discover that everyone in a community of faith plays a

critical role."

The emphasis on "seeker friendly" services. The call of Hybels has always been to create a "church for the unchurched." In the youth group, a high priority was placed on reaching the lost. That continued when, on October 12, 1975, Hybels and his coworkers opened the doors of the Willow Creek Theater in Palatine, Illinois (another Chicago suburb) for the first service of Willow Creek Community Church.

The idea of seeker-friendly services is to create a "safe place to hear an unsafe message." The relevance of the Bible is stressed to the realities of everyday life: the use of money, what God has to say about marriage, the impossibility of being "good enough" to get into heaven. "Seekers" are encouraged to come in an anonymous setting and explore their questions about the Bible, God, and spirituality. The Christian message is presented in its most basic terms: "Christianity 101 or 201." (For Christians seeking doctrine, midweek services delve deeper into the Bible.)

In seeker-friendly services, however, relevancy is achieved from a variety of sources. Music is contemporary and deals with real-life issues. Drama is presented and, through a backdoor approach, pricks a seeker's conscience and heart with a "hey, that's me" sense of connection.

In seeker-friendly services, Willow Creek does not apologize for being entertaining. At the same time, however, the church seeks not to compromise the integrity of biblical doctrine. Eventually the seeker comes face to face with the fact of sin, a need for repentance, and the absolute necessity of the intrusive and life-changing grace of God.

Each person "matters to God"

"We strongly believe in John 3:16," Hybels says. Each person, no matter what his circumstances, is important to God, so important that Jesus Christ died for him or her.

More than two hundred people showed up during the first seeker-friendly service of the church held at Willow Creek Theater.

> *Within a year, the church had more than one thousand people coming on weekends.*

Mostly, in a curious twist, it was kids dragging their parents to church.

There was also the deep sense of community. Of "us." "Willow Creek is really the product of community," says Hybels. "In its very essence. No one single person was responsible. There was just a nucleus of people who brought their strength and vision and shared it with the group. We learned from early on what the Bible means by community—that relational dimension where there is warmth, vulnerability, closeness, transparency, commitment and loyalty."

Like Son City, the results were also the same. Lives were being changed. Within a year, the church had more than one thousand people coming on weekends. By 1979, that number had nearly doubled, and the church was bursting the seams at each of the three weekend services. By 1990, the church had moved to its present campus in South Barrington and was soon drawing thousands.

On the brink of failure

All of this is not to say that Bill Hybels has a magic touch, that all ministry he touches turns to gold. Far from it. In 1979, four years after starting Willow Creek, the wheels

fell off. The church—beset by burnout, little or no accountability, spiritual and emotional immaturity, and what Hybels calls an "addiction to fruit bearing"—experienced a painful split. Holmbo, the co-founder, and most of the people who formed the "creative guts" of the church left.

"We were all obsessed with ministry and paid no attention to the pace of our lives," Hybels says. Many fell into sin.

But the church split was not all that Hybels was dealing with. During the latter part of 1978 and on into 1979 several crises affected Bill Hybels's life: his father died, his wife had a miscarriage, the church staff disintegrated, his marriage fell into shambles, people began to question his motivation, his best friend became involved in sin, and the church fell behind in its fund-raising efforts.

Everything was unraveling. Except Bill Hybels's faith.

Face down on the carpet, alone in the middle of the night, Hybels remembers a Gethsemane-like prayer. He had to make a call: Were they going to go on with the church or not? It had reached that point. Possibly for the first time in his life, he experienced a situation that was beyond his

> ## *The pace was allowed to slow down.*

control. Even his father's training had not prepared him for this.

He deeply felt the weight of his own sins and shortcomings: modeling an unhealthy pace; failing to confront; a lack of emotional, psychological, and spiritual maturity; and, at times, a failure to show compassion. After a period of confession, he prayed: "We don't deserve You giving us another shot, but if You give us one more round, we'll do it right."

It was, he says, a critical moment. "I made a commitment that this was going to be God's church and we were going God's way and we were going to teach God's Word."

What he sensed was a feeling of surrender. "It was in God's hands," he says.

The crisis did not disappear overnight. For nearly two years, 1979–1981, the church hung on by a thread. "We were always just one service away from extinction," says Hybels. Yet in many ways, despite its blackness, the era was one of the most important in the church's history. The lessons learned and the changes implemented, restored perspective and shaped the church's future. The overriding consideration in decision making became: "God has to be in this."

"There was a lot of confession and brokenness before the Lord," says Hybels. "There was a deep sense of humility and dependance on God."

Sacrifice

There were crucial changes: the leaders, tried under fire, became the ruling body of the church. Staff structure took on a well-defined chain of command to make accountability possible. Expectations for staff and leaders were outlined: no longer would it be enough to just have a gift or proficiency. The pace was allowed to slow down. Relationships and caring for people, once again, became the core of the church.

But, more than anything else, it was a period deeply marked by sacrifice. There was a belief, beyond all logic, that Willow Creek Community Church would not only survive, but would play a key role for the kingdom of God. In the hearts of many, the vision still burned.

Several years and many transformed hearts later, the vision still burns. It is the vision of a church that belongs to Christ.

Rob Wilkins

PASSIONATE ARTIST

Steve Green

1956–

Steve Green was born to Charles and Jo, missionary parents, on August 1, 1956, in Portland, Oregon. He spent his formative years in Argentina. He was home schooled for a year by his Mom, spent another year in public school, then spent the next six grades (third–eighth) at a Christian boarding school away from home. He attended high school both in the United States and in Argentina.

Charles and Jo did a good job with their kids. Their daughter Barbara is married to Mark Bailey, a professor of Bible exposition at Dallas Theological Seminary. Their other daughter, Grace, is married to Rev. Jerry Hill, who is a pastor in New Jersey. Steve and his brother David are both involved in music ministry. David is the administrator for Steve Green Ministries. Randy, Steve's older brother, with his wife, Marlene, and kids, is a missionary in Venezuela.

Coming to know the Lord

One Sunday afternoon in Argentina, Steve Green's life was changed forever. Though only eight years old, he began to recognize his need for forgiveness, for a Savior. On that red-letter day Steve had just returned from church and was required to take a nap. To pass the time he read his Sunday school paper and was touched by one of the testimonies. The Holy Spirit used this simple, unpretentious event to bring conviction of sin and realization of the need for forgiveness and cleansing. Steve knelt by his bed in a room all by himself and asked Christ to be

> *He opened himself to receive God's eternal truth, he accepted in childlike faith, and he made it his own.*

Behind the boyish, clean-cut good looks of Steve Green lies a passionate artist and a man who desires to live in genuine spiritual integrity. Since signing with Sparrow Records in 1983, he has sold more than two million records. He has won six Dove Awards and four Grammy nominations. Many of his Christian radio singles, such as "People Need the Lord," "He Holds the Keys," and "Find Us Faithful," have become standard favorites.

His concerts can thrill and inspire, bring goose bumps, tears to the eyes, and a lump in the throat. Just listen to him sing, "I Know That My Redeemer Liveth," or "Symphony of Praise," or "He Holds the Keys," and you will know what I mean.

Yet there is so much more to know about Steve. His life is not only about moving performances. He is not a one-dimensional man. He has a broad, well-rounded life, a warm, fulfilling family context, and a disciplined spiritual walk. It is this walk that informs his life and work and makes him very special among contemporary Christian musicians. Moreover, he is committed to sharing Christ through his music because "People Need the Lord."

his Savior. He saw clearly that being part of a Christian, missionary family was not enough. He appropriated the fundamentals of the historic Christian faith (the death, burial, and resurrection of Christ) in a profoundly simple and personal way. He opened himself to receive God's eternal truth, he accepted in childlike faith, and he made it his own.

Getting started in music

The whole Green family in Argentina was musically inclined. Steve's father, Charles, played trumpet and sang. Steve's mother, Jo, played piano and accordion, and possessed a beautiful voice. Steve's brothers played guitars, and Steve played B-flat clarinet. They were able to make little family orchestras for church events and special meetings. Charles would often take his family to small Argentine villages to perform as an attention grabber and crowd builder. He was a master of using music to build a bridge to people. He would then follow through with a dynamic presentation of the gospel.

Of all the kids, Steve had the strongest predisposition to music. He was drawn to it like a magnet. In high school, both in the States and in Argentina, music became a important part of his life—maybe even too important. It became a way of escape from the real world and a way to understand and express new and strange adolescent emotions of loneliness, homesickness, frustration, and even rebellion. Lost in the isolation of his bedroom, he could get high on the mesmerizing painkiller of pop music. He stoked this habit by buying and listening to tapes and by hearing the Voice of America Countdown every Saturday night in Argentina for the latest American hits.

Yet, even with all of that, Steve never thought of music as a career. It was a hobby, a communications tool in church work, or a personal, aesthetic enjoyment. He thought he would attend Grand Canyon University to pursue a medical or legal profession. He certainly never sat with a clipboard writing out goals relating to how to become a B.M.O.C. (big man on campus) in the music business.

Other people—professors, friends, and musicians—affirmed and confirmed his musical gifts. College life was enriched with choir, private voice lessons, and participation in small musical groups. Personal ambition was not a factor at all in Steve's aspiring involvements in music.

One night, Steve and a friend went to hear the touring group, Truth. His friend also went to audition for possible membership in the group. But Roger Breland, the group's leader, needed a tenor and asked to hear Steve. This led to a two-year stint with Truth (1976–1978) during which he sang

> ## Steve sees children as on loan from God.

alongside a lovely, talented brunette named Marijean. This work with Truth led to singing backup for The Bill Gaither Trio and becoming an original member of the Gaither Vocal Band (1978–1983). In 1983 he signed with Sparrow Records as a solo artist, and, as they say, "The rest is history."

Family life

After touring the United States with Truth, Steve and Marijean were married in 1978. They now have two children, twelve-year-old Summer and eight-year-old Josiah. Marijean home schools the children, and they tour together as a family. "We are thankful that this lifestyle has been conducive to growth for them. We take every other day on the road off, so we enjoy great family times," Steve says.

Steve sees fathering as one of the most sacred privileges and tremendous responsibilities that God entrusts to men. He sees his children as on loan from God, and he sees his responsibility as nurturing and instilling an understanding of the character of God, our heavenly Father. He finds great joy and lasting fulfillment in being a father and has enjoyed every aspect of it.

Summer is a seventh grader who is an aspiring gymnast. Josiah is a second grader who is nuts about basketball. Both of them have professed faith in Christ, and both are starting to get involved in recording and videos in order to help motivate children to memorize Scripture.

With all of Steve's responsibilities and pressures he still has quality time for his family and close friends. He also enjoys gardening and working in his yard, which he attacks with a vengeance. He has an eye for God's creation in nature as he rides his Harley down the historic Natchez Trace Highway.

Randy's confrontation

Gracing the headquarters of Steve Green Ministries in Nashville is DiCianni's artist proof, "The Prodigal." It is a regular reminder of a period of personal turmoil that led to a turning point in Steve's life. It was a cataclysmic event that began a new life in

> *There was no harmony in his soul.*

ministry for Steve.

Back in high school days, Steve began a double life. There was no harmony between his internal reality and the external image he projected. Inside and outside were in dissonance with each other. Outside, he was involved in ministry, especially sensitive to people, and going through the motions of Christian ministry. Inside, he was rebellious, autonomous, hard-hearted, and disobedient. There was no harmony in his soul.

Starting in high school he began to be obstinate and willful. He wanted to be free from parental restrictions and to distance himself from authority and supervision. He began to experiment with things that tear down rather than build up: questionable films, unhealthy friendships, impure thoughts. His upbringing was a restraint, but for all the wrong reasons. He looked good on the outside but was rotting within and was unaware of his own spiritual disintegration. The "lust of the eyes, the lust of the flesh, and the pride of life" ruled his life. Sensuality, impurity, lust, and confusion took control as he rationalized his carnal lifestyle.

But the Lord, rich in mercy and love, used Steve's older brother, Randy, lovingly to confront him. While riding one day in the car, Randy began exhorting his brothers about the importance of submission and communion with the Lord. Steve's response was to interrupt his older brother with wisecracks and witty sarcasm. He finally said, "I don't want to talk about this. Let's talk about something else!" Steve then went from irritation to anger to telling his brother to shut up. His family was shocked, and with tears in his eyes Randy said, "Steve, you're not resisting me, you're resisting the Holy Spirit!"

As Steve began to think about that, he felt exposed and humiliated in front of his family. A host of confusing and convicting emotions and thoughts surged through his being.

Later that night, Steve's defensive, self-righteousness turned to deep hurt, guilt, and desire for forgiveness. He threw himself upon the mercy, love, and grace of Jesus. He admitted and faced his hypocritical lifestyle,

The Life of Steve Green

1956	Born in Portland, Oregon
1964	Professes faith in Christ on the mission field in Argentina
1976–78	Performs as member of music group Truth
1978	Marries Marijean McCarty
1980	Becomes an original member of Gaither Vocal Band
1978–83	Sings backup for The Bill Gaither Trio
1981	Daughter, Summer, born
1983	Signs as solo artist with Sparrow Records
1985	Son, Josiah, born Organizes Steve Green Ministries

USA

• Nashville
TENNESSEE

his pretense, and personal deception and cried out to the Lord for forgiveness.

That turned out to be not just a fleeting emotional experience but an epiphany that produced a sea-change in personality and practice. He confessed not only to God but to people. He made restitution. He unveiled his real self and personal sins to his wife, Marijean. With brutal honesty he spent two weeks making things right. And God in His great faithfulness lit a revival flame deep inside of Steve that burns brightly and consistently to this day. It is *that* which makes

Steve so unique and special. His close friend, songwriter John Mohr, sums it up in this lyric:

Oh sleeper awake!
Come out of the night.
Throw open the door and step into the light.
For sin is undone and worry is made right.
We've been set free!
Come and see!

Spiritual disciplines

It is fair to say that Steve is a serious, consistent, growing Christian. He works faithfully on his walk with the Lord every day—not for salvation but to cultivate intimacy with his Lord and Master.

Five habits of holiness stand out in Steve's walk. First, he has a regular time of reading God's Word. Second, he memorizes the Word. Not just verses, but whole chapters and books as well. Third, he's involved in journaling—even to the extent of writing out his prayers. Fourth, he is personally involved in his local church. Unlike many artists enveloped in public ministry, Steve is involved in discipleship, missions, worship, and evangelism. He is not reclusive and withdrawn when he comes home. He is an active, involved, serious Christian. He goes to meetings (even prayer meetings) and church suppers, and participates freely and regularly in local church fellowship. And finally, he is a concerned disciple looking to older, mature mentors (such as John DeBrine of Boston's Songtime Ministries) for guidance, encouragement, and wisdom.

An evening in concert

Every artist has a message coming through if you listen to his songs. Steve believes this is the life-message coming through. The life-message, Steve says, "is the sum total of who God has made me to be and what He has given me to do." Moving, vital songs such as "People Need the Lord," "He Holds the Keys," "Enter In," "For God and God Alone," "Find Us Faithful," and "The Mission" were chosen with that mandate in mind. They were also chosen because they reflect and authenticate Steve's calling. They

> *God lit a revival flame*
> *deep inside of Steve.*

> *He wants to be known as*
> *a person who loves his Lord*
> *with all of his heart.*

express his life-message, his pilgrimage in growth, and his particular focus and emphasis for a given year of music ministry. Steve's songs, structured around central biblical ideas, touch people deeply and teach theological truth to them.

Steve has seen real evidence that the Lord is using his ministry. One example would be the many homes that have been healed and put back together again. One lady, facing the signing of divorce papers the next day, came to a concert in the North. She spoke to Steve and told him that the Lord had convinced her during the concert not to do this and to seek reconciliation. A few weeks later, her own husband attended another concert in the Southwest, and the Lord began to work in his heart. They were soon reconciled and subsequently were able to attend a Steve Green concert together. They now treasure a picture taken of themselves with Steve after that concert.

Steve's overarching goal and desire is to allow the Holy Spirit to make listeners' hearts tender and to lead them to revival. He wants to create a stir in people's lives, to motivate loving obedience, and to inspire people to witness. He believes it is God's truth that frees people from bondage. He believes strongly that God's eternal, objective truth is what transforms people, and Christ-centered music will take this message deep inside of people in a unique way.

Standing ovations, sold-out rooms, emotional intensity, and high-class entertainment are hollow substitutes for personal revival and genuine worship and praise of our transcendent Savior.

Ministry to Hispanics

Steve has recorded three Spanish records in addition to his other thirteen records and has brought his tour to Mexico, Guatemala, Costa Rica, Brazil, Venezuela, Chile, Argentina, Ecuador, the Dominican Republic, Bonair, and Spain. These exposures have made him one of the most listened-to artists in Hispanic countries around the world. Along with regular performances to Spanish-speaking people in the United States, he does

a yearly foreign tour. This is something he looks forward to with great delight because it helps him to be refreshed and refocused in his career and service for the Lord.

Handling high visibility

Steve seems to have handled national recognition, the rewards it brings, and professional awards with godly wisdom and balance. A small prayer support group provides accountability, and a carefully selected group of pastors oversees Steve Green Ministries.

Steve does confess to a certain ambivalence about professional awards. He doesn't cast a personal vote in the Gospel Music Association's Dove Awards. He is not comfortable doing that because these awards are not the focus of his motivation and values. Yet, he admits to disappointment and concomitant hurt pride on occasion if he is nominated but someone else wins. How does he handle that? "The Lord rebukes me," Steve says. "The Lord says to me, 'You say these awards don't mean much to you, but apparently they do! What's going on here? What's your problem?'" Steve confesses that these kinds of things make up the stuff of life and that it is a constant battle. He wants his motivation to be pure. Some days that's as clear as a bell; some days he falls into pride, insecurity, and making comparisons. Well, just like other Christians, he's an earthen vessel containing Christ's treasure. It's comforting to know this outstanding Christian leader is human as well.

Advice to young musicians

As Steve tours the country, young aspiring writers and performers ask him for advice. He usually shares the following principles. "First, *determine your calling*. Find out what your gifts are and how they relate to the Body of Christ. Second, *be patient.* Do not hurry to be on stage and then have nothing to say. Wait until the Lord extrudes you into a place of service. Third, *study, practice, and work.* Seek wisdom, sharpen your skills, and practice discipline for God's glory. Fourth, *be content where God has placed you.* Guard against looking for the bigger place and working to enlarge your platform." He adds, "Little becomes much when God is in it," as the old gospel song says.

"Finally, the work of the kingdom of God is not accomplished through the means of this world. God does not depend on human power, prestige, intimidation, impressiveness, or popularity to carry out His will. Rather, it is through weak vessels, those who tremble at His Word, that His power is demonstrated."

Looking to the future
As Steve looks ahead, he is sensitive to the needs of his wife and family. He has personally witnessed some of the hurts of the children of well-known Christian leaders. They bear the scars of the neglect and workaholism of their parents. He is guarding vigilantly against making that mistake.

On almost a daily basis he is trusting God to provide for his calling and vision and to enable ministry with spiritual and musical sensitivity. Though he has lots of challenges and opportunities, he is experiencing a joyful journey and attempting to serve with distinction into the twenty-first century.

He wants to be remembered for leaving behind a trail of people who were encouraged and blessed through his music ministry. He wants to be known as a person who loves his Lord with all of his heart. Abraham was "the friend of God." Moses knew the Lord "face to face." King David, the chief musician of the Old Testament, was "a man after God's own heart." And the apostle Paul was known as a "finisher of the race." Steve told me, "Those are all great titles. I'd take any one of them!"

Steve is attempting to maintain the highest standards of spiritual and musical excellence. That is obvious in observing what Steve loves: the Lord, His Word, family, close friends, and people who slip into one of his concerts. They are in for a great aesthetic and musical experience and maybe even personal revival.

Steve knows what this old world desperately needs. He knows what people need. He knows what he personally needs. "People need the Lord!"

Don Wyrtzen

South America

APOSTLE TO THE LOST TRIBES

William Cameron Townsend

1896–1982

Cam Townsend and "Robby" Robinson were assigned to Guatemala by the Los Angeles Bible House with instructions to work closely with the Central American Mission (CAM) and three other evangelical missions. A member of the CAM welcoming committee in Guatemala City confided to his colleagues, "Robinson will do fine, but that skinny Townsend won't last two months." Cam himself soon realized his unpreparedness. Following instructions from an evangelism manual, he asked a man, "Do you know 'Senor' Jesus?" The man shrugged and replied, "No, I'm a stranger in town myself." Cam hadn't realized that in Spanish "senor" may mean either "Lord" or "Mr." and that "Jesus" is a common name in Spanish-speaking countries. Cam fled to his room and cried, "Lord, I'm a failure."

Cam recovered. He and a native escort, Francisco, set out on a missionary journey. Arriving in a town, Cam showed his gift for public relations. He first looked up the mayor, gave him a Spanish New Testament, and asked permission to sell others in the town for a small price. Cam quickly learned that most Guatemalans spoke native Indian languages and understood little Spanish. The illiterate Indians, he also noted, were forced to work for Spanish-speaking "ladinos" for virtual slave wages.

"Aren't there any Indian schools?" Cam asked Francisco.

"Ha," Francisco replied bitterly. "Who would teach us, when the ladinos say it is a disgrace to even talk to an Indian? Even the missionaries go to the Spanish-speakers. Not one evangelizes the Indian in his own tongue." Francisco looked hopefully at Cam. "Don Guillermo [Mr. William], why don't you come and be our missionary? I will teach you our language."

The start of translation work

Cam decided to do just this. Meanwhile, on trips back to Guatemala City, he got acquainted with Elvira Malmstrom, a musically talented CAM mission secretary from Chicago. Shortly after Cam started the first local Indian mission school in Central America, he and Elvira were married on Cam's twenty-third birthday, July 9, 1919.

Cam moved his bride into a cornstalk house near his school in the Cakchiquel Indian village of San Antonio. They appeared to be perfectly matched. Cam studied the native language and directed the school. Elvira played the portable organ and taught singing, organ, and sewing. Unfortunately, Elvira suffered from drastic mood changes. From being a sweet and loving wife, she could swing in a minute to a harsh and abusive scold. Missionary acquaintances realized the problem, but none knew how to help her.

Though Francisco died from malaria, Cam kept working on the unwritten Cakchiquel language. Far from being primitive, he found Cakchiquel to be incredibly complex. "I'm trying to analyze the grammar," he told a visiting American archaeologist, "but this language doesn't work the way you'd expect. It puzzles me."

"Perhaps you're trying to force Cakchiquel into the Latin mold," the archaeologist suggested. "Dr. Edward Sapir, the famous University of Chicago linguist, recommends

> *"Don Guillermo [Mr. William], why don't you come and be our missionary? I will teach you our language."*

a descriptive approach."

Cam's puzzlement turned into a smile. "Of course. Each language must have its own pattern!"

"Exactly. Take the Cakchiquel viewpoint, and you'll find a regular and logical development of the language."

That proved to be the key. Cam found that Cakchiquel was built by attaching prefixes and suffixes to word roots. A single Cakchiquel verb could indicate time, number of subjects, number of objects, location of the doer, several aspects of action, and many other ideas.

Finally Cam completed the gospel of Mark. When printed, the Cakchiquels exclaimed, "Now God speaks our language!"

W. Cameron Townsend in his early twenties.

The man whom many consider the greatest missionary strategist of the twentieth century was born in a California farmhouse, July 9, 1896, to poor, God-fearing, farm parents. Will and Molly Townsend named their son William for his deaf father and Cameron for his minister uncle.

Twenty years later, the skinny young student at Occidental College didn't quite know what he wanted to do with his life. Cam Townsend felt a pull toward foreign missions and applied for membership in the Student Volunteer Band. But when asked to state his reason for wanting to join, he mumbled, "I'm not sure why I wish to belong."

When a National Guard recruiter came to the campus in the fall of 1916, Cam enlisted, thinking the United States would soon enter the European War and he would be drafted anyway. Then he and his friend, "Robby" Robinson, who was planning to enter officer's training school, met furloughing missionary Stella Zimmerman.

The angular, blond missionary exclaimed, "You cowards! Going to war where a million other men will go and leaving us women to do the Lord's work alone! You are needed in Central America to sell Bibles to people who walk in darkness."

"Let's go, Cam," Robby urged.

To Cam's surprise, the captain of his Guard unit, said, "Go. You'll do a lot more good selling Bibles in Central America than you would shooting Germans in France."

The captain's words proved incredibly prophetic. With just three years of college, the unpromising Cam Townsend became the greatest mission strategist of the twentieth century while founding the first distinctive Bible translation mission in the history of Christianity. Propelled by an audacious faith, deep sensitivity to oppressed peoples, and uncommon common sense, he did this without any preplanned program or the backing of any denomination or major Western missionary organization.

A new support worker

Cam scheduled a Cakchiquel Bible conference and invited Leonard Legters, a missionary to the Comanches in Oklahoma, as the visiting speaker. Legters was amazed at the response of the people when his English sermons were translated into Cakchiquel. "You've found the way," he told Cam. "You've got to translate the whole New Testament into Cakchiquel." Leonard returned to the States and began raising financial support for the Cakchiquel ministry.

But trouble was brewing. The Cakchiquel work was in Central American Mission (CAM) territory, and many CAM missionaries thought the Indian work divisive. The Indians should learn Spanish, they said. Cam's school should be integrated into the CAM's Spanish-speaking ministry.

Cam disagreed. "If the work is integrated," he maintained, "the ladinos will continue to dominate and discriminate against the Indians. When the Indians attain education and economic freedom, they can meet the ladinos as equals." To his relief, the CAM council voted six to two in Cam's favor.

With Elvira typing and Indian language helpers checking, Cam finished the Cakchiquel New Testament in 1929. A dedication service was held at Cam's home, the Church of the Open Door, in Los Angeles. Cam gave an impassioned plea. "Over a thousand years passed before the New Testament was translated into English. Nearly 2,000 years have elapsed until now it is given to the 200,000 Cakchiquels. How much time will you let go by before the other 500 or more languages in Latin America have the Gospel?"

Cam and Elvira mailed the manuscript to the American Bible Society. While waiting for it to be printed, Cam talked up an aviation support program for Bible translation advance in Amazonia. Leonard Legters added his voice: "If the wild jungle tribes of Latin America are to be reached for Christ in this generation, this is the only way it can be done. We need those planes."

Gaining leader's endorsements

When the printed Cakchiquel New Testaments arrived, Cam wangled an audience with the Guatemalan president. In a palace ceremony, Cam presented a leather-bound

Wycliffe Bible Translators Lynne and Naabiro Istor teach first aid in Kenya.

> *Any preaching or study*
> *of Indian languages would get*
> *them expelled immediately.*

inscribed copy, then persuaded the head of state to pose with the New Testament for a picture.

When the money didn't come in for missionary aviation, Cam proposed a specially-designed steamboat that could carry Bible translators and their cargo up and down Amazon streams. "It could be taken apart and carried over places where portage was necessary." To his fellow missionaries, Cam's new idea seemed as impractical as missionary airplanes.

Not long after that a visiting Mexican educator named Moises Saenz stayed overnight with the Townsends. Cam unloaded his vision for the Indians: "The key to Indian education is in their mother tongue. Help them learn and become proud of their language and heritage. Give them the Bible to set them free from vice and superstition. Once they have dignity, spiritual freedom, and self-assurance, they can move into the Spanish-speaking world as equals with the ladinos."

The Mexican was impressed. After returning home, he wrote back to Cam: "Come to Mexico. Our revolutionary leaders will help you."

CAM leaders urged Cam and Elvira to stay with the Cakchiquels and make "occasional exploration into unoccupied fields." Cam objected to working under "missionary bosses."

Other pressures came down on Cam. His mother died. He fell ill with tuberculosis, and his doctor ordered five months of bed rest in California. After arriving in California, Elvira was told a heart condition gave her only one year to live.

Legters came for a visit and found Cam doing housework. In a discussion of strategy, Legters urged Cam to start in Mexico "where there are at least fifty Indian tribes without the Bible. I'll help raise support."

Opposition in Mexico

News came from Mexico that a new government, headed by socialist president, Lazaro Cardenas, had taken control of all religious

Translators in Mexico put language lessons on computer.

properties and ordered foreign missionaries home. Legters traveled to the East Coast where on August 10, 1933, he participated in a Day of Prayer at the Keswick Bible Conference for Mexico and Cam's Bible translation dream.

Undismayed, Cam sent Elvira to stay with her family in Chicago while he and Legters met in Dallas and headed for the Mexican border. Denied entry, Legters sat on a bench humming a song about faith. After a while Cam fished from his bag the letter from Dr. Moises Saenz and showed it to a border official. After checking with others, the official gave them permission to enter, but warned that any preaching or study of Indian languages would get them expelled immediately.

After a few days in Mexico City, Legters returned to the States. Through an amazing series of contacts, Cam met Rafael Ramirez, the director of rural education. Ramirez

> "We follow the example of our Master who came to serve and give His life for others."

gave Cam a permit to "study our rural education system . . . and maybe write an article about what we are doing with the Indians." Cam was elated. He made a six-week tour and returned home to write two glowing articles for publication in the *Dallas News and School and Society Magazine.* Cam sent the articles to Ramirez who replied with warm thanks.

The start of SIL
Assured that Mexico was going to open, Cam and Legters held the first three-month "Camp Wycliffe" in an Arkansas barn during the summer of 1934. The three students and four faculty sat on nail kegs. Subjects ranged from "Indian Orthography" to "How to Work with Others."

When news came that President Cardenas had dismissed several atheists from his campus, Cam was sure that Christian workers would be permitted to work in the country. Cam and the ailing Elvira, with Cam's niece, Evelyn Griset, as Elvira's nurse, headed for the border with four students. They were not only permitted into Mexico but were given a police escort through Mexico City traffic. "It's just like the Lord rolling back the waters of the Red Sea," Cam exulted. "I wish some of the skeptics could see us now!"

After dispatching the students to tribal assignments, Cam drove south to an Aztec village that he had heard was the most backward Aztec settlement in the state of Morelos. After pulling the trailer into the town square, he showed Mayor Martin Mendez his papers from the Ministry of Education. "We've come to learn your language and help your people in practical ways," Cam said. The mayor subsequently became the first Christian believer in the town.

Cam's practical ways included reading classes and a garden to teach the Indians how to improve their economy. President Cardenas heard about the innovations and came calling. After showing him around, Cam presented his hope of bringing translators to Mexico to put the Bible into Indian languages. Cardenas's eyes swept over Cam's garden. "Will they help the Indians in such practical

ways as this?" Cardenas asked.

"Certainly, Senor Presidente," Cam declared. "We follow the example of our Master who came to serve and give His life for others."

"Then bring in all you can," the president invited.

Cam and Cardenas became warm friends and Cam later wrote his biography. "Of all those who come to see me," Cardenas told Cam on one occasion, "you are the only one who talks to me about my soul."

Legters, Cam's most important associate in the Mexican advance, was always "Mr." or "Rev." When the question of address was put to Cam, he chuckled and said, "Well, my niece Evelyn calls me 'Uncle.'" He was "Uncle" Cam ever after.

Cam and Legters didn't always agree. Legters wanted tougher physical and mental standards for workers. Cam would accept almost anybody who was willing. Later he would say, "We're interested in everybody except the bartender. We'll take a second look at him when he gets converted."

The two argued over sending teams of single women to tribes. "Think of the criticism we'll get if something happens to them," Legters said.

"The Lord will take care of them," Cam insisted, adding that women were just as capable as men in Bible translation.

A new type of mission
Legters pushed Cam for an organization. Cam, who had not been schooled in Western missionary methods, didn't want the group placed under a paternalistic stateside organization that might not understand what the translators were doing.

Nevertheless, Cam got his field group together and showed them a letterhead he had had printed up with the name Summer Institute of Linguistics. "A suspicious country wouldn't consider this a threat. And we do train during the summer." Cam also proposed that "SIL" be incorporated in Mexico. "Let's run our own affairs from the field under the Lord's leading," he said.

After being elected director Cam proposed that he answer to an executive committee—something new in the history of missions: a founder-director telling a crew of young members they could have the final say. The incorporation papers were signed in the fall of 1936. For the first time in history an organization had been formed to reduce languages to writing and translate the Bible for the world's tribal groups.

When the SIL group grew larger, Legters pleaded with Cam to open an office in the United States for channeling gifts from the United States. Shortly after Pearl Harbor, Cam and Elvira drove to California to talk with associates about a support office. Cam suggested twin organizations with interlocking directorates. SIL would handle training, field work, and associations with foreign governments and universities. Wycliffe Bible Translators (WBT) would receive and forward funds and publicize the field work. With Cam leading the way, the incorporators voted to transfer the training camp from Arkansas to the University of Oklahoma campus. Oklahoma, Cam believed, could be the first of many universities providing facilities for the training of future linguists. Seeing the need of prospective teachers, Cam further encouraged young SIL/WBT scholars to take time to earn their doctorates in linguistics and associated fields. Cam saw all of this as helping fulfill the vision for reaching every tribe the Lord had given him in Guatemala.

Facing criticism

Cam's personal life remained as clean as the proverbial "hound's tooth." His servant demeanor tended to disarm those who disagreed with him. Yet—particularly from Mexico on—he was never without critics, and some could be virulent.

A missionary in Mexico became furious after learning that WBT/SIL workers were listed as linguistic investigators on immigration forms. "You're in the country under false pretenses," he charged.

"The government knows we will translate the Bible," Cam countered.

"Perhaps so, but you're doing other things besides linguistic work. You're deceiving your home supporters."

The critic went back to the United States to warn churches about the "fakery" and

"dishonesty" of Cameron Townsend.

Cam was also criticized by some of his own people for asking them to keep a low profile in evangelical churches. "Stick to translation," he urged, "and avoid sectarian involvement."

Cam was also lambasted by some missionaries for working with and receiving aid from a socialistic government. Cam's reply: "We are in Mexico to serve and not to dictate policies to the government." At a banquet given to the SIL group by Cardenas, Cam said, "Each of us wants to follow Jesus Christ by serving the Indians . . . and assisting your government in its program of bettering the masses. We have found, too, that it helps to translate God's moral and spiritual revelation into the Indian language." Cardenas responded by assigning rural schoolteachers' salaries to eight translators.

Relations between Cardenas and the United States government were not good at

"Uncle Cam"— W. Cameron Townsend.

> *For the first time in history an organization had been formed to translate the Bible for the world's tribal groups.*

this time, principally because of Mexico's takeover of foreign oil companies. Cam wrote a small book defending Mexico's action and offered to go to the United States and plead Mexico's side. Cardenas bought him a car. Cam was rebuffed at every turn in Washington and New York. He kept the car and drove it almost 300,000 miles during the next thirty-five years.

On Christmas Eve, 1944, Elvira suffered a fatal heart attack while Cam was at a friend's house in Hollywood, working on his biography of Cardenas. Cam had to be led away from her bed. In a statement read at her funeral, Cam termed her "a love gift" from God "to the people of Latin America and to us. . . . By His grace my devotion . . . to my Lord's service . . . shall be my passion from now on."

The move into Peru

Cam had little time to mourn. An invitation came from the Peruvian minister of education to begin work in Amazonia. Cam flew to Lima for talks with officials and then hopped over the Andes to check out a proposed jungle base.

While making preparations to enter Peru, Cam married Elaine Mielke, an SIL member who had been an outstanding educator in Chicago. President and Mrs. Cardenas were best man and maid of honor, respectively, at the wedding.

Back in the United States, Cam urged Dawson Trotman, head of the Navigators, to help fulfill the vision for the tribes by urging discharged Christian veterans to become part of the WBT/SIL Peru Corps. While in Trotman's office, Cam met aviatrix Betty Green, who had flown during the war and was now helping start Missionary Aviation Fellowship (MAF). Flying to see the new work in Peru, she became the first woman to pilot a plane over the Andes.

Ultimately, MAF decided to concentrate on helping regular missionaries. For the translators, Cam set up Jungle Aviation And Radio Service (JAARS) as a subsidiary of WBT/SIL. JAARS operated as a jungle airline, flying translators and supplies to tribal locations and assisting anyone else who needed transportation.

"Anyone else" included Catholic missionaries. This brought a barrage of criticism that JAARS was helping the enemy.

> "In helping the Indians, we promote Christian faith and no special brand of it."

Hard-nosed Catholics, for their part, demanded that the translators teach the Indians Catholic doctrine. Cam countered to all who would listen: "We serve everybody in a non-sectarian way."

The new airline had to have planes. A genius in fund-raising, Cam set up an "International Goodwill" program in several major cities in the United States. When enough money had been raised to purchase a plane, a dedication ceremony was held, with the mayor or some other prominent person speaking. The plane was then flown to Lima for another ceremony, and the property was deeded over to the Peruvian government, which assigned the property to JAARS. All the way, it was vintage Cameron Townsend who said, "I've never asked anyone to contribute to personal support. But when the Lord leads me, I'm willing to ask one government to help another. Or for a wealthy man to help buy an airplane for the people of another country."

Cam and Elvira had no children. Elaine gave him four—Grace, Elainadel, Joy, and Billy in Peru. Grace, the oldest, was dedicated in a non-sectarian ceremony in the Mexican embassy in Lima with many government officials present. To no one's surprise, Cam worked in a testimony about the "young pioneers" who were serving the jungle tribes.

By 1963 "Uncle Cam" was serving as general director of more than 1,100 WBT/SIL members. That year the government of Peru awarded him its Order of Distinguished Service. Cam moved his family to pioneer again in Colombia, where passions ran high between Catholics and Protestants. While there, he promoted the candidacy of a young American Catholic translator for WBT/SIL membership. When this effort was rejected, Cam arranged for the young man to serve as a hired staffer at the Colombia base.

As in Guatemala, Mexico, and Peru, Cam cultivated friendships in high government circles, saying, "In helping the Indians, we promote Christian faith and no special brand of it." He got a contract to begin work with Colombia's tribes.

Beyond Central America

As WBT/SIL expanded into Africa and the Pacific Islands, Cam continued to give primary attention to Latin America. He trusted others—many of whom he had trained himself—to supervise expansion outside of the Americas.

In 1966, with help from Oklahoma's Senator Fred Harris, Cam persuaded the United States House and Senate to name September 30 as Bible Translation Day. Four years later, he was welcomed into the Oval Office by Richard Nixon. "Mr. President," Cam announced, "we've just entered our five-hundredth language."

"What an achievement," Nixon declared. "You're doing two things: Giving them the Bible and teaching them to read. What can I do to help?"

"Mr. President, there are still more than 2,000 language groups without Scripture, or even an alphabet. We need 8,500 new recruits. Would you write a letter that we can use in challenging young people to volunteer?" Nixon promised to do just that.

As far back as 1940 Cam had been thinking of the tribes in the Soviet Union. In explaining why he did not criticize atheistic policies in some departments of the Mexican government, he told his associates: "If they would let me teach the Bible in Russia, I would gladly abstain from censorship of their policies that I did not like."

In 1956 he visited the Soviet embassy in Washington and proposed to a diplomat a cultural exchange, with Soviet linguists coming to lecture at SIL's summer school and SIL people going to the USSR. The diplomat urged him to go to Moscow and present the idea to the Soviet Academy of Science. Cam had other fish to fry at the time, but kept the USSR on his mind.

Twelve years later he wrote the Academy, requesting an invitation to visit for six months. The invitation came and in September 1968 he and Elaine flew there. After a warm reception in Moscow, they flew to the Caucasus region and learned of dozens of languages spoken in the USSR. When Cam asked permission to translate portions of the Bible, one of his hosts said, "We are atheists. We would never allow that."

Again, Cam suffered criticism from fellow American Christians. One caller lambasted him for "helping the Communists." Others

The Life of William Cameron Townsend

1896	Born in California, July 9
1917	Goes to Guatemala as Bible distributor
1919	Marries Elvira Malmstrom, July 9
1931	Townsend's translation of the New Testament in Cakchiquel is published
1934	First three-month Bible translators school in Arkansas
1936	Summer Institute of Linguistics (SIL) incorporated in Mexico
1942	SIL moved to University of Oklahoma campus
1944	Elvira Townsend dies, December 24; Townsend later marries Elaine Mielke
1963	Number of WBT/SIL workers reaches 1,100; Townsend receives Order of Distinguished Service from government of Peru
1982	Cameron Townsend dies, April 22
1985	Number of WBT/SIL workers reaches 6,000 working with 1,000 language groups

USA

MEXICO

GUATEMALA

PERU

> ### *"Finish the task.*
> ### *Translate the Scriptures*
> ### *into every language."*

said the Soviet government would never permit the Bible to be translated into the minority languages there. Cam told one doubter privately, "In that case, I guess the Lord will have to change the government over there."

Undaunted, Cam and Elaine began studying Russian in preparation for the anticipated new advance. They continued their language work after moving to a "retirement" home on the U.S. JAARS base in North Carolina. From there Cam made frequent trips to the Soviet Embassy in Washington. One weekend, a Russian diplomat brought his family down to visit Cam and Elaine. It was Cam's way of building friendships to pave the way for workers to enter more tribal groups and translate the Bible.

After moving to North Carolina, Cam and Elaine became the first white members in the history of a black church. Since 1917, Cam had spent most of his life outside the United States. Now he urged WBT/SIL members to build friendships with blacks and recruit black translators.

In 1985 WBT/SIL, more than six thousand members strong, entered their one-thousandth language group. Seven years later two Dutch members began linguistic work in the former Soviet Union. William Cameron Townsend never lived to see these dreams fulfilled. At eighty-five he died from leukemia in a North Carolina hospital. In his last conscious moments he was still suggesting ideas for completing the task launched in Guatemala.

His body is entombed on the JAARS property between the Mexico and the Alphabet museums. The passion of his life is inscribed on the stone: "Dear Ones: By love serve one another. Finish the task. Translate the Scriptures into every language. Uncle Cam."

James Hefley

Translators Jim Leonard and Fred Nolema check proofs in Kenya.

Further Reading

Hefley, James. *Uncle Cam: The Story of Cameron Townsend.* Waco: Word, 1974.

Wallis, Ethel E. *Two Thousand Tongues to Go: The Story of Wycliffe Bible Translators.* New York: Harper and Broth, 1959.

THE IMPACT OF

The Auca Five

In December 1957 a young Marine climbed aboard a bus bound for Camp Pendleton in southern California. Chuck was depressed and dejected and felt that God had forgotten him, even though he had seldom included God in his life. He would soon leave Cynthia, his bride of two years, and family and friends for service in Okinawa. His brother, seeing his panic and need of help, gave him a book and admonished him to read it. Chuck rolled back his eyes and muttered, "Oh sure." "What kind of book does he want me to read now?" Chuck wondered. However, once on the bus he opened the book and began to read. The story of five men willing to give up their lives for God captured his interest, especially since they were not much older than he was.

The bus arrived at the marine base long before he had finished the book, but he couldn't put it down. He found the only light available—in the washroom—and there he stayed until he had finished the book. The book, *Through Gates of Splendor* by Elisabeth Elliot (1957), recounted the story of five missionaries who were speared by the Aucas in the jungles of Ecuador in January 1956, and it became the turning point in Charles Swindoll's life.

He telephoned his wife to tell her she must read the book, saying, "God has gotten my attention and has calmed my panic." God used the book and its story of five men obedient unto death to confirm a sense of call to him. He wanted to be available just as those five men were in whatever way God might choose. After Okinawa, Swindoll attended Dallas Theological Seminary. Since then God has used his life and ministry as a preacher, author, and radio host to reach thousands of people.

Though almost four decades have passed

A secret mission to reach a primitive tribe with the gospel ended abruptly one Sunday afternoon as five young men lay dead on a sandbar along the Curaray River in the jungles of Ecuador. The news that five young missionaries had been speared to death by Auca Indians on January 8, 1956, shocked the world.

One of the five missionaries was Nate Saint, an innovative veteran pilot with Mission Aviation Fellowship. His frequent flights into the jungles had often taken him near the large Auca territory. He had prayed that their small villages could be located and their elusive, savage inhabitants reached for Christ. His friend, Roger Youderian of Gospel Missionary Union, had already successfully reached the hostile Shuar Indians and was eager now to evangelize the Aucas. The other three were with Christian Missions in Many Lands. Jim Elliot and Pete Fleming were boyhood friends.

The five went to Ecuador together with the hope of reaching the Aucas. Pete gave up a promising academic career through which he had hoped to serve Christ. Jim, a young man of fervent spirit, had gone to Wheaton College, where he knew Ed McCully, a prelaw student. They shared a deep devotion for the Lord.

The five converged in Ecuador. Although their intended mission ended prematurely, God's work through their lives has continued in amazing ways.

was talking to one of the widows. Similarly, many years ago a German woman in an obscure farm village was surprised to learn that staying in her home was one of the widows. She had heard about the five martyrs years before when her minister in a small Lutheran church told the story. Each woman was encouraged in her faith as God brought someone from the story into her life.

Three of the "Auca Five." Left–right: Jim Elliot, Pete Fleming, Ed McCully.

since members of a little-known tribe swarmed a sandbar on the Curaray River and murdered five men, their widows still hear from people whose lives were impacted by their sacrifice. Some of these stories are from well-known Christian leaders like Charles Swindoll; other accounts are from lesser-known persons who on occasion serve in obscure areas of the globe. We will never be able to measure fully the impact on world evangelization of the deaths of the "Auca Five": Jim Elliot, Pete Fleming, Ed McCully, Nate Saint, and Roger Youderian. But it has been significant.

Unexpected meetings
Over the years, each of the five widows has met many people who have told how the death of the men affected their lives. Here are three from the writer's own experience: Recently, in a Chicago suburb, a woman from a small town in Mexico related how her family had prayed for the families of the five men. Their story was again impressed on her memory as she read *Through Gates of Splendor*. She was stunned to learn she

Tokyo

A few years ago in Tokyo a young Japanese former airline pilot told how the story of Nate Saint in *Jungle Pilot* changed the direction of his life. He gave up his career and went to seminary in Tokyo to prepare to become a missionary pilot.

Secular news media

What is there about this story that touched a generation so powerfully? And why does it continue to affect people today? Certainly one reason was the imagery of five young men on a heroic adventure to an unknown, primitive jungle tribe. Their daring missionary efforts were recounted over and over again in Christian books and magazines by Elisabeth Elliot, Jim's widow, and by others. But there was another factor: the amazing worldwide coverage given to the "Auca

Jim Elliot and Nate Saint attempt to communicate with Auca by the Curaray River.

> *The pictures of primitive Indians with five young Americans captured the public's heart.*

Five" through the secular news media. This is a tale in itself.

To avoid signaling those who might wish to exterminate the savage Auca tribe, the men kept secret the discovery and approach to the Aucas. How, then, did such a quiet mission become known to the media? The story began to unfold on the morning of January 9, 1956. Nate had not made a promised radio contact from the beach the previous afternoon nor returned as expected at night. Marj, his wife, knew something was wrong. The following morning the other mission pilot flew out to the river and saw the small plane on the beach stripped of its fabric. At the same time a pilot with Wycliffe Bible Translators stopped by the Saint house in Shell Mera and quickly realized that something was wrong. Marj and I told him our worst fears. He felt that HCJB, the missionary radio station in Quito, should know immediately. HCJB—then, as now—had powerful transmitters beaming the gospel internationally. Through this station Christians around the world first heard the news of the missing five men. The pilot also made a call for help to the United States Air Rescue Service in Panama for their help. Once they received the call and the order was issued for them to go to Ecuador, it was not long before the media picked up the story and sent it to papers around the world.

Media support

Without the extensive news coverage most people would never have heard about the five men. But why would a *missionary* story receive such worldwide attention? The year 1956 was one of the quiet interludes in the Eisenhower administration. With the Korean War over and the space age only talk (Russia would launch Sputnik in 1957), there was little major news. Television had improved and people could now see events developing within a few hours. The media were all in place, hungry for news, when the story of five missionaries missing in the jungles of Ecuador broke. People heard the

daily accounts of the rescue party's search for the five men until the last body was found four days later and they were all buried next to the river sandbar. People in the secular world who knew little about missions were following the news reports. They talked with friends about the courage of the five.

One of the members of that search party was the celebrated *Life* magazine photographer, Cornell Capa. In Central America when the story broke, he immediately flew to Ecuador. At that time *Life* was a major news source through vivid photo journalism, and their January 28, 1956, issue portrayed the whole story of Operation Auca from the beginning flights over the Auca houses to the final tragic death of the men. Readers were visually transported to the jungles. They read a step-by-step account of the well-planned operation from the men's diaries and letters. They saw what the men saw as they flew over the Auca huts. People were taken right to the beach where the missionaries had their first friendly visit with the Indians. The pictures of primitive Indians with five young Americans captured the public's heart. Water-stained film recovered from a camera found in the river intensified the impact. The poignant pictures of friendly naked Aucas sprinkled alongside Capa's photos of the massacre two days later heightened the emotional response.

Through Cornell Capa's pictures and personal account, people experienced the tension of the rescue effort, the trauma of finding the bodies and the fear of the search party as they buried the bodies and faced the long trip back up the river through hostile Auca territory. Through pictures he captured the grief of the five widows and the nine fatherless children. But he also captured "life as usual" in a picture of the long lines of diapers hung up to dry back at the mission station where the families waited. As magazines in other countries carried the story, the world became aware of a quiet attempt to reach a remote tribe in Ecuador with the gospel.

> *Elisabeth Elliot and Rachel Saint were invited by the Aucas to live with them.*

Far-reaching impact

The Ecuadorian government acknowledged the impact of evangelicals on the country. President Ibarra invited representatives of all the evangelical missions to the palace where he presented a plaque to the missionaries. All of this appeared in the newspapers. Shortly after this presentation permanent visas that had long been awaited by new missionaries were issued. A few years later the Ecuadorian government commemorated the death of the five men by issuing five postage stamps with their portraits, one for each missionary.

The widows and mission agencies received letters from people around the world, telling of the impact the men's sacrifice had on them. In Christian schools and colleges young people by the hundreds were committing their lives to missions. Many wanted to replace the five men. Christians were able to use the event as an opportunity to witness to their neighbors and business associates because nearly everyone knew the story.

The impact was equally powerful in other countries. A missionary in Japan, for instance, was ministering on a small island. He visited a local school and found on the bulletin board a newspaper clipping of the story of the "Auca Five." This was the opening he needed, and he retold the story of the men's reason for facing death.

Life photographer Cornell Capa kept the story before the world with another report a year later as to what the widows were doing. Then in 1958, when Elisabeth Elliot and Rachel Saint were invited by the Aucas to live with them, Cornell had yet a third story.

One never knew who was listening in to conversations by two-way radio in the jungles. Marj and I were being interviewed a few years ago on radio station WMBI, Chicago, when a man called in to say that he had heard the last radio transmission between Nate on the Curaray River sandbar and his wife, Marj, at the Mission Aviation Fellowship station just before the men were killed. He was far from the jungles, manning a radio station with a 500-foot antenna at the Polar Cap. On Sunday, January 8, 1956, he was monitoring the radio and picked up the conversation taking place on a weak radio frequency deep in the jungles thousands of miles away. He set his alarm for the time Nate said he would call back and listened once again. But there was silence.

(Left) Roger Youderian, (right) Nate Saint.

Ambassador's wife

In 1970 a missionary in Europe met the wife of the Ecuadorian ambassador to one of the European countries. The missionary asked the woman if she had heard of the five men killed in Ecuador by the Indians. Immediately the lady's face fell. She remembered the story well because she felt in some way responsible for the deaths of two of those men. In 1951 her husband was the ambassador to the United States, and they lived in New York. "I met a nice young man on the subway. When he found out I was from Ecuador, he told me that he and his friend wanted to go there as missionaries but were having a hard time getting their visas. I told him that I would talk to my husband to see if he could help." The two waiting for visas were Pete Fleming and Jim Elliot. Not long after they left New York, they both received their visas. The woman did not know which of the men she had talked to, but knew they were two of the men killed by the Aucas. The woman felt that there was something supernatural about the event. The missionary had an opportunity to assure the woman that she was not responsible, and was able to tell her about the Lord.

Life-changing impressions

The stories continue to come in, each with its own fascination. Barbara Youderian met a cowboy chaplain who was a bronco and Brahma bull rider. After he saw the film *Through Gates of Splendor,* he decided to go back to church where he heard the gospel and received Christ as Savior. Instead of giving up the rodeo he took the message of salvation to his workplace and became a chaplain to cowboys.

Recently Elisabeth Elliot was interviewed by Josh McDowell, who told her of his experience while he was a student at Wheaton College. During a special chapel honoring the five men he was moved by the story. At that time he surrendered his life completely to God, and said, "If I can glorify You through death I'm willing." He said that since that time his life has been threatened at least twice, one attempt nearly succeeding. Each time he remembered his specific commitment at Wheaton.

Don Stephens, president of Mercy Ships, a ministry of Youth With A Mission, was impressed as a child with the death of the

> *We can never know the "ripple effect" of the death of the five men.*

five men. His family heard the news over the radio and he later saw the pictures in *Life.* As a family they prayed for the Aucas and for the families of the five men. It made a great impression on the young boy. He wanted to be used to replace those five men. God did lead him into missions, and twenty years later he was standing at the Port of Los Angeles with the first Mercy Ship moored behind him. In *Shadow of the Almighty* there is a picture of Jim and Pete standing on a pier just before they boarded a ship for Ecuador. It was the same pier.

"I realized that in some degree, I had become part of the fruit of the five men as mentioned in John 12:24. The three ships in the Mercy Ships fleet are somehow a part of the continuing legacy of their lives."

A story from Timbuktu

Perhaps the most unusual story about the Auca Five's legacy comes from Timbuktu, that city in Saharan Africa so remote that many think its name is fictitious. Nate Saint's son, Steve, was stranded there in 110° heat one day in 1986. With the last seats on the return flight taken by two UNICEF doctors, and with the Sahara stretching out on all sides, Steve searched for a way out. He also searched for God's way, because although Steve was a strong believer, he was still deeply perplexed over his father's death. *Did it have to happen?* Now, in Timbuktu, he again wanted a revelation of God and His love such as his father had known.

The doctors later decided not to return that night, freeing space for Steve. But that was a minor matter compared to an extraordinary conversation that took place during the afternoon. Steve had previously learned that this Islamic city of twenty thousand had a small Christian church. In trying to find it, he was led instead to a young man, Nouh Ag Infra Yatara, who, in turn, took him to a missionary. A fascinating story unfolded as the missionary interpreted Nouh's narrative. Nouh had been converted through a former missionary, was persecuted, and had courageously stood for his faith. What had given him that courage? The missionary had given him some books about others who suffered for their faith, including a book on the five Auca missionaries.

Reflecting on this, Steve writes, "Nouh and I had gifts for each other that no one else could give. I gave him the assurance that the story that had given him courage was true. He gave me the assurance that God *had* used Dad's death for good. Dad, by dying, had helped give Nouh a faith worth dying for. And Nouh, in return, had helped give Dad's faith back to me" ("To the Ends of the Earth," *Guideposts,* January 1991).

Elisabeth Elliot has remarked that we can never know the "ripple effect" of the death of the five men. It would be impossible to mention all those who have been impacted by the story of the five men and how God has used their lives for His glory.

Where it all began

But what about the effect of the death of the "Auca Five" on the very people that the missionaries tried to reach? By the end of 1958 Rachel Saint and Elisabeth Elliot were in the tribe with Dayuma, the Indian woman who had run away from her tribe because of all the killings. Dayuma, taught by Rachel and Elisabeth, explained God's Word to her people. Translation of the New Testament began, and one by one over the years the Indians believed the word they heard and trusted in Christ. Today all five Indians who had killed the five missionaries are not only believers in Christ but also in their own way spiritual leaders among their people.

June 11, 1992, was a day of celebration for the Waorani (the Aucas' real tribal name). They received the New Testament in their language. Rachel Saint, who has lived with these people for thirty-four years, rejoiced and prayed that "it will have a strong impact on their hearts." Catherine Peak and Rosi Jung saw the fruit of their years of translation as they handed the Indians their New Testaments and heard the Waorani reading.

At the same time the New Testament in the Pastaza Quechua language was presented to those Indians by the translator, Carolyn Orr. Jim, Pete, and Ed, before they were killed, had lived and worked with the Quechua. They began translating Scripture into the Quechua language and had taught the Indians to read. Now the work is completed for both tribes of Indians.

The new generation of Waorani are readers and now all of them have the availability of God's Word. But how had the older generation remained so strong in their faith? The Waorani men involved in the killing, along with others who witnessed it, were deeply affected by two things that transcended their own experience.

The first was the fact that the white men refrained from using their guns, thereby sparing the Indians and leaving themselves vulnerable. Had the missionaries' intentions been benign after all? The second was even further beyond their comprehension. The killers heard singing—not from the beach, where the missionaries' bodies now lay, but from above the trees on the riverbank. Looking up they saw an array of bright lights. Frightened, they kept this vision to themselves. Later, as Christians, they began to understand their experience of the supernatural that day. It was not until my visit there in 1989 that they openly shared their remarkable vision (*Unfolding Destinies,* Zondervan, 1991). From the very day the men died to the present, God has been at work, lives have been changed, and history testifies that the Auca Five did not die in vain.

Olive Liefeld

Further Reading

Capa, Cornell. "'Go Ye and Preach the Gospel,' Five Do and Die." *Life* (January 30, 1956): 10–19.

Capa, Cornell. "The Martyrs' Widows Return to Teach in Jungle." *Life* (May 20, 1957): 24–33.

Elliot, Elisabeth. *Shadow of the Almighty.* New York: Harper, 1957.

——. *The Savage My Kinsman.* New York: Harper, 1961.

——. *Through Gates of Splendor.* New York: Harper,1957; Wheaton: Tyndale, 1981.

Liefeld, Olive Fleming. *Unfolding Destinies.* Grand Rapids: Zondervan, 1990.

A FARMER READS THE BIBLE

Victor Landero

1924–

> *Victor Landero, a farmer who also owned a tavern cum house of prostitution, was trying to keep cool on this hot, dusty afternoon in the northern Colombia village of Providencia, which often served as a refugee for outlaws. Some called the village donde matan sin licencia ("where they kill without license"). Victor happened upon an itinerant preacher, Don Pedro Guiterrez, who was selling Bibles. When Guiterrez told Victor that this book would tell him how God made the world, Victor purchased a copy—even though he couldn't read. Little did Victor know that the God who made the world had a plan for his life: to be an ambassador for Christ.*

Some years after Victor Landero bought a Bible from an itinerant preacher, he learned to read. Then, through a remarkable series of circumstances, God brought Victor into contact with Eliecer Benavides, a recent graduate from a Bible institute in Sincelejeo, Colombia. Between reading the Bible and Eliecer's explanations, Victor committed his life to Christ.

At that time he employed three prostitutes and also lived with three different women at the same time, not married to any of them. There were no churches, no missionaries, no pastors where Victor then lived. His only source of spiritual growth was his own reading of the Bible and the sovereign work of the Holy Spirit in his life.

Complete change
With amazing quickness Victor began to grow. He first led his whole family (father, mother, eight brothers and sisters) to the Lord. He began to clean up his moral life,

dismissing his prostitutes and turning his tavern into a general store. He dismissed two of the three women he lived with and married the mother of his five children. He also established a thriving little church on his farm. When the church was well established, he persuaded his brothers Gregorio and Claudio to take responsibility of the church and to buy out his portion of the family farm.

Corozalito
With the proceeds from the farm he moved far up the San Jorge River region, bought property, and began to hack a new farm out of the forest. His purpose was to present the gospel in a new area where no witness had previously been given. The small hamlet where he lived was known as Corozalito, and within a short period he had led ninety-two of the ninety-four residents to Christ.

From Corozalito the message of salvation began to spread out as Victor visited other villages and farms. Within a very few years hundreds of people had come to Christ, and dozens of churches or small congregations had sprung up in the forests and rural areas. The remarkable gift of evangelism with which the Holy Spirit had endowed Victor was being used constantly and effectively. The daily burden of his heart was to lead others to Christ, which he did with inexhaustible energy and fervor.

Gifts and balance
A few years after his conversion he began to see some of the more spectacular gifts of the Holy Spirit being manifested in his ministry

> *He first led his whole family (father, mother, eight brothers and sisters) to the Lord.*

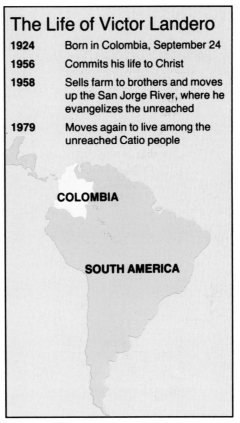

The Life of Victor Landero

1924	Born in Colombia, September 24
1956	Commits his life to Christ
1958	Sells farm to brothers and moves up the San Jorge River, where he evangelizes the unreached
1979	Moves again to live among the unreached Catio people

COLOMBIA

SOUTH AMERICA

Victor Landero, evangelist farmer of Colombia.

as well as in the lives of others who had come to the Lord. Such things as speaking in tongues, words of prophecy, healings, and casting out of demons became very prominent in the churches. For a while these gifts were overemphasized to the point of being used in unbiblical ways and causing rifts and splits within some churches.

However, God gave Victor and some of his more mature converts amazing gifts of discernment and insights into understanding the Word of God. Little by little, and not without some very painful turmoil, they were used of God to bring a more balanced understanding and a more orderly exercising of these gifts in the church. Victor was clearly a gifted leader, even though he had never attended school.

Unreached tribe

Victor's vision for reaching those who had never heard of Christ kept him constantly traveling to places where Christ was unknown. After fifteen years of faithful witnessing in the San Jorge River region, he realized that everyone in that vast area had not had an opportunity to hear the gospel. So he began to look beyond the Spanish-speaking population to the Catio, an unreached Indian tribe deep in the jungles near the border of Panama.

Finally he moved his family to a remote hamlet in the heart of Catio territory. With no education and without the help of any formal language school, he began to learn the Indian dialect by hard work and identification with the Indians themselves. His witness to these Indians was every bit as fervent as had been his witness to his Spanish-speaking friends.

But the results were woefully different. Whereas he had had the joy of leading hundreds of people to Christ and seeing hundreds more spiritual "grandchildren" plus planting dozens of churches, he was unable to plant even one church among the Catio. He found them to be nomadic in their cultural life making it difficult to have ongoing

> *The remarkable gift of evangelism with which the Holy Spirit had endowed Victor was being used constantly and effectively.*

> *Victor has been faithful to the trust placed in his humble hands.*

relationships. More important, the Catio were volatile and resistant to the gospel message. Whereas he had worked for years with very responsive people, he now found himself among an unusually resistant group.

Victor says that he will spend the rest of his life among these Indians, in spite of the lack of tangible results, because he knows this is where God wants him. He had been God's instrument in a great people movement during the first fifteen years of his Christian experience. Now he had been placed again as a sower rather than a reaper. There will be thousands of Colombians in heaven who trace their spiritual roots to Victor Landero. Among them may be a few Catio Indians who will thank the Lord for Victor's faithfulness.

Unheralded
While Victor remained relatively isolated and unheralded beyond his own immediate remote surroundings, his brother Gregorio, whom Victor led to Christ, was gifted as an outstanding preacher and organizer. Gregorio organized creative holistic ministries to meet the needs of poverty-stricken people, initiated an amazing pastoral training program that trained hundreds of pastors and lay leaders, and engaged in pastoral and evangelistic ministries in Columbia and elsewhere. He even preached twice at the InterVarsity Urbana missions conventions held in America, even though, like Victor, he had never had formal schooling himself. Victor, instead of being jealous of his younger brother's fame, rejoiced with him in God's gifts and encouraged him to use them faithfully.

When one thinks of Victor Landero the words of 1 Corinthians 4:2 come to mind: "Now it is required that those who have been given a trust must prove faithful." Victor has been faithful to the trust placed in his humble hands.

David Howard, Sr.

SLAIN BY THE SHINING PATH

Rómulo Sauñe

1953–1992

Ayacucho was a flurry of activity. Christians paraded through the streets; musicians held outdoor concerts. The focal point was the arrival of God's Word—both the Old and New Testaments in a language these Ayacucho people could understand. On September 3, 1987, Quechua believers streamed down the mountain by the thousands to attend the joyous celebration. At city hall, the mayor, the bishop of the Roman Catholic church, and representatives of the Peruvian Bible Society took their places at the dedication ceremony.

For many years, Rómulo Sauñe had worked with missionaries from Wycliffe Bible Translators and the Presbyterian church to translate the entire Bible for his Quechua people.

Hunger for the Word of God

At the end of the ceremony, Christians crowded around the Bible Society booth to purchase Bibles. They pressed forward. Some people had walked great distances for a Bible, but the stacks of Bibles were disappearing rapidly. "How can we get these Bibles to the people if they can't get a copy today?" Rómulo wondered. Suddenly he had an idea.

The next week Rómulo went to Lima and visited his good friend, Wycliffe missionary Al Shannon. As he sat in Al's office, Rómulo laid out his concern. "This Bible is still too expensive for my people. Even at three dollars, it's too much. What can we do?"

"Look, Rómulo, for every Bible you sell for one dollar, I'll match it with two dollars." Al was convinced that at a subsidized price, Rómulo would sell only a few hundred Bibles. That many sales Al could easily cover with his personal savings.

"That's fantastic, Al," Rómulo said.

Tucked into the South American Andes mountains of Peru is a city called Ayacucho. In the Ancient Inca language, it means "Corner of the Dead." From this city came one of the most brutal terrorist groups in the Western Hemisphere—the Shining Path. Thousands of Christian believers in this area have met violent deaths for their faith in Jesus Christ.

Rómulo Sauñe grew up in a small shepherd village near Ayacucho. As a young boy, Rómulo was kicked in the head by a horse. The people called Rómulo "Deaf and Stupid One." No one thought he would amount to much.

Yet years later on June 23, 1992, in Manila, Philippines, Rómulo Sauñe accepted the first Religious Liberty Award from the World Evangelical Fellowship. The award recognized Rómulo's courageous efforts: to proclaim the gospel of Jesus Christ; for his translation work through Wycliffe Bible Translators and the United Bible Society; and his servant leadership of TAWA, and indigenous ministry to the Quechua people of Peru.

Only a few months after the award, Rómulo returned to Peru. In spite of the dangerous risk of meeting the Shining Path, in September 1992 Rómulo and other family members traveled to a small village near Ayacucho. They were visiting the grave of Rómulo's grandfather who had been brutally murdered by the Shining Path two years earlier. During their trip home from the small village, the Shining Path set up a roadblock, and killed Rómulo, plus more than twenty others. After shooting Rómulo, one of the terrorists said, "We got him!"

> *To get their own Bible,*
> *they even took the clothes*
> *off their backs and sold them*
> *in the streets.*

When they heard of the plan, the Peruvian Bible Society directors agreed to advance as many copies as Rómulo could sell during the special offer. News of the two-day sale was announced on Quechua radio with plenty of advanced notice.

One evening Al told his wife, Barbara, "I admire Rómulo's faith, but the country is in shambles. Most of the people don't have one dollar to spare for food, much less for a Bible."

On the day prior to the official sale, Al received an anxious telephone call from Rómulo. "Al, we need your help!"

Al's first thought was that the Shining Path terrorists had stolen the Bibles. "What's the matter? Is something wrong?"

Rómulo laughed. "Nothing's wrong, Al; we've just sold all 5,000 of the Bibles. We don't have any to sell at the sale. Could you send up another 5,000 by tomorrow?"

Relieved, Al replied, "No problem. I'll get those up to you by air first thing in the morning." He called the Bible Society and made the arrangements. But then it suddenly struck him, "Wait a minute! I don't have that kind of money! That's going to cost me a fortune. What have I gotten myself into? Help, God!"

But miles away, Rómulo Sauñe was laughing. The people were ready to receive these Bibles, and he had known it all along. The next week, Rómulo came back to Al's office. Tears streamed down Rómulo's cheeks as he told about the distribution.

"Al, the people would do anything to get their own Bible. They even . . ."—he choked back the tears—"took the clothes off their backs and sold them in the streets to get the money." In one week, Rómulo and the other brothers had sold 11,000 Bibles, a new record for the Peruvian Bible Society.

In the coming weeks, people continued pouring into Ayacucho to buy more Bibles. Soon the entire first run of 20,000 were sold out. The Bible Society immediately ordered another 20,000 Bibles. When they arrived, the Quechua church leadership held another

sale, and all 20,000 were sold. The Bible Society officials in Lima shook their heads in disbelief. But the timing was perfect. As the weeks passed, the violence from the Shining Path in this area of Peru increased and made Bible distribution nearly impossible.

An unexpected visitor
The home of Rómulo Sauñe and his wife, Donna, was quiet for the night. Although terrorism reigned throughout Peru, the Sauñes lived simply without any guards or security. They settled their children for the night and listened to their nighttime prayers.

Suddenly there was a rap at the door. The Quechua community often turned to the Sauñe house for help. Rómulo hesitated for a moment then called out, "Who is it?"

"Is the pastor there?" a voice asked. Since the pastor of the small church had gone off for the night, Rómulo replied, "He's not here." Then he heard footsteps walk away. He didn't recognize the voice so he thought nothing of it.

As his custom, Rómulo got up at 4 A.M. to spend time with the Lord in prayer. After breakfast, Rómulo heard a knock at the door. He opened it, and there stood a young man with a gunny sack over his shoulder.

"Good morning," Rómulo ventured.

"Is the pastor here?" It was the same voice Rómulo had heard the night before.

"No, the pastor doesn't live here," Rómulo said. "Why do you ask?"

"Are you Rómulo Sauñe?" Rómulo nodded.

"Why didn't you open your door last night? If you had, things would have been quite different. I came by with two of my comrades. We were going to kill you."

Rómulo stared at him wide-eyed. Then with measured words he said, "You're not fighting against me. You're fighting against the God of the universe. And that God didn't allow me to open my door last night."

"But, Rómulo, from your university studies, you know the detailed preparation of the Shining Path. I've worked hard in recent months spying on the church. I even memorized Bible verses so you would think I was a part of the congregation. But I've also taught other comrades how to set dynamite and destroy churches."

Rómulo had never seen the young man

Rómulo Sauñe (center) with his father, Enrique, and mother, Maria, in Peru, September 1991.

before, but he believed him. "Why are you telling me this now?"

The terrorist breathed a heavy sigh. "Last night I was tortured by those Bible verses that I had learned. They were like a hammer pounding inside my head. Finally I couldn't stand it anymore. So this morning I decided to come and talk with you about your faith, about your God. I don't want to kill you anymore."

Rómulo reached for his Bible and sat down next to the man, "God is working in your life. You need to repent of your sins. You need to stop wasting your life and give it to Jesus instead of the Shining Path. It's the only way to stop this torture in your head."

The young man began to sob. He couldn't speak. But Rómulo gently began to lead him in a prayer. After they had prayed together, Rómulo smiled. "God's Word says that the angels rejoice when someone enters the kingdom of God."

As an act of celebration, the man gave Rómulo the brown gunny sack. Inside was a small gun and a handful of ammunition. His story wasn't an idle threat. On this occasion, the Sauñe family had been spared violence from the hands of the Shining Path.

But on September 5, 1992, Rómulo Sauñe was not so spared. He was slain by the terrorists of the Shining Path. One of the Lord's choicest servants went to his heavenly home to be with his Savior whom he loved so dearly. Nor will the distribution of the Bible in Peru and elsewhere in Latin America be thwarted by bullets. In fact, Rómulo's death may prompt a whole new generation of young people to commit their lives to winning Latin America for Christ.

Terry Whalin

The Life of Rómulo Sauñe

1953	Born on January 17 at Chakiqpampa
1974	Graduates from high school
1977	Marries Donna Jackson on August 13
1978	Receives diploma from Latin American Bible Institute
1979	Returns to Peru from United States
1982	Ayacucho Quechua New Testament dedicated in January
1987	Ayacucho Quechua Bible dedicated on September 3
1992	Receives the World Evangelical Fellowship Religious Liberty Award in Manila on June 23
1992	Killed by Shining Path in Peru on September 5

PERU

• Ayacucho

SOUTH AMERICA

This chapter is taken from One Bright Shining Path, *by W. Terry Whalin and Chris Woehr, Copyright 1993, pages 168–70; 173–74, 216. Used with permission of Good News Publishers, Crossway Books, Wheaton, Illinois 60187.*

(Rómulo Sauñe was affiliated with the Wycliffe Bible Translators, United Bible Society, Open Doors International, TAWA (an indigenous Quechua organization), and to a lesser extent with Evangel Bible Translators, Christian Hope Indian Eskimo Fellowship (CHIEF), the Presbyterian Church of America, and the Jesus film project.)

Further Reading

W. Terry Whalin and Chris Woehr. *One Bright Shining Path, Faith in the Midst of Terrorism, The Life and Testimony of Rómulo Sauñe.* Wheaton: Crossway, 1993.

CARIBBEAN CHURCH LEADER

Dieumème Noelliste

1952–

Mama, I want to learn to read. Ple-e-ease," Dieumème begged.

His older sister listened sympathetically as his mother answered: "I very much want you to be able to read. Then you could read the Bible for us during family worship times—but I just don't see how."

She knew her illiterate family was poor even by rural Haitian standards. Besides Dieumème, there were a brother and two sisters to feed.

Dieumème's own uneducated father, a believer who died one month after Dieumème's birth, had named him "Dieumème" in the mistaken belief that it meant "Gift of God" in French. Instead, its actual eyebrow-raising meaning is "God Himself." Noelliste's mother had remarried, but her second husband had also died not long after.

Mrs. Noelliste explained to Dieumème that the private school for basic reading in the village charged one United States dollar for the course—far beyond what they could afford.

It was then that Dieumème's sister made a startling offer. She would sell her only rooster to make it possible for him to go to reading school.

An education, step by step

That was how Dieumème started school. He went on to public school in the town of Petite Rivière. Although tuition was free, sending him was still a hardship because there was the cost of books, uniforms, and shoes.

The evangelical church in the city of Grand Hatte established branch ministries

> *She would sell her only rooster to make it possible for him to go to reading school.*

Tourists love to go to the Caribbean islands. But the fact that tourism is this fragmented region's main business shows how economically depressed it really is.

This is the story of Dieumème Noelliste, who overcame a desperately impoverished upbringing in Haiti, the Western Hemisphere's poorest nation, to pursue an education and master the skills to direct the first advanced school for pastoral training in the Caribbean. It is also the story of how God prodded him along the way.

Today, besides presiding over two seminaries, Noelliste is vice president of the Evangelical Association of the Caribbean and president of the Caribbean Evangelical Theological Association. Most important, he has contributed to the improvement of the quality of church leadership in the Caribbean.

in outlying areas, including one near where Dieumème's family lived. Dieumème placed his faith in Christ at age thirteen during a vacation Bible school. His own older brother was the teacher.

Dieumème moved to the capital, Port-au-Prince, to enter a secondary school operated by Unevangelized Fields Mission. He studied there for the five years of academics it then offered. This fell one year short of the preparation necessary for the Baccalaureate I exams under the French educational system (similar to high school entrance). But he and three others tutored themselves from the texts during their fifth year and took the exam a year early. Dieumème and two others passed.

The Life of Dieumème Noelliste

1952	Birth at Petite Rivière, Haiti, September 20
1973–76	Attends Haiti State University school of law
1979	Awarded Th.B. by William Tyndale College Marries Gloria Jean Charleston
1982	Awarded M.Div. by Trinity Evangelical Divinity School
1985	Dr. Zenas Gerig offers deanship of Caribbean Graduate School of Theology (CGST)
1986	CGST is formally launched in September; in December accepts the deanship
1987	Awarded Ph.D. by Garrett Seminary-Northwestern University Family moves to Jamaica
1988	Hurricane Gilbert devastates CGST campus
1989	First CGST class of eight graduates
1991	Elected president of Caribbean Evangelical Theological Association
1993	Installed as president of both CGST and the Jamaica Theological Seminary (combined enrollment of 209) Elected vice president of the Evangelical Association of the Caribbean

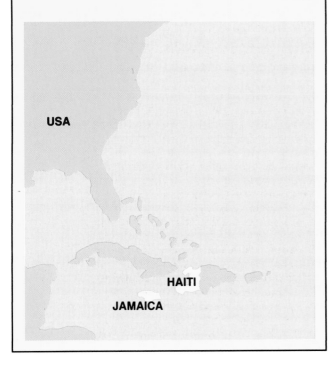

USA

HAITI

JAMAICA

He then took what is normally the seventh school year at Lycée Toussaint Louverture and passed the Baccalaureate II exams. By this time, Dieumème's older brother had entered the ministry, becoming pastor of the Petite Rivière church. Observing his subsistence-level existence, Dieumème decided the ministry was not for him. He would enter a profession and provide for his extended family.

He enrolled in the school of law at the Haiti State University. During the three years of the four-year course he completed, he earned his way by working as a news announcer at Radio Lumière, the World-team-operated Christian station. When Dr. Harold Merchant of Detroit visited the radio station, he was impressed with Noelliste's potential and offered to sponsor his coming to the United States to study Bible at Detroit Bible College (now William Tyndale College).

In love with theology

Dieumème, not attracted to the idea of coming to the United States, nearly rejected the offer. But studying there carried prestige, and his older brother urged him to accept. He did, but only half-heartedly. However, in Detroit, Noelliste rapidly fell in love with the study of theology. He abandoned all thought of a law career.

During his second year, he took an evening course and met Gloria Charleston, a local African-American evening school student. She had never been to the Caribbean but had made tentative plans to go to Haiti as a missionary. Noelliste graduated from William Tyndale College in May 1979, and he and Gloria were married that same month.

Noelliste had decided to pursue a graduate degree and applied to several seminaries. He was accepted by several schools, but favored Trinity Evangelical Divinity School in Deerfield, Illinois, because he wanted to study philosophy under Dr. Norman Geisler, then a professor there. Even though he had not been accepted by Trinity, he took his bride with him to

> *Noelliste rapidly fell in love with the study of theology.*

> *In Haiti, evangelicals*
> *were now thought to be*
> *a quarter of the population.*

Deerfield and enrolled anyway, only to discover that Dr. Geisler had just moved to Dallas Theological Seminary.

Noelliste feels certain that the way he was directed to Trinity was providential. When he moved to Deerfield, a far north suburb of Chicago, he did not realize that twenty-five to thirty thousand Haitian immigrants lived in the Chicago area—mostly clustered in Rogers Park, at the north edge of Chicago, and in adjacent Evanston.

Dieumème and Gloria began to work in that community. In 1982 they launched the Haitian Evangelical Baptist Church with seven adults and two children. By 1986, the Creole-speaking congregation had grown to sixty adults and twenty-five children. It then rented facilities from the Rogers Park Lutheran Church.

While Noelliste studied at Trinity, Gloria worked as an accountant. Two of their four children were born then. Dieumème graduated in 1982 and moved to Rogers Park. He enrolled at Garrett Seminary-Northwestern University in Evanston to begin doctoral studies in theology.

Because of its location in the neighborhood of his congregation, Garrett-Northwestern was a logical school for Noelliste to study in. But he was an evangelical shaping his thesis on "The Role of the Church in Human Emancipation" under the supervision of three liberal scholars. Noelliste believes that he did not compromise any essentials, but it took skill and tact to avoid offending his proctors. Getting the first chapter of his thesis approved was especially difficult.

A call from the Caribbean

Meanwhile, a committee to form a Caribbean Graduate School of Theology (CGST) was searching for a qualified Caribbean scholar to serve as dean. Project coordinator Zenas Gerig had pursued several promising leads, but none of the candidates was approved. The Haitian member of the school's academic committee knew about Dieumème Noelliste but had never volunteered his name. This Port-au-Prince Bible

Dr. Dieumème Noelliste.

School president hoped to add Noelliste to his own staff. But in early 1985 he gave in and shared Noelliste's name with the committee.

Dr. Gerig visited Noelliste soon after and offered him the position. Dieumème was skeptical. He had become wrapped up in the Haitian church and expected to remain its pastor. The dean's salary was not tempting, and the school was still only a concept.

But he did not close the door. Dieumème and Gloria visited Kingston, Jamaica, in December 1985. Although not attracted to the position, he could not escape the urgent need for affordable pastoral training at an advanced level within the Caribbean region. Over the last two decades there had been rapid church growth. In his native Haiti, for example, evangelicals were now thought to be a quarter of the population. But most of those who went abroad to study were not returning to their economically depressed homelands. As a result, the quality of church leadership was actually declining.

And Noelliste—fluent in English, French, Creole, and Spanish, the major languages of the region—had to admit that he was ideally prepared for a Caribbean-wide education role. He increasingly came to feel God was calling him to the position. But it took almost two years for him to "become broken" enough to submit.

When the Caribbean Graduate School of Theology was launched in September 1986, with an initial student body of twenty, the Noellistes were once again guests of the school, but Noelliste was still not ready to accept the position of dean. So Dr. Gerig served as acting dean for the school's first academic year.

Finally in December, Noelliste sent word of his acceptance. He returned to the school's campus the next February to teach a module on Old Testament theology. It clicked. He loved teaching and there was an immediate positive chemistry between him and the student body. He returned to the United States, completed his doctoral program, and resigned from the church he had founded.

Enlarging the school

Dr. Gerig had provided a solid foundation by spearheading planning for a graduate-level school, purchasing an acre of property adjacent to the college-level Jamaica Theological Seminary (JTS, which he had directed for years) to create a combined five-acre campus, and launching an ambitious funding campaign to expand the shared facilities.

Dr. Noelliste lost no time in building the superstructure. During his first year at CGST he taught three modules (all day, five days a week, for three weeks) in the residency phase. By the second year he had added supervision of the thesis writing phase—which follows residency—for all

> *Dieumème Noelliste deals relevantly with liberation theology, Marxist influence, and pervasive poverty.*

students. Today the school has master's degree programs in theological and biblical studies, Christian education and Caribbean ministries, and counseling psychology. It received accreditation from the Caribbean Evangelical Theological Association in 1991.

With contagious enthusiasm, Noelliste embarked on a series of promotional visits around the Caribbean. CGST was at first little known outside Jamaica. But in the second entering class, students from Spanish-speaking areas joined their English-speaking counterparts.

He demonstrated administrative skills as he directed the school and recruited and scheduled first-rate, qualified scholars from the Caribbean and North America as resident and visiting faculty, and developed a scholarship program for qualified students who could not afford the school's modest tuition charge.

In September 1988, Hurricane Gilbert ripped the roofs off five of the campus's nine buildings, damaging the men's dormitory beyond repair. Security fences worth $100,000 were destroyed. And all electrical, water, and telephone services were cut off. Yet CGST and JTS opened their doors according to their original schedules—the only advanced-level schools on the entire island to do so.

Dieumème Noelliste understands the Caribbean region, giving evangelical theology a Caribbean flavor that deals relevantly with liberation theology, Marxist influence, and pervasive poverty.

In January 1993, he was promoted from dean of CGST to president of both CGST and JTS, with a combined enrollment of more than two hundred. The sale of the rooster by Dieumème's sister turned out to be one of the soundest investments ever made.

Harry Genet

Australasia

SERVANT IN SUMATRA

Ludwig Ingwer Nommensen

1834–1918

Three of the most notable missionaries of the German Protestant Church were Bartholomaus Ziegenbaig (1682–1719), who worked in India, Johan Ludwig Krapf (1810–1881), who ministered in East Africa, and Ludwig Ingwer Nommensen (1834–1918). Of the three, Nommensen may have been one of the most successful missionaries ever to preach the gospel.

During fifty-six years of tireless work in Sumatra, he helped the Batak church come into existence. It is presently one of the largest Protestant churches in southeast Asia. Nommensen led this church with great skill until his dying day. From the very beginning, he employed natives and was eager to ground church life deeply in the social structure of the country. In Sumatra, Nommensen is honored as the "Apostle to the Bataks."

The second largest of the Indonesian Great Sunda islands, Sumatra, lies off the Malaysian peninsula. By the middle of the seventeenth century, the Dutch had gained a foothold there and acted as an exploitive colonial power. None of the colonists thought much about the spiritual needs of the pagan population. Efforts to win the natives, however, began in 1820 by three Baptist missionaries, but they saw no fruit. In 1834 a second attempt took place. Two missionaries, Lyman and Munson, sent by the American Board of Commissioners for Foreign Mission, ventured into the interior in order to reach the Batak, an ancient Malayan tribe.

One evening, after a strenuous journey through the jungle, they were approaching a small village. Suddenly they were attacked and killed by a number of outraged warriors. Following Batak custom, the cannibalistic murderers proceeded to eat their bodies.

In that same year, on February 6, Ludwig Ingwer Nommensen was born on the North Frisen island Nordstrand (Schleswig). His father, Peter, served as the lock keeper of the island, but he died when Ludwig was fourteen. The boy's mother, Anna, had her work cut out for her raising her wild, but intelligent boy. But she always knew how to treat him. At age twelve he had an accident that confined him to his bed for almost one year. During this time, he became a heartfelt Christian through reading the Bible. He took a vow to become a missionary if God brought him back to health. After his recovery, he worked as a farm laborer, then for the railway helping to build the first railway line in Schleswig, and eventually as an assistant teacher.

When Nommensen was twenty years old his mother agreed to his plans to become a missionary. Motivated both by his youthful Christian enthusiasm and his lack of finances he traveled to Fohr, intending to sign up as a sailor in order to go overseas. Instead, however, through the help of a minister he started a four-year course in the missionary seminary of the "Rheinische Mission" in Wuppertal-Barmen. While there, the theologies of two mission directors, Freidrich Fabris and Ludwig von Rhoden, exercised a formative influence on Nommensen's thinking.

Finally Nommensen was sent out as a missionary. On Christmas Eve 1861, he

> *The cannibalistic murderers proceeded to eat their bodies.*

began his journey to the mission field on board a sailing ship traveling from Amsterdam to Sumatra. On the way, he wrote a significant entry into his prayer diary. He entrusted himself, without reservation, to his heavenly Father: "Today, in the middle of the Indian Ocean, I renew the covenant which I have made with you, my God and Father. ... You have chosen me to be an apostle of the Gospel to the heathen. Therefore, I give my life to you. Seal up my covenant with you in heaven, as I seal it in this book on board the ship. ... Sealed and signed on 13th April 1862."

The beginning
Four weeks later, Nommensen landed in Padang on the northwestern coast. He lived for a time in Barus and then in Angkola, a place in the Islamic south of the Batak region where four missionaries had already worked. On October 7, 1861, they had held their first conference in Sipirock which marks the birth of the Batak church.

This church reached its most crucial juncture in May 1864. Nommensen turned toward the central mountains in the north and settled down in the region of Saitnihuta, a part of the very fertile and densely populated high valley in northern Sumatra. At

The Life of Ludwig Inwer Nommensen

1834	Born February 6 on Nordstrand (Schleswig)
1861	Sails to Sumatra on Christmas Eve to begin missionary service
1865	Baptizes first converts in Silindung Valley
1866	Marries Karoline Gutbrodt
1878	Translates the New Testament into Batak
1886	Penetrates the Toba Lake region
1887	Karoline dies
1911	Active during the fiftieth anniversary of the Batak church
1918	Dies on May 23; 180,000 members of the Batak church
1993	2.5 million members in the Batak church

SUMATRA

AUSTRALIA

this time, Silindung was politically independent and influenced completely by the old Batak tribal culture, which emphasized the social rooting of the individual in his or her family and tribe. No Dutch influence pervaded the Silindung villages; instead, the Batak's animistic religion dominated, with its belief in the spirituality of all nature and spirit worship. The life of the Bataks was well-ordered by the "adat," which was the

Ludwig Ingwer Nommensen (1834–1918).

> *The missionary was to be offered as a sacrifice to the ghosts.*

Opposite:
Ludwig Nom-
mensen with
his wife and
daughter in
Sumatra.

The church was integrated into the village community.

base of law and custom handed down through families.

Into this valley came Nommensen. Although he was under the protection of the chief Pontas Lumbantobing who later became his friend, he was not warmly welcomed by the inhabitants. Supposing that Nommensen was a precursor of the colonial government, they rightly feared for their independence. Thus they mocked and threatened him: "We will cut off your legs and throw you into the river." But Nommensen was not intimidated.

When their threats proved futile, they tried to take his life. During a large celebration of ancestor worship the missionary was to be offered as a sacrifice to the ghosts. But he walked imperturbably through the furious crowd so that nobody dared lay a hand on him. This made a great impression on the crowd.

His many efforts to gain the confidence of the villagers did not remain without effect. Often he would play the violin to them and tell stories. At great cost to himself he would care for the sick and in spite of little medical knowledge he was successful in effecting cures, using homeopathic remedies. Later, he was able to introduce a vaccination against smallpox which frequently wreaked havoc in the valley. Even more than their physical well-being, however, he was concerned about the spiritual well-being of the people; he attempted to convince them of God's love and power through a simple preaching of the gospel and personal conversations always adapted to the Bataks' way of thinking.

Finally, he gained a hearing. On August 27, 1865, he baptized the first people from Silindung, four couples and five children. Consequently, they were cast out of their tribe, the "adat" community. Then they lost their property and were threatened by their fellow tribesmen. So, Nommensen took them into his small mission base and helped them to plant new rice fields. Despite bitter hostility and predatory attacks, more and more Bataks joined the new Christian community so that the base called "huta Dame" was gradually transformed into the com-

munity of the "new religion" protected by ramparts and trenches.

Nommensen received his own reinforcements in 1866, when his fiancée, Karoline Gutbrodt, arrived from Hamburg to become his wife and a fellow Schleswig countryman Peter Hinrich Johannsen arrived to work at Nommensen's side as a teacher and Bible translator. A little later, Ludwig started a second mission base in Pansurnapitu in the southeast end of the valley, followed by the planting of other small churches. In his diary Nommensen described his daily activities: "In the morning, a short passage from the Bible is explained and then we eat. Thereafter, everybody gets down to work. My usual tasks are first to look after the sick, then translation work is done followed by teaching in school. Towards the middle of the day, people will usually come to talk about God's word. Regularly, however, there are quarrels and arguments to arbitrate. In the evening we gather together again in school."

A new era

After a decade of opposition with the tribal religion there was a gradual change in the Silindung valley. By 1876 there were more than two thousand Christians; now the number of Christians grew quickly. More and more chiefs turned to Christianity—and with them entire villages. In the middle of the 1870s, the Dutch colonial power annexed the area, and the number of converts grew quickly. Individual baptisms were replaced by group baptisms. A new era had begun! With great skill, Nommensen built Batak churches and translated Luther's *Small Catechism* and the New Testament into the Batak language. In 1881 he established new church statutes with special consideration of the Sumatran circumstances.

Now, Nommensen turned to the Toba region, a pagan area in the north which he had explored in 1876 accompanied by friendly chiefs. Upon his first view of this magnificent country he wrote in his diary with prophetic vision: "In my spirit I can already see Christian churches and schools all over the place. . . . Young and old alike I see walking to the church and hear the church bell ringing everywhere." After the Dutch government had subdued this area and suppressed revolts led by the High Priest Singsmangaradja XII, a bitter enemy of

Christianity, Nommensen and his missionaries moved in.

In 1886 Nommensen finally settled down in Sigumpar on the eastern shore of the Tobe Lake, making it the center of his work. With a sailing boat he shuttled tirelessly across the lake in order to get to know the chiefs and to start mission bases. After a little while these bases had developed into flourishing churches, which Tobas now joined with entire families and tribes. But in the course of this growth, the superficiality of the Christianization process became apparent to the mission.

As in Silindung, Nommensen was asked to guide the mass movement into a national Batak church. He gave wise counsel, focusing on the self-preservation of the local churches. From the beginning he trained natives to be elders and pastors and especially teacher-preachers who became the backbone of the inner church work. With great care, the church was integrated into the village community by keeping the social structure of the "adat," thus making the Christian and the civil community almost one. This, of course, made Christianization much easier.

"Forward march!"

Within two decades the Toba region was also penetrated with the gospel, and the Batak church numbered nearly fifty thousand members. At this point, Nommensen intended to expand his mission up the east coast to the Simalungun-Batak region. For some time proponents of Islam had been busily at work there. This made the mission all the more urgent. When Nommensen asked the mission center in Wuppertal regarding his plans, he received a telegram in the Batak language: "Tole," meaning "march forward." His answer, in which he asked for a further twenty-eight missionaries, was: "Here, it has always been tole! Forward march and never back!"

Thereafter Nommensen insisted on making the first big venture to Simalungun in order to prepare for well-ordered and structured church planting. During the following years the mission gained a foothold. But the success was less impressive than in the other areas. Despite his great age, Nommensen was not only concerned with finding missionaries for the new areas but, as a leader

of the entire Batak mission, he also continued to visit the large mission field extending up to Angkola. In 1911, in the fiftieth year jubilee of the Batak church, more than fifty missionaries worked there. In the same year, Nommensen was awarded the title of an "officer" of the Dutch order of Orania-Nassau. Already on his seventieth birthday in 1904 he had received an honorary doctorate in theology from the University of Bonn.

Nommensen's joy about the promising developments of his mission was, however, shadowed by grief. Already in 1887, Karoline, Ludwig's first wife had died. In 1910 his second wife died as well. Early on he lost his four children too.

On May 23, 1918, at the age of eighty-four years, Ludwig himself died. The Batak church he had planted (Toba-Batak Church since 1930: Huria Kristen Batak Protestant) numbered 180,000 members in more than five hundred churches, with thirty-four ministers and nearly 800 teacher-preachers. Today the church has 2.5 million members.

The name of the "Apostle to the Bataks" lives on in "Nommensen University" founded in 1954. Nommensen had proved to be the "Apostle to the Bataks" by his pioneer spirit, his qualities as a leader, his imperturbable patience, and his courageous Christian faith. Once, in a letter to the mission center in Wuppertal he wrote describing what any ambassador of Christ should be like: "They must be the most efficient people, no hot-tempered, choleric types, but patient, friendly, self-sacrificing, loving men . . . who count on God's word as they count numbers." He himself was such an ambassador.

Werner Raupp

Further Reading

Petersen, Paul B. *Batak Blood and Protestant Soul: The Development of National Batak Churches in North Sumatra,* 1970.

Schreiner, Lothar. "Ludwig Nommensen Studies: A Review." *Mission Studies* IX (1992).

SHE LOVED THE CHINESE BEST

Lottie Moon

1840–1912

"She is Melanie and Scarlet in one package." That is how Irwin Hyatt described Southern Baptist missionary Lottie Moon. Cultured and gentle, a Southern belle, she had a flair for the independent and unconventional. Literary portraits oscillate between sentimental transcendent perfectionism and captivity to race-associated sexual frustration, a psychological caricature of late nineteenth-century Southern Protestant white women. Nearer the truth is this: Lottie Moon was a real Christian with average weaknesses, above-average strengths, involved in a life-long process of real sanctification punctuated by a fair number of rather exotic adventures.

Born the fourth of seven children, Lottie was reared with the privileges of antebellum Virginian aristocracy. The Moons had servants and kept a tutor in the home for languages and classical literature. An uncle, James Barclay, who owned Jefferson's Monticello, became the first missionary of the Christian Church to Jerusalem. Lottie's sister Orianna the first female medical doctor south of the Mason-Dixon line, followed him there and was baptized in the Jordan River. Lottie's father died when she was thirteen, leaving Mrs. Moon in charge of a large family and a large estate.

In 1854–55 Lottie attended Virginia Female Seminary, where her academic record read "very good in Latin, superior in French" but "very deficient" to "tolerable" in natural science and math. Her spiritual disinterest may have been evidenced by twenty-six absences from chapel during the final two quarters.

After one year back at Viewmont, she set off to Albemarle Female Institute near Charlottesville, Virginia. There she met C. H. Toy, who taught English and ancient languages. Her literary brilliance (Toy said, "She

Lottie Moon as a young woman.

Born in Viewmont, Virginia, in 1840 as the fourth of seven children, Charlotte Digges Moon was reared in a world of social and racial divisions perpetuated by school, church, and commercial interests. Though the family was settled in Baptist convictions, religious contacts with Quakers, Presbyterians, Methodists, and Catholics created both diversity of thought and rebellion in the Moon children. However, Lottie was brought to saving faith in Christ in 1858.

Though the Civil War destroyed most of the external trappings of social and racial partitions, many of Lottie's friends found stronger emotional ties to their social and racial prejudices after the war. Meanwhile, Lottie was experiencing an antidote to this prejudice in the form of a rapidly increasing desire to see the spread of the kingdom of her Savior. In 1873, she became a missionary to China. A lingering cultural elitism crumbled under the weight of the word of reconciliation; proud sectionalism melted before the warmth of a concern for world Christianity. Her commitment to reach the greatest number of Chinese with the gospel in the most effective way aided in establishing a stable indigenous witness in the Shantung province.

Lottie's clear and ingenious literary techniques dedicated to the task of encouraging, shaming, and arousing Southern Baptists did more than any other single factor in wedding that denomination to the call of foreign missions as its most defining and unifying activity.

A Christmas offering for foreign missions was created in 1888 as a result of the continued insistence of Lottie. From that date until 1992, the special offering, now called the Lottie Moon Christmas offering, has collected $1.33 billion. Every penny has been used immediately to meet needs on the foreign mission field.

> *Lottie Moon was a real Christian with average weaknesses and above average strengths.*

writes the best English I have ever been privileged to read") was perhaps matched by her spiritual cynicism. Sundays were for Shakespeare in the straw, not sermons in the church; and the "D" in her name stood for "Devil," she said, not "Digges." But in December of 1858, God changed her scoffing to praying and brought her to saving faith under the witness and prayers of her friends and the counsel of John A. Broadus. Mrs. W. E. Hatcher observed her subsequent activities and closely noted the difference "in those details of the daily life which at last afforded the most delicate test of Christian character."

In 1860, Lottie Moon returned for a fourth year to Albemarle just so she could exhaust the curriculum. Awarded an M.A. upon graduation, she was now, according to Broadus, "the most educated woman in the South."

A child of the lost cause

The Civil War dealt a death blow to many implicit assumptions that regulated the Southern way of life. Lottie Moon was as Southern as grits. Her cousin Jim rode with Mosby's Raiders, and two female cousins served as spies for the Confederacy, posing as Irish washer women. Her attitude toward the war's consumption of Southern manpower showed brutal patriotism: "Let them go, I say. The women and children can take care of themselves, and far better all perish than bow the neck to the tyrant's yoke."

Her recognition of the sanctifying power of suffering also increased as she observed the mounting sorrow of friends. Character receives "its fullest and most beautiful development" only as it passes through "the fiery furnace of affliction." Trouble comes in season, and "we ought to be just as thankful for sorrows as for joys."

"Blight our dearest hopes," she could pray, "that we may learn more fully to depend on Thee." The lesson that she admired from afar, God would force her to learn up close.

Following the Civil War, Lottie taught in Danville, Kentucky, and Cartersville, Georgia. Personally and financially involved in creative

The Life of Lottie Moon

1840	Born in Albemarle county, Virginia
1854–56	Attends Virginia Female Seminary (Hollins Institute)
1858	Conversion and baptism
1863–72	Teaches in Virginia, Kentucky, and Georgia
1873	Joins her sister, Edmonia, in China as a Southern Baptist missionary
1876	Accompanies her sister back to United States; renews romantic friendship with C. H. Toy
1877	Returns to China
1883	Abandons schoolwork to concentrate on itinerate evangelism
1885	Begins work in P'ingtu
1900	In Japan during Boxer Rebellion
1912	Begins sympathy fast; dies of starvation in Kobe Harbor, Japan

P'ingtu •

CHINA

Lottie Moon's coworker Pastor Li conducts a baptism around 1910.

outlets for Christian missions, she stirred Southern women to the same. "Our Lord does not call women to preach," she wrote, but He surely commands them as well as men, "Go work in My vineyard." She advocated a deaconness system in Baptist churches to care for destitute women and children.

When her sister Edmonia, a correspondent for a Richmond missionary society, went to China, she called for Lottie: "I cannot convince myself that it is the will of God that you shall not come." Her picture of the urgency and opportunities of the field reinforced several other promptings in Lottie's

life. In 1873, Lottie sailed to China, where with the exception of a few furloughs she would spend the rest of her life.

Provincial pride

According to Southern observers, a woman of "fine intellect, rare culture, and splendid social gifts" had given herself to lead the "darkened and degraded to the true light." She herself was not free of this sense of contradiction.

"Narrow minds and degraded morals," she wrote in 1873, were typified by the Chinese women's bound feet. A March 1875 trip to Shanghai prompted a description of

> ## "Narrow minds and degraded morals" were typified by the Chinese women's bound feet.

the energy and uplifting character of the British, compared with the "dark, crowded, filthy, streets" and the odors and sounds of the "native city." "Where the Caucasian goes," she asserted, "he carries energy, and an inferior race is roused by the contact."

In 1876, after three years of missionary labor, Lottie sent H. A. Tupper a letter shy of her typically brilliant style. Stopping short of finishing one of her narratives she exclaimed, "I wonder if all this interests you! If not pray excuse it on the score that much mingling with the heathen makes one stupid."

Astute social observation is one thing. Prejudice is another. Lottie was good at both. Personal gifts and privileges and cultural aloofness, perhaps encouraged by an incipient social Darwinism from her friend C. H. Toy, made a fine Southern recipe to cook up such statements of prejudice. God's guidance, however, and the nature of her call eventually caused Lottie to lose this superior-inferior viewpoint.

Debtor to Greeks and barbarians

For the Christian ambassador, "mingling with the heathen" has its own power to produce true humility. Cultural disdain increasingly gives way to sober reflection on the destructive power of sin and idolatry. Racial pride succumbs to unspeakable joy in the reconciling work of the gospel. But also securities of the past must crumble.

Several well-placed blows of Providence rattled Lottie's framework of earthly support and crushed her cavalier spirit. In 1876, Edmonia's severe mental and physical decline forced her permanent return to America. Lottie accompanied her. This American respite renewed friendship with C. H. Toy. The dream of marriage, however, dimmed by degrees. In 1879, Professor Toy resigned from Southern Seminary because of his changing views of biblical inspiration. Still hopeful and patient, Lottie set up a protest when the appointments of two young mission volunteers, T. P. Bell and John Stout, were rescinded because both held Toy's views on inspiration.

It was clear; Toy could never join her on the mission field. But might she join him at Harvard? By 1882, her personal study of the theological issue involved evoked a clear no. In addition, N. W. Halcomb, an effective missionary with several years' service, resigned his charge in 1886. In spite of Lottie's efforts through Bible study to get "his feet ... upon a foundation that nothing can shake," she saw "the strongest man we have" leave the field because of a theological struggle over the deity of Christ.

From the very beginning of her labors, Lottie was dominated by a sense of urgency to people "who literally sit in darkness," bound by the "folly & sin of idol worship." Just as urgently, as an "Ambassador for Christ," she implored those back home not to allow the heathen to "sink down into eternal death without one opportunity to hear that blessed gospel which is to you the source of all joy & comfort."

Urgency toward the heathen soon was joined by a sense of unity with the heathen. In 1877 she could write, "I love the Chinese best." Her constant contact with children, women, and men, and her involvement in sharing catechism, hymns, gospel tracts, portions of Scripture, and evangelistic conversations broke down barriers, both in her mind and theirs. By 1884, she was encouraged by the change she saw in attention span, religious concepts, and openness to friendship. Her work was with the "respectable poor and the middle classes," while "the aristocracy still regard us with lofty disdain." Now instead of a perpetrator, she shared the reproach of such disdain.

She had come to see in the men "much to admire" and in the women and girls "many sweet and lovable traits of character." She had not experienced a "more graceful, hearty hospitality than that of the Chinese" in any land. She admired greatly Christians such as a "noble young woman" who endured "much persecution for her Lord's sake," and she felt compelled to chide gently but seriously those who vaguely spoke of the heathen, "picturing them as scarcely human, or at best, as ignorant barbarians." By 1890 she commiserated with the Chinese over the absence of "foreign brethren" to help in pastoral situations. "No matter," she encouraged them, "we natives will do the work."

> *Racial pride succumbs to unspeakable joy in the reconciling work of the gospel.*

Sitting in darkness, carrying the light

Even when she was under the spell of her narrow ethnic views, Lottie's confidence rested in the unfettered power of the gospel. Insurmountable difficulties hindered Chinese conversions because of the devastating impact of error and idolatry. "Their spiritual darkness," she would say, "is inconceivable to one who had not seen it." Equally disastrous for missionary success was "wealth hoarded in Christian coffers" and Baptist "money lavished on fine dresses

An irrigation project in Africa supported by the Lottie Moon Christmas offering.

Lottie Moon with missionaries Ella Jeter (left) and Jessie Pettigrew (right) around 1905.

> *She had become*
> *one of the "natives"*
> *that she might win some.*

and costly living." The power of God's grace, however, and the certainty of the promise that "the heathen shall be given Thy Son for an inheritance and the uttermost parts of the earth for a possession" gave her comfort.

Like most missionaries, Lottie had a great desire to see the former heathen standing "firm in one spirit, contending as one man for the faith of the gospel" (Philippians 1:27). Her move to P'ingtu at age forty-five ignited a series of conversions and saw her great *desideratum* fulfilled. These Christians radiated not only sweet and lovely character and hearty consecration to God's service, but "Their one chief absorbing thought seems to be the glory of God, and the salvation of souls." The fruit grew and multiplied long after she returned to Tengchow.

The most celebrated coworker was Pastor Li. Li was a young Confucian scholar when an older friend heard the gospel while standing on the perimeter of one of Lottie's lessons for women. He went to Li for help in understanding the New Testament the missionary gave him. Li, intending to ridicule the book, was gripped by its message and went to Lottie as an inquirer. His commitment to the Christian faith led to brutal treatment at the hands of his brothers for refusal to worship at the graves of his ancestors. Subsequent to this persecution and prior to his baptism, C. W. Pruitt remarked, "I never heard a more earnest and thorough Christian experience. Let us thank the Lord for that brother. He is so humble and true that we feel greatly encouraged to hope for a wide influence."

Ten years later, during the Boxer Rebellion, thousands of Christians, Protestant and Catholic, were tortured and killed brutally and pitilessly by the political insurgents. Li and a group of fellow Christians were tied by their queues to horses and pulled at a gallop more than twenty-five miles to Laichowfu. Lottie made a dangerous and ingenious trip to P'ingtu to encourage the persecuted before the evacuation of American missionaries to Japan. The witness of Pastor Li continued, however, and his zealous activity for the gospel extended beyond Lottie's lifetime. Eventually he baptized ten thousand converts, five hundred in the year of Lottie's death. While the poignant, lingering death of Lottie Moon has some elements of the bizarre in it, one factor cannot be overlooked. She had come to identify her life so closely with that of Chinese Christians that she could not detach her activities from theirs. When she learned that many were on the verge of starvation during the famine of 1912, she stopped eating. And just before she died on board a ship docked in Kobe Harbor in Japan, she smiled and gave a Chinese greeting to friends whom she would soon join in the presence of their common Savior.

She was no longer the "most educated woman in the South." She had become one of the "natives" that she might win some. And by God's grace, she did.

Thomas Nettles

Further Reading

Allen, Catherine B. *The New Lottie Moon Story*. Nashville: Broadman, 1980.

Hyatt, Irwin T., Jr. *Our Ordered Lives Confess*. Cambridge: Harvard Univ., 1976.

Lawrence, Una Roberts. *Lottie Moon*. Nashville: The Sunday School Board of the Southern Baptist Convention, 1927.

ALL BY FAITH

James Hudson Taylor

1832–1905

James Hudson Taylor was born on May 21, 1832, in Barnsley, Yorkshire, England, the only son of a druggist and apothecary named James Taylor and his wife, Amelia. The elder Taylor was a lay Methodist preacher as well as a druggist. As a small child Hudson often heard visiting ministers and others talk about faraway lands. Foreign missions often came up in discussions around the dining room table and in the parlor.

Talk of the mysterious land of China especially fascinated young Hudson. From his earliest childhood days he decided he would someday go to China as a missionary. This conviction had not yet ripened into a call from the Lord, but it was to become the dominant theme and focus of his life.

But Hudson Taylor was a frail child, not even able to attend school until he was eleven, and then only for a brief time. His education continued at home.

At age fifteen he went to work as a clerk in one of the best banks in Barnsley. He was there for only nine months before inflammation of the eyes forced him to resign his position and return home.

It was time enough, however, for an older clerk to laugh at Hudson's old-fashioned spiritual views and to woo the younger man with his skeptical, freethinking views. Taylor began to distance himself from a faith in Christ. His family became deeply alarmed and prayed for him regularly.

Called to faith and service

At age seventeen, while serving as an apprentice to his father, Taylor had the decisive spiritual experience that was to mark his life and place him on the road to a lifetime of pioneer missionary service.

The historic day came in June 1849. Taylor was on holiday and picked up a tract

Known worldwide as the founder of the China Inland Mission, now called Overseas Missionary Fellowship, J. Hudson Taylor wielded a spiritual influence far beyond China. He is rightly regarded as one of the pioneers of the modern world missions movement.

Taylor's influence extended across continents as he made appeals to the United States and other countries for missionaries to China. The hard lessons he learned from the deficient support he had received from the missionary society sponsoring him during his early years on the field were reflected in the way the China Inland Mission was later organized. Taylor's views on matters such as the raising of funds for ministry became normative for generations of Protestant missionaries.

As a world traveler, Taylor had ample opportunities to tell the story of Christian missionary efforts in China. The thousands of gifts that poured in for his work testify to the effectiveness of his ministry in generating financial support as well as recruiting young men and women for missionary service. By 1895, Taylor's China Inland Mission had become the largest Protestant mission in China.

At Taylor's death tributes poured in from Christian leaders around the world. In our own day thousands of Christians have been deeply affected by reading about Taylor's perspectives on Christian discipleship, the "exchanged life," and about his now well-known "spiritual secret."

The Life of Hudson Taylor

1832	Born at Barnsley, Yorkshire, England
1849	Converted
1854	Arrives for first time in China
1858	Marries Maria Dyer
1865	Establishes the China Inland Mission (CIM)
1866	First CIM party sets sail for China
1870	Maria dies
1871	Marries Jane Faulding
1881	Prayer and appeal to double CIM missionary force
1895	CIM becomes largest Protestant missionary body in China
1902	Retires as general director
1905	Dies at Changsha, Hunan

CHINA

Shanghai●

Changsha●

Opposite: (top) James Hudson Taylor in 1889; (bottom) Changsha, capital of Hunan, where Hudson Taylor died.

> *"The conviction never left me that I was called to China."*

the state of mind that had dominated him for some time, and back to the familiar "territory" of faith. He knew at once that he was also called to serve, and he knew where. He recalled years later that as he offered himself fully to Christ, "the conviction never left me that I was called to China."

Submitting to hardship

So the frail teenager began to train himself for missionary service to China. He obtained a copy of the gospel of Luke in Mandarin and began to teach himself the language. He also engaged in physical exercise and tried to rid himself of as many comforts as possible in the belief that this preparation would help toughen him for life in China. He threw himself into numerous forms of ministry, convinced that he must be a soul-winner at home before he could become one in China.

A year after his conversion and call to China, Taylor believed it was time for even more rigorous preparation. He wanted to earn his own living and to pursue medical studies. He moved to Hull to become an assistant to one of the busiest doctors in town. His mentor was a good doctor and a "consistent Christian," but Taylor felt that living in his luxurious house was not the way to learn to endure hardness. He moved to the working-class slums of Hull, taking a small and sparsely furnished room.

Later, Taylor said of that period, "I felt that one's spiritual muscles need strengthening. When I get out to China I have no claim on anyone for anything. How important, therefore, to learn before leaving England to move man, through God, by prayer alone."

The discipline of faith

As assistant to Dr. Hardey of Hull, Hudson Taylor had ample occasion to practice this principle. The kind but very busy doctor often forgot to pay Hudson. The young man, however, determined never to remind him, but to learn to live each day not knowing whether he would have money for the next.

On one occasion, Taylor gave his only coin to the family of a starving woman who

to read as he sought something to fill the idle hours. The tract emphasized the finished work of Christ. The text, "It is finished," hit the young Taylor like a thunderbolt. He realized that if the work of redemption was finished and the debt of sin fully paid, there was nothing left for him to do but accept this salvation. And he did!

Taylor's conversion brought him out of

came to him for help. He struggled mightily with the decision, feeling on one hand that God wanted him to give it all, but knowing that he did not have enough food at home for more than a few meals. He finally gave the family the coin and said that obeying the Lord on that night saved his spiritual life from wreckage on the rocks of disobedience and unbelief. The next day, he received in the mail a larger coin tucked in a pair of kid gloves, from a donor whose identity he never learned.

By 1852 Taylor wondered in a letter to his sister Amelia if he should not resign his position and work for his passage to China. The Chinese Evangelization Society and his father in Barnsley offered their financial help. Oddly enough, he turned down both offers.

How Taylor determined that these offers were not part of God's provision for his needs, when a coin from an anonymous donor in fact was, is not clear.

Taylor went to London to further his medical studies. Unfortunately he caught a disease from handling an infected cadaver. He nearly died. But he made a miraculous recovery. The stirrings to go to China became stronger than ever. Political changes in China seemed to throw open the doors of that huge empire to Christianity, and Taylor was eager to begin his ministry.

Alone in China

On September 19, 1853, after much prayer and preparation, Hudson Taylor boarded a ship destined for China at Liverpool. His mother and a few friends waved their handkerchiefs from the pier as his ship departed. It was a long trip; the ship did not drop anchor at Woosung, China, until March 1, 1854.

In England Taylor had left behind his unfinished medical studies and the girl he had hoped to marry. She had refused to come with him.

For six months Taylor lived in Shanghai in the home of missionaries from the London Missionary Society. As the weeks passed he felt a growing urge to find a place of his own and to get established in his own work.

Those early months in China were filled with hardships. No financial support or instructions came from the Chinese Evan-

> *Taylor's deepest longing was to penetrate China's interior.*

gelization Society, so Taylor's funds dwindled. His frustration and impatience with the Society grew as more months went by with no word.

Taylor's deepest longing was to penetrate China's interior, which most foreigners had never even been permitted to see, let alone minister in. Buffeted by many fears and feeling depressed due to the departure of his only fellow missionaries, Taylor never wavered in his determination to go inland. He learned enough of the Chinese language to make his way and even began preaching to the people.

Still the Chinese Evangelization Society left the young missionary to fend for himself. The inadequate support of his home base threw Taylor back on faith and prayer for his support. He lived as he had back in Hull. He learned one of the lessons he is famous for imparting to others: "Depend upon it. God's work, done in God's way, will never lack for supplies."

To China's interior

Taylor began to take itinerant preaching trips along inland canals in defiance of the ban on foreigners—a very dangerous practice. During these trips he sensed the incredible spiritual needs of the inland Chinese people. His heart had found its home.

Taylor also decided to adopt Chinese dress, a practice unheard of among Europeans except for temporary purposes. As he wrote to his family, his plans were "Chinese dress, a little place in the interior, and above all a future left in the hands of God." Years later he made identification with the Chinese people a rule for the missionary society he established.

Taylor worked in Shanghai, Swatow, and Ningpo from 1854 to 1860. In 1857 he fell in love with an English girl named Maria Dyer. She was one of two sisters who served in Ningpo with a woman named Miss Aldersey. Miss Aldersey had founded and still operated the first Protestant missionary school for Chinese girls ever established.

Maria returned Hudson's affection, but both Miss Aldersey and her older sister discouraged the relationship. Miss Aldersey viewed Taylor as a "young, poor, unconnected Nobody," all the worse because he wore Chinese dress.

The missionary community was opposed to their eventual engagement, even when Maria's uncle back in England gave his consent. Still, the couple were married on January 20, 1858. God blessed their home with the birth of a dearly loved daughter, Grace, on July 31, 1859.

Five years in England

But six years of service in China had pushed Hudson Taylor to the limit of his physical endurance. He returned to Britain in November 1860 with Maria and Grace. Taylor spent the next five years translating the Bible into the Ningpo dialect, writing a book on China, and praying for missionaries for inland China.

He also completed his medical training and urged existing missionary societies to consider the needs of inland China, but in vain. During these years, however, his own burden for China's millions without Christ grew even stronger.

By now Taylor realized that the only way he could fulfill his vision for China was to establish his own mission. But the idea seemed so burdensome that by the summer of 1865 he was approaching a nervous breakdown.

The Brighton beach prayer

Instead, Hudson Taylor experienced a breakthrough. It happened as he was walking alone one day on Brighton beach. The thought came to him that if he and the missionaries he might take to China were going in obedience to God, then "the responsibility [for their needs] rests with Him, not with us!" That day, June 25, 1865, Taylor prayed for "twenty-four willing skillful laborers," two for each unreached province in China.

Taylor was physically weak and financially impoverished, but he threw himself upon God's ability. Nearly a year later, on May 26, 1866, the Taylors sailed for China with seventeen new missionary recruits. Some had gone on ahead, and others would follow. The interdenominational China Inland Mission (CIM) was born.

Despite intense opposition and even slander from other missionaries, some internal dissension, and several riots, the CIM estab-

Hudson Taylor and his wife Jane.

lished itself as the "shock troops" of the Protestant advance in China. The pressures and slander were almost too much. Taylor seriously contemplated the "awful temptation even to end his own life." Only Maria's love held him back. However, the Taylors did suffer a loss as their daughter, Grace, died in 1867.

Peace in abiding

Taylor's intense personal struggle led to what has been called "Hudson Taylor's spiritual secret." In fact, it had been pointed out to him by one of his own CIM missionaries, who told Taylor he had discovered the secret of Christian living: "To let my loving Saviour work in me His will. ... Abiding, not striving or struggling." Taylor was overjoyed.

"As I read I saw it all. 'If we believe not, He abideth faithful.' And I looked to Jesus and saw (and when I saw, oh, how joy flowed) that He had said, 'I will never leave you.'" The secret was not to struggle for strength or peace, but rest in the strength and peace of Christ. Said Taylor: "I have striven in vain to abide in Him. I'll strive no more. For has not He promised to abide with me—never to leave me, never to fail me?"

> *He made identification with the Chinese people a rule.*

Taylor became a new man spiritually. When his beloved Maria died in 1870 a few days after giving birth to a son—who also died—he was able to rest his deep grief on the Lord. Eighteen months later he married Maria's best friend, Jane Faulding, another happy marriage that lasted until her death nearly thirty years later.

The growth of the work at home and other circumstances made a return trip to England necessary for Taylor, but he was back in China by the end of 1872. He was able to stay only for a year or so before the work of the China Inland Mission and continued poor health demanded another trip to England.

Advance in inland China

In 1876 every region of China was opened to Westerners as never before. Hudson Taylor seized the moment. The pioneering missionaries of CIM went everywhere. The goal was to bring the gospel to every person. Taylor was happy to see other missionaries reap where his pioneers had sown, although many CIM stations did become permanent.

By 1881 there were seventy mission stations with as many missionaries. But more workers were needed, so it was agreed to pray for seventy more missionaries during the next three years. By the end of that time, the prayer had been answered.

Taylor was very active in famine relief, opposed the opium trade, and was ahead of his time in his willingness to work with other mission bodies, in allowing women to pioneer on their own, and in his desire for a Chinese-led church. Taylor's writings, travels, and dramatic appeals for missionaries stirred the churches of Britain and North America.

By 1895 the CIM had become the largest Protestant body in China with 641 missionaries, about half of the entire Protestant force in China. During the Boxer Rebellion of 1900, CIM also suffered the greatest number of martyrdoms.

Taylor's great spiritual qualities and the caliber of the CIM, together with his writings and world travels, gave him an influence far beyond China and led to the founding of similar faith missions.

Among his chief emphases were identification with the people (all CIM missionaries had to wear Chinese dress), the direction of the mission to come from the field rather than from the home base (a painful lesson he learned from his early experience), efficiency in administration, and the deepening of Christian life in the home churches as a means of encouraging future missionaries.

On June 3, 1905, J. Hudson Taylor died at age seventy-two in Changsha, the capital of the last province to open. His work was completed, the call that he felt since his early youth was now fully answered. His heart had been set early on service to God in China, and his years of rigorous preparation and faithfulness on the field and at home bore fruit in a lifetime of ministry.

At his death, Hudson Taylor left behind 205 CIM stations with 849 missionaries and 125,000 Chinese Christians—and a legacy that will last until the Lord returns.

Phil Rawley

Further Reading

Broomhall, Marshall. *The Man Who Believed God: The Story of Hudson Taylor*. Chicago: Moody, 1929.

Pollock, John C. *Hudson Taylor and Maria: Pioneers in China*. New York: McGraw-Hill, 1962.

Taylor, Dr. and Mrs. Howard. *J. Hudson Taylor: A Biography*. Chicago: Moody, 1965.

TAPPING GOD'S POWER

John "Praying" Hyde

1865–1912

Prayer was not uppermost in John Hyde's thoughts as he paced the deck of the American ship bound for India in 1892. He was indignant. No, *indignant* was too mild a word for the emotional turmoil raging within him. How could anyone, much less a cherished friend, imply that he was not fit for missionary service! He, a pastor's son, was a young man who had been devoted to God almost all his twenty-seven years.

The friend's words burned into Hyde's mind: "I shall not cease praying for you, dear John, until you are filled with the Holy Spirit." Not filled with the Holy Spirit? Of course he was, he'd thought as he crumpled the letter, flung it onto the floor, and stalked out of the room.

Pacing the deck brought no peace. In desperation John returned to his cabin, dropped to the floor to retrieve the crumpled letter and, smoothing it out carefully, read it again and again and again. Could his friend possibly be right?

Days of misery followed until in despair John turned to God and asked to be filled with the Holy Spirit. "The moment I did this," he wrote later, "the whole atmosphere was cleared up. I began to see myself and what a selfish ambition I had."

Longing for power

He had wanted to serve God, he realized, but he had also wanted to be a great missionary. Now he was determined to be filled with the Holy Spirit at any cost, even if it were to mean the humiliation of failing language exams or the anonymity of working quietly, unnoticed by others.

God took him at his word. John *did* labor unnoticed for many years. He *was* slow in learning Indian languages, not because of linguistic ineptitude but because God made

> **Something is wrong here,** *thought John Hyde as he listened to an evangelist pouring out his heart to a complacent audience scattered among the empty seats in a British meeting hall. "That man needs help!"*
>
> *Help was something John knew how to get, even though he was just a visitor in town. A couple of days later, early on a Monday morning, his hotel room became a prayer chapel where he spent the entire day on his knees before God.*
>
> *That evening the meeting hall was packed. When the invitation was given, fifty people responded by turning their lives over to Jesus Christ. That was just the beginning. The Holy Spirit came in such power in subsequent meetings that barriers were broken down, and men and women were convicted. All over the hall people began confessing sin and crying out for mercy and salvation.*
>
> *John Hyde found these results awesome but not unusual. He had seen such things happen before because he was a man who had learned to tap into God's mighty reservoir of power through prayer.*

knowledge of the Bible a priority for him. (In time, after intense Bible study, John did become fluent in several languages and dialects.)

From the time of his arrival in India, John began praying for revival. Preaching and teaching were preceded by early morning prayer meetings when Indian brothers learned to pray with him.

"If our hearts and lives are right before God we shall receive a great blessing," he

The Life of John Hyde

1865	Born in Carrolton, Illinois, November 9
1892	Graduates from McCormick Seminary, Chicago Sent to India by the Presbyterian Board
1902	First furlough to the United States
1904	First Sialkot Convention, India
1910	Organizes Feoszepore (Moga) Training School for village workers
1912	Dies in Northhampton, Massachusetts, February 17

• Sialkot

INDIA

A wrestler with God

During this barren year John's vision was enlarged. "I determined to ask God to give us one real Israel, a wrestler with God, a prince prevailing," he wrote. That turned out to be a dangerous prayer, for God revealed to John that *he* was to be that Israel.

Meanwhile, he continued steadily his quiet work, teaching Bible in a boys' high school. His free time he spent traveling from village to village leading people to Christ and dealing with converts who had quarreled or fallen into various sins, even lapsing into idolatry. Patiently John would gather these stumbling converts together to pray with him. On his knees, often with his face to the ground, he would spend up to two or three hours, much of the time silent before God. Usually the erring ones would break down and confess their sins, seeking forgiveness and deliverance.

In 1899 John wrote, "I have felt led to pray for others this year as never before. I never before knew what it was to work all day and then pray all night." Often he would rise at four or five o'clock in the morning or stay up till well past midnight to pray. "In college or at parties at home I used to keep such hours," he explained, "and can I not do as much for God and souls?"

Sometimes John would get so involved in talking or praying with a needy person that he would completely forget to eat or sleep. That was fine when he was alone but did little to build harmonious relationships when he was staying with a family or in a boarding house. One hostess expressed her struggles with irritation at such inconsiderateness, yet added, "On coming back he is so unselfish, so willing to go hungry rather than make any trouble that I forgive him and go to extra trouble to see that he has what he needs."

In 1904 after a decade of untiring work interrupted by debilitating bouts with various ailments, John was suddenly overwhelmed with homesickness. Work became drudgery. Yet he wrote, "To keep a-plugging away I think is the finest quality we may have in Christian service."

In July, John and a friend (later joined by another friend) began a thirty-day prayer vigil for a spiritual life convention to be held in August in Sialkot, India. During the ten-day convention two rooms were set aside for

wrote, "and if it be delayed, it will be like holding back a strong-flowing river which will come with mighty power when let go."

Trickles of blessing came as John saw a small but steady stream of conversions. Then in 1896 the trickle dried up. "Why?" agonized John. One reason emerged: tension in his relationship with a couple of co-workers. After much prayer the three people involved came together to work through their difficulties. Afterward John exclaimed, "Wasn't that good!"

> *"I began to see myself and what a selfish ambition I had."*

John Hyde (1865–1912).

Below: The Sialkot Convention, 1922; (inset) the Audience Hall, Sialkot, where the first three conventions were held.

prayer, one for men and one for women. They were never empty day or night. Most of the time John was among those praying.

Sparking a revival

One evening he was asked to speak at a men's meeting. The men arrived and seated themselves on mats in the meeting tent, but no speaker appeared. The congregation began to sing one hymn after another. Still no speaker. More hymns. Finally John slipped in quietly and seated himself on a mat at the front. The singing came to an end but John remained motionless and silent. After a considerable time he rose to his feet and began speaking in a quiet voice.

"Brothers, I did not sleep last night and I have not eaten anything today. I have been having a great controversy with God. I feel that He has wanted me to come here and testify to you concerning some things He has done for me, and I have been arguing with Him that I should not do this. Only this

evening a little while ago . . . have I agreed to obey Him."

John then "very quietly and simply told some of the desperate conflicts that he had had with sin and how God had given him the victory," wrote one of those present. "I think he did not talk more than fifteen or twenty minutes, then sat down, bowed his head for a few minutes, and said, 'Let us have a season of prayer.'

"I remember how the little company prostrated themselves upon the mats in the Oriental manner, and then how for a long time, man after man rose to his feet to pray, how there was such confession of sin as most of us had never heard before and such crying out to God for mercy and help."

That was the spark that was to ignite revival in the Indian church. The scene was repeated many times: long, intensive periods of prayer, open confession followed by an outpouring of God's Spirit transforming the lives of His people. John Hyde, a pivotal figure in it all, became known as Praying Hyde.

At Sialkot conventions in the following years, John spent most of his time in the prayer room, accompanied sometimes by only a handful of people and at other times by hundreds. Prostrated with his face on the floor, he would quietly, earnestly lift his petition to God. Then he would lapse into a patient, watchful silence that was pulsating with longing. Again he would present his petition and wait silently. Then again and again, until finally his soul was filled with assurance that God had answered.

People were attracted to him. Often he would be surrounded by Indians seeking Christ. Occasionally he would interrupt his praying, rise to his feet and single out someone in need. With an open Bible in one hand and his other arm around the man's shoulder, John would earnestly point him to Christ.

Mingling tears with joy

Often pleading for them with sobs, he never lost sight of the thousands of Indians without God and without hope. His pleading consisted of "dry, choking sobs that showed how the depths of his soul were being stirred," commented one observer, deeply moved.

Yet there were also times when John

> *John's desire was to burn out rather than rust out.*

would be so full of praise that he would burst into song. The prayer meeting might even turn into an all-night rejoicing party with those praying. He included marching around the room singing, shouting, clapping hands, tossing hats into the air, and reveling in praise to the Lord. One of Hyde's favorite cries was, "*Bol Yisu Masih, Ki Jai!*" (Shout the victory of Jesus Christ!).

John's desire was to burn out rather than rust out. In 1911, growing increasingly frail and ill, he finally returned to the United States a dying man. En route he stopped off in Britain to visit friends and there attended the preaching mission described at the beginning of this article.

When John returned to his friends after that week of intercession, he was so exhausted and in such pain he could hardly speak. "The burden was heavy," he admitted, "but my dear Savior's burden for me was heavier. It took Him down to the grave."

Soon afterward in the United States he underwent an operation for a brain tumor. It was malignant. On February 17, 1912, as he passed into the presence of the Lord, he uttered a feeble yet triumphant cry, "*Bol Yisu Masih, Ki Jai!*"

Elaine Rhoton

Further Reading

McGaw, Frances A. *Praying Hyde.* Philadelphia: Sunday School Times, 1923. Abridged edition: Moody Press Acorn Booklet.

Miller, Basil. *Praying Hyde, A Man of Prayer.* Grand Rapids: Zondervan, 1943.

MISSION TO HINDU WOMEN

Pandita Ramabai

1858–1922

Ramabai was born to Anant Dongre and Laxmibai, Hindu Chitpawan Brahmins, the highest caste in southern India. Her father was a sastri, a master of Sanskrit and teacher of *sastras*, or sacred Hindu scriptures. He had studied under the best gurus in Mysore, Benares, and Puni. Young men flocked to study with him, but his two passions were the study of the Sanskrit texts and religious pilgrimages.

When he was forty-four, Anant married Laxmibai (his first wife had died), who was nine years old, and despite scriptural prohibitions and excommunication from his fellow Brahmins, he began to teach her Sanskrit and the sacred Puranas. The study of these was forbidden on pain of death for men of the lower castes and for all women. Ostracized by his peers, Anant and his wife made their home in a remote forest and set up an *ashram*, where they studied the sacred texts together. It was here that Ramabai was born in 1858, and here she was instructed by her mother in the forbidden sacred language and scriptures.

Reduced to poverty by their disdain for wealth, the fraud of their relatives, and their gifts to Brahmin priests to please the gods, Ramabai's parents left their forest home to wander through the cities and villages of India. They recited the scriptures as *puranikas*, that is, traveling bards who went from village to village reciting the sacred Puranas in Sanskrit. They lived off the gifts of appreciative audiences.

The years of Ramabai's youth were years of hardship and suffering. She later noted that she and her family visited the important Hindu shrines across India and worshiped the Hindu gods daily, but they found no peace of heart. "We stayed [at the great temple at Ghatikachala] for nearly a year, but did not see a single person whose prayers

She was a widow at fifteen. . . . Her fine linen was replaced by the coarse garment which was henceforth to be the badge of shame. Her head was shaven and every possible indignity was heaped upon her. . . . Filth, instead of food, was thrown into her little basket. Mocking, taunting words were the only answers to her piteous appeals. Three times she resolved to put an end to her miserable existence; but the fear of another incarnation into womanhood restrained her. She heard of Ramabai's school and came to it, notwithstanding the curses of her people, who threatened her with excommunication, loss of caste and religion, and with all the plagues they could invoke. She came and was happy.

Four years later, she became a Christian, married again, and became the mother of a number of distinguished sons.

This is only one of the many thousands of stories of widows and orphans rescued by Pandita Ramabai in her remarkable ministry of liberating women from the curse they suffer under Hinduism. It is hard for us now to understand the terrible suffering endured by women in many societies before Christianity came. Studying Pandita's life helps us see the transforming effect the gospel has on human societies.

> *The years of Ramabai's youth were years of hardship and suffering.*

The Life of Pandita Ramabai

1858	Born to the highest caste in southern India but grows up in poverty
1870	Has memorized much of the Puranas (Hindu scriptures); eventually learns four languages
1876–77	Father, mother, and sister die of starvation
1880	Brother dies Marries beneath her caste and is rejected by the reformed-minded Hindus
1881	Daughter born; husband dies
1882	Moves to Puni; begins work for widowed women
1883	Begins studies in England and, later, in the United States Professes faith in Christ
1887	Forms the Ramabai Association in Boston
1889	Returns to India and opens Sarada Sadan (Home of Wisdom) to provide for and teach widowed women
1900	Builds Mukti Sadan (Place of Salvation) thirty miles west of Puni
1921	Daughter dies
1922	Dies April 5

INDIA

• Puni

were answered nor one who had not suffered much by coming there. Still we went on with our service of the god."

Throughout these pilgrimages Ramabai continued her studies of the sacred Puranas. In traditional fashion, she first mastered the intricacies of Sanskrit by memorizing the grammar and dictionary set in verse. Then she memorized the Puranas, the scriptures of Hindu Bhakti. At twelve she could recite eighteen thousand verses of the Bhagavata Purana and was acquainted with the intricacies of Sanskrit. She also learned Marathi, Kanarese, Hindustani, and Bengali.

The wandering family was caught in the great famine of the Madras Presidency (1876–77). Despite their prayers and austerities, Ramabai saw first her father, then her mother and sister, die of starvation within a few months of each other. Before he died, her father took her in his arms and told her to remember how much he loved her and how he taught her never to depart from the way of righteousness and to serve God all her life. Little did her parents know where this exhortation would lead her.

Encounter with Christianity

Ramabai and her brother, Srinivasa, sought refuge from the famine in Calcutta. There her lectures in Sanskrit attracted a great deal of attention and provided the two of them with a livelihood among reform-minded Hindus of the Brahmo Samaj. Her remarkable learning, quick wit, and ability to compose extemporaneous poems in Sanskrit caused a stir in the world of the learned and won her the title Saraswati from a council of pundits at Puni. Thereafter she was known as Pandita Ramabai. Pandita is the feminine form of *pandit*, or teacher.

But Ramabai faced strong ridicule and opposition from the orthodox religious establishment, which accused her of the death of her parents and of destroying Hinduism and the Indian family by her study of the Hindu scriptures.

By this time, Ramabai and her brother had lost faith in Hinduism and were groping for a new path. Invited by a converted Brahmin, they went to a Christian social gathering. The experience and the worship were strange and incomprehensible to the two young seekers. Ramabai wrote,

> "This great grief drew me nearer to God. I felt He was teaching me, and that if I was to come to Him, He must Himself draw me."

Pandita Ramabai, missionary to Hindu women.

We thought the Last Age, the Kali Yuga, that is, the age of quarrels, darkness and irreligion, had fully established its reign in Calcutta, since some of the Brahmans were so irreligious as to eat food with the English. . . . After a little while one of them opened a book and read something out of it and then they knelt down before their chairs and some said something with closed eyes. We were told that was the way they prayed to God. We did not see any image to which they paid their homage, but it seemed as though they were paying homage to the chairs before which they knelt.

In May 1880, Srinivasa fell ill and died, leaving his sister with no relatives to care for her. A number of prominent Brahmans families wanted her as a wife for their sons, but she married Bepin Bihbari Medhavi, a Bengali Sudra and friend of her brother. Her marriage to a low-caste man shocked the Brahmin community. For this outrage there was no forgiveness. By it she put herself beyond the pale of fellowship with orthodox Hindu communities.

Ramabai's husband was a lawyer in Assam, and the two lived happily for nineteen months. There Ramabai gave birth to her daughter, Manoramabai (Heart's Joy). Then Bepin died of cholera, leaving Ramabai a widow. "This great grief," she wrote, "drew me nearer to God. I felt He was teaching me, and that if I was to come to Him, He must Himself draw me."

Two experiences during the happy time with her husband in Assam remained vivid in Ramabai's memory. In her husband's library she had seen St. Luke's gospel in Bengali and had begun to read it. Also, Mr. Allan, a Baptist missionary at Silchar, visited her and explained to her the basic teachings of Christianity. She later wrote:

Having lost all faith in my former religion, and with my heart hungering after something better, I eagerly learnt everything which I could about the Christian religion, and declared my intention to become a Christian, if I were perfectly satisfied with this new religion.

But that satisfaction was to come later.

In 1882, Ramabai moved with her daughter to Puni, the capital of Maharashtra to fight for women's freedom and education in Indian society.

Men look on us women as chattels: we make every effort to deliver ourselves from this situation. But some will say that this is a rebellion against man, and that to do this is sin. To leave men's evil acts unrebuked and remain unmoved before them is a great sin.

Her allies were Hindu reformers such as Bal Tilak and Mahadev Ranade, who saw women's education as the means to change the status of women in India. Her accusers were the great majority of orthodox Hindus, who denounced her as a destroyer of the family and of Hinduism.

Ramabai traveled widely speaking about the need to educate women. To promote this she founded the Arya Mahil Samaj, a society for Indian women. Her pleas for women physicians to treat women, prevented by their husbands from going to male doctors, impressed Queen Victoria and led to the establishment of the Dufferin Hospitals.

But Ramabai was uncertain of her own role in the reform movement for women until a Brahmin widow age twelve was brought to her.

She was very dark, had cross eyes and was very unattractive in many ways. . . She was given in marriage when five years old, but the boy husband died a few days after the marriage was performed. Her mother-in-law would not look at her. She said the girl had eaten up her son and was a great demon.

As I looked at that little figure my vague thoughts about doing something for my sisters in similar conditions began to take shape. . . . I began to place a plan for starting a Home for Hindu widows before my countrymen and to ask for their help. . . . I tried my best to get help, but could not.

Thereafter Ramabai battled for the care of widows and the prohibition of child marriage. She estimated that there were twenty-three million widows in India in 1880, fifty-one thousand below nine years of age, ten thousand below four. Many of the child widows were originally married to old men who had lost their first wives.

The plight of these widows was terrible. Their heads were shaved, and they had to wear white saris. They were accused of causing the deaths of their husbands, beaten, and forced to do menial labor and beg for their food.

To fulfill her vision, Ramabai went to England for further training. In 1883 she enrolled at Cheltenham Ladies' College. There, befriended by some devout Christian women, her faith and her vision took shape.

After my visit to the Homes at Fulham, where I saw the works of mercy carried on by the Sisters of the Cross, I began to think that there was a real difference between Hinduism and Christianity. I asked the Sister who instructed me what it was that made the Christian care for, and reclaim, the "fallen women." She read the story of Christ meeting the Samaritan woman, and His

> ### Ramabai battled for the care of widows and the prohibition of child marriage.

wonderful discourse on the nature of true worship, and explained it to me. She spoke of the Infinite Love of Christ for sinners. . . I realized, after reading the 4th Chapter of St. John's Gospel, that Christ was truly the Divine Saviour He claimed to be, and no one but He could transform and uplift the downtrodden womanhood of India and of every land.

That year she confessed her faith in Christ by baptism.

Early ministry

Her vision now clear, Ramabai spent two years in the United States studying educational methods, writing about the status of women in India, and raising support for a school. In 1887 the Ramabai Association was formed in Boston with the goal of educating high-caste child-widows in India.

Ramabai returned to India in 1889, and opened Sarada Sadan, the Home of Wisdom, with one student, a child-widow who had suffered much after the death of her betrothed husband. In three months there were twenty-two students under her influence.

One such widow was a child of thirteen, taken by her mother-in-law as a child. When her husband died, she was accused of having killed her husband by some sin committed in a former existence. She was starved, beaten, and hung from the ceiling. When she came to the Home of Wisdom the light had gone out of her large dark eyes, and her head was bowed as under a great burden.

From the beginning Ramabai made clear that she was a Christian, but to attract students from the hostile Hindu community and to gain the support of the Hindu reformers, she agreed that there would be no open proselytizing in her school. She continued her own Bible study and prayer, however, and did not turn away students who wished to join her. Her attractive personality and her love for the students won their hearts. Not surprisingly many students began to join her in her early morning devotions, and a number of them became followers of Christ.

Rumors of the conversions spread, and

Pandita Ramabai addresses pupils at Sarada Sadan, Puni.

attacks by newspapers increased until it was no longer safe for the home to remain in Bombay. In 1890 Ramabai moved to Puni with eighteen widows, but the vehement opposition continued. A major storm broke in 1893 when the leading Hindu reformers resigned from her board. Of the fifty-three girls studying in the Home at the time, twenty were withdrawn by irate parents. Most of the widows remained because Hinduism had no home for them.

The break with reform-minded Hindus freed Ramabai openly to invite her students to follow Christ. In November 1895, twelve of them were baptized. Word of her ministry was spread, even by her critics. Her daughter, Manoramabai, wrote:

The little widows all over the country heard the gentlemen talking about a dreadful woman named Pandita Ramabai, who was a friend to widows, and many thought to themselves, "If there is a place where a widow is welcomed, I should like to go there."

In addition to growing opposition from the outside, these years were ones of spiritual struggle for Ramabai. Dissatisfaction with her own spiritual condition burdened her greatly. She found release on reading *From Death into Life* by Mr. Haslam, an evangelist. Her faith, which had been largely intellectual, now became intensely personal. Her spirit was renewed, and she was freed from her intense burden of sin.

The famine years

At the end of 1896 another severe famine swept India. Recalling her own bitter losses in the previous famine, Ramabai determined to see for herself the condition of widows in North India. She disguised herself as a pilgrim and went to Brindaban, a great center for the worship of Krishna. She saw thousands of widows, young and old, who had fallen into the hands of lecherous priests and who were cast out when they no longer pleased these men. She wrote back of their misery:

There is no shelter for the unhappy creatures, clothed as they were in dripping rags, suffering intense pangs of hunger along with the bitter cold of the wind. They were huddled shivering under trees and beside walls: men, women, and children, old and young, all sorts of people, enduring a living death.

Pandita Ramabai felt called to minister to the thousands who were dying, but she lacked the finances to broaden her ministry. About this time she read the life stories of George Müller, Hudson Taylor, and John Paton. She was moved by their faith and determined to follow their example and trust God to provide for her work.

> *On one day alone,*
> *seventeen cartloads of*
> *young women went for*
> *baptism to a river*
> *six miles away.*

Because of her limited resources, friends suggested that she limit the number she brought back to Puni to about six hundred. She answered,

It is true that my resources are limited; not only that but I am literally penniless with no means of any kind. I own nothing on earth but a few clothes and my Bible. . . I am poor and needy, yet the Lord thinketh upon me. His resources are limitless, and He has promised to supply all my needs.

Soon hundreds of young women and girls, victims of the famine, arrived at Puni in need of care.

When cholera swept the town, Ramabai moved the starving to temporary shelters at Kedgaon, thirty miles west. There she built Mukti Sadan (Place of Salvation), a haven for those rejected by society. She and her assistants patiently taught the girls the gospel, and many responded. On one day alone, seventeen cartloads of young women went

for baptism to a river six miles away "singing all the way for very joy." But most, by now, were from the lower castes and needed to be taught how to cook their food, clean their rooms, care for their health, and read the Scriptures.

In 1900 there were more than 1,900 people and 100 cattle whose needs she had to supply. There were 1,350 Gujarati girls: 150 under seven years of age, 500 from ages seven to fourteen, 600 from ages fourteen to twenty, and the rest older.

Later ministry

The years following the great famine were fruitful and tiring ones. Ramabai was not content merely to sustain the lives of those under her care. She organized schools to educate them and teach them trades, found jobs for them, and arranged their marriages. She built schools for the blind, orphan boys and village children, and a refuge for the homeless. None were ever turned away from the door at Mukti Sadan.

The work in Ramabai's homes and schools was organized into departments, and she supervised these programs in great detail. Her day began at four each morning with prayers and ran late into the night, when she presented to God the needs for the

Mukti Bible women set out to visit neighboring villages.

next day. She wrote:

I feel very happy since the Lord called me to step out in faith, and I obeyed. . . . There are over 1500 people living here. We are not rich, nor great, but we are happy, getting our daily bread directly from the loving hands of our Heavenly Father, having not a pice [Indian coin] over and above our daily necessities, having no banking account anywhere, no endowment or income from any earthly source, but depending altogether on our Father God; we have nothing to fear from anybody, nothing to lose, and nothing to regret. The Lord is our Inexhaustible Treasure.

Ramabai also had a deep passion for Bible translation. She understood little of the first Bible given to her because it was written in an archaic version of the Marathi language. Determined that the common people be able to read the Scriptures for themselves, she learned Greek and Hebrew, then worked hard on a vernacular translation that was published by the Mukti Sadan press.

In 1921 Manoramabai died. Pandita was heartbroken, for she had hoped that her daughter would take over the work. But she accepted it as the hand of God. By now she was almost deaf. Her body was weakened by years of relentless service. On the morning of April 5, 1922, Pandita Ramabai slipped away to be with her Lord, and a telegram was sent abroad saying, "Ramabai Promoted."

No one has done more than Pandita Ramabai to call attention to the evils done to India's women and to create a conscience that demands that these wrongs be righted. In her time she was one of her country's great liberators. The king of England awarded her the Kaiser-i-Hind gold medal, the highest honor given in the British Empire.

Few have led so many people of that great land to faith and life in Christ. Her legacy is not in buildings and institutions but in the lives of people she helped to transform. From her homes and schools there have

> *Her legacy is not in buildings and institutions but in the lives of people she helped to transform.*

come thousands of women who have served as evangelists, Bible women, and godly mothers. They have played a very important role in the life and outreach of the church in India.

Sadly, however, many of the evils perpetrated against the women of India during Pandita's time still persist. It is important that Christians there as well as the world over hear the story of this courageous woman so that they will be inspired to follow her example and in the name of Christ resist the oppression of women.

Paul Hiebert

Further Reading

Butler, Clementia. *Pandita Ramabai Sarasvati: Pioneer in the Movement for Education of the Child-widow of India.* New York: Revell, 1922.

Dyer, Helen S. *Pandita Ramabai: The Story of Her Life.* New York: Revell, 1900.

——. *Pandita Ramabai: Her Vision, Her Mission and Triumph of Faith.* Glasgow: Pickering & Inglis, 1900.

Fuller, Mary Lucia Bierce. *The Triumph of an Indian Widow: The Life of Pandita Ramabai.* New York: Christian Alliance, 1928.

MacNicol, Nicol. *Pandita Ramabai.* London: Student Christian Movement, 1926.

Ramabai, Pandita. *A Testimony.* 9th ed. Kedgaon, Poona Dist., India: Ramabai Mukti Mission, 1968.

FOUR GENERATIONS OF

The Guinness Family

On his twenty-first birthday, Henry Grattan Guinness noted in his diary that his only ambition was "to live preaching and to die preaching; to live and die in the pulpit; to preach to perishing sinners till I drop down dead." In him was all the drive and forcefulness of the entrepreneurial Guinness spirit mingled with the creative, magnetic qualities of the Cramers (to whom his mother was related). It was an irresistible combination, and Grattan was learning how to employ those qualities to the fullest effect. He had but to walk into a room to command attention. He was a deeply intense man, unable to laugh easily, but the intensity added drama to his personal charm.

In 1860, when Grattan was twenty-five, he married Fanny Fitzgerald. Grattan felt at ease in her presence from the moment they met. But life as a itinerant evangelist's wife was not easy. By the time she was twenty-nine, hard work and slender means had taken their toll. However, necessity, which had robbed her of her youth, had made her capable and competent, but never cold or hard. There was too much of the Irish in her to curb her fire and zest completely. Whenever she opened her mouth to speak, there was a sudden warmth and vivacity about her.

During a trip to Armagh in 1872, the future course of Grattan's life became clear to him. His vision was for a college for theological training that would require no fees. It would run by faith. God would provide the house, the staff, the students, and the food to feed them. Because Grattan was a visionary, Fanny knew that the practical details of such a venture would be left to her. With six children to care for, the implications were too enormous to contemplate.

The East End of London

Within months the family had moved to the East End of London, a poor and unsavory area. One reason for choosing the East End was that Grattan believed no young man or woman, if he or she could not cope with life among London's poor, could honestly say he could cope with missionary work in China or elsewhere.

By the end of 1873, new accommodations were essential, so the Guinnesses and their students moved into Harley House in Bow. Harley House (officially, the East London Institute for Home and Foreign Missions) was ideally situated as far as Grattan and Fanny were concerned, not only for the children but also in terms of practical work for the students. It was surrounded by factories, it was near the Tower, and directly opposite stood the dreaded Union Workhouse. The opportunities for caring for people's needs were limitless, and the Guinnesses were closely tied to a myriad of inner city initiatives, alongside friends such as the great, reforming Earl of Shaftesbury. Grattan also shared with Shaftsbury a deep concern for the Jews and, like him, was a faithful promoter of the Zionist cause.

Grattan and Fanny (who became known as the "Mother of Harley") were zealous for world missions, especially missions to China, so it was not surprising that missions quickened the heart of their college, Harley House. One person who greatly influenced the Guinnesses was their friend Hudson Taylor, one of the pioneer missionaries to China. Wherever he went, his descriptions

> *The opportunities for caring for people's needs were limitless.*

Rev. H. Grattan Guinness.

of China had an enormous impact.

Grattan and Fanny shared Taylor's ideals entirely: his missionaries were to live simply, serving the people; to identify completely they must adopt the national costume; his society was interdenominational. It accepted working-class men and women with no formal academic education or training other than what they received at Harley College.

In 1875 the first twelve students went to the mission field from Harley House—to India, France, South Africa, China, Japan, and Burma. When letters arrived, Fanny read them aloud to the children. The descriptions of lively Japanese towns, junk-traversed Chinese waters, the scorching plains of India or Burma, and work on the West Indian plantations held them enthralled. But most thrilling of all were the descriptions in the newspapers of Stanley's discoveries in the hitherto unexplored continent of Africa as he searched for David Livingstone.

Just before he died, Livingstone wrote of Africa, "May Heaven's richest blessings come down on everyone, American, English or Turk, who will help heal this open sore of the world." Dying on his knees, stretched

In recent years the missionary ideal of the nineteenth century has been criticized for confusing Christianity with imperialism. Civilizing the savages meant importing a British Christian culture that was not as superior as the Victorians believed. But that is a sweeping generalization. Britain's colonializing tendencies wreaked havoc long before most missionaries arrived in India, China, or Africa. Adventurers, traders, soldiers, and government representatives imported alcohol, drugs, and guns in a deliberate effort at subjugation of the native peoples.

The famous Hudson Taylor deplored such abuses, but so did his less well-known, though no less significant, colleagues in the Guinness family—the Christian branch of the Irish brewing family. Henry Grattan Guinness and his wife, Fanny, established a college for missionaries in 1873 based on Taylor's ideals. In later life, Grattan wrote books and responded to speaking invitations from all over the world. Grattan and Fanny's children, Harry, Lucy, Geraldine, and Whitfield, served on the mission fields of Africa and China, promoted the missionary ideals of sacrifice and service, and criticized the government for allowing practices harmful to the people in its overseas possessions.

Whitfield's son, Henry Whitfield Guinness, and his wife, Mary, followed his parents as missionaries to China. After being captured by the Japanese in World War II, they lost two of their three young sons in the desperate conditions brought on by the Japanese occupation. Their surviving son, Os, went on to become a well-respected Christian apologist and cultural critic in the second half of the twentieth century.

Opposite: The family of Harry Guinness.

out across his bed in prayer for Africa, the great, godly man had thrown down the gauntlet to the students of Harley Institute. By the middle of 1878, the Livingstone Inland Mission had been set up, with Grattan and Fanny as founder committee members. Several Harley students pledged their lives to Africa, and over the next few years they braved the disease and dangers of the "dark continent" to bring its inhabitants the gospel message.

Tragedy

In 1879 tragedy struck the Guinness family. Six-year-old Agnes and her sister Phoebe died of diphtheria. The other four children were spared. Fanny wondered why she and Minnie should be spared and the two little ones taken. Why were Lucy and Whitfield providentially out of the way? Perhaps it meant that God had some special work for them to do. The thought was a tiny ray of hope piercing the pain.

As it turned out, eldest son Harry, a medical doctor, took over the running of Harley House. In 1889 he set up the Congo and Balobo Mission, and later spent two years in the Congo establishing mission stations. Outraged by the appalling consequences of Belgian colonialism, he carried his fight for justice to the king of Belgium himself. Geraldine and Whitfield became missionaries to China. A fourth child, Lucy, also helped out at Harley House. In addition, she was a writer who condemned unjust practices by the British overseas, such as the selling of opium to the Chinese, and stirred up interest in the missionary endeavor through her books.

Grattan and Fanny's children believed implicitly that not only wealth changed the world. God could do it with any man or woman willing to take the risk. Each determined to be that man or woman.

When Mary Geraldine decided to become a missionary to China, she wrote to tell her parents. Fanny responded with warmth. It was all she had ever desired for her children. Her father was less happy. At her public farewell in 1888, he said that this was the "gladdest and saddest" gathering he had ever attended. "It is one thing to send out other people's children, but quite another to send out your own." Geraldine eventually married Dr. Howard Taylor, son of Hudson Taylor and also a missionary in China, and

Dr. H. Grattan Guinness.

wrote Hudson Taylor's biography. In later years, she was a highly effective and sought after missions speaker and writer.

Guerrilla priests

Whitfield, after becoming a medical doctor, followed Geraldine to China in 1897. When he arrived, he found wearing Chinese dress a trial. The cumbersome shoes and long gown cramped his athletic style. He hated shaving his head and wearing a pigtail, but his vocation required it. Wherever the Harley missionaries went, they lived as simply as possible, identifying with the people as fully as they could, laying down their lives when called upon to do so. They were the "guerrilla" priests of their day, siding with the people against the tactics of the British government in China and particularly in Africa, where the Europeans walked in and took control.

Boxer riots

The main problems in China were drought and famine. By the turn of the century the situation was so severe that the Boxers, supporters of the Dowager Empress against the young Emperor Kuang Hsu, easily stirred up

DESMOND.

HOWARD.

GORDON.

H. REED.

GERALDINE.

J. GRATTAN

GERALD.

VICTOR.

EILEEN.

The Guinness missionaries

1835	Rev. Henry Grattan Guinness born
1860	Henry Grattan Guinness marries Fanny Fitzgerald
1861	Dr. Harry Grattan Guinness born
1862	Mary Geraldine Guinness born
1863	Lucy Evangeline Guinness born
1869	Dr. Gershom Whitfield Guinness born
1873	Harley House established
1875	First missionaries sent out from Harley House
1878	Grattan and Fanny help found the Livingstone Inland Mission
1879	Grattan and Fanny lose two young daughters, Agnes and Phoebe, to diphtheria
1880	Grattan becomes director of the Livingstone Inland Mission
1886	Lucy writes first booklet
1887	Grattan writes first book
1888	Geraldine goes to China as a missionary
1889	Harry sets up the Congo and Balobo Mission
1894	Geraldine marries Howard Taylor, son of Hudson Taylor
1897	Whitfield goes to China as a missionary
1899	Grattan establishes The Regions Beyond Missionary Union
1900	Whitfield escapes the Boxer massacre
1908	Henry Whitfield Guinness born
1910	Henry Grattan Guinness dies
1918	Harley House closes
1941	Os Guinness born
1942–44	Henry Whitfield and wife, Mary, survive Japanese occupation of China but lose two sons

Harley College, Bow, London.

> *He hated shaving his head and wearing a pigtail, but his vocation required it.*

hatred against Europeans. In June 1900 she decreed the destruction of all foreigners. Howard and Geraldine were safe, having already left China, later to join Hudson Taylor, who was recovering from a slight stroke, and his wife in Switzerland. But Whitfield was ministering in the middle of Boxer territory with the Conways, who had a new baby, and Miss Watson, a single missionary. A thousand miles of Boxer-infested country separated them from the coast.

When the Boxer rioters arrived in the village, the five slipped out the back door of the mission station and made their way to the relative safety of a neighbor's attic. Their home was burned to the ground, but for the moment they were safe.

Within a short while their neighbor appeared and informed them that it was too dangerous to stay there. Mrs. Conway asked him about a deserted-looking building in his backyard. That, he said, was his haunted loft. They were welcome to it.

"The more haunted the better!" Whitfield said, and under cover of darkness they ran across the courtyard and made their way up into a tiny, filthy loft. The missionaries hid in the loft with little food or drink, in stifling heat and high humidity for six days. Several times rioters climbed ladders in an attempt to peer into their small enclosure or tried to push their way through the trapdoor on which Whitfield sat.

On the sixth day Whitfield wrote on a scrap of paper, "We have no change of clothing; and day by day, living in a temperature of 90–100 you may imagine our condition—all four in one room with a baby. The Lord grant it may be soon over." That night a torrential downpour fell. Mr. Li, their protector, appeared. "Truly your God is wonderful. Only this night I have made terms with Mr. Wang, and now under cover of this rain and darkness I will get you to his house."

They made it to Mr. Wang's, but to their immense disappointment the rainfall was insufficient to fill up the parched waterway. On the eleventh day, however, they heard shouting. The dried-up river was filling with water. Rain must have fallen back in the hills. That night they crept and rode a cart to the river, where a boat was waiting. The normally five-day journey downriver took ten days. They spent hours shut up in the cabin as they passed customs check after customs check.

At last the foreign settlement of Han-k'ou came into view, and they passed out of Boxer territory. Gownless, dirty, and unshaven, Whitfield went on ahead to the China Inland Mission-house, thirty days after the riot began. Only then did he discover that seventy-five of their fellow missionaries had perished in the massacres.

Later, as he was recovering from his ordeal in Shanghai, Whitfield met the lovely young Swedish woman who would become his wife. She was Jane af Sandeburg, the daughter of a Swedish prince and a fellow missionary in China. They had three children—Isabel, Mary, and Henry Whitfield.

End of an era

By 1918, the Harley Institute closed its doors, but in its time it was an exceptional venture, having trained more than one thousand missionaries. And though Harley House was gone forever, the Guinness family was not. Henry Whitfield Guinness and his wife, Dr. Mary Taylor, were also missionaries to China, the last Europeans in Nanking when the Communists took over the city. They spent a year under house arrest.

At the outbreak of the Second World

> *"Living in a temperature of 90–100 you may imagine our condition—all four in one room with a baby."*

War, they were still working at the China Inland Mission Hospital at Kai-feng, which Henry's father had founded thirty years before. The Japanese invasion of Kai-feng forced them to join the Long March. In desperate conditions of flood, famine, and plague, they lost two of their three boys—Arthur Gerald and Brian Reginald—and were forced to bury them in hastily dug graves along the way. But their third surviving son, Os, lived to establish a reputation as an academic and outstanding contemporary apologist in the seventies and eighties. "The vision and example of previous generations of Guinnesses," he wrote, "is never far away from my awareness of what my wife and I are about."

Joe O'Day

[This chapter is mostly taken from Michele Guinness, The Guinness Legend (London: Hodder & Stoughton, 1989).]

Further Reading

Elgin S. Moyer. *The Wycliffe Biographical Dictionary of the Church.* Chicago: Moody, 1982.

CRISS-CROSSING CHINA

Jonathan Goforth

1859–1936

In 1893, R. P. MacKay, foreign mission secretary of the Presbyterian Church of Canada, wrote to Jonathan Goforth, a five-year veteran of the China mission field: "Do you find it hard to keep up enthusiasm? Are you as red hot as you used to be? Or do the unresponsive Chinamen quench the flame that a more appreciative audience cherishes?" Goforth's reply is lost, but the record of his service more than underscores his ongoing enthusiasm and high spirits, which increased with each passing year.

His daughter later recalled that the Chinese fondly referred to him as "the flaming preacher." A letter home to his son in Canada, dated January 7, 1928, revealed the heart of the firebrand: "It is a joyful way— the way of soul saving. As far as I can discern I was used to lead two men to Christ this forenoon on this west side of the railway, and this afternoon on the east side I led four young men to Him. Their ages were from nineteen to twenty-eight." He noted, in conclusion, that it was "joyous to be used every day to lead souls [to] Christ Jesus."

The hand of God

Goforth's zeal for souls, exuberance for missions, and power in ministry were corroborated by more than his own testimony. Indeed, those who knew him were amazed at his energy and optimism about God's desire to open doors, knock down barriers, and reach the lost. When the seventy-seven-year-old missionary died in 1936, *Moody Monthly* eulogized him with these words: "The hand of God was upon Goforth in a mighty way, and his ministry was almost like that of Charles G. Finney and Evan Roberts combined." A colleague from China spoke of his "buoyant hope, joy, and expectancy in connection with the work," and his son, Paul, remembered him as "a man in action ... [whose] inexhaustible energy was characteristic of him to the last."

This man whom God used so mightily in China was born in rural Ontario, Canada, in 1859. Although his father was not a professing Christian until late in life, he never discouraged Jonathan from going to church with his mother. Even though the youngster faithfully attended years of worship services, the message of the gospel didn't become clear until he was eighteen. A visiting preacher with a gift for evangelism presented the good news of Christ's death for sinners, and he impressed upon his listeners their urgent need to respond while there was still time. Goforth gave his heart to the Lord Jesus Christ that day and the effects of his response were rapid and wide-ranging.

Robert Murray M'Cheyne

Eager now to know the Lord personally and be a faithful disciple, Goforth began teaching Sunday school and studying the Bible. Eventually two circumstances intervened to cause the young Christian to lay aside his dream of a legal and political career and instead spend his life on the mission field. The first life-changing event was reading the *Memoirs* of Robert Murray M'Cheyne. The radical nature of M'Cheyne's commitment to Christ, in particular his self-sacrificial attempts to evangelize European Jews, stirred Goforth's heart.

An aged missionary's sermon

Then Goforth heard a message preached by a missionary on furlough from his outpost in Formosa. He told of the great needs in

> *"His ministry was almost like that of Charles G. Finney and Evan Roberts combined."*

Jonathan Goforth (1859–1936).

A few years before his death in 1936, Jonathan Goforth wrote By My Spirit, *a memoir of his missionary experiences in China. This book has stirred countless numbers of souls to rely more fully upon the Holy Spirit, and to allow Him to use them in worldwide evangelism. This little book has been in print more than half a century, and it still inspires men and women to dedicate their lives to vocational ministry—especially foreign missions.*

For forty-six years (1888–1934) Jonathan Goforth and his energetic, intelligent wife, Rosalind, criss-crossed China in order to preach, teach, and make disciples. Wherever they ministered, pagans became Christians, indolent disciples of Christ were aroused to fruitful service, and indigenous men and women were trained to do the work of evangelism, teach the Bible, and make disciples. During their last eight years they concentrated their efforts on Manchuria, where they stayed until 1934 when Jonathan's blindness and Rosalind's failing health forced them to return to their native Canada. In the wake of their ministry, they left sixty-one full-time Chinese evangelists and Bible teachers, two resident mission stations, and thousands of baptized and discipled converts.

In the early 1980s, a half century after the Goforths left China, their daughter, Mary Goforth Moynan, returned to China to see the sites where she grew up. With deep gratitude and joy she reported that revival was once again spreading in China, and some of the people God was using were spiritual heirs of the fires that her father, whom the Chinese Christians called "the flaming preacher," had started many decades before.

Asia and how he had traveled the length and breadth of Canada trying to recruit volunteers for this important work. With a heavy heart, Dr. G. L. Macray said he could not find even one young man to return to Formosa with him. The aged missionary knew he would die within a few years, and there would be no one to take his place.

Training and trials

From that night forward, Jonathan Goforth set his sights on evangelizing China. In preparation, he moved to Toronto to study theology at Knox College. While there, he worked to support himself, yet still found time to evangelize the poor people in Toronto's slums and jails. To his surprise, however, most of his fellow students—even those who were preparing for careers in the pastorate—made fun of his evangelistic zeal, his unquestioning confidence in the Scriptures, and his childlike faith in God to meet his needs.

If his urbane fellow students laughed at his home-tailored clothes and his simple faith in the Lord and the Bible, they eventu-ally grew to admire his sincerity and love for the poor and hurting. By 1886 he completed studies at Knox College and was ordained in the Presbyterian Church of Canada. The following year he met and married Rosalind Bell Smith, an attractive, talented, and well-educated woman who was born and reared

The Life of Jonathan Goforth

1859	Born on a farm near Thorndale, Ontario, Canada, February 2
1877	Responds to a preacher's invitation to surrender his life to Jesus Christ
1879	Called to vocational ministry
1886	Ordained a Presbyterian after several years of study at Knox College
1887	Marries Rosalind Bell Smith
1888	Jonathan and Rosalind Goforth become missionaries to China
1900	Nearly killed in the Boxer Rebellion; returns to Canada to recuperate
1901	Returns to China
1907	Personally witnesses the great Korean revival
1908	Launches an itinerant revival and evangelistic ministry in Manchuria and China
1927	Begins a major evangelistic and disciple-making outreach in Manchuria
1934	The Goforths return to Canada in December
1936	Dies, October 8

Rosalind and Jonathan Goforth's first home in China.

> *They lost*
> *nearly everything they owned*
> *during the 1900*
> *Boxer Rebellion.*

in a prosperous London family.

In 1888 the couple moved to China where God allowed them to endure many painful trials in preparation for some of the most significant work done in that great country during the twentieth century. Besides the usual difficulties faced by all missionaries of learning a new language and adjusting to a markedly different culture, the Goforths carried the additional burdens of death and the ravages of war. Rosalind Goforth bore eleven children, but she and her husband buried five in the soil of China during their early years on the field. Added to this heartache was the loss of nearly everything they owned during the 1900 Boxer Rebellion. At the turn of the century, many Chinese began rebelling against foreign exploitation of their natural and human resources. "Foreign devils" became the targets of angry bands of Chinese soldiers. Thousands of foreigners were massacred during the Boxer War, including large numbers of Western missionaries.

In 1900 the Goforth family and other missionaries were driven from their northern outpost. As they began to flee southward to safety, a band of armed warriors attacked them. Jonathan, being the most fluent in Chinese, implored the soldiers to spare their lives. Although the angry men ignored most of the little group, they brutally beat Jonathan and then hacked his head, neck, and back with long, broad-blade swords.

In what can only be described as a miracle, Jonathan's wounds were not mortal. Despite the loss of much blood, he continued as spokesman for the group as they made their way to the south. Eventually they were forced to sail back to Canada where Goforth spent several months convalescing and seeking God's guidance for the future.

The search for power

The Goforths returned to China in the autumn of 1901. Jonathan had recovered rather well from the physical wounds received during the Boxer ordeal, but his

> "Pentecost was merely a
> specimen day."

remembered, "the spirit of judgment was made manifest. Wrongs were righted and crooked things made straight."

heart ached over the coldness of Canadian Christianity. While pondering the great need for revival in his North American homeland, he became increasingly dissatisfied with what he saw in China. Modernism was infecting the mission stations and schools there, and a carnal Christianity was pervading far too many of the churches. In brief, Goforth observed that powerlessness and coolness toward Christ had become the common condition of most believers.

The Lord led him to study the Scriptures more intently until, according to his own words, "every passage that had any bearing upon the price of, or the road to, the accession of power became life and breath to me." He also read a number of books on revival, but Charles Finney's *Revival Lectures* and *Autobiography* stirred him the most. As Goforth began to pray for direction in his own work, he felt God impressing upon him that revival would be poured out upon any servant who sincerely called upon the Lord in prayer, confessed sins, genuinely repented, and obeyed everything commanded by Christ.

When word came in 1904 of the great revival in Wales, he poured over the story with intensity. He became convinced that a lack of faith and general disobedience, rather than God's refusal to bless, is the cause of powerlessness in the Christian life. Furthermore, he acknowledged with Moody that "Pentecost was merely a specimen day."

In 1906 while preaching at one of his outstations, Goforth fell under massive conviction to reconcile his difference with a Christian brother, even though their strained relationship was the fault of the other man. Goforth tried to argue with God, but the prodding never stopped. While preaching without freedom and anointing, he stopped and promised the Lord he would reconcile as soon as the meeting closed. Instantly the atmosphere changed. People became receptive, the meeting opened to prayer, and confessions and repentance spread throughout the tear-filled congregation. In the wake of this meeting came several months of similar occurrences. "At each place," Goforth

Witnessing revival

A year later, the foreign mission secretary of his denomination asked Jonathan to accompany him to Korea in order to witness firsthand the spreading revival on the Korean peninsula. "Korea made me feel, as it did many others, that this was God's plan for the world aflame." What impressed Goforth most was "the practical nature of the movement." This was no mere "gust of religious enthusiasm" that died when the winds of emotions ceased. On the contrary, thousands of Christians repented and manifested transformed lives. Wrongs were righted, reconciliations became commonplace, and people hungered for more of the Lord Jesus Christ. This craving for Christ was seen in the miraculous spirit of prayer and the insatiable hunger for the Holy Word.

Goforth returned to China with a new agenda. He was confident that God wanted remote areas of interior Manchuria. He lived to call the indolent Chinese church to

Rosalind and Jonathan Goforth in 1935.

> *More than thirteen thousand new converts were baptized between 1908 and 1913.*

renewed focus on the holiness of God, the righteousness of Jesus, and the need to confess sins and repent. This work he did until his physical blindness and Rosalind's poor health forced them to return to Canada in December 1934.

His faithful response to this call from God was not undertaken without powerful resistance. At first Rosalind opposed the rigors and hardships of traveling in the rural areas of the vast country. She argued that more of their children would surely die because of the deprivations they would face. After months of reassurances from her husband that no place was safer than the path of God's will, she relented, and indeed the children prospered.

Family opposition ceased by 1908, but now the Goforths met with strong antagonism from the established Presbyterian mission and church structure. Countless missionaries and pastors, both in Canada and China, disagreed with Jonathan's focus on the need for confession. Younger denominational leaders blanched at his preaching on judgment and hell. They likewise found unpalatable his constant references to the entire Bible as God's inspired and inerrant guide to salvation and life. Finally, his colleagues deemed his call for everyone to be baptized with the transforming power of the Holy Spirit to be the ultimate in poor taste.

Opposition neither deterred Goforth's mission nor dampened his enthusiasm. The skeptics notwithstanding, revival spread through the Presbyterian wing of the Chinese church. As a result, God raised up more than sixty Chinese men and women who served full-time as evangelists and Bible teachers. Thousands of new converts were baptized (more than thirteen thousand between 1908 and 1913 alone), and thirty new missions out-stations were established that ultimately became command posts for planting small churches.

The full impact of Goforth's faithfulness will not be known this side of heaven, but it should inspire us to realize that in the 1980s, a half-century after the Goforths left China, their daughter, Mary Goforth Moynan, could testify to the impact of her parents' selfless service.

Lyle Dorsett

Further Reading

Goforth, Jonathan. *By My Spirit*. Grand Rapids: Zondervan, 1942.

Goforth, Rosalind. *Climbing: Memories of a Missionary's Wife*. Toronto: Evangelical Publishers, 1940.

———. *Goforth of China*. Grand Rapids: Zondervan, 1937.

———. *How I Know God Answers Prayer*. Philadelphia: Sunday School Times, 1921.

Goforth's papers are located in Billy Graham Center Archives, Wheaton College, Wheaton, Illinois.

TRIUMPH IN DEATH

John and Betty Stam

1906–1934 and 1907–1934

A clump of pines silently stood guard over the terrorized crowd on a hill just outside Miaosheo, south Anhwei Province, China. In the crowd witnessing the sentencing of the young American missionary couple, a Christian Chinese medical doctor pressed his way forward and fell on his knees imploring the Communist leaders to spare the lives of the newly arrived missionaries. Angrily repulsed by the Marxist invaders on that fatal morning, December 8, 1934, the doctor was dragged away to die for daring to appeal for mercy for the Christian foreigners, "imperialists."

Barefoot and stripped of his outer clothing in the cold winter morning, John Stam turned to the Marxist leader, urging mercy for the doctor while Betty, his wife of almost fourteen months, shivered along side him. Her thoughts must have been on her baby, Helen Priscilla, not yet three months old who had been left alone in a house in Miaosheo.

John was commanded to kneel. Betty quivered, fell to her knees. The sword flashed twice. Both were "with Christ which is better by far." Their baby remained alone in the strange, deserted house.

Throughout the world the media broadcast the news of the martyrdom of John and Betty Stam and the rescue of "the Miracle Baby," Helen Priscilla.

Family heritage

John and Betty Stam had given their lives totally to the lordship of Christ, long before that deadly day in 1934. They had inherited the vigor of strong Christian families. John's family was involved in the Star of Hope Mission in Paterson, New Jersey. Betty's parents were Presbyterian missionaries to North China.

John's parents were immigrant Holland-

> *John and Betty Stam's martyrdom in Anhwei Province at the hands of ruthless Chinese Communists on December 8, 1934, stirred the Christian world to renewed missionary commitment in the midst of the Great Depression. The Stams' main accomplishment was modeling compassion and mercy so effectively that scores of young people of their generation wanted to know the will of God in the same fashion that John and Betty Stam had known the will of God in their lives.*
>
> *A retired mission executive recently remarked, "I personally know of hundreds of volunteers of all ages who gave their lives to the Lord for missionary service because of the death of John and Betty Stam."*

ers, parenting seven sons and three daughters, one of whom died in infancy. John was the seventh child.

On arriving in America, John's father, Peter, was given a Dutch-English New Testament, his great helper in learning English and becoming a Christian. Mother Stam descended from the French Huguenots, religious refugees of the French Counter Reformation. The Stam family life was strongly characterized by godliness. Culture developed through music and books and expressed itself in community service.

Unpaid service to the poorest of Paterson set the standard for the entire family, father Peter leading them in visitations to hospitals, jails, and almshouses. Peter Stam was a

> *The Stam family life was strongly characterized by godliness.*

The Lives of John and Betty Stam

1906	Elisabeth Alden Scott born in Albion, Michigan, the first of five children, February 22
1907	John Stam born in Paterson, New Jersey, the fifth of six sons, January 8
1931	Betty graduates from Moody Bible Institute and sails for China
1932	John graduates from Moody Bible Institute and sails for China
1933	John and Betty Stam marry, October 25
1934	Helen Priscilla Stam born, September 11 John and Betty martyred, December 8

CHINA

Shanghai •

Christian businessman driven by the love of Christ to use his skills as a contractor in serving the less fortunate. He and his wife were role models of Christian faith and loving outreach for all the family.

The Star of Hope Mission

John's father converted a livery stable into an auditorium that accommodated six hundred. It became the Star of Hope Mission where thousands of deprived citizens found food and hope, comfort and strength, forgiveness and reconciliation by trusting Jesus Christ as Savior and Lord. The family orchestra participated regularly in evangelistic meetings at the Star of Hope Mission as it served the homeless in a family commitment to assuaging human need. Here was created a climate for the maturing of John Stam.

Nonetheless, John's response to the rescue mission influence was slow. Such transformations as he had repeatedly observed were not required of him. He knew the gospel and enjoyed a cultured, supportive family. Consequently business became his priority and the business college diploma his goal.

New perspective, new goals

However, a blind evangelist preaching at the Star of Hope Mission opened John's eyes to the subtlety of sin and the reality of a Christless hell. At age fifteen he committed his life to Christ and developed as a Christian during his six years in business school and in office positions in New York City.

Although John was retiring and self-effacing, his experience of the new birth brought him to a new plateau of self-assertion, including grassroots street corner evangelism.

This renewal in evangelism was balanced by commuter Greek lessons as John rode the train daily to Manhattan from Paterson in a group with three other young men, one of whom was a Greek specialist. The Greek studies climaxed in John's applying to Moody Bible Institute in 1929 to prepare to serve Christ. His spiritual development brought him to a position of leadership among the students at the Bible institute. His daily morning meetings with God, and many monthly prayer meetings with his peers in the Student Missionary Union vitally contributed to his academic and personal growth.

Elizabeth Alden Scott

Elizabeth Alden Scott had been studying at Moody one year when John appeared. Betty was a direct descendant of the John and Priscilla Alden family of *Mayflower* fame. Betty's father and mother, Dr. and Mrs. Charles Ernest Scott, were well-known in missionary circles as Presbyterian missionaries in Shantung Province, North China. The Scotts were serving as Presbyterian home missionaries in Albion, Michigan, when Betty was born. Six months later the

John and Betty Stam.

Scotts moved to North China as evangelistic and Bible teaching missionaries. They were a closely knit family with five children playing, studying, and praying together. Daily family prayers, physical exercises, and reading periods after the evening meal were routine.

Inflammatory rheumatism during her last months in high school left Betty with a severely weakened heart requiring prolonged bed rest. During this time of recuperation she discovered a gift for writing poetry. She developed this ability during her student days at Wilson College, Chambersburg, Pennsylvania, where she was elected president of the Literary Society and appointed as associate editor of the Wilson College literary publication. She also participated actively in the Student Volunteer Movement, serving as a cabinet member.

The influence of the message and ministry of the Keswick Conferences in New Jersey was evident in her life. The "exchanged life" (Hudson Taylor), the teaching of surrender to the lordship of Christ, and faith that issues in daily spiritual victory directed her to "giving my life to Jesus" and taking Philippians 1:21 as her life's verse, "To me to live is Christ, and to die is gain."

Focusing on the vision

Following graduation from college in 1928, Betty enrolled at Moody Bible Institute for practical evangelism and Bible instruction. Her understanding of prayer and her sensitivity to the needs of others is reflected in her "Sonnet on Prayer," based on Jeremiah 31:12:

I passed a thorny desert soul one day,
A soul as fruitless as a painted mast—
So harsh and hard and dry I stood aghast,
And would have helped, but had no time to
    stay,
Yet, half in doubtfulness, began to pray
To Him the Source of living streams. At last,
Returning, I beheld a velvet-grassed,
Abundant garden; saw the rainbow spray

Of fountains, shimm'ring high against the
    trees;
Saw old-time flowers, pansies and sweet
    peas,
Pink-hearted phloxes, heliotrope,
    heartsease.
Clustering roses hung from arches there;
The scent of hidden orchards filled the air,
And there were children's voices everywhere.

Her thoughts were focused on the lepers in Africa for whom it seemed so few really cared. Also, her own China tugged at her heart. The China Inland Mission (CIM; now the Overseas Missionary Fellowship) sponsored a weekly prayer fellowship under the leadership of its local representatives, Mr. and Mrs. Isaac Page. Betty noticed the tall, attractive John Stam, a new regular at the China prayer group after his enrollment at Moody Bible Institute (MBI).

John took the opportunity to minister to a small, rural Ohio church two hundred miles east of Chicago on a biweekly basis. His pastoral gifts developed as he visited in the community, preached on Sundays, led the congregation in singing and in Scripture memorizing. Meanwhile he sensed the "burden for China" becoming weightier. He became acquainted with Betty Scott, and a relationship developed in spite of the reserve exercised by both of them.

Marriage and God's will

The will of God was primary for both, especially in marriage. Betty finished her studies at MBI in 1931 and was accepted by the CIM. Although they talked about marriage, no formal engagement was possible. John had another year of study remaining when Betty concluded her course and was accepted for missionary service. As she left Chicago with China her ultimate destination, an "understanding" existed between them.

During her late teens Betty had written a serious poem, "My Ideal," revealing her heart's desire:

> ## Thousands of deprived citizens found food and hope, comfort and strength, forgiveness and reconciliation.

> ## "The faithfulness of God is the only certain thing in the world today."

I'll recognize my true love
    When first his face I see;
For he will strong and healthy,
    and broad of shoulders be;

His interest is boundless
    in every fellow man
He'll gladly be a champion
    as often as he can:
O, he'll be democratic
    and maybe shock the prude
He will not fawn before the great
    nor to the low be rude.

He'll be a modern Daniel
    a Joshua, a Paul
He will not hesitate to give
    to God his earthly all.

O, if he asks a Question,
    my answer "yes" will be!
For I would trust and cherish
    him to eternity.

Before she left Chicago, John and Betty met with the CIM representative, Isaac Page, and shared their hearts with him, indicating their relationship was "in the Lord's hands." Fairness to God and to each other required them to place a priority on reaching the unevangelized world. Marriage should not hinder this biblical goal.

Eight months after Betty's arrival in China, John addressed his graduating classmates and their guests. He reminded them...

... that the Great Commission was never qualified by clauses calling for advance only if funds were plentiful and no hardships or self-denial were involved. On the contrary, we are told to expect tribulation and even persecution, but with it victory in Christ... The faithfulness of God is the only certain thing in the world today. We need not fear the result of trusting Him... Does it not thrill our hearts to realize that we do not go forward in our own strength? Think of it, God himself is with us.

By July 1, 1932, John had concluded his six-week candidate visit to the CIM headquarters in Philadelphia where he was accepted as a member of the Mission. He now was at liberty to ask Betty to join him in marriage so that they might serve Christ together. He wrote her. But no reply arrived from Betty before he sailed to China on the *Empress of Japan*.

China at last

The delayed return of Dr. and Mrs. Scott from their stateside furlough and the on-time arrival of the *Empress of Japan* with John aboard developed into a providential coincidence. Infected tonsils had brought Betty back to Shanghai for medical help just in time to meet her parents—and to welcome John upon his arrival. John and Betty had affirmed the reality of the promises of the Lord, "Seek first His kingdom . . . and all these things will be given to you as well." Their engagement was formally approved and announced.

John headed for language study in Anking, southeast Anhwei Province, while Betty returned to Fowyang in the northwest district of Anhwei. In five months and one day John completed his language studies, passed three examinations on three consecutive days, and received his mission designation from the CIM director, C. E. Hoste, during Hoste's administrative visit to Anking. John was assigned to Suancheng with the senior North American missionaries Mr. and Mrs. George A. Birch.

Developments in China

In 1922 an anti-Christian movement developed in China. Between 1924 and 1934 twenty-seven Protestant missionaries were killed, fifty-nine were kidnapped for ransom, twenty-one imprisoned, and two died in captivity. Intense anti-Christian hostility and banditry prevailed. By 1927 hundreds of missionaries were evacuating China, closing schools and hospitals. The new non-Christian Chinese intellectuals and the uneducated residents of the interior joined in anti-Christian acts, killing missionaries and destroying their properties.

Two years later, in spite of the hostility, the CIM appealed for two hundred new workers to be on the field in two years. CIM opened twenty new stations in one year in hitherto unreached territory.

The violence in Anhwei Province, how-

Helen Priscilla Stam.

ever, did not begin in the 1920s. As early as 1867 an agent of the British and Foreign Bible Society was killed. In subsequent decades many cases of anti-Christian activities were reported. In 1922 Russian Stalinists and the New Tide/Renaissance appeared. China's intellectuals were now emphasizing the scientific method and rationalistic anti-foreign aggressiveness. Chinese students organized an Anti-Christian Federation in 1922. Mission schools were viewed as instruments of student denationalization. Thus, nationalism was fusing the anti-Christian movements and fostering opposition to all religious education in the schools.

The Great Depression in the West also militated against sending and supporting missionaries. Nevertheless, the China Inland Mission sent two hundred new volunteers during the early 1930s.

In this context, during the summer of 1932, after two months of orientation under the direction of his senior missionary George Birch, John Stam found himself alone at Suancheng. He worked with Chinese church leaders while continuing language studies for his second examination, and he began a study of the gospel of John with a group of young men. He also taught choruses in Chinese tunes to the children.

John and Betty serve Christ together

The one-year-engagement policy of CIM, dating from the time that missionary duties were assumed, was fulfilled. During that period Betty maintained her language study for her third set of examinations and departed Fowyang in northwest Anhwei for her parental home at Tsinan to prepare for her wedding. CIM coworkers made up the bridal party. Betty's roommate at Wilson College, Marguerite Luce, now a missionary nurse at the Presbyterian Chefoo Hospital, was her bridesmaid. Rev. R. A. Torrey, Jr., Presbyterian missionary in Tsinan and son of the famous evangelist, officiated at the outdoor ceremony on the tennis court of the mission, on October 25, 1933.

After their wedding trip to Betty's childhood area on the rocky seascape of Tsingtao, the bridal couple arrived at Suanchang in time for Betty to complete her final language exams within the three-year limit. They participated in joint ministries with their Chinese coworkers at out-stations and preaching points. A ten-mile trip in a six-hour period was not uncommon.

Their ultimate goal was to relocate at Tsingteh, sixty miles southwest of Suanchang, to replace Mr. and Mrs. S. J. Warren who were leaving for furlough. Ten miles from Tsingteh, over the mountains, was Miaosheo, where Evangelist Lo and his Christian Chinese family kept the light of the gospel burning.

At the beginning of the Miaosheo gospel witness a solitary Bible fell into the hands of a schoolteacher, Mr. Cheng, thanks to an itinerant peddler. As a result eighteen persons had affirmed the reality of salvation by faith in Christ. John and Betty observed this tiny minority during a twenty-four-day trip to that region.

Helen Priscilla was born to John and Betty Stam on September 11, 1934, at the Methodist hospital in Wuhu.

Rumors
Rumors of Communist activities created concerns among the CIM administration. The Stams' nearest missionary neighbor, E. A. Kohlfield, and John followed superintendent W. J. Hanna's request to investigate conditions relative to the Communists'

> They tied up John
> and dragged him off
> to their headquarters.

activities and the Stam family safety if the family were to move to Tsingteh. The Chinese magistrates assured them there was no danger of a Communist attack. Besides, they (the magistrates) would provide protection. So the Stams moved. A letter to supporting friends in Paterson, dated December 6, 1934, the last day of their short residence in Tsingteh, stated:

Things are always happening otherwise than one expects. . . . The Lord help us to be quite satisfied, whatever He sends our way this day. Whether our hopes for study or work are realized or not, may He help us to be satisfied with His plan for the day, as He unfolds it to us.

"For this cause . . ."
Earlier John had written an Easter meditation on John 12:24–28 for the Anking student magazine: the corn of wheat falling into the ground to die brings forth much fruit. He applied Jesus' statement "for this cause came I unto this hour."

Whether we face suffering or joy . . . whatever we may face we may say, "for this cause came I unto this hour." . . . All has been to prepare us to meet the present circumstances.

Captive
On December 7, 1934, a surprise Communist attack was made by two thousand troops that crossed the mountain range on seldom-used trails behind the regular army sixty miles south. The alarm from passing citizens sounded as Betty was bathing baby Helen Priscilla. The family paused to pray with the household helpers. When the Communists swept into the mission compound, Betty served them tea and cakes. In spite of her courtesy they tied up John and dragged him off to their headquarters, returning shortly for Betty and the baby. A letter from John to the CIM Shanghai headquarters briefly explained their plight.

The following morning, December 8, 1932, the reinforced Red Army, now six thousand troops, took Miaoshao with John and Betty and Helen Priscilla in tow, discussing openly whether the infant should be disposed of to avoid the inconvenience of her care. An unknown farmer in the crowd protested the slaying of the infant, whereupon he was advised it would be his life for hers.

To this he agreed. He was killed on the spot. Helen Priscilla was allowed to live.

At Miaoshao the Stams were placed in the custody of the postmaster who inquired, "Where are you going?"

"We don't know where they are going," said John, "but we are going to heaven." John wrote another letter to CIM in Shanghai, updating headquarters on the demands of $20,000 ransom. Courage and calm prevailed in the letter and in the Stams' behavior.

Sharing Christ's cross

They were quartered for the night in an abandoned house of a wealthy owner who had fled. John was tied to the post of a heavy bed while Betty was free to care for baby Helen Priscilla in the cold winter night. The silence of that dark night still speaks of the light of God's grace and love.

Witnesses to the events of the next morning spoke to the calm and composure of John and Betty. The pines on the hilltop sighed in the breeze as their roots embraced the fallen bodies.

Meanwhile an old woman whispered to Evangelist Lo that a foreign baby had been left alone for almost a day and a half in the deserted house. In spite of danger from the Communists, he cautiously entered the house, found Helen Priscilla, and committed her to the care of his Christian wife. Another Christian woman, Mrs. Wang, and her son cared for the bodies of John and Betty. After a treacherous foot journey of one hundred miles, hidden in a rice basket, baby Helen Priscilla was presented in good health to her grandparents, Dr. and Mrs. Charles Ernest Scott. Incredible!

John's parents received a telegram from one of his schoolmates:

"Remember, you gave John to God, not to China."

Peter Stam responded in *Moody Monthly* to the great number of communications received, which supported the family with a great volume of prayer:

These many friends need not feel that their prayers were unanswered. They were answered, for Betty and John were released—from the pain and toil of life and brought gently into the presence of the Savior whom they loved so dearly. We are earnestly praying that it will all be for God's glory and for the salvation of souls.

Betty's father, Dr. Scott, reported on two memorial services held for John and Betty— one in Chinese at Tsinan, conducted by the Chinese Presbytery, and the other in English conducted by Rev. R. A. Torrey, Jr. One devout layman remarked:

Their death is in truth a sharing of the Cross of Christ—the same love over the same evil, and not overcome, but victorious.

In Dr. Scott's Princeton Mission Lectures, which he delivered early in the twentieth century, he said:

Because the weakness of God is stronger than men, the Almighty is continually using a humble, unexpected means or instrument to attain a great object. "God chose the weak things of the world that He might put to shame the things that are strong."

Twenty-five years later this statement could be applied to his daughter and her husband, who in weakness triumphed as they entered the presence of the Lord whom they were serving!

Will Norton, Sr.

Further Reading

English, Eugene Schuyler. *By Life and by Death: Excerpts and Lessons from the Diary of John C. Stam.* Grand Rapids: Zondervan, 1938.

Hockman, W. H. "Our Martyrs," *Moody Monthly* 35, no. 6 (February 1935).

Huizenga, Lee S. *John and Betty Stam—Martyrs.* Grand Rapids: Zondervan, 1935.

Scott, Clara, and Charles Ernest Scott, "In Memory of Elizabeth Alden Scott Stam," *Moody Monthly* 35, no. 6 (May 1935).

Taylor, Mary Geraldine Guinness. *John and Betty Stam: A Story of Triumph.* Chicago: Moody, 1935, 1982.

AN INDIGENOUS CHINESE CHURCH

Wang Ming-tao

1900–1991

Wang Ming-tao has been widely recognized in both mainland China and overseas as one of the most influential figures in the Chinese church. His respect for biblical authority, his example of moral integrity, and his defense of the Christian faith have won the admiration of Chinese Christians around the world. For more than twenty years he was confined to prison due to his refusal to compromise and cooperate with the Communist government. His suffering for the Lord strengthened the faith of many Chinese Christians during periods of social turmoil and religious suppression in China in the past four decades. When news of his death (July 28, 1991) reached the outside world, memorial services were held in several big cities where Chinese Christians have a sizable population. Although Pastor Wang has passed away, he continues to speak to the Chinese church today.

The Chinese world into which Wang was born in 1900 suffered from much sociopolitical turmoil. Since the middle of the nineteenth century the Ch'ing Dynasty had been incompetent to deal with successive foreign aggressions and civil rebellions. Eventually, in 1911, under the leadership of Dr. Sun Yat-sen the Republican Government replaced the dynasty. China then emerged as a new nation in international politics. However, because of internal divisions provoked by local warlords and external aggression by foreign powers, the country was far from united. The weakness of the nation was blamed on traditional Confucianism due to its alleged inability to modernize the Chinese society.

The quest for wealth and power precipitated an intellectual revolution, called the May Fourth Movement (1915–23), which emphasized science and democracy as the means to build the young nation. These developments greatly affected the sensitive mind of Wang Ming-tao.

Political ambitions

Educated and baptized in the church run by the London Missionary Society in Peking, Wang grew up in a conservative expression of Christianity. Like most young intellectuals of his generation, he felt the obligation to participate in the task of national salvation. At first he wanted to become a well-known politician, a "Chinese Lincoln." He did not aspire to be a Christian minister, partly because he knew pastors received low salaries and were not greatly respected. But in 1918 the direction of Wang's career was dramatically changed during a period of sickness which threatened his life. He promised God to give up politics for the Christian ministry if he could survive. Wang did recover and was faithful to his promise.

From the mid-1920s on, Wang labored to build an indigenous church upon the threefold principle of self-propagating, self-governing, and self-supporting (in that order). His church began in a household gathering in Peking where a few people gathered for Bible study, prayer, and fellowship. This group grew, and in 1937 the Christian Tabernacle—the name of Wang's church—was constructed with the donations of his own congregation. Visible spirituality was the criterion for membership; this kept the size of his congregation small. In 1949 when mainland China came under Communist rule, the Christian Tabernacle had a membership of only about 570.

Scripture and Spirit

Several features characterized Wang's church. Simplicity in Christian life and service was emphasized to the extent that anything not mentioned in the Bible should not be done. No form of tradition or denominational liturgy was acceptable to Wang. No cross was found in the entire church building. During the worship service, there was no choir or circulation of offering bags. Christmas was not celebrated. Wang himself did not like to be called "Pastor," which, he thought, had no biblical warrant.

Wang Ming-tao received no formal university education or seminary training. Yet he was extremely well versed in Scripture. Moreover, he was constantly open to the guidance of the Holy Spirit in personal decisions. In his understanding, both Scripture and Spirit were adequate in the making of God's servant. His preaching was practical and powerful. As a speaker, he was in great demand among churches in various provinces. Throughout his itinerant ministry Wang unreservedly attacked the worldliness of Christians and the apostasy of the churches. He knew that he might not be invited a second time, but the enthusiastic response to his preaching proved the opposite. It was his ideal that he should become a model for Chinese pastors, and that the Christian Tabernacle should be a model church.

The battle against liberalism

Doctrinal purity was given first priority in the ministry of Wang. He did not often invite outside speakers to his pulpit lest erroneous doctrines be taught to his congregation. For the same reason not many contributors were welcomed in his quarterly magazine, *Spiritual Food,* which enjoyed a wide circulation.

In both preaching and writing, he was a strong opponent of theological liberalism, which was gaining popularity in some denominations in China in the 1920s. The theological controversy between liberals and

Wang Ming-tao
(1900–1991).

> *Wang unreservedly attacked the worldliness of Christians and the apostasy of the churches.*

conservatives in American churches had been transplanted to China by the missionaries. Wang helped create the Bible Union of China, which was an effort to consolidate conservative forces to combat liberalism. Wang criticized the liberal wing of the Chinese church for preaching a different gospel.

Many Chinese liberals were interested in searching for a gospel which could speak relevantly to the needs of the Chinese people. Some accommodated Christianity to traditional culture; others advocated a radical program to revolutionize the Chinese society; still others promoted pioneering service to rural areas. To Wang these efforts, though capable of doing good to reconstruct the disintegrated society, should never be

The Life of Wang Ming-tao

1900	Born in Peking
1918	Sickness Gives up political ambitions and dedicates his life to Christian ministry
1937	Construction of Wang's Christian Tabernacle
1955	Imprisoned for religious beliefs by the Chinese government
1979	Released from prison
1991	Dies in Shanghai

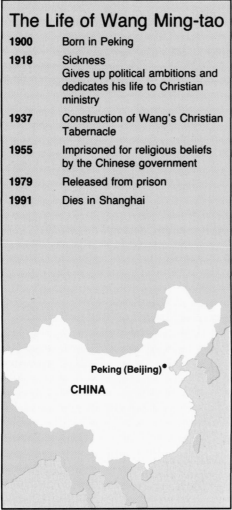

Peking (Beijing)•

CHINA

The church must be separated from the state because of the functional differences between the two.

corruption. The church must be separated from the state because of the functional differences between the two. The state should not be allowed to interfere with the affairs of the church. This principle of separation was closely followed in Wang's response to political repression in the 1940s and 1950s.

During the Sino-Japanese War (1937–45), Peking fell under the control of the Japanese army, which sought effectively to control the churches of North China. Wang was invited to join the Japanese-led Chinese Christian Federation of North China, but he declined on the ground that the Christian Tabernacle was already an indigenous church, not pro-Britain or pro-American, and that his theological position differed from that of some members in the Federation. He kept a coffin in his house for the possible consequence of his stance: receiving the death penalty. Indeed, his refusal incensed the Japanese authority which, however, took no action against Wang. This amazing turn of events, interpreted by Wang as divine protection, perpetuated his view of political noninvolvement and strengthened his willingness to be a martyr. Undoubtedly this prepared him for a bigger crisis in the 1950s.

identified with the gospel itself. Such identification betrays the essence of Christianity and is a Chinese version of the social gospel. Wang single-handedly produced in his many writings an apologetic that has preserved the integrity of the evangelical faith for the Chinese church. Its impact is still discernible today.

Political noninvolvement

Ever since Wang had abandoned his political ambition for a total commitment to the gospel cause in China, he took a firm stand against any form of political involvement. Christianity must be separated from Chinese politics which, in his view, could never save the people in adversity. Only the gospel of Jesus Christ can deliver them from sin and

Struggling for survival

When the Communists came to power in 1949, the Christian church in China faced the problem of survival under an atheist government. To the Communists, religion is the opiate of the people and has to be eliminated. In order to purify the church of "imperialism" and establish complete independence, all foreign missionaries were asked to leave the country. And Chinese Christians were instructed to render their contribution to the socialist reconstruction of the nation. Love for their country should come before loyalty to their religion. Under the directive of the Communist Party, the Three Self-Patriotic Movement (TSPM) was organized to control the nationwide Christian church.

Confronted with the unfavorable religious

policy implemented by the TSPM, Wang Ming-tao remained calm. Convinced that the future of the Chinese church was in the hands of God, he continued to stay away from politics. He knew that the TSPM was a government instrument designed to suppress the church, and he refused to give in. Such nonconformity was hardly acceptable to the totalitarian regime. It led to his imprisonment in the summer of 1955 after a formal accusation was launched against him. His friends daringly organized an "Oppose the Persecution of Wang Ming-tao" campaign, which was reported all over the country. In jail Wang was interrogated unceasingly by two government officers until in September 1956 he signed a confession and was released. But afterward Wang was exceedingly sorry for what he had done. He thought he had betrayed his Lord. He and his wife decided to appear before the government where they revoked the previous confessions. They were imprisoned again. Only in December 1979, decades later, were they finally set free.

In 1979 China entered into a new era of Four Modernizations under the leadership of Teng Hsiao-ping. A more tolerant religious policy was adopted which brought about Wang's release. During the 1980s the Wangs lived in Shanghai, welcomed visitors to their home and shared their experience of suffering for Christ. An invaluable lesson Wang had learned in prison was forgiveness. Although he was betrayed, accused, and scandalized by his enemies, he was able to forgive them all with the love of Christ.

Regeneration

The central doctrine of Wang's theology was regeneration in Christ, upon which Christianity stands or falls. Whereas the liberals preach an earthly kingdom of God to be established through human efforts, and whereas the Communists envisioned a utopia through revolutions, Wang affirmed that only a changed person through genuine rebirth could change society. This teaching has greatly affected the Chinese church today in its outlook on world missions and social involvement. Wang's own willingness to be a prisoner for Christ decade after decade in a Communist prison cell gives an enormous validation for this teaching's reality.

Lam Wing-hung

Further Reading

Wang Ming-tao. *Treasuries of Wang Ming-tao.* 7 vols. Edited by C. C. Wang. Taipei, Taiwan: Conservative Baptist Press, 1976–78.

Lam Wing-hung. *Wang Ming-tao and the Chinese Church.* Hong Kong: China Graduate School of Theology Press, 1982.

Lyall, L. *Three of China's Mighty Men.* London: Overseas Missionary Fellowship, 1973.

MIRACLE AT MIDNIGHT

Sister Annie

1911–1992

When the people carrying the idols saw the two women, the procession halted, the drums stopped beating, and two men ran toward the women.

They were waving their arms and shouting, "Take off your hats!"

The tall woman with the blonde hair and

Two women were approaching the village in the mountains of northwestern China. The smaller one was at the back. She was skinny and slight in person, hardly five feet tall. A wide-brimmed straw hat covered her straight, black hair. The woman in front towered six feet above the narrow track, which bent its way between stones and trees up toward the first low houses of the village. A slight breeze was playing with the blond curls underneath the tall woman's straw hat.

When the two women reached the town entrance, they met a long procession of mumbling women and men. The people were carrying wooden idols between them, while hollow drumbeats boomed along the valley.

A drought had ravaged the small mountain village for weeks. By this time the soil was so dry that there would have to be rain within a few days. Otherwise the whole year's crop would be destroyed.

The taller of the two women was Annie Skau Bernsten, a Norwegian missionary nurse to China. Unknown to Annie, she was about to experience a life-and-death test concerning her faith in the God of Christianity.

the blue eyes did not understand what the men meant.

"Hurry up, get those hats off immediately."

"But why, honored procession leaders?" asked the shorter, Chinese woman.

"You know that our gods cannot bear seeing dry grass on somebody's head when there is a drought in the village. When they do, they get furious and send even more drought over our poor fields. Please, take off your hats at once, otherwise we will tear them off you and burn them!"

The tall woman kept her hat on. She replied: "Listen, idol worshipers. I cannot take off my hat as a salute to your idols."

The oldest of the men turned to the others. "Then we will kill her!" Twelve to fifteen men lifted heavy sticks over their heads.

The promise of rain

"Wait!" The tall woman continued. "My God can give you rain; your idols cannot!" She stared the oldest one straight in the eyes.

"Your God!" the man hissed back. "We do not know any gods other than our own!"

"Just wait and see, and He will turn the drought into rain. Wait and see," answered the tall woman.

The oldest man got the rest of the group to encircle the two strangers, and they once again lifted their sticks in a threatening way.

"I promise you rain before midnight!" said the tall woman. There was no tremble in her voice.

The old man turned to the others: "The giant-woman is promising rain, do you hear that? Let her show us what this God of hers can do. Let her show us that she has a God better than our gods. But if the giant-woman and her God cannot provide rain before midnight, we will kill her!"

Sister Annie at "The Hope of Heaven," Hong Kong.

Then the two women were permitted to continue their walk. When they reached a small mission late in the evening, they recounted what had happened and what they had promised.

"You should never have promised such a thing," exhorted an elderly Christian at the mission. "If there is no rain in the village before midnight, it means that you have scorned the idols in the village, and one who does that will have to pay with his life tonight."

"I can only believe that it is God's will that I shall live and continue to preach the gospel in this country. Therefore I trust Him to show who is the one and only God—also in the village between the mountains," replied the tall woman.

The few remaining hours of the evening lumbered slowly on. In a small room in the old mission building, the giant-woman was on her knees praying. Yu Chin, her companion, was kneeling next to her.

Half an hour before midnight the door was thrown open brusquely. It was the oldest person at the mission who came running in.

"The rain is coming! The rain is coming! God be praised! You have saved your lives."

The Life of Sister Annie

1911	Born in Oslo, Norway
1938–51	Serves as missionary nurse in China
1953	Begins work in the Rennie's Mill refugee camp, Hong Kong
1955	Founds "The Hope of Heaven" rehabilitation center, Hong Kong
1979	Receives distinction as "Member of the British Empire"
1992	Dies in Horton, Norway

CHINA

Hong Kong •

"The rain is coming! The rain is coming! God be praised! You have saved your lives," he shouted and fell on his knees.

"Tomorrow you can continue safely, and you can tell the village people about a God who sends rain to those who need water and sun to those who are floodstricken. . ."

The thirty-year-old Norwegian nurse, Annie Skau Bernsten, folded her hands and prayed, rejoicing in the faithfulness of her heavenly Father.

This all happened one day in June 1941

> "Tears were rolling down my cheeks when Grandma prayed for me and my parents."

somewhere in northwest China. As so many times before, Sister Annie had put all her confidence in prayer to the God of all creation. Once again her faith had been strengthened.

From Marx to Christ

Annie Skau Berntsen, born in Oslo, Norway, in 1911, was in her early years a leader in her Karl Marx youth club in the small town of Horten, to which her family had moved when Annie was a little girl. Later on, she decided to become a nurse. While attending nursing school, the one-time Marxist became a Christian.

"But I received my first sign from God at the age of seven when I spent Christmas with my grandparents," she remembered. "Grandma and I knelt to pray several times that Christmas. We prayed to God, and it was Grandma who spoke. I had never learned how to pray at home. Never before had I heard anyone pray freely, and I had never done that myself. Tears were rolling down my cheeks when Grandma prayed for me and my parents."

"Ask Jesus to save Mum and Dad and you, dear Annie," Grandma said.

"I was not certain that God cared for me," Annie recalled, "but I thought that perhaps God's power was in me even though I did not understand much of it.

"I felt an inner security which I had never felt before, a strange feeling of belonging to a community. Before long, I was praying too, just as intensely as Grandma. It seemed perfectly natural to me to pray to be saved and to be allowed to serve Him who guides all things."

"The seed has been planted in your heart, dear Annie," said Grandma. "One day it will grow, and there will be both leaves and flowers."

Leaves and flowers

Annie Skau Berntsen participated in the China Inland Mission missionary training program in 1937–38, taking a course on tropical diseases. In 1938 she was sent to China where she worked at the Shanghsien and Lungchuchai mission in Shensi province for thirteen years, until 1951.

Then the Communists came to power. Annie and all other foreign missionaries were forced to leave the China mainland.

In China, Annie had met Gladys Aylward, the legendary English missionary who devoted her life to work with the Chinese.

Annie encountered Gladys for the first time in Fengsiang, in the western portion of the Shensi province. When Gladys Aylward had gone to the missionary field, she was supposed to work together with an older missionary who had been in the country for years. But after a time he died. As a young nurse, Annie was the only missionary left in the area.

Gladys Aylward was on the run when Annie met her. She had managed to get across the Yellow River with a group of small children. The Japanese were approaching and made the conditions at Gladys's own mission unsafe. But even through the hardship Gladys kept her smile, her friendliness, and her dignity. And her belief. Annie was much impressed by Gladys's genuine Christian faith.

Hong Kong
From 1953 to 1955 Annie worked in Hong Kong at the Rennie's Mill refugee-camp where the Christian Children Fund had established an aid program. The Scottish nurse and missionary Helen Wilson joined the clinic later, together with Hanny Gronlund from Norway.

In 1955 Annie founded "The Hope of Heaven" Hospital in Hong Kong where thousands of refugees from mainland China have been treated at the rehabilitation center. Today the hospital remains one of the principal rehabilitation institutions of Hong Kong.

For her sacrificial work, Sister Annie was honored with the Norwegian King's St. Olaf's Orden and the Florence Nightingale Medal. In 1979 she was named a "Member of the British Empire" for her tireless labors in Hong Kong.

Toward the end of her life Annie reflected

Sister Annie was honored with the Norwegian King's St. Olaf's Orden and the Florence Nightingale Medal.

upon what she had done with the opportunities for service God had given her: "It has been an adventure—and a toil.

"But to be allowed to wear oneself out serving God, that is the greatest happiness. That is why I would have chosen exactly the same path if I were to be young again. What I would have changed were all the stupid and clumsy things I have done.

"I have always been in the fortunate situation that I have not had to look for tasks; the tasks have always been put in front of me. Working out here [in the Far East] has taught me that cooperation is necessary to solve even the smallest problem. We who work in a foreign country have not been sent here to preach to a congregation. We are here to preach about Jesus. We cannot sit on separate hills; we have to pray together, and we have to love Jesus together."

Fearless in death
Nor did Annie Skau Berntsen fear death. Though her "miracle at midnight" spared her once, she welcomed death as a time to see her Lord. Yet, before she died and joined the Lord in 1992, she was full of concern for those who worried about their own last day. She listened to their fears and tried to relieve the worries of the frightened.

"Even if I am not scared of death myself, I can understand those who are," she said.

"Standing before death we stand in front of something totally unknown. Nobody knows what death contains, we can only believe. My belief is so strong that I have no fear. Now I just look forward to meeting Jesus. The most magnificent thing which can happen to me is to be allowed to serve Him day and night in His temple. Nothing in the world is as glorious as serving the Lord Jesus Christ!"

Arvid and Gudveig Møller

MAORI PROPHET AND EVANGELIST

Muri Thompson

1930–1992

Muriwhenua Thompson was the oldest of six children born to a Maori family in the small village of Mamaranui, near Dargaville, in northern New Zealand. His father, a seaman turned sheep farmer, died when Muri was only nine, leaving Muri's mother, Meriana, sister to the Maori bishop of Aotearoa, to raise her large family alone. Meriana had dreams of her son Muri becoming an Anglican clergyman, but Muri's major desire was to become a leader of a dance band. At sixteen he went off to Auckland to finish his schooling in the big city, and Meriana arranged for him to board at the United Maori Mission, under the godly leadership of the well-known Maori evangelist, Charlie Bennett.

Life in the big city took an unexpected turn for Muri. The sincerity and genuineness of Bennett deeply impressed the young man. One Sunday evening he attended an evangelistic meeting in the YMCA, and someone said to him, "Why don't you receive Christ?" His response was, "All right, I'll give it a go." The pragmatic Muri thought to himself, *I'll give it all I've got till I find out if it works or not.* He wasn't conscious of an immediate change, but slowly a change in mind and heart did take place.

Born with a hole in his heart, Muri was often quite ill. But propped up in bed, he would devour the biographies of famous preachers and evangelists that Charlie Bennett unloaded on him. And so a new dream started to form in his mind: to become an evangelist for the Lord.

Budding evangelist

On January 22, 1954, there landed in Auckland a man in his early forties, keen to promote a more effective kind of open-air evangelism. Jim Duffecy, of Open Air Campaigners (OAC), was a colorful character,

cheerful and audacious, willing to try anything. His quick wit and humor appealed to young Muri. It gave him confidence to be his own Maori self, aggressive and unorthodox in style, and still bring Christ to his own people.

At the end of Jim's visit, a New Zealand branch of OAC was established, and Muri became one of its first evangelists. A year later, when Duffecy took a team from Australia to establish OAC in North America, Muri joined the team and spent the better part of a year in Chicago and Toronto. But his heart was giving him problems while he was in North America. He wondered how long he would live. As his plane flew him back home from Canada, his eyes filled with tears as he prayed, "Lord, if You will give me my life, I will serve my Maori people by preaching the gospel to them."

Some time after his return, he was sent to Greenlane Hospital Cardiac Unit. The doctors there told him he had only a 50 percent chance of surviving an operation, his heart was so bad. Muri didn't like the "*other* percent," as he called it, so he checked out of the hospital, trusting God for whatever life God might give him. At that time, several Christians prayed specifically for Muri's healing, and Muri gained strength. He actually returned to Greenlane for the operation in 1974, some seventeen years later.

Those years were fruitful ones of evangelism. Muri gathered a team of musicians around him, who called themselves the Maestros. Muri, very musical himself, demanded perfection and made them practice and practice. In Whaengarei in an early

> *Born with a hole in his heart,*
> *Muri was often quite ill.*

crusade, Muri stayed at the home of a Mrs. Hansen and was impressed by the musical gift of her daughter Ena, a pianist. He invited Ena to play alongside the Maestros in their first big crusade in Tauranga.

After an initial refusal, she did finally agree and played not only in Tauranga but for many subsequent crusades. A friendship with the "hell-fire and brimstone" preacher ripened into love, and they were married in 1963. Ena proved a loyal support and strength through nearly thirty years.

Looking back on those early crusades, Muri recalled that he didn't have a great number of sermons—just enough to see him through a crusade. But he repeated his messages with fervor, and the Lord made those messages remarkably effective in place after place.

A new breath of the Spirit
In 1970 Muri accepted an invitation to conduct crusades in the Solomon Islands for the newly independent South Sea Evangelical Church. A letter sent to the pastors of some three hundred churches read, "Muri

Peter Robertson was a confused young man. It was 1976, and Peter had been seeking God for some years. He had come to trust Jesus as his Savior but was desperately seeking God's direction for his life. He was feeling he had lost his way, fearing he had totally and utterly "blown it."

One Wednesday night, not knowing why, he went to a Presbyterian church in East Auckland, New Zealand, and heard a little Maori man speak from the pulpit. He seemed earnest. He seemed genuine. Perhaps this man could help him in his quest.

After the service, he went up the aisle, put out his hand, and said, "Gidday, my name's Peter."

The preacher stopped dead, looked at him fixedly, and exclaimed, "Don't move! Stay just where you are!" Then he turned and paced up and down the church praying and making what to Peter were all kinds of strange noises. Peter was scared. Was this funny guy seeing something evil, something threatening, that Peter could not see?

Then the preacher stopped, turned abruptly, and said to him, "Do you believe God brought you to this church tonight?"

Peter gulped and said, "Yep, I do."

The preacher then said to him, "All day the Lord has been speaking to me, and saying, 'Today you will meet a man called Peter. Go and anoint him.' Peter, you are that man, and so I will pray for you."

The preacher was Muri Thompson, a man who had learned to listen to God, a man prepared to be sent day by day, moment by moment, wherever God chose, and to bring God's message to small or great, to a lonesome, lost individual, or to a whole nation that had forgotten God.

Thompson, a Maori evangelist from New Zealand, will be here for a number of crusades during July and August. Have your people pray every day. Pray for Revival, a mighty pouring out of God's Holy Spirit upon His people so that people from all

Muri Thompson (1930–1992), Maori prophet.

churches and missions will be eternally built up in Christ."

Muri, accompanied by Rex Tito and John Pipi, spent two months visiting centers on many islands, traveling on the *Evangel* with missionary George Strachan. Halfway through the time, Muri was asked to speak

The life of Muri Thompson

1930	Born in Mamaranui, New Zealand
1946	Comes to Auckland
1954	Joins Open Air Campaigners (OAC)
1956–57	Comes to North America with OAC
1958	First crusade in Kaikohe, followed by crusades throughout New Zealand
1963	Marries Ena Hansen
1970	Ministers in the Solomon Islands
1972	Speaks at Jesus marches in New Zealand
1974	Has major heart surgery
1975–91	Waitangi celebrations
1992	Dies on March 29

● Auckland

NEW ZEALAND

Opposite: Muri
Thompson at
an evangelistic
rally.

at a conference of missionaries and national leaders. The Holy Spirit moved in that conference in a remarkable way. There was brokenness, with confessions of sins of bitterness, of attitude, of resentments, jealousies and hurt feelings going back over many years and crippling God's work.

In the crusades that followed, a team of about forty went from place to place, seeing the power of the Spirit increasingly evident. At Kobiloko, on the northeast coast of Malaita, on August 23, Muri was finishing his address. He started to say, "If anyone wants to come forward . . ." but was prevented from completing his statement as the entire congregation of six hundred rose and surged forward, men and women in tears, crying out to the Lord. For ten minutes there was no other sound. Then Muri said, "Praise the Lord!" and outbursts of joy and praise took over. George Strachan wrote, "The whole situation was in the perfect control of the Holy Spirit: no hysteria, no panic, but simply joy unspeakable and full of glory. The Holy Spirit came down—God was visiting His people."

At Sifolo, a little village of 150 people, the church had been extended sideways and lengthwise to hold two thousand, and yet, on August 27, it overflowed. After his message, Muri asked for a time of silent prayer. In the hush that followed, he heard a sound. At first it was just a whisper, seeming to come from the sky, but it grew louder and louder till it was a roar like a great gale blowing up. It was Pentecost repeated.

The New Zealand evangelists left a week later, but the revival in the Solomons continued. The islands were full of prayer and praise. People were healed, many confessed long-cherished sins, and people threw their fetishes into the sea. Life after life was delivered from the power of Satan.

And for Muri, it was a turning point. He returned to New Zealand with a burning hope that God's power might be likewise demonstrated in his own land.

The Jesus marches

The early 1970s in New Zealand saw the growth of the permissive society. People took to the streets in demonstrations for all sorts of things, some reasonable, and some painfully immoral and anti-Christian. In 1972, Christians throughout the land

decided to "march for Jesus" in demonstrations for a moral and spiritual revival. Marches were held in twelve major cities throughout New Zealand. Seventy thousand marched, holding aloft placards such as "Righteousness Exalts a Nation" and "Jesus is Alive!" and "Change the Heart to Change Society." Muri was the chief spokesperson at the rallies that concluded each march.

To a crowd of twenty thousand on the grounds outside Parliament in Wellington on Sunday, October 8, Muri proclaimed: "We are not here telling the government what to do. We are telling the government and the nation what we intend to do. We are not telling other New Zealanders how to live and how to act. But we are covenanting before God to pray for this city, to pray for this nation, and to praise God in purity and happiness."

Prophet to his people
New Zealand is unique among colonizing powers of the nineteenth century. In 1840 an agreement between the Queen of England and the indigenous tribes of New Zealand was signed at Waitangi in the Bay of Islands. The Treaty of Waitangi guaranteed to the Maori people their rights to land, to the means of livelihood, and to preservation of their culture.

Sadly, the terms of the treaty have not always been adhered to, and over the last thirty years "Waitangi" has become a word of contention. Sometimes there have been impossible demands for redress from radical Maoris. And sometimes these have been met by implacable, unreasonable resistance from diehard Europeans.

In this situation Muri Thompson was a mediating and reconciling voice. Always ready to listen to both sides, however extreme. He was able to understand and empathize with rightful grievances, but in all to look for the reconciliation that he believed could only finally come in Christ. He was accepted and trusted by radical and reactionary alike. Year after year, on February 6, he attended the Waitangi celebrations, and on the Maori marae and on the hill in front of the ceremonial flagpole, he proclaimed Christ to the people as the One able to unite Maori and non-Maori together in love around the foot of the cross.

David Stewart

Further Reading

Gibson, Nepia. *Tohunga o Wairua: The Life of Muriwhenua Thompson.* Unpublished essay, Univ. of Auckland, 1993.

Griffiths, Alison. *Fire in the Islands!* Westchester, Ill.: Harold Shaw, 1977.

Shaw, Trevor. *The Jesus Marchers.* Auckland, N.Z.: Challenge Publishers, 1972.

Not in Vain. Missionary magazine of South Sea Evangelical Mission, 1970 volume.

TWO JAPANESE MISSIONARIES

David and Joshua Tsutada

1906–1971 and 1939–

T he election of Joshua Tsutada as the new chairman of the Evangelical Fellowship of Asia (EFA) in Feburary 1989 was headline news among Christians in Japan. It was a miracle of God's grace and demonstrated to the world that Christ's love can bury dark memories of war years in the deepest sea.

David

God had taken great pains to prepare Joshua for his responsibilities. One could say that this process began with his grandfather, a dentist, who made a name for himself in Singapore. In 1906, Joshua's father, David, was born into an internationally minded family. He was the second son of eleven children. David received an excellent education. After basic schooling in Japan, he traveled to London to study law at King's College. On board ship David spoke with a friend who was a born-again Christian. At the time, David was greatly perplexed by his friend's comments, since he, like his father, considered himself a Christian. In fact, David was serious about life and was looking forward to serving society in the name of Christ. Later in London a pastor pointed out to David that Christ's kingdom would not come on earth through human effort but through the second coming of Christ. This was startling and shocking news to the law student, who meant to change society by his humanitarian efforts. Ironically, while he was in London, a Japanese evangelist had the privilege of leading the earnest young man to a saving knowledge of Christ.

As the time approached for David to return to Japan, he faced a difficult choice. He knew how eagerly he would be wel-

Dr. Joshua Tsutada is a spokesperson for the emerging evangelical leaders of the nineties. In 1987 he was elected vice chairman of the Evangelical Fellowship of Asia (EFA) and in 1989 became chairman of EFA. In 1992 he was also elected as member from Asia to the International Council of the World Evangelical Fellowship. His countrymen hold him in high esteem as a stalwart Christian leader.

But Joshua Tsutada's story cannot be exhausted by simply referring to distinguished leadership positions he has held or to his faithful missionary work in India. Rather, his Christian walk was greatly influenced by his godly father, Dr. David Tsutada, one of the church leaders who was imprisoned during World War II because of his uncomproming faith. Thus, to understand Joshua Tsutada's remarkable ministry, we also need to reflect upon the life of his father, who risked all to follow Christ.

comed home. Political circles and the government had their eyes on him. David envisioned himself as one day becoming Japan's prime minister. This was not an unrealistic ambition according to his friends, who knew of his ability and integrity. But God, too, had His eye on David. He

He wrestled with the two life callings, unable to come to a decision.

David Tsutada.

JAPAN Tokyo

Hiroshima

felt God calling him to full-time Christian service.

He wrestled with the two life callings, unable to come to a decision. He turned for advice to his father, who was in Singapore. When the fourteen-page letter arrived, his father called together the staff and servants for an all-night prayer meeting. The next morning a cable was sent with just two words: "Obey God."

Prison

David was reminded of this crisp message some years later when agents of the secret police came for his arrest. He was principal of his denomination's Bible college then, and as was his daily custom he had begun the day in his prayer room. His wife interrupted the quiet of the morning to inform him of the dreaded secret police at the door. Quickly the parents went into the children's room and offered prayer. Then David was taken away in the pouring rain. Two truck-

The Life of Joshua Tsutada

1939	Survives difficult delivery on November 14
1949	Commits life to Christ; receives call to India when only nine
1961–66	Studies at Yavatmal Union Biblical Seminary in India
1967	Marries Esther N. Hasegawa
1972–75	Serves as registrar at Yavatmal Union Biblical Seminary
1975–77	Pursues graduate studies at Aberdeen University in Scotland
1981–present	President of Immanuel Bible Training College in Yokohama, Japan
1987–89	Becomes vice chairman of the Evangelical Fellowship of Asia
1988–present	International Relations Commission member of the Japan Evangelical Association
1989–present	Becomes chairman of the Evangelical Fellowship of Asia
1992–present	Becomes member from Asia of the World Evangelical Fellowship

Edible grass, roots, snails, and other "delicacies" supplemented a meager menu.

When his tormentors realized that persuasion would get them nowhere, they changed their tactics and for eighteen long months placed him in solitary confinement. It was a tiny, dingy, damp basement cell. A peeping window allowed guards to watch his every move. Twice a day he would receive his daily ration consisting of a bowl of rice and a bowl of soup through this window. Oh, how he longed for news from the family!

The quiet of the nights was interrupted only once when strains of "What a Friend We Have in Jesus" came from the ventilation window. It must have been a courageous member of his church who played the accordion to comfort his pastor behind bars. Or was it an angel?

A mission born in a prison cell

In a real sense Immanuel General Mission was born in that prison cell. God's presence had been so real that it transformed this cold, damp room into the palace of the King. "Immanuel, God with us," David would repeat. It would become the name of the organization David would found should God see fit to set him free. God honored David's faith and vision.

The denomination has grown to 117 churches in 1993 with an additional ninety branch churches. Eighteen missionaries serve in seven countries around the world.

Two highlights in David's postwar activities were his participation in the 1952 Youth for Christ World Congress in Tokyo as congress vice chairman and later in 1967 his leadership of the Tokyo Billy Graham Crusade. How pleased David would be if he could look down from heaven to see his oldest son, John, serving as one of the vice chairmen of the 1994 Tokyo Billy Graham Crusade at the Tokyo Dome.

Joshua

Joshua is fond of talking about his rich heritage. How evident God's leading has been in the Tsutada family. He is also keenly aware of the fact that were it not for the mercy of God he would not have survived even his first day on earth on November 14, 1939.

loads of priceless books and sermon notes were also confiscated and never returned. For David this was the beginning of a two-year ordeal of interrogation and imprisonment.

What crime had he committed to deserve such treatment? He was accused of treason. How could a Japanese pastor refer to Jesus as King of kings and Lord of lords? Was such honor not reserved for the Emperor, the descendant of the Sun-Goddess Amaterasu-oomikami? Who after all was greater, the Emperor or Jesus Christ? And what about this talk about Jesus' return to earth? David's training in law school was a big help, of course, but it was God who gave David confidence to stand up with conviction.

Joshua
Tsutada.

That same year two missionaries from India spoke at the church. When the appeal for workers from Japan was made, it was Joshua's "Macedonian Call" from India. It kept ringing in his heart from that day on. Later the continent of Africa was added to Joshua's vision. Then during high school God's call to full-time service was confirmed.

Although his older brother, John, had gone to Houghton College, Joshua chose to attend Rikkyo University (St. Paul University), where he majored in English literature.

India
Then the door opened for service in India. Dr. F. J. Kline, the founder of Yavatmal Union Biblical Seminary, had come to Joshua's father with a special request. It had been brought to his attention that two students from the Immanuel Church had left a deep impression on the Houghton College campus. Dr. Kline expressed the hope that this could be repeated at Yavatmal. David Tsutada accepted the challenge, and in 1961 he and two other young men set out for India.

This marked the beginning of the overseas missionary work of the Immanuel Church. For Joshua India would become his place of service for seventeen years. God gave him a love for the people of India. The first five years of study seemed to pass by quickly. Then he was invited to remain at the seminary as a member of the faculty and later as registrar.

A divinely arranged marriage
It is not uncommon in Japan to have arranged marriages. In the case of Joshua, his father had been looking for just the right partner. It was Esther N. Hasegawa. Her father had been killed during the war, leaving behind Mutsuko, his wife, and three little girls. Mutsuko became a Christian as a child. One day she told God that she was willing to serve Him as a missionary. That day seemed very distant on the morning the despondent widow with her three youngsters received official notification of her husband's death at the Hiroshima municipal

A critical decision had to be made. The doctor in charge of the delivery informed Joshua's father that it would be medically impossible to deliver the baby without risking the life of the mother. He put it bluntly: "Which life shall we save?" For David, who believed that all areas of life are in God's hand, there was only one answer: "Save them both!" God honored such faith.

Joshua grew up during difficult days. When he was only four years old his father was imprisoned. The war years brought untold hardship as Mother struggled to raise the five children. There was no food to feed hungry mouths. Edible grass, roots, snails, and other "delicacies" supplemented a meager menu. But God saw them through.

Conversion and a call to service
Then came the end of the war. The family was at last reunited, and once again Joshua's father could preach the Word. It was a time of sowing and reaping. At age nine Joshua was among those who accepted the Lord.

office. There was no ray of hope as the four boarded the train home. Mutsuko saw no way out except suicide. The train would cross a river, and from that bridge she would jump with the children firmly in her grip. But God intervened and spoke to her just as the train approached the bridge. Had she not given her life to Him? Had she not promised to serve Him? Had He ever let her down? Could He not provide what was needed to feed three hungry mouths? Clearly it was God's voice: "Entrust them to me. One day they shall be missionaries and go where you couldn't go and do what you couldn't do." In tears Mutsuko repented of her selfish ways and committed her little flock into His hands.

It was not to be the last crisis for the family. Though Mutsuko had found much-needed employment at a downtown hospital run by relatives, it seemed to her that God was telling her to quit the job, leave Hiroshima, and flee to the mountains. She first kept these thoughts to herself but felt compelled to share them with her relatives. They only laughed. It was ridiculous to leave Hiroshima. The city was of little strategic military importance and had been spared bombing thus far. Continue to work in the hospital and support the family, everyone urged. Mutsuko followed this advice. Then one day the voice she heard was louder and more urgent. This time, without notifying anyone, she fled. The atomic bomb was dropped on Hiroshima the next day.

Joshua heard these amazing stories of God's leading in the Hasegawa family for the first time when his mother-in-law visited the Tsutadas in India, after he was married. Who would have thought that one day Esther would become a missionary to India, while her two sisters served God in Jamaica and Kenya? God kept His part of the agreement. Joshua's marriage to Esther was indeed divinely arranged.

Opened and closed doors

In 1975 the door opened for the Tsutadas to leave India for Aberdeen University in Scotland. There Joshua would pursue graduate studies in New Testament exegesis with the

> **The atomic bomb was dropped on Hiroshima the next day.**

> **The total project cost 6.5 million dollars.**

hope of returning to Yavatmal Union Biblical Seminary to teach there. It was not to be. Repeated efforts to apply for a reentry permit were refused. Joshua accepted this as a sign from God that his work in India had been completed. The time was ripe for the Indian church to carry on without outside help.

The years in India were excellent preparation for Joshua's international leadership as chairman of the Evangelical Fellowship of Asia and as Asian member of the International Council of the World Evangelical Fellowship. Joshua would also play an important role on the International Relations Commission of the Japan Evangelical Association.

Another miracle

With India's doors shut tight, the Tsutadas returned to Japan. First, there was a call to pastor a flock in Kyushu. Then in 1981 an invitation was received to become president of Immanuel Bible Training College. It was a great challenge since it was a time when the school needed to expand in terms of land and facilities. There were a few choice pieces of land adjacent to the campus, but there was none for sale. Landowners with holdings that are kept in the family from generation to generation feel obligated to their ancestors. Moreover, land prices in Japan are exorbitantly high.

In 1987 Joshua was burdened to bring this need to the entire college family during weekly Monday evening prayer meeting that runs until after midnight. As usual, the first two hours of prayer focused on Scripture reading, meditation on the Word, and prayer for personal needs. The remainder of the evening is taken up with intercessory prayer. Joshua proposed that the latter portion of the service focus on the need for land, with specific emphasis on the neighboring landowners, that they would be moved on their own to offer the land. An hour or so had passed when Joshua received assurance from the Lord that the prayer had been answered. He rose to share this news with the congregation. The service concluded with praise to the Lord.

The next morning Joshua's routine in the office was interrupted by an unexpected visit. One of the neighbors entered apologetically. He had failed to make an appointment, but there was an urgent matter that needed immediate attention. The previous night he had met with his three brothers to discuss how to pay the huge inheritance tax on the land their father, who had passed away six months ago, had left them. They had the choice of selling any one of twenty plots but had reached the unanimous decision to sell the one next to the college. As a neighbor, they thought, the school should be given first choice. Joshua found it hard to contain himself. It took strong effort to maintain a poker face and to reply calmly, "Thank you for sharing this information. We will consider."

Answered prayer

Joshua spent much time in prayer. One and a half million dollars seemed like an unsurmountable sum to him. But all things are possible with God. After all, He owns the land. Why then take out a twenty-five-year loan? Would it not make sense to ask God to give it all in one lump sum? What a testimony it would be to hand the neighbor the total amount in cash in exchange for the land. Once again he had assurance of God's help.

Routine office work occupied Joshua all day. That evening he had to attend to another item of business at the Tokyo headquarters of the Wesleyan Mission. It had been a long day. Joshua was already at the door as everyone filed out. The newly appointed mission director tugged lightly on Joshua's shoulder. "Josh, do you have a minute? I would like to pass something by you. Our mission headquarters is located in a very choice section of Tokyo. There is no strategic benefit, however. I have been thinking of relocating—perhaps to Yokohama; in fact, I already had an estimate of the property. The sale would generate more than the cost of relocating. Off hand, I would say that we would have a surplus of a million and a half dollars. Would there be any specific project in which the college could use the funds?"

Joshua listened in amazement as God's answer to his prayer unfolded before his eyes. God's generosity showed itself even more clearly when it turned out that the actual figure would be 25 percent more than promised.

What a day of rejoicing it was when in November 1989 the new property, with a large chapel and two additional buildings, was dedicated debt free. The total project cost 6.5 million dollars. The lovely new chapel has opened its doors on Sundays to the community. Presently attendance ranges from 150 to 160. Most parishioners are converted and have been baptized.

Joshua Tsutada especially rejoiced that from the community each year at least one young person is admitted to Immanuel Bible Training College and that about 65 percent of the total church income is being channeled to missions. Truly when God closed the door to India for Joshua and Esther, He opened the door to Japan and the world.

How faithful the Lord has been to David and Joshua Tsutada of Japan, and their families! How faithful He is to all who will trust in Him!

Siegfried Buss

Africa

MARTYR BISHOP IN UGANDA

James Hannington

1847–1885

God turned a boyish prankster into a courageous pioneer of the gospel. Although other missionaries actually served longer and may be better known, the Church Missionary Society stated that "Bishop Hannington did more for Africa in his death than in his life." James Hannington, who was concerned "more about saving souls than saving money," led Anglican evangelization in East Equatorial Africa for less than two years before a fearful Ugandan king ordered his killing. Many young people decided to become missionaries after learning about Hannington's martyrdom.

SEEKING CAREER: *Handsome, wealthy young man, full of fun, loves travel, has military commission.*
JOB OFFER: *Missionary to help open Central Africa to the gospel. Applicant must be prepared for deprivation, illness, and possibly violent death.*

Only God could bring those two statements together. And therein lies the story of James Hannington, first Anglican bishop of East Equatorial Africa.

James got his start on September 3, 1847, as the youngest of eight children in a wealthy businessman's family in Sussex, England. His father and grandfather were stern disciplinarians, but uppermost in James's young mind seemed to be mischief and fun, coupled with fearlessness. For instance, one day at the age of seven, James was found dangling by the seat of his pants from the top of the mast of his father's yacht—a place he had no business to be. On another occasion James lost a thumb when he used dynamite to destroy a wasp nest.

His father, Charles Hannington, sent teenager James off to private school to groom him for the family business, but the headstrong lad had no stomach for academics. Schoolboy pranks were more to his liking, and on a single day he endured canings for misdemeanors twelve times. However, James was also known for dependability and truthfulness.

James found his real interest in sailing, military service, and travel. Before he turned seventeen, he was commissioned as a second lieutenant in a volunteer regiment. The dashing young Englishman cut a popular figure on trips to the continent—Paris especially. Companions tended to look to Big Jim as a natural leader.

From prankster to priest

Then at the age of twenty-one, he stunned everyone by entering St. Mary's Hall, Oxford, to study for the Anglican priesthood. He failed his first try at the bishop's examination, but passed on a second try.

So the fun-loving boy became a parish priest. But a boyhood friend, who also became a curate, knew that James had one vital lack in his life—personal salvation. Rev. E. C. Dawson prayed much for him and finally wrote, telling how he himself had come to personal faith and urging James "to make a definite surrender of himself to the Savior of the world and join the society of His disciples."

Hannington did not appreciate the letter, but could not shake off feeling under growing conviction. After thirteen months he finally wrote Dawson desperately: "I have no faith! I can lay hold of nothing and I feel I have no right to preach to others. Shall I

James was also known for dependability and truthfulness.

> *He jumped out of bed*
> *praising God for salvation.*

The Life of
James Hannington

1847   Born on September 3

1877   Marries Blanche Hankin-Turvin

1882   First trip to Africa

1884   Consecrated bishop of East
Equatorial Africa on June 24;
Second trip to Africa

1885   Killed on October 29

AFRICA

UGANDA

ever be able to say, 'Jesus is mine and I am His'?"

Dawson kept praying for his friend. One night as Hannington was reading a booklet, *Grace and Truth,* Christ's forgiveness of sin became personally real. He jumped out of bed praising God for salvation.

Called to Africa

Although Hannington was never known as an eloquent preacher, he had a great heart for evangelism. That involved him with evangelistic missions of the Anglican Church Missionary Society (CMS), and he became aware of the spiritual needs of countless people in other lands.

James and a young lady from his parish, Blanche Hankin-Turvin, had in 1877, launched what proved to be a very happy marriage, blessed with three children. But he became drawn increasingly to evangelism.

It was the murder of two CMS missionaries on the shores of Lake Victoria Nyanza in the 1880s that challenged Hannington to consider foreign missionary service.

Hannington had read the appeal of the explorer Henry Stanley for more missionaries to enter Uganda, and the personal request of the ruler, Mtesa I. In 1882, the year of the first Protestant baptism in Uganda, Hannington responded to the challenge and led an expedition of six to Africa. He kept a detailed diary, recording customs and experiences, illustrated with graphic pen sketches and sprinkled with humor. The party was attacked by wild animals and warriors, but with typical fearlessness, James trekked on. Once when his porters fled from two hundred menacing warriors, Hannington marched up to them alone and unarmed. "Why do you want to kill a white man?" he demanded—as the nonplussed marauders slunk into the bush.

What did defeat Hannington were fever and dysentery. Twice he was left for dead but revived. Eventually, however, ill health forced him back to England, arriving June 10, 1883. Doctors forbade him to go anywhere for six months, and never again to Africa.

James Hannington was a skilled illustrator. A humorous sketch he made showing how he crossed a stream in Africa.

Return to East Equatorial Africa

But in two months the middle-aged Hannington was asking the CMS for another assignment in Africa. The bishops felt the need for closer supervision of the widely scattered emerging churches in East Africa, and decided that James had the right qualifications: "authority to command, wisdom to organize, and character to ensure obedience." They consecrated James Hannington as bishop of East Equatorial Africa June 24, 1884, and the new bishop arrived in Mombasa, Kenya, January 24, 1885.

"People seem to stand in awe of a bishop," he wrote to his wife, who stayed in England with the children, "but they need not, for I am an exceedingly meek and unpretentious individual!"

By this time God had taken the cockiness out of Hannington while preserving his leadership qualities. (He never lost his sense of humor, seeing the funny side in even the worst plights.) But this Englishman did not go to Africa for adventure or to extend colonial empire, or out of cultural arrogance—as critics of missions allege. His diary and letters show that his main concern was for the spiritual need of others—fellow Christians as well as the unevangelized.

"I want to hear more about saving souls than saving money," he urged his missionaries and clergy. He was impatient with sterile officialdom, complaining that letters from headquarters in Britain lacked spiritual input: "Oh that someone would enquire after our souls and draw out the depths of our hearts!"

Into Uganda

A trek inland to Mount Kilimanjaro convinced Hannington he was fit to attempt another expedition to Uganda, to encourage the missionaries and believers. He decided that a different route through the northeast would be better than the usual tedious journey around the malaria-infested lake. Knowing that Masai warriors could be a threat, he decided not to risk the lives of his missionary colleagues but set out with a veteran African chaplain, Rev. William Jones, and two hundred porters on July 23, 1885.

But Hannington apparently was unaware of a greater danger to his expedition than roving Masai warriors. King Mtesa had died, and his ruthless son, eighteen-year-old Mwanga, was haunted by an ancient prediction that the kingdom would be overthrown by a white man invading from the northeast. The young king's fear was increased by reports of German annexation of lands in

East Africa. Arab traders persuaded him that missionaries were imperial agents.

Mwanga turned out to be as murderous as his father, killing innocent people on any whim. Upset by Christian condemnation of these murders, he lashed out at the church. The refusal of Christian pageboys to submit to his homosexual passions also enraged Mwanga, who burned thirty-two of them to death in one day.

Then messengers brought word that a white man was approaching from the northeast with two hundred men. The CMS leader in Uganda, Alexander Mackay, listened with concern as he heard a description of the white man: "Tall, bearded, with only one thumb." Mackay knew it was the bishop. He dispatched runners with a warning to Hannington, but they were unable to intercept him.

James Hannington had already reached the north shore of the lake with fifty selected porters, leaving the others encamped with Chaplain Jones in Kenya.

When Hannington reached the lake, a vassal of King Mwanga, Chief Lupwa, beat and robbed the party, imprisoning them while awaiting instructions from Mwanga. Within a few days three messengers arrived with orders—to free the captives, Hannington was led to believe. But on October 29, as they were led out to anticipated freedom, the prisoners were speared to death.

The price of the road

Bishop Hannington had kept his journal right up to the end, and a survivor of his party smuggled it and eyewitness details of the bishop's final hours back to Chaplain Jones.

"Tell your king that I have purchased the road to [Uganda] with my death!" the missionary had told his assailants before crumpling to the ground in a pool of his blood.

"Hannington did more for Africa in his death than in his life," stated CMS headquarters. "Within a few weeks after the news came to England, fifty men had offered themselves to CMS for service in the mission field; and Hannington's name has continued to be a great inspiration to many."

In fact, the faithfulness and courage of Hannington and other Christian martyrs, black and white, have provided the soil for

Another sketch by Hannington, showing the interest he evoked from Africans.

virile church growth and spiritual revival in Uganda. Often this has been under great persecution, from King Mtesa's day to the more recent tyranny of General Idi Amin. From the church in Uganda, God has raised up strong evangelical leaders, such as Bishop Festo Kivengere, who have blessed the world.

The road to Uganda, opened for the gospel at the great cost of blood, has become a two-way street of powerful Christian testimony.

Harold Fuller

Further Reading

Berry, William Grinton. *Bishop Hannington, The Life and Adventures of a Missionary Hero.* London: Religious Tract Society, 1910.

Dawson, E. C. *James Hannington, A History of His Life and Work.* London: Seeley, 1887.

Michael, Charles D. *James Hannington of East Africa: The Merchant's Son Who Was Martyred for Africa.* London: Pickering & Inglis, 1920.

VISION FOR THE SUDAN

Rowland Bingham

1872–1942

More than a hundred years ago, a Scottish-Canadian widow began praying for the millions of unreached people in a vast stretch of Africa known then as the Sudan. As a result of Mrs. Gowans's concern and prayers, her son Walter and two of his friends sailed to Nigeria to begin a work that was to become known as the Sudan Interior Mission. Within a year, Walter Gowans and Thomas Kent died of malaria in Nigeria. The third man, Rowland Bingham, returned to Canada alone and broken, but determined to carry on the vision of opening the interior of West Africa to the gospel.

From a mother's prayers and tremendous sacrifice emerged a mission that has a strong 100-year history of spreading the gospel throughout the world. It is now known as SIM (Society for International Ministries) and works in twenty-three countries of Africa, Asia, and South America. SIM's nineteen hundred missionaries represent more than thirty home countries and more than fifty denominations. Its ministries include evangelism, church planting, Christian education, healthcare, development, theological education, Bible translation, radio, and literature. There are eight thousand SIM-related churches around the world, and many of these churches are also sending out their own missionaries for cross-cultural ministries.

Mrs Gowans's prayers continue to be answered today.

Rowland Bingham was only twenty years old when he and his two companions, Walter Gowans and Thomas Kent, first landed in Lagos, Nigeria in 1893. Their burning passion was to penetrate the interior of Nigeria and of the whole area known then as the Sudan—a continent-wide region stretching across the bulge of Africa from the Atlantic Ocean to the horn of Africa. Up to this point, missionaries had reached only the coastal areas of West Africa. Veteran missionaries warned of certain failure and probable death if the three pursued their determination to go interior: "Young men, you will never see the Sudan; your children will never see the Sudan; your grandchildren may."

The white man's grave

As they prepared for their journey, Bingham suffered a severe attack of malaria. Because he was so weakened, the three decided that he should stay on the coast to get supplies and to maintain contact. The other two began the journey inland. Soon they would experience firsthand why this area was called "the white man's grave." Within the year, both Gowans (age twenty-three) and Kent (age twenty-five) died of malaria.

Five months later, Bingham returned to Canada with nothing to show for his effort but two graves. He told of visiting Mrs. Gowans to give her the few personal belongings of her son: "As I was shown into her parlour, she met me with extended hand. We stood there with hands clasped in silence for a while. Then she said these words that I will never forget: 'Well, Mr. Bingham, I would rather have had Walter go out to the Sudan, and die there, all alone, than have him home today disobeying the Lord.'"

Bingham went through a crisis of faith when he returned from his failed mission.

> *Within the year,*
> *both Gowans and Kent*
> *died of malaria.*

He had left two faithful colleagues buried in West Africa. Why should those most anxious to take the gospel to millions in darkness be cut off right at the beginning of their careers? He struggled for months before he was finally "brought back to the solid rock."

He devoted the next few years to study, first a six-month course in medical studies and then theological education at A. B. Simpson's New York Missionary Training College (which later became Nyack College). He served as a student pastor during this time and continued to promote the cause of evangelizing the Sudan.

On May 24, 1897, Rowland Bingham and Helen Blair were united in marriage. Four years earlier, Helen's father had depleted his bank account to help finance Bingham's first journey to Africa. Now he also gave him his daughter. Three days after the wedding, Bingham officially organized the interdenominational board of the Sudan Interior Mission.

Rowland and Helen Blair Bingham.

The Life of Rowland Bingham

1872	Born in England, December 19
1888	Conversion
1889	Emigrates to Canada
1890	Joins Salvation Army
1892	Commits life to foreign missions under ministry of A. J. Gordon
1893	First effort to enter the interior of Nigeria
1896	Enters New York Missionary Training College
1897	Marries Helen Elizabeth Blair Organization of Sudan Interior Mission board
1900	Second failed attempt to enter the Sudan
1901	First mission station established in Patigi, Nigeria
1904	Begins *Missionary Witness* magazine
1911	Magazine becomes the *Evangelical Christian*
1912	Becomes founder of Evangelical Publishers
1924	Establishes Canadian Keswick Bible Conference
1941	Sudan Interior Mission grows to four hundred missionaries
1942	Death of Rowland Bingham, December 8
1960	Death of Helen Bingham

AFRICA

NIGERIA

The ill-fated
Patigi party en
route for
Nigeria.

The second attempt

In 1900, Bingham and two others made another attempt to enter the Sudan. This time he left behind his wife and two-week-old daughter. Within three weeks of their arrival, Bingham was again stricken with malaria. Doctors at the government hospital ordered him home, not expecting him to live. As he was carried to the ship on a stretcher, his two companions assured him that they would carry on. But discouragement set in, and they followed on the next boat.

Later Bingham wrote, "It would have been easier for me, perhaps, had I died in Africa, for on that homeward journey I died another death. Everything seemed to have failed, and I went through the darkest period of my whole life."

Bingham recovered remarkably and continued to pursue his vision for opening the interior of the Sudan. By the beginning of 1901, four new recruits were ready to sail for Nigeria. Bingham did not join them this time, but stayed in Liverpool to organize the mission's British council. The party of four successfully established a mission station at Patigi. But within two years, two were sent home ill and a third was buried in Nigeria. Only one, A. W. Banfield, was able to continue in Africa.

It was about this time that medical science proved that mosquitoes transmit malaria. The discovery that quinine could cure malaria dramatically changed the whole record of death and failure in tropical countries. It was literally a new day for missions.

Growth of the mission

Once established, the Sudan Interior Mission grew steadily. Even during the years of the Depression, the mission doubled in size. By 1933, the mission had 230 members drawn from Britain, North America, New Zealand, and Australia. Churches, hospitals, and schools were established in Nigeria, French West Africa, and Ethiopia. By the time of Bingham's death in 1942, the mission had grown to four hundred missionaries, the largest "faith mission" in Africa.

Bingham traveled to Africa six different times to encourage the missionaries and to plan new outreaches. On one tour in 1914, he trekked fifteen hundred miles on foot, horseback, and cycle. It was on this trip, after twenty-one years of sacrifices and losses, that he began to see the fruit of all the struggle. Guy Playfair, a missionary to Egbe, Nigeria, described Bingham's reaction when he first met a group of fifteen hundred believers in that area: "He was overcome with sheer joy. The fountains of the deep were literally opened within his heart as tears of joy flowed down his cheeks. This was the supreme moment of his life and repaid all the sacrifice and heartaches of the past."

Bingham also traveled extensively in North America, Britain, Australia, and New Zealand. He promoted missions wherever he went and challenged many young people to give their lives for the cause of Christ. In fact, Bingham believed that the greatest need in *foreign* missions was a revival in the *home* churches. This conviction led him to serve as editor of a Christian magazine known as the *Evangelical Christian* from 1904 until his death in 1942. This became a tool for challenging Christians in the home countries to committed discipleship. It was also sent to missionaries all over the world, encouraging them in their task. A missionary in Baghdad was asked what helped him most in overcoming loneliness. The missionary answered, "Somebody sends me a paper, the *Evangelical Christian*, from Canada, and I get more spiritual help from that than from any other outside influence."

His concern for revival in the home churches also motivated Bingham to establish the Evangelical Publishers in 1912 and the Canadian Keswick Bible Conference in 1924. This summer-long ministry encouraged a deeper spiritual life and challenged people to respond to the needs of the world. Bingham also used Keswick as a training ground for new missionary recruits.

In all of Bingham's projects—the mission, the magazine, the publishing house, and the Bible conference, he emphasized the need to work across denominational lines. "The lines of fellowship must be drawn horizontally," he said. He recognized that "some of the best saints that God and grace have made" were to be found in various denominations. He believed that God would be honored by cooperation and fellowship within the whole church of Christ. While insisting on loyalty to the fundamentals of the faith, he urged Christians to take their place as servants under one common Lord, forgetting their minor differences.

Throughout Bingham's ministry, his wife, Helen, was a strong and capable partner. She was on the boards of the Sudan Interior Mission, Canadian Keswick, and Evangelical Publishers. During the early years of the mission, she often functioned as the acting

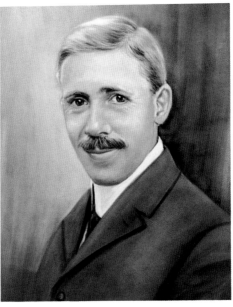

Rowland
Bingham
(1872–1942).

administrator during Rowland's lengthy journeys. As head of the Toronto mission home, she played a key role in evaluating missionary applicants. She also wrote a book, *Irish Saint*, and played an important role in the editorial details of the *Evangelical Christian*.

If Bingham could visit Africa today, he would find strong churches making an impact on their nations. In Nigeria, he would find more than twenty-five hundred SIM-related churches, and he would meet the leaders of one of the world's largest indigenous missions, the Evangelical Missionary Society, with more than nine hundred Nigerian missionaries in cross-cultural ministries. For one whose passion in life was missions, there could be no greater joy than to know that the churches he helped to begin also have a vision for cross-cultural outreach.

James and Carol Pluedemann

Further Reading

Bingham, Rowland. *Seven Sevens and a Jubilee!* Toronto: Evangelical Publishers; Grand Rapids: Zondervan, 1943.

Hunter, James. *A Flame of Fire: The Life and Work of R. V. Bingham.* SIM, 1961.

Root from Dry Ground: The Story of the Sudan Interior Mission. SIM, 1966.

"I CANNOT DENY MY JESUS!"

Evangelist Wandaro of Ethiopia

*c.*1910–1991

The simple youth from the hills may have seemed most unlikely material for an evangelist, but he probably won more people to Christ than anyone else in southern Ethiopia—during a time of tremendous persecution. His name was Wandaro. Amazingly enough, he had formerly been a Satan worshiper.

"Curse Jesus!" yelled the Ethiopian official, grabbing Wandaro by his beard. "I cannot deny my Jesus!" Wandaro replied, his teeth clenched with pain as the official yanked out a fistful of hair.

Only ten years before, Wandaro had been following Satan. His father was the witch doctor on Mount Humbo, among the Wolayto people of southern Ethiopia. What a radical change. Now he would risk death for Satan's conqueror, Jesus Christ. What had happened?

One rainy day on his way to market, Wandaro had noticed a clinic erected by a newly arrived white man and woman who gave sick people a different kind of medicine than his father dispensed. The white man, Earl Lewis, beckoned Wandaro and several others to take shelter from the deluge. Inside, Lewis began reading from a strange book.

A book—brought by a foreigner! Was this what the Ethiopian prophet Asa had prophesied long ago? Wandaro wondered. *A foreigner would bring a book telling about the Creator, whom people should worship instead of Satan.*

The next week Wandaro returned for more of this news, and eventually, in Ethiopian fashion, declared, "I renounce Satan to follow Jesus." Fear of evil spirits vanished, and for the first time he felt "joy in his stomach."

Wandaro longed to read more about God for himself, but he had never been to school. Mrs. Lewis helped him learn the 256 characters of the Amharic alphabet. Wandaro was the slowest in the group, but his love for his Savior burned strongly. In 1933 he and nine others became the first Wolaytos baptized.

One Sunday he stood up in the worship service and pointed out that the clinic was too small for the increasing number of believers. Everyone liked his suggestion that they build a house for God just as they built their own grass houses—all the neighbors giving a hand. Wandaro's next project was to build a meeting hut in his own town of Humbo.

Wandaro's baby boy

Then fever struck Wandaro's baby boy. His father, the witch doctor, predicted that unless Wandaro sacrificed to Satan, the infant would die. "I love my baby boy, but I will not sacrifice to the demons again!" Wandaro declared.

The child did die, and all of Mount Humbo turned out to wail, gashing their faces and chests. "Stop!" Wandaro pleaded. "I miss my child, but God has given me peace in the face of death. I believe that my son is safe in the arms of Jesus."

His teenage wife could not understand Wandaro, nor could she withstand the pressures of her Satan-worshiping family. She left her husband. Eventually, however,

"I love my baby boy, but I will not sacrifice to the demons again!"

she returned to Wandaro because of the amazing changes she saw in his life, and she too believed.

Chief Dana Maja

Once a slave trader was examining his tobacco crops down in the lowlands, when a gangly hillbilly walked up to him. Chief Dana Maja was startled as well as offended, for strangers avoided him lest he capture them as slaves. But this shabby peasant didn't even prostrate himself before the area's most notorious slaver! And what the

Evangelist Wandaro of Ethiopia.

man was saying shocked Dana Maja even more.

"Master," Wandaro said very simply and directly. "Some day you will die. If you do not repent and believe on Jesus Christ, you will go to hell. You will burn in the lake of fire that never goes out!"

Never had Dana Maja heard anything like this. Trembling, instead of ordering his bodyguards to capture Wandaro, he asked the evangelist what he meant. Wandaro explained the gospel message very simply.

Later, when Italian warplanes dropped bombs from the sky, the terrified chief was certain that eternal judgment had begun. In panic he sought for Wandaro and found him at a river in the midst of a baptismal service. Several of the new believers were slaves who had escaped from Dana Maja, and when they saw the chief, they scrambled out on the opposite bank of the river. But now the slaver was seeking only the Savior. And Wandaro, beaming with a smile the shape of a new moon, was there to welcome him into the kingdom. Dana Maja eventually became

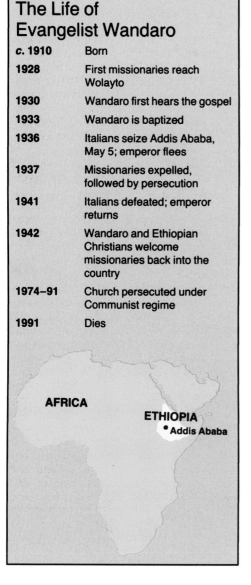

The Life of Evangelist Wandaro

c. 1910	Born
1928	First missionaries reach Wolayto
1930	Wandaro first hears the gospel
1933	Wandaro is baptized
1936	Italians seize Addis Ababa, May 5; emperor flees
1937	Missionaries expelled, followed by persecution
1941	Italians defeated; emperor returns
1942	Wandaro and Ethiopian Christians welcome missionaries back into the country
1974–91	Church persecuted under Communist regime
1991	Dies

AFRICA

ETHIOPIA

• Addis Ababa

a dedicated leader of the Word of Life churches started by the Sudan Interior Mission.

Persecution

When the government fell to the invaders in 1936, Italian soldiers marched into Wolayto country. The Roman Catholic invaders and Ethiopian Orthodox priests found common cause in attacking evangelicals. Corrupt officials, resentful of evangelical witness, saw their opportunity to get rid of foreign missionaries.

SIM (then Sudan Interior Mission, now Society for International Ministries) had reached Wolayto in 1928. One year after the invasion, in 1937, they were forced out, leaving only forty-eight baptized believers. Tears rolled down Wandaro's cheeks as the missionaries were evicted. Through their own tears, the missionaries called back, "We are leaving you, but God is not leaving you!"

Once the foreigners were gone, persecution descended on the believers like a baptism of fire. They were rounded up and beaten, their churches were burned, and their leaders imprisoned. They worshiped in secret, hiding their precious Bible portions

> *He ordered him to be beaten and his church torn down.*

in buried pots. But what puzzled the invaders and their Ethiopian collaborators was the continued growth of the churches. Pagan bystanders were convicted as they heard the testimony of Christians being beaten for their faith, and they too trusted in Christ.

Enraged at the spread of the gospel, one Amharic official, Fiturari Dogesa, from Mount Humbo, decided he would make Wandaro an example. He ordered him to be beaten and his church torn down.

"Now will you give up this religion?" Dogesa shouted, shaking the evangelist by the beard.

His face bleeding, Wandaro replied, "Never!" Furious, Dogesa tied up Wandaro in the marketplace.

"Do not listen to Wandaro—see how he is bound!" he declared to everyone. "Do not go to his church. It is torn down!"

Although tied up like a criminal, Wandaro witnessed to the throngs in the marketplace: "This rope is not the final judgment—it is only placed on me by man!" he called

A Christian gathering in Ethiopia.

out. "Believe on the Lord Jesus Christ and you will be freed from sin!"

Three-hour flogging

The official ordered his guards to scourge the evangelist with the cruel hippo hide whip. "The foreigners have all gone," Dogesa taunted. "They aren't here to help you. Give up!"

"I am not serving the missionaries, but the God who sent them." Wandaro testified. "He will strengthen me."

What was supposed to be a public warning that would stop the spread of the gospel had now become a contest between a powerful official and a powerless believer. Dogesa turned up the heat. The next day he appointed five men to take turns publicly flogging Wandaro for three hours. Then they threw the evangelist's flayed body into the bamboo lock-up. For several days Wandaro hovered on the brink of death as his family and friends wept and prayed for him. Finally he sent them a message: "I think I will live. Do not weep. The Lord is with me."

For a year Wandaro was imprisoned, but he was such a model prisoner that at times the guards left him in charge while they took time off duty. Upon being released, one of his first acts was to gather the believers to help Dogesa harvest his crops. Even after that, Dogesa challenged Wandaro to a debate with the Orthodox priests, declaring that if the evangelicals lost the debate, three of them must die. Before the appointed day, Dogesa fell over backward and died. The debate was never held.

When other officials placed a price on Wandaro's head—dead or alive—his friends advised him to go into hiding; they needed him alive. When the Italian invasion ended in 1941, the authorities had to focus on other urgent matters, and Wandaro continued preaching the gospel across the valleys and over the hills of central Ethiopia.

Missionaries return

Missionaries were allowed back into Ethiopia in 1942, and they cautiously inquired about the few believers they had left in Wolayto. They were astounded to learn that the forty-eight they had left had multiplied to ten thousand, with possibly one hundred churches! Their number grew to fifteen thousand by the time the missionaries reached Wolayto in 1943. Vast crowds of believers turned out to meet them, this time with tears of joy.

And among them was Wandaro—his body covered with scars but his face wreathed in that familiar wide smile.

"Welcome, welcome!" he cried, embracing the missionaries. "This is like heaven! God has sent you back. We need you to teach the new believers. See how many there are now, but they are untaught!"

Amazed, the missionaries looked up and saw lines of white-shawled believers streaming toward them over the hilly paths, chanting antiphonal hymns. God had used Wandaro to win many of them to his Jesus.

These had come to spiritual birth in an era of suffering—an era that would be repeated with even greater ferocity during the Communist regime of the 1970s and 1980s. And still encouraging them to stand true was Wandaro, then an old man but with the same solid faith and simple smile.

Harold Fuller

Further Reading

Cotterell, F. Peter. *Born at Midnight.* Chicago: Moody, 1973.

Davis, Raymond J. *Fire on the Mountains.* Scarborough: Sudan Interior Mission, 1980.

Fuller, W. Harold. *Run While the Sun Is Hot.* Chicago: Moody, 1967.

PASSIONATE MISSIONARY DOCTOR

PASSIONATE MISSIONARY DOCTOR
Dr. Helen Roseveare
1925–

Helen Roseveare is a woman who lived ahead of her time. In the 1950s when most women aspired to marriage, children, and keeping house, she chose a career as a doctor and medical missionary. Instead of staying home in England, she moved to Africa where she built medical centers, practiced medicine, and trained medical personnel.

A pioneer at heart, she risked her personal safety for her work. Consequently, she refused to leave the Congo when civil war broke out and most whites moved to Kenya. Soldiers attacked, raped, and imprisoned her along with other missionaries and foreigners. After five months of captivity, she went home to England and vowed never to return. But she went back because the African medical personnel needed her.

Working with doctors from other mission boards, Helen helped establish the Evangelical Medical Center, a hospital and training college in northeast Congo. In conjunction with that hospital, she established bush clinics and a flying doctor service to provide needed care in local areas.

Helen realized the culmination of her dream for medical work in Africa when the government granted accreditation for the training school so nationals could practice medicine with a Christian perspective. In the same year (1971), the first man she trained became the medical director at her first hospital, placing it under national control.

For Helen, Christians will be missionaries when they fall in love with Christ again.

I want people to be passionately in love with Jesus, so that nothing else counts," declared Dr. Helen Roseveare, former missionary doctor in the Congo (now called Zaire). "I'm a fanatic, if you like, but only because I believe so strongly that nothing counts except knowing your sins have been forgiven by the blood of Jesus. We've only got this short life to get others to know the same truth."

Helen has lived this philosophy since she came to know Christ as her Savior when she was a college freshman. Reared in a non-Christian home, she was conscious of God and her need for Him while a child. Although she was confirmed, went to church services, and participated in religious activities, she did not have a personal relationship with God. When she attended college at Cambridge, she met students whose faith in God was genuine and relevant to daily life.

The last night of her first Christmas break, she met God through reading Scripture. And that same night she asked Him for the privilege of being a missionary for Him. "From the moment I fell in love with Him, everything else was secondary to one thing—becoming a missionary."

That single-mindedness carried her through medical school, even though she did not like medicine. Becoming a doctor was her father's dream. Although she wanted to be an evangelist, she recognized that God had called her to be a medical missionary.

Doctor in the Congo
Eight years after her conversion, she stepped on African soil, sent by Heart of Africa Mission, later known as Worldwide Evangelization Crusade (WEC). Her first assignment was at the Ibambi, Congo, station. There she set up a dispensary and began to practice

Dr. Helen
Roseveare.

The Life of Helen Roseveare

1925	Born in Haileybury, Hertfordshire, England, September 21
1945	Conversion
1951	Graduates from Newham College, Cambridge, with a medical degree Worldwide Evangelization Crusade (WEC) accepts her as a missionary candidate
1953	Arrives in the Congo (now Zaire), sets up dispensary in Ibambi Builds hospital and trains African nurses
1958	Takes first furlough for more medical training
1960	Returns to the Congo two weeks before independence is declared
1964	Rebel soldiers capture her in the Congo civil war
1965	Leaves the Congo after being freed from captors, vows never to return
1966	Returns to the Congo to establish Evangelical Medical Center
1971	Government accredits medical training school Turns hospital in Nebobongo over to African leadership
1973	Leaves the Congo and returns to England Travels to represent WEC
1976	Joins WEC staff, first as a teacher at WEC Missionary Training College in Glasgow, Scotland, then as home base staff, speaking and writing for the mission board

AFRICA

CONGO (ZAIRE)

medicine. "I knew none of their language, they knew none of mine. The ink was hardly dry on my medical diploma and overnight I became the Senior Chief Consultant of everything from pediatrics to geriatrics and everything in between. But this [situation] in itself forced me back on God."

Helen worked at an obsessive pace, fiercely dedicated to her work. Africa was still primitive in those days, and she treated diseases that were only descriptions in her school's medical books. Many times she improvised care without drugs or proper instruments, depending on God for healing. And when she had opportunities, she told her patients about Christ and His provision for spiritual healing. Medicine was for her a way to introduce an unreached audience to Christ.

Six months after she arrived, a sixteen-year-old African Christian named John Mangadima appeared at the clinic. He changed Helen's vision of medical work in the Congo and provided a way to enlarge her audience. John wanted her to teach him to be a doctor.

> *"I want people to be passionately in love with Jesus, so that nothing else counts."*

So Helen taught John medicine, and John helped her become fluent in Swahili, the language of her patients. But more important, John's request crystallized a dream to train nationals to care for their own people. To accomplish that dream, Helen needed a hospital with trained nurses. So she recruited others to train with John and supervised the building of a thirty-two-bed hospital. Eighteen months later, four of her five students passed the government exam for the aid nurse diploma.

But the other missionaries on her station were not as thrilled as she was at this accomplishment. Instead, the field committee asked her to move the medical center to Nebobongo because they did not view medical training as missionary work.

That move necessitated building a new hospital and assuming the leadership of a station by herself. But Helen's dedication to the medical work God had given her resulted in a larger hospital and training center within a year.

One of Helen's main frustrations was not being able to evangelize like she wanted to. "I longed to lead souls to the Lord and be used in straight evangelism. At one stage I was overwhelmed at just being a doctor—twenty-four hours a day, seven days a week—I was never getting to evangelism at all. There were six qualified African evangelists and their wives working at our hospital, and they were leading souls to the Lord every week. They had to show me that we can't all be the last link."

Two years later, another doctor joined her at the station as her superior. When he took over some of the administrative duties, Helen had time to establish out-station clinics staffed by trained nurses. She visited them monthly to diagnose diseases and treat patients who had problems beyond the nurses' abilities.

Loss of passion

At the end of five years in the Congo, Helen Roseveare felt like a failure. Her strong will, impatience, pride, and dictatorial nature had antagonized fellow missionaries. And in spite of her accomplishments, she did not think she had succeeded at anything. Furthermore, a lack of spiritual peace and fulfillment prompted her to consider resigning from the mission. So she gratefully accepted

> *A lack of spiritual peace and fulfillment prompted her to consider resigning from the mission.*

an early furlough.

During her two years in England, Helen completed more surgical training. She also thought much about her work in Africa. In the process, God gave her added confidence in medicine and peace in her spirit. By mid-1960 Helen was ready to return to the Congo.

Captive in the Congo

But the Congo was not the same country she left. The people were anticipating independence from Belgium, and the Belgian colonial administration had left the country. Whites were leaving, not entering, the Congo to escape the riots and violence. Getting in was difficult, but Helen insisted it was her home and ignored warnings to stay out.

Three weeks after returning, civil war broke out and violence against whites began. Mission boards ordered their staffs to leave. Helen refused to depart. Instead, she continued her medical work in the midst of the turmoil and lawlessness. God had called her, and she was needed.

However, staying in the Congo turned into a nightmare. In the next four years, Helen was attacked, beaten, raped, and finally arrested by rebel Simba soldiers. She and the other prisoners lived with the constant fear of being murdered as most foreigners were. During the five months of captivity she continued to tell people about God and the peace He wanted to give them. Because she had experienced rape, she was able to comfort and witness to other rape victims. In addition, she boldly talked to her captors about God.

Finally, at the end of 1964, a group of international mercenary soldiers found Helen's group of women and children and freed them. On New Year's Day, she flew out of Africa to England. Helen vowed never to go back to the Congo. The terror and violence of the past few months had frightened and frozen her.

But in August, Helen received a letter from John Mangadima in Congo. He wrote

Dr. Roseveare
with a new
Land Rover on
her return to
Congo (Zaire)
in 1966.

about the destitute conditions at the hospital at Nebobongo and compared the Congo to the time before the first missionaries. That letter was a turning point for Helen; she decided to go back.

Return to the Congo
Seven months after receiving Mangadima's letter, Helen returned and discovered that John Mangadima had replaced her as the doctor at Nebobongo. Although the people had lost nearly everything, they still had their faith in God.

That term she worked with a doctor from another mission board to establish the Evangelical Medical Center—a hospital, training college, airstrip for a flying doctor service, and four bush clinics in northeast Congo. The goal was to consolidate the medical efforts of several missionary organizations and to gain government accreditation of the school.

In less than a decade, her plans became a reality and surpassed her twenty-year-old dream of a network of clinics throughout that area of the country. In 1971, she appointed John Mangadima as the hospital director at Nebobongo, thus turning the leadership over to the nationals. The same day she received the news that the government had granted her school the coveted accreditation.

Challenge to Christians
Two years later, Dr. Helen Roseveare left the Congo for the last time, broken instead of rejoicing. Failing to resolve a student strike, she resigned as director of the medical college three months before she was due to leave.

But God gave her another avenue for service in which she is still involved. Helen travels and writes as a representative for WEC. God had, as Helen said, "given a new 'baby' to nurture, in making known the urgent needs of millions throughout the world, as yet unreached by the gospel of God's redeeming love, and the endless opportunities available, for those who would enter God's service with this one burning desire in their hearts, to make Christ known."

Through her speaking, God has called young people to missionary service and challenged older people to pray for missions. But as materialism has changed Christians, her message has changed. "Now I tell Christians, wherever they are, that they must 'refall' in love with Jesus. Christianity in the West today says we must have a bigger church and a bigger car and a better suit. Once Christians fall out of love with that and in love with Jesus, I won't need to talk mission; they will become missionaries because they love Him."

Lin Johnson

Further Reading

Burgess, Alan. *Daylight Must Come: The Story of a Courageous Woman Doctor in the Congo.* New York: Delacorte, 1974.

Roseveare, Helen. *Doctor Among Congo Rebels.* Fort Washington, Pa.: CLC, 1965.

——. *Give Me This Mountain.* Leicester, England: Inter-Varsity, 1966.

——. *He Gave Us a Valley.* Leicester, England: Inter-Varsity, 1976.

——. *Living Faith.* Minneapolis: Bethany House, 1987.

——. *Living Holiness.* Minneapolis: Bethany House, 1986.

——. *Living Sacrifice.* Minneapolis: Bethany House, 1979.

Tucker, Ruth A. *From Jerusalem to Irian Jaya.* Grand Rapids: Zondervan, 1983.

THE MAN AND THE MESSAGE FOR AFRICA

Tokunboh Adeyemo

1944–

President of Nigeria by 1973—that was what eighteen-year-old Tokunboh Adeyemo dreamed about as he graduated with honors from L.A. Teachers College in Ibadan, Western Nigeria, in 1962. Nothing was going to stop the ambitious and disciplined young Muslim from reaching his goal. He prepared and adopted a rigorous ten-year plan that would have culminated with him "occupying the presidential chair of my country."

Several hours a day devoted to private study, as much time invested in public political and social activity as possible, and a locally visible position of head of a school meant that Tokunboh's plan was on schedule. An uncle who served in Nigeria's first post-independence parliament became his mentor and nurtured Tokunboh's dream. Soon Tokunboh was elected to a party position at the local level.

Sidetracked to the unknown
But in 1966, a bloody coup rocked Nigeria. Many people in political positions were killed; others were put in jail. Adeyemo was in a sense fortunate; he was placed under house arrest, but his dream was shattered.

With his movements and activities curtailed and his very life tottering in the balance, the dreamer slowed down and began to reflect on deeper questions of life. "I started to ask questions . . . about life. . . . What is reality?"

At this time Tokunboh Adeyemo was in his early twenties. He had been born into a wealthy and royal Muslim family on October 1, 1944. Though the second-born in a family of eight, he was the first son and therefore was destined to be chief among his people in Nigeria's Oyo State.

Nigeria is the most populous country in Africa, and more than a third of its people

> *His credits as a world Christian leader are sterling: chairman of the World Evangelical Fellowship (WEF) Executive Council since 1981; general secretary of the Nairobi-based Association of Evangelicals of Africa and Madagascar (AEAM); one of the three editors of* Transformation *magazine; former acting principal of Nairobi Graduate School of Theology; much-appreciated speaker at international meetings of Christians. But something else makes these credits even more impressive: as a young man Tokunboh Adeyemo was a Muslim.*
>
> *How did the power of the gospel change a very talented Muslim into a Christian leader whose ministry the Lord has blessed in a very special way?*

are Muslim, mostly in the north. Though nearly half of the people claim to be Christian, evangelicals compose only about 14 percent of the population.

Despite his strong political ambitions, Adeyemo did not depart from his Muslim upbringing. He prayed five times a day, fasted during Ramadan, the Muslim holy month, and stayed away from practices forbidden by Muslim law. "Humanly speaking, I was righteous and pure," he says, but still, "I realized that something was lacking in my life."

During the period of house arrest, his quest for meaning and purpose become even more urgent. "What is the purpose of human existence? Where are we going?" he asked himself. At this critical moment Islam failed to satisfy his inner spiritual needs.

Earlier, Adeyemo had brushed aside an invitation to a church meeting extended to

The Life of Tokunboh Adeyemo

1944   Born in Nigeria, October 1

1962   Graduates from teachers college

1966   Conversion and baptism

1967   Becomes licensed evangelist by Evangelical Church of West Africa

1973   Graduates from Igbaja Theological Seminary

1976   Receives M.Div. and Th.M. from Talbot School of Theology

1977   Elected general secretary of the Association of Evangelicals of Africa and Madagascar

1978   Receives Th.D. from Dallas Theological Seminary

1979   Receives Ph.D. from the University of Aberdeen, Scotland

1981   Marries Ireti Ayelaagbe
Becomes chairman of the World Evangelical Fellowship (WEF) Executive Council

AFRICA

NIGERIA
• Ibadan

> *Adeyemo's passion is fueled by a fervent prayer life.*

him by one of his subordinate teachers. But, after the house arrest, Adeyemo accepted an invitation to attend a tent meeting. The preacher was E. White, a South African missionary. His message, based on John 10:10 ("The thief comes only to steal and kill and destroy; I have come that they may have life, and have it to the full"), left Adeyemo "captivated and arrested." "The message gripped my soul," he says.

He stayed after the service for a one-to-one talk with the preacher, who finally led him in the sinner's prayer. "Though I did not fully understand the full implication of what was going on, I knew beyond doubt that I was choosing to follow Jesus, the one who offers abundant life." That day was September 13, 1966.

The power of the gospel

The power of the gospel immediately took effect in Adeyemo's life. He had a deep desire to study the Bible, to pray, and to evangelize. "I could not contain my discovery within me. ... Every opportunity was seized to share the good news with others."

Adeyemo's passion for personal evangelism has not diminished since. Even as general secretary of the Association of Evangelicals of Africa and Madagascar (AEAM), a job requiring travel worldwide, Adeyemo still makes the effort to witness to at least one person per week.

Another aspect of Adeyemo's passion in ministry likewise began at his conversion and has not changed since. It is the desire to see people of the Muslim faith brought to the saving knowledge of Jesus Christ.

Adeyemo's passion is fueled by a fervent prayer life. At the Nairobi (Kenya) church of which he is an elder, he attends all-night prayer meetings. It is also his common practice to devote most of his Fridays to fasting, prayer, Bible reading, and meditation.

Adeyemo's entry into ministry followed an interesting path. Soon after his conversion, he enrolled in a "Back to the Bible" correspondence course in which he did so well that it was suggested he consider seminary. "Back to the Bible" founder Theodore Epp offered Adeyemo a scholarship to

Igbaja Theological Seminary in Nigeria in 1969.

Adeyemo's move into the ministry was therefore more of a natural progression than one based on a specific call. "I have never had what you may term a 'call'; my desire started at conversion."

To the United States

Adeyemo had said to God that if He gave him the opportunity for further training he would work hard and advance as far as possible. During his first night at Igbaja, Adeyemo says, "God showed me that He was taking me to America." And it happened. At the end of his course at Igbaja, a door opened for him to begin graduate studies at Talbot School of Theology in California in 1973.

The first year at Talbot was not at all easy. As Adeyemo himself puts it, he arrived with "no money, no apartment . . . nothing." Each time the bills came in he made a secret trip to the chapel to "spread it before God like Hezekiah." He often said, "Lord, You have to supply. I do not know anybody in this land." And God was always faithful; money came in mostly from unknown sources. At Talbot, Adeyemo excelled, doing a four-year program in three years and receiving the highest awards for both the M.Div. and Th.M. programs.

After Talbot, Adeyemo attended Dallas Theological Seminary for the Th.D. program, which he pursued between September 1976 and December 1977. This was a record time to finish a doctorate. At graduation he received the highest award for scholarship. Two years later Adeyemo finished further research and earned the Ph.D. from the University of Aberdeen in Scotland.

Leadership in the African church

In 1975, Byang Kato, then general secretary of the AEAM and one of Africa's outstanding evangelical leaders, died suddenly in a swimming accident. In 1977, at the AEAM general assembly in Ivory Coast, Tokunboh Adeyemo was elected to succeed Kato as general secretary.

Stepping into Byang Kato's shoes was not an easy task for the young, single, and untried Adeyemo. "I had never been a

Tokunboh Adeyemo in Manila, 1992.

> "The future of Africa
> is in your hands as
> a woman or man of God
> and of prayer."

national figure; I came from nowhere," he says. Adeyemo had only one assurance: "The hand of the Lord was upon me."

Indeed God's hand seems evident upon Adeyemo's ministry at AEAM, in his services as chairman of the international council of World Evangelical Fellowship, and as a speaker at international conferences.

But Adeyemo's Christian leadership roles have not led him to forget his Muslim family and background. His conversion to Christ greatly affected his Muslim family. When he was converted in 1966, most of his family was outraged. Particularly offensive was his zeal for prayer, fasting, Bible reading, and outreach. "My people could not take it any longer. They called a meeting to decide what they were going to do with this traitor."

Before the meeting, Adeyemo withdrew to a mountain for a three-day period of prayer and fasting during which the Scripture "Though my father and mother forsake me, the Lord will receive me" (Psalm 27:10) was impressed upon his heart. He would follow Jesus at all cost.

He was thrown out of the home and denied the privileges of the oldest son in a royal family. For three years he lived in an apartment rented with his teacher's stipend. But Adeyemo had no regrets. "Those three years were used to solidify my faith and to ground myself in the Word of God."

He was eventually reunited with his family and many relatives. His mother, brothers, and sister have all become Christians. From this personal experience Adeyemo has concluded that what Muslims need is a "demonstration," not a "definition," of the power of the gospel.

While he was studying in the United States, an uncle who is a chief wrote to him saying, "I have watched your life; I have seen consistency in your life."

A few years later when Adeyemo married his bride, Ireti Ayelaagbe, the same uncle, who himself remains a Muslim, repeated his comments about Adeyemo's Christian testimony. "Tokunboh," he said, "I have watched your life since you said you became a Christian and you have been consistent. You have impressed me. You are serious and dedicated."

Tokunboh and Ireti enjoy a happy family life. They have two boys: Samuel Bamidele (born 1982) and Salem Modupe (born 1984).

He began with the dream of becoming the leader of Nigeria. But as AEAM general secretary, Adeyemo now carries a Christian burden for all of Africa—a continent ravaged by civil war, political corruption, foreign exploitation, famine, and poverty—for which many see no hope.

For Adeyemo, the answer to Africa's woes is not in political ideologies or economic theories but in the fervent prayer of Christians in Africa. "The future of Africa is not in the hands of secular politicians, economists, developers, or financial institutions (with all of their good intentions), but in your hands as a woman or man of God and of prayer." This is a man of God, and this is a message Africa needs to hear.

Isaac Phiri

Mid East

APOSTLE TO ISLAM

Samuel Marinus Zwemer

1867–1952

Samuel Zwemer was born in Michigan on April 12, 1867, the thirteenth child of fifteen born to immigrant Dutch parents. His father was a pastor in the Reformed Church. Both father and son graduated from Hope College, Holland, Michigan. Four of Samuel's five surviving brothers became pastors; sister Nellie was a missionary to China. Adriaan and Catherina Boon Zwemer had produced a Christian family of which they could be justly proud.

An Arabian mission

After his college days Samuel Zwemer attended the seminary of the Reformed Church in America in New Brunswick, New Jersey. While there, he and a friend, James Cantine, became absorbed in the idea of missionary work in Arabia. After much prayer, and with the support of Hebrew and Arabic professor John G. Lansing, they developed plans for the Arabian Mission, intending it to be a self-supporting mission arm of the Reformed Church. Disappointed by their Mission Board's negative response, they still proceeded, convinced that God wanted them in Arabia. Zwemer was ordained on May 29, 1890.

Lack of support

Zwemer saw Arabia for the first time on January 12, 1891. During a brief stop at Jeddah, he visited the Muslim "tomb of Eve" shrine on the outskirts of Mecca. Then it was on to Yemen for two months with colleague and Arabian Mission co-founder James Cantine. "We were down with malarial fever," he wrote, "and our finances were never before or since in such straitened condition. We prayed and even fasted one

whole day. . . . The answer came in a long overdue remittance for salaries."

After almost ten years of hard missionary work in which he rode camels across the hot deserts of Arabia to reach yet more Muslims with the gospel, Zwemer found that widespread support for mission to the Muslims in the United States was lacking: "There is a general failure among Christians to realize the number and importance of the missionary promises in the Old Testament." He asked, "Is it not remarkable that nearly all of these Old Testament promises are grouped around the names of countries which now are the center and strength of the Muslim world?"

But in spite of all the biblical promises, Zwemer emphasized, "Arabia . . . is not a field for *feeble* faith. . . . The promises are great because the obstacles are great; that the glory of the plan as well as the glory of the work may be to God alone."

Marriage

Zwemer went to the mission field single, but the Lord had other designs. Jokingly, he spoke of having to follow local custom to "purchase" a wife, referring to the dowry system that still prevails today. He had been invited to teach Arabic to two Australian nurses who had come to Arabia under the umbrella of the Church Missionary Society (CMS). It was not long before Samuel proposed to one of them, Amy Wilkes, whom he married in 1896. But, in order for this to happen, he had to reimburse CMS her travel expenses, the required "dowry" for his spouse.

After marrying in Baghdad, the young couple moved to Bahrain, an independent

> "*There is a general failure among Christians to realize the number and importance of the missionary promises in the Old Testament.*"

island off the eastern coast of Saudi Arabia. They experienced a deep, deep sorrow there, for when they moved away fourteen years later, they left behind a tiny gravestone inscribed, "Worthy is the Lamb to receive riches." Under it were the remains of their two little daughters, both of whom perished within eight days of each other in July 1904. Their uncle, Peter Zwemer, missionary to Muskat had died six years earlier, as had other co-workers. Year after year in those early days, there was one burial after another from one disease or another, and yet the workers kept coming—a marvelous testimony to the spirit of sacrifice the gospel engenders.

Sam spent his last months in Bahrain alone while Amy was in the States with their four children. Theirs was a typical missionary separation, the need for children's schooling. This problem was soon relieved, for they all began living together again when the family moved to Cairo in 1912.

Both Amy and Sam had a great sense of humor and a way with words, gifts that proved useful during long years in foreign mission fields. Anecdote after anecdote can be told, but one will suffice. During a visit to Iran, Amy was enjoying an after-dinner cup of strong Turkish coffee when another missionary lady asked, "Mrs. Zwemer, do you drink coffee at night with impunity?"

"Why, no," she replied. "I drink it with cream and sugar."

Shortly after celebrating their fortieth wedding anniversary, Amy died suddenly, leaving a very lonely Samuel, who by this time had returned to the United States and was teaching at Princeton Theological Seminary. Some years later he married Margaret Clarke, a New York City spinster introduced to him by his old friend and coworker, James Cantine. She also proved to be a faithful helper, traveling regularly with Samuel and assisting with his writing. After ten years of wedded companionship, Zwemer said farewell to her, also. Three years before they had celebrated his eightieth birthday, Margaret, all four children, and fifteen grand-

Samuel Zwemer, an "apostle" to Islam, was one of those remarkable persons who not only learned a foreign language and culture well but, while carrying on an active evangelistic vocation, found time to do a great deal of writing—more than thirty books and a flood of articles. These matereials enable us to draw upon his rich experience while constantly challenging us to take seriously the Muslim world around us.

Zwemer enjoyed advantages that many modern missionaries to the Muslim world do not have. Today, distributing the Bible or gospel tracts is forbidden in many Muslim lands in spite of the fact that the Quran speaks highly of the earlier Scriptures. Zwemer, working closely with the British and Foreign Bible Society, sought permission from Turkish government officials to distribute the Bible, more often receiving permission than not. Although the door for this kind of activity was more open in Zwemer's time, this does not mean he never faced suspicion or danger.

During his thirty-year experience in Basra, Bahrain, and Cairo, Zwemer distributed thousands of Bibles and tracts. He was, moreover, much more than an ordinary book salesman. He saw Bible distribution as a way to open doors to introduce Muslims to the "living Word," Jesus. Zwemer's prayer for Muslims reveals his great love for them:

Make Thy people willing in this new day of opportunity. Send forth reapers where the harvest is ripe, and faithful plowmen to break furrows in lands still neglected. . . . Give all those who labor among Muslims the tenderness of Christ, so that bruised reeds may become pillars of His Church, and smoking flaxwicks burning shining lights. Make bare Thine arm, O God, and show Thy power. All our expectation is from Thee.

children at his side.

The year before Margaret's death, they visited Kuwait to celebrate the sixtieth anniversary of the founding of the Arabian Mission, making stops in Beirut, Iraq, and Bahrain. They greatly rejoiced at what God had accomplished through this mission.

The measure of the man

Perhaps more than any other legacy, Samuel Zwemer left behind a burning love for the Muslim world. That deep love sparkles from the pages of his extensive writings, continually challenging the church to continue to carry the gospel into a world so hurting for God's love. He wrote, "It is only when Christian things have been done in an unChristian way, or when unChristian things have been done by Christians, that Christianity has appeared as a bitter foe to our Muslim brethren."

Unlike those who feel that Christians should muster an array of forceful arguments to demolish Muslim attacks on Christian truths such as the Trinity and the sonship of Jesus, Zwemer argued more for a "ministry of friendship," pleading for "less of the spirit of controversy and more of the spirit of the Cross." He called "not for less assault on the citadel of error, but for more ministry of healing to the wounded and dying." "The nearest way to the Muslim heart," said Zwemer, "is the way of God's love, the way of the Cross." This friendship and this love, Zwemer suggested, ought to begin with Muslim leaders.

Friendship with Muslim leaders

Zwemer strove to accomplish something few Christians work at nowadays, to build friendships with Muslim leaders. "The postwar world," he surmised, "will bring America and Europe in closer touch with Islam than ever before." With this anticipation in mind, he challenged Christians of all vocations—"men of the consular service, orientalists, merchants, tourists, and missionaries." He continued: "It is supremely important to understand the soul of a people and their popular religion and folk traditions. To achieve this, we must know their spiritual leaders. My conviction . . . is that the key to understanding of the masses lies in personal friendship with their clergy, the so-called *imams, mullahs,* and *sheikhs.*"

The life of Samuel Marinus Zwemer

1867	Born April 12
1890	Ordained by the Reformed Church in America
1891	Initiates work in Arabia
1896	Marries Amy Wilkes
1897	Settles in Bahrain
1904	His two daughters die in July; survived by four other children
1912	Relocates to Cairo
1929	Begins teaching at Princeton Theological Seminary
1937	Amy dies
1938	Retirement
1940	Marries Margaret Clarke
1950	Margaret dies
1952	Dies April 2

• Cairo

• Bahrain

SAUDI ARABIA

Zwemer argued for a "ministry of friendship," pleading for "less of the spirit of controversy and more of the spirit of the Cross."

Samuel
Zwemer
(1867–1952).

Furthermore, said Zwemer, "The clergy and priesthood of Islam demand the respect of those who desire to help the masses or have dealings with them." "This," he repeated, "applies to tourists, orientalists, political officials, and merchants no less than it does to missionaries. It applies most of all to the latter because it is from among the clergy of Islam that opposition often arises, and also some of the strongest and most distinguished Christian converts have come from this very class."

"We decided never to attack Islam or the religion of anyone present," Zwemer once remarked in a gathering of students and missionaries at Princeton. Instead, he said, we try to "state positively the claims of Christ and invite them lovingly to accept him as Lord of their life." When asked by a missionary what he would say if pressed for an answer as to what he thought of Muhammad, Zwemer responded, "I would reply I consider Muhammad the greatest Arab who ever lived and next to the New Testament he gave the greatest witness to Jesus Christ. Then I should point them to ... where the Quran calls Christ 'The Word of God.'" This approach by no means signified that Zwemer was hesitant to present the gospel forthrightly.

Evangelism more than "sharing"

Zwemer expressed deep misgivings when the word "sharing" began to creep into the missionary vocabulary:

It is well to go back to the real issues. All things are of God. He reconciled us to Him-

> *"The more elaborate the organization of missions the more indispensable is the presence of the Spirit of God."*

self by Jesus Christ. He gave us the ministry of reconciliation. This ministry committed unto us is called "the word of reconciliation." Because we are the custodians . . . the ambassadors of the word of Christ, we beseech the world that knows not this message, in Christ's stead, to be reconciled to God. . . . The acceptance of this message transforms life and produces a new creation.

Councils and committees

Zwemer was also clearly disturbed by the trends toward more committee work, collection of and analysis of statistics, all of which he saw as encroaching upon valuable missionary time and detracting from the real task in hand. He called for "not more technique, more machinery, but more power. The more elaborate the organization of missions the more indispensable is the presence of the Spirit of God." He went on to conclude, "We are in dreadful peril of being dominated by the machinery we have created. . . . We spend more time at councils and committees than we do in prayer. We *survey* every department and every province and publish the statistics, when what we most need is to '*survey* the wondrous Cross on which the Prince of Glory died.'"

Such is a brief glimpse of one of God's faithful ambassadors to the Muslim world. In spite of the endless camel back rides, the scorching mind-bending heat, all the heartache, the uncertainty, the risk, and the danger, Zwemer could reflect years later—with deep gratefulness to God, "The sheer joy of it all comes back. Gladly would I do it all over again in some unoccupied seaport of Arabia."

James Dretke

Further Reading

Tucker, Ruth. *From Jerusalem to Irian Jaya.* Grand Rapids: Zondervan, 1983.

Vander Werff, Lyle L. *Christian Mission to Muslims.* Pasadena, Calif.: William Carey Library, 1977.
(Vander Werff gives a full list of all Zwemer's writings.)

Wilson, J. Christy. *Apostle to Islam.* Grand Rapids: Baker, 1952.

Zwemer, Samuel M., and James Cantine. *The Golden Milestone.* New York: Revell, 1938.

A LATIN VISION FOR MUSLIMS

Pedro Carrasco

1948–

The uproar could be heard several blocks away as Pedro hurried to the site of the demonstration. He was on his way to join a number of his fellow Marxist agitators who were closing down the Mexican university he attended. As he approached the riot, his path was suddenly barred by soldiers who had cordoned off the area as they prepared to fire on the mob. While the crowd ran in all directions to escape the hail of bullets, Pedro felt his world crumbling. "Who am I?" "What drives me into the streets to fight the authorities?" Shaken, he drifted back to his own neighborhood.

Conversion and change

"You can't change society if there is no change in you," someone had once pointed out to him. "You won't be part of the solution if you're still a part of the problem." Provoked by those thoughts he entered a small evangelical church where a simple gospel message was being preached. Yes, he had heard it before, but this time God touched his heart. Screwing up his courage, he responded to the altar call. With the others who that day wanted to get right with God, he walked up the aisle to the astonished looks of those who knew him.

During the days of the ensuing student strike at the polytechnic university where he was studying engineering, Pedro had a lot of time to think. Over breakfast one morning, Pedro's father talked to the family about Jesus' call to Matthew. Turning directly to Pedro he said, "Are you going to serve the Lord or continue to study?" The question left Pedro speechless. He had not considered that his decision to follow Christ might mean sacrificing his studies. His parents, who had high vocational expectations of him, knew what his decision might mean to

Pedro Carrasco was born in 1948 in Mexico City. Shortly before his birth, his parents accepted Christ. Although he grew up in an evangelical home, Pedro's university career was marked by Communist activism. His eventual disillusionment with this revolutionary world set the stage for his conversion. Subsequently, through his service with Operation Mobilization, he received his calling to mobilize Latin Americans for missionary service to Muslim areas of the world.

In 1982, Pedro began exploratory trips which would lead to the founding of a Latin American mission to Muslim peoples. The young organization first focused on regions of North Africa but has since broadened its horizons to the whole of the Muslim world. PM International, as it is now known, is currently entering fields among Muslims in former Soviet Central Asia. Pedro directs the growing mission from Europe, where he and his family are living.

> *"Are you going to serve the Lord or continue to study?"*

his career. Confronted directly with the question, like Matthew, he chose to follow Christ. His mother started to cry, and his father left the table without another word.

His parents' pain at his decision left Pedro feeling bad for them and angry at God for having provoked the situation. In retrospect, however, he knew it was God's way of testing his resolve to follow Him. During the ensuing days of suspended classes, Pedro thought, read, and prayed. By the time school resumed, he was convinced that God wanted him back at the university. He also knew he was called to serve Him there and anywhere else the Lord might lead him.

His life at the university changed dramatically. The group of Christian students in which he participated felt a deep desire to evangelize in every way possible. Pedro explains: "From the day we handed out thousands of Bible portions at the exit to the Azteca Stadium where the World Cup soccer tournament was being played, we felt it was a small world to reach with the gospel."

With a friend, Roberto, he began praying for his city, his country and then, over maps, the world. During those early morning prayer sessions, the Lord promised that He would go before them, "breaking down gates of bronze." Such was the certainty of this calling that they got passports, talked with their pastor, informed their families, and began looking for a mission agency that would take them—to India! So convinced were they that this would happen, that they left their jobs, dedicating themselves to prayer and Scripture reading.

> *Pedro and Janie sold everything.*

Operation Mobilization

The Lord indeed did answer. Responding to an invitation to go to an Operation Mobilization (OM) meeting in the United States, they lined up what they needed and attended. The only part of the conference translated for them was a message on how God divided the waters of the Jordan so that Israel could reach the Promised Land. Their Jordan, however, was the Atlantic Ocean. With that thought in mind, they volunteered to go to Europe with OM, and the cost of the trip was miraculously provided through an anonymous gift.

God used that year in Europe to deal with Pedro's pride. He wondered if he wasn't wasting his engineering degree handing out tracts from door to door. He had decided to return to Mexico when God again spoke to him very pointedly. Reading the biblical account of Joshua, he realized there were places to conquer and giants to overcome, but he needed to decide whether he would let God use him or not. Shortly thereafter,

Pedro Carrasco was brought up in Mexico.

Pedro Carrasco
prayed over a
map of the
world.

he accepted a challenge to join a team being sent to Muslim countries. With four other young people, he traveled across Europe to the Arab world.

God instills a vision for Muslims
God used the following two years to give Pedro a clear understanding of the spiritual need of Muslims as he traveled and ministered throughout the region. It wasn't always easy to get from place to place. On one occasion, having traveled extensively to reach a North African country, his European companions were allowed to enter, but he was told he needed a visa which could only be obtained in an embassy six hundred miles away.

After journeying all night by ship to reach the embassy, Pedro found that he would have to wait one month for his visa. With no money and no contacts, what was he to do? Where was God's guidance? Was He closing the door, or was this an attack from the enemy? After the Lord granted him peace and assurance, Pedro found a temporary job and place to stay while he waited for the visa. When at last he returned to the Muslim land, the Lord again showed Himself faithful by guiding him to his teammates who

had temporarily settled in a distant part of the country. Through all of this, a clear vision and calling for Muslim evangelism was developed in Pedro.

Latin Americans enter the vision
Three years after Pedro and Roberto set off by faith, they returned to Mexico. Their families received them joyfully, proud of their sons' achievements. Pedro began working on his engineering thesis, and during an evangelistic campaign on the United States and Mexican border, he met for the third time Janie, whom he would marry a year later. The young couple moved to Puebla, Mexico, where Pedro began working in his engineering profession. Three years later, when he had just started getting comfortable in his work, he received a call from OM to serve on the evangelistic ship *Doulos*, which was visiting Latin America for the first time.

Pedro and Janie sold everything they had and moved onto the ship with their baby girl Natasha. They had just begun to settle into their new life when they were sent to Spain to organize a special event for seventy Latin Americans. Through this activity, Pedro began to visualize the potential Latins have for reaching the Muslim world. Following their own sense of calling, Pedro and Janie decided to remain in the south of Spain, nurturing the vision of Latin mobilization for Muslim ministry.

The following three years were spent in church planting in Spain and researching mission possibilities in North Africa. Two more children were also added to their family, Yousef and Yamila. Their youngest was born with Down's syndrome just before their planned move from Spain to a Muslim country. Again, Pedro questioned God's guidance and leading for their lives. Assured that they were indeed on the right course, they moved to North Africa.

The early years in Tashban were very difficult. Short on funding and personnel, they often felt like orphans as they sought by word and example to inspire Latins to Muslim ministry. Slowly God began to reward their faithfulness. One by one, Latin workers were added to their numbers. From Argentina, Brazil, Uruguay, Mexico, Venezuela and other Latin countries, harvest laborers began to arrive. Through faith and perseverance, Pedro's pioneer vision began to be fulfilled.

Reflecting on the growth of the young mission, Pedro writes, "Once more I find myself a spectator, observing what God is doing. He keeps on loving and saving Muslims. In so doing, He's raising up His servants from Latin America to penetrate the 'impenetrable wall' surrounding the Muslim world."

(The name "Pedro Carrasco" is a pseudonym designed to protect the identity of the person described and his ministry.)
Jonathan Lewis

Europe

BREAKING DOWN BARRIERS IN RUSSIA

Frederick W. Baedeker

1823–1906

Frederick Wilhelm Baedeker, a German who became a naturalized Englishman, was a product of the evangelical revival of the second half of the nineteenth century who himself became a preacher. He played a unique role in the religious movement in tsarist Russia associated with Lord Radstock and Col. Paschkov.

His particular distinction was his ability to evangelize among the many elements of society, from the leaders, on the one hand, to the convicts in the prisons, particularly in Siberia, on the other. His life demonstrates the power of the gospel in the hands of a dedicated, single-minded, and caring individual to break down social, linguistic, and racial barriers.

Said to have been in poor health at the time of his conversion, he traveled extensively in Scandinavia, Eastern Europe, Russia, and Siberia (which he crossed three times). His work illustrates the unusual evangelistic and missionary endeavors inspired by the Brethren movement.

Frederick Baedeker, the son of famed ornithologist F. W. J. Baedeker, buried his bride of only three months in 1851. Heartbroken, he spent the next eight years restlessly traveling in Europe, Tasmania, and Australia before settling in England at Weston-super-Mare, where he set up a private school and became a naturalized Englishman. Eleven years after his first wife's death, he married a young widow, Harriet Ormsby. But real inner peace would not come until four years later when he first met Lord Radstock, who was to influence his life profoundly.

Conversion

The Earl of Cavan, one of numerous members of the upper classes drawn into the Brethren movement, had invited Lord Radstock (an evangelical Anglican who sat lightly to denominational constraints) to conduct an extended mission in Weston. Baedeker was persuaded to attend, and one evening Lord Radstock put his hand on his shoulder saying, "My man, God has a message through me for you tonight." Later, Baedeker remarked: "I went in a proud German infidel, and came out a humble, believing disciple of the Lord Jesus Christ." Harriet also was converted.

The Baedekers were introduced to the Brethren network, and spent a year in Bristol where George Müller, also of German origin, was running his orphanage. Baedeker gained some medical knowledge there, presumably by "walking the hospital."

Called to preach

Soon after his conversion, Baedeker began to preach. While in Berlin in 1874, Lord Radstock suggested he should interpret for an American evangelist. As a result, he was invited to conduct his own evangelistic tour—the first of many. One of his converts in Berlin was Fräulein Toni von Blücher, who immediately commenced evangelistic and social work, and later founded the famous Central Mission.

Lord Radstock also introduced Baedeker to his life work in Russia. After the Crimean War ended in 1855, reforms, such as the abolition of serfdom (1861), prompted demands for more radical changes. Members

The Life of Frederick W. Baedeker

1823	Born at Witten, Westphalia, Germany, August 3
1851	Marries Auguste Jacobi, who dies three months later
1859	Becomes a naturalized British citizen
1862	Marries Harriet Ormsby, widowed mother of one of his students
1866	Converted at Weston-super-Mare, England
1874	Begins evangelistic ministry in Germany
1875	Introduced by Lord Radstock to the evangelical nobility of St. Petersburg.
1887	Introduced to prison evangelism in Finland by Baroness Mathilde von Wrede; begins eighteen years of fruitful evangelism in Russian prisons
1906	Gives his last evangelistic address at Kewstone (Somerset); dies, October 9

RUSSIA

• Moscow

> *"I went in
> a proud German infidel,
> and came out
> a humble, believing disciple of
> the Lord Jesus Christ."*

Dr. Frederick Baedeker in Russian costume.

of the intelligentsia led a populist movement, Trek to the People, which gained the support of some of the nobility. But government resistance fostered a mood of skepticism and hopelessness. The church, with its formalism, spiritual dryness, and medieval outlook, did little to help.

Lord Radstock

Into this situation came Lord Radstock (1874, and again in 1875 and 1878), whose simple Bible expositions given in the drawing rooms of the great and with emphasis on such fundamental gospel truths as justification by faith in the atoning death of Jesus Christ, drew an immediate response. Some of the converts, like Col. Paschkov, Colonel

Baedeker
supplied Bibles
to Russian
prisoners.

of the Guard, and Count Korff, were men of immense wealth who sprang into action. They built hospitals and schools on their estates and cheap lodging houses and tea rooms in St. Petersburg. They set up the Society for the Encouragement of Spiritual and Ethical Reading (1876), which published several million tracts and pamphlets on religious and moral subjects. Radstockist meetings were held in some forty aristocratic homes, and the movement aroused interest and opposition in newspapers, periodical literature, and the writings of literary giants like Dostoevski and Tolstoy.

This was the milieu into which Baedeker was introduced by Lord Radstock in 1875. With his wife and adopted daughter, Baedeker spent three years in Russia, ostensibly to preach to German-speaking Russians, but also assisting the movement commenced by Lord Radstock. Even after the latter's expulsion from Russia (1878), Baedeker continued low-key evangelism in noble households. He often stayed with Princess Nathalie Lieven, residing in the Malachite Hall with its magnificent malachite mantelpiece and pillars. Meetings were held in the huge white drawing room of the princess's palace, and in the homes of numerous other princesses, counts, and barons. Baedeker had access to generals, ambassadors, and even the grand duchess. The palatial country homes of the nobility

were also open to him. He and his wife were present at the remarkable conference of Stundists and other dissidents convened by Paschkov in an attempt to bring about united action. The 1884 conference was broken up by police, and Paschkov and Korff were exiled from Russia.

Visiting prisons by "special command"

His introduction to prison visitation appears to have been given him by Baroness Mathilde von Wrede, daughter of a former governor general of Finland, who had been converted to an evangelical faith and had begun prison visitation at age nineteen. In 1887, Baedeker preached to hundreds of prisoners in Helsingfors, Tavastehus, Abo, and Wilmanstrand. He also spoke to university students and visited numerous counts, barons, and members of the royal family.

In Russia, through the influence of an unnamed countess, Baedeker obtained a permit from the director of prisons stating that he was under special command to visit the prisons of Russia, and to supply the convicts with copies of the Holy Scriptures. The permit was renewed every two years, usually with enlarged privileges, such as permission to visit prisoners in their cells. Initially Baedeker faced obstruction from some prison officials, but attitudes softened with the years.

In 1890, Baedeker made his first epic trip

across Russia and Siberia, leaving St. Petersburg on May 8 and arriving at Nicolajwesk, "the Land's End of Great Russia" as he described it, on September 7. He subsequently visited the prison island of Saghalien before returning to England by sea.

Traveling by *tarantass*

He traveled by boat, down rivers and across Lake Baikal, but for two stretches of about a thousand miles each he used the roads, such as they were, traveling by *tarantass*. This vehicle he described as "something like an old-fashioned family coach." The body was made of wickerwork, lined with carpet. Overhead was a movable leather hood. Lacking springs, the body rested on long poles that provided some elasticity. Drawn by three swift Siberian horses, the carriage rattled along rough roads from post station to post station. Boxes of Bibles and New Testaments were packed first, then luggage (including food, for little but hot tea was available at post stations), and finally mattresses and pillows. With him traveled an interpreter, for though he spoke German, English, and French fluently, he knew little Russian and less of the local languages. Additional supplies of books were dispatched ahead.

The prisoners he addressed and to whom he distributed Bibles and New Testaments included religious and political exiles, as well as common criminals. Baedeker seems to have communicated with them as effectively as he did with the nobility.

Though he confided to his diary that he would never travel such a distance again, he did it twice more. And he visited the prisons in Caucasia, as well as Finland and Sweden.

Ingenuity

As an evangelistic preacher, Baedeker used considerable ingenuity. Forbidden by police to hold religious services in Riga, for example, he obtained permission to *lecture* on "Sin and Salvation" in halls seating two and three thousand; they were crowded, night after night. He spoke in schools and universities (e.g., Helsingfors), and there were few countries in Europe which were not visited by this dedicated preacher.

Baedeker received his Ph.D. degree from Freiburg University, although it is not

Baedeker often stayed with Princess Lieven and her family.

known in what field. A cousin of the Baedeker of *Continental Guide Book* fame, he contributed to several of the guides. And yet his chief aim was not to be an academic or a famous writer. Rather, he was moved by a compelling desire to proclaim the gospel of Christ to Russians, whether they be in a prison house or in an aristocrat's reading room.

Harold Rowdon

Further Reading

Heier, E. *Religious Schism in the Russian Aristocracy, 1860–1900 Radstockism and Pashkovism.* The Hague: Martinus Nijhoff, 1970.

Latimer, Robert Sloan. *Dr. Baedeker: and His Apostolic Work in Russia.* London: Morgan & Scott, 1907.

GIVER OF PATIENT, GENTLE ANSWERS

Edith Schaeffer

1914–

Edith Schaeffer in 1956.

After fame and recognition came to Edith Schaeffer as the world-famous "missionary to the intellectuals" (a phrase that *Time* magazine once used to describe my parents), she never saw herself differently than she had long before anyone heard of her or her ministry. United States ambassadors might call, Christmas cards adorned with personal, handwritten presidential greetings from the White House might arrive, but my mother never delegated the task of being a physical or spiritual good Samaritan. To the thousands of young people who looked to her for help, she was on call twenty-four hours a day. To anyone in need of spiritual answers or emotional and intellectual help, Edith Schaeffer's door was never shut.

Family life and youth

Edith Schaeffer was born on November 3, 1914, in Wenchow, China. Her parents, George Hugh Seville (1876–1977) and Jessie Maude Merritt Seville (1876–1958), were called to the China Inland Mission and served for many years in the Checkiang Province before China's fall to Communism.

When Edith was five years old her parents returned to the United States, bringing Edith and her two older sisters, Elsa and Janet, with them. They left behind the tiny grave of a young son.

Edith's education was a priority to her refined, scholarly father and her talented, genteel mother. Edith attended the Stevens School for Girls in Philadelphia, then, when her father took a teaching job in California, the Orange Avenue School in Monrovia. Edith's high school years were divided between the North Toronto College School in Canada and Newburgh High School in Newburgh, New York. Edith's last formal educational experience was at Beaver Col-

Edith Schaeffer in 1956.

lege in Jenkintown, Pennsylvania.

Like many pastors' children, Edith had to get used to move after move as her father relocated from one ministry to another. Her childhood was a series of interrupted friendships and postponed hopes and dreams. But Edith learned that the only consistent part of life was God's never-failing love.

Marriage

While in her first year at Beaver College, Edith met a young man named Francis Schaeffer. The manner of their meeting was a foreshadowing of events to follow. Edith noticed a young man standing up to challenge a stridently liberal theological guest lecturer at a nearby college. Francis made an impassioned defense of traditional ideas of biblical truth in the face of liberal claims

The Life of Edith Schaeffer

1914	Born in Wenchow, China, November 3
1935	Marries Francis Schaeffer on July 6
1937	Birth of Priscilla Schaeffer
1941	Birth of Susan Schaeffer
1945	Birth of Debra Schaeffer
1948	Departs for Europe
1952	Birth of Frank Schaeffer
1955	Settles in Huémoz, Switzerland Founds L'Abri Fellowship
1962	First of sixteen books, L'Abri, published
1984	Francis Schaeffer dies on May 15
1985	Resides in Rochester, Minnesota

SWITZERLAND
• Huémoz

ITALY

My mother is no respecter of persons! I well remember the time she kept the United States ambassador to Switzerland waiting in our living room. Mother was standing on one foot in our small crowded chalet kitchen, comforting a distraught seventeen-year-old girl who was high on drugs and threatening suicide.

My father, Francis Schaeffer, had sent me to find out why my mom was taking so long with the ambassador's tea. When I walked up the narrow, old staircase from our living room to the kitchen, I heard the sound of sobbing. As I came around the corner I saw Mom gently holding a crying girl in her arms. The ambassador's tea tray lay forgotten on the kitchen table.

My mother stroked the young woman's long, greasy locks that fell over a torn, filthy T-shirt above threadbare jeans.

The girl was one of many of the flotsam and jetsam that the "hippie" movement of the late 1960s had thrown upon L'Abri Fellowship's doorstep. She had been hitchhiking across Europe with a boyfriend who had left her pregnant and hooked on hard drugs. They had been on an intercontinental "search for truth" and had made their way from St. Louis, Missouri, to Switzerland via a Hindu ashram in India.

The distraught girl was not unique. By the 1960s many like her had found their way to L'Abri, or "The Shelter," and many more would follow. The United States ambassador and his wife could wait. To Edith Schaeffer there were no "nobodies."

that the Bible could not be taken literally. The seventeen-year-old Edith Seville inquired of mutual friends as to how to meet "that wonderful young man." Three years after they met that night and fell in instant and abiding love, Francis and Edith were married on July 6, 1935, in Germantown, Pennsylvania.

Edith left college a year early and worked hard in the rough and tumble of the depression era to support herself and her young husband as he pursued his seminary studies. Edith's dressmaking and leather goods (belts, buttons, and handbags) as well as other creative handicraft work, put food on

the Schaeffer table and paid the tuition bills as the Schaeffers prayed that God would lead them to the place of His choosing.

After graduation from seminary Francis pastored a number of Presbyterian churches, including ones in Grove City and Chester, Pennsylvania, and in St. Louis, Missouri. During these formative years Edith concentrated on working with young people. She founded numerous summer Bible schools and wrote a Summer Bible School Curriculum for grades K through 12.

In 1937 Edith's first child, Priscilla, was born. Susan, her second daughter, followed in 1941. Debbie made her appearance in 1945.

Ministry in Europe

In 1948 the Schaeffers' prayers for the Lord's leading were answered, and they were sent to Europe as missionaries to the young people of bomb-ravaged cities. These were lean and difficult years as Edith and the girls lived in shabby rented rooms, first in Holland, then in Switzerland, while Francis traveled and organized Bible classes and Bible camps all over Europe.

Finally the Schaeffers settled in Champéry, Switzerland, where they lived from 1949 to 1955 and where an important local leader made a profession of faith and started attending the Schaeffers' in-home Sunday church services. Because of this the Schaeffers were driven from their home when the Roman Catholic authorities had them and their infant son, Frank (born in 1952), expelled for having a "religious influence" on the village. Ironically, the man whose born-again experience got the Schaeffers expelled had been an atheist, not a Roman Catholic. But the local bishops and priests were not about to sit by and see their flock become evangelical Christians.

The Schaeffers' expulsion took place at a time of severe testing for the family. Only one year before, in 1954, their son, Frank, had been diagnosed with polio and was still severely paralyzed (a condition from which he later recovered).

L'Abri

In 1955 the Schaeffer family's prayers were again answered when they were given residency permits to live in the Protestant part of Switzerland. (Switzerland is divided into Protestant and Roman Catholic "cantons," or states.) They settled in Huémoz in a chalet called Chalet Les Mélèzes, where they would reside for the next thirty years and which became the headquarters of L'Abri Fellowship.

L'Abri started very informally. Indeed, it never was "planned" but unfolded as God opened doors. It all began when

> They were expelled for having a "religious influence" on the village.

Priscilla began to bring friends home from the University of Lausanne for long weekends of discussion, fellowship, and Bible study.

Soon the word got out in the local university population that Edith and Francis Schaeffer were unusual people who would always find time to answer sincere questions, from Christians and non-Christians alike, about philosophy, theology, and modern culture. Moreover, the Schaeffers had an open home to all comers and would invite people to stay with them in their growing Christian community.

Edith and Francis both took a keen interest not only in Bible study but in all aspects of their contemporary culture. Thus they were specially prepared to make biblical truth relevant to students and others to whom very few Christians were speaking in the fifties, sixties, and seventies.

Edith's love and understanding of art, literature, and creativity of all kinds made her especially well-equipped to speak to a generation of secularized seekers to whom many other Christians, less interested in the arts and humanities, had failed to communicate. In fact, many Christians had begun to give up on reaching rebellious students with the gospel. But Edith was not about to "give up" on anyone, however long the hair or beard, or however short the miniskirt. Thus, in the 1950s many an outcast "beatnik" found Christ in L'Abri. And in the 1960s hundreds of "hippies" and other experimenters in "alternative lifestyles" accepted Jesus at Edith's knee, along with countless other young people from all over the world. For Edith the so-called generation gap did not exist.

In the 1970s hundreds, then thousands, of people began to arrive each year at L'Abri for study and fellowship with the Schaeffers. Edith presided over the hospitality side of the work and the all-important personal one-on-one encounters with the many lost and searching young people who now looked to her and her husband for honest answers to honest questions about life's meaning.

Schaeffer
family reunion,
1981.

Writing

Soon Edith's lifelong love of literature began to show itself in a new way. She began to write. Edith's first book was *L'Abri*, the story of her ministry. It was written in 1962 and chronicled the miraculous development of the work. Other books soon followed. *Hidden Art* was about the hidden creative ability each homemaker has. *Christianity Is Jewish* recounted the wonderful plan of salvation God unfolds through the Old Testament and how it is fulfilled in the New Testament. *What Is a Family?* is a classic work on family life. *Affliction* is a volume that many have called the best book on coping with suffering ever written. Edith wrote sixteen books in all, many of which became inspirational bestsellers.

After Edith's ever-popular books were published, naturally many speaking invitations began to arrive. Suddenly Edith was in demand all over the world. As her books were translated into more than twenty languages, she began to speak in churches, colleges, and schools from Hong Kong to London.

Francis falls ill

The sacrificial life of extraordinary outreach, public ministry, and plain hard work took its toll on the Schaeffer family. In 1978, Francis contracted lymphoma, a cancer of the lymph glands. Edith and Francis were told by his doctors that Francis's illness was related to the stress associated with a life of sacrificial full-time Christian service. But cancer notwithstanding, neither one of them saw fit to retire or to scale back their outreach to the lost and seeking. In fact, it

> *Many Christians had begun to give up on reaching rebellious students with the gospel.*

Edith Schaeffer with her twelfth great-grand-child.

Between frequent speaking trips and her work at the various branches of L'Abri in England, Switzerland, and Holland, Edith found time to establish a branch of L'Abri in Minnesota as well as to work with many patients and families who came to the Mayo Clinic.

A life of Christian service

Since her beloved husband's passing, Edith's call has been the same as always: to give honest answers to honest questions, believing that Christianity is truth and not just a "religious experience." Edith's books, life, and message all proclaim one vision: Christ can be the Lord of *all* of life, not just the "religious" parts of it. Whether it's writing a book or being a homemaker all we do must be to the glory of God. That is the message that Edith Schaeffer spent a lifetime sharing with her own children, her spiritual children, and her millions of readers.

It was the message she shared with the weeping seventeen year old who kept the ambassador waiting. And it was that truth that led the same girl out of the slavery of the drug culture, away from intellectual despair, and convinced her to keep her baby.

As to the ambassador—well, in the end he got his tea and fresh-baked oatmeal cookies. He spent that mid-June afternoon in 1969 asking Francis and Edith Schaeffer questions about how Christianity could be reconciled to modern existential philosophy. Like the weeping girl the ambassador received patient, gentle answers to his questions.

Frank Schaeffer

was *after* Francis was diagnosed with cancer that both Edith and Francis redoubled their efforts in a new direction of the Lord's work. In the late 1970s they became the leaders of the evangelical prolife movement.

Up to the time when the Schaeffers began to speak out on the issue of the sanctity of human life, many evangelicals had ignored the issue of abortion or remained silent about it. It was Edith and Francis Schaeffer who led millions of Christians to reconsider, then reject, their apathy regarding the issue of protecting the unborn. Edith's many speeches, lectures, and articles, as well as her appearances on numerous television and radio shows, did much to complement her husband's ground-breaking work in regard to protecting unborn children. Moreover, she was a founding board member of the Christian Action Council, an organization responsible for operating more than 450 crisis pregnancy centers.

In the 1980s, Edith and Francis began to spend more and more time in Rochester, Minnesota, at the Mayo Clinic where Francis was being treated. After Francis's death in 1984, Edith made her home in Rochester.

Further Reading

Schaeffer, Edith. *L'Abri*. London: Norfolk, 1969; Wheaton, Ill.: Tyndale, 1972.

———. *The Tapestry*. Waco, Tex.: Word, 1981. (an extended autobiography of Edith and Francis Schaeffer)

RUSHING TO RUSSIANS

Peter Deyneka, Sr. and Jr.

1898–1987 and 1931–

In the body of Christ, Peter Deyneka, Sr., was a vocal cord. Peter, Jr. is a ligament.

After emigrating from Russia in 1913, the senior Deyneka found Christ as his personal savior at Moody Memorial Church in Chicago. God soon ignited a fire in him to witness to anyone who would listen, but especially to Russians.

Peter discovered Russians in Chicago, then in North Dakota, Canada, Alaska, and South America. After World War II, he and his helpers ministered among two million Russians in displaced persons' camps in Germany and Austria.

In American churches his animated speaking style and intensity earned him the endearing nickname, "Peter Dynamite." He constantly urged Americans not to forget that Russians were a mission field, challenging people with the importance of prayer—as a life, a commitment, and a means of walking close to the Lord. He often declared, "Much prayer, much power"—giving the alternatives as "little prayer, little power" and "no prayer, no power." Thousands answered his call for commitment to full-time Christian service.

His own prayers also had a "dynamite" intensity. At 2 A.M. one night the hotel manager at Winona Lake Bible Conference asked him to tone down his praying a few decibels. "You know, Peter, God isn't deaf," the manager observed.

Peter answered, "No, but he's not bashful, either!" Peter continued to beseech the Lord with all his heart, unabated.

Peter wasn't bashful about asking God for opportunities to serve Him. He claimed

> "Much prayer, much power—
> little prayer, little power—
> no prayer, no power."

The Russia of today is a land of tremendous opportunity for the advance of the gospel. And two of Russia's most active evangelists have been Peter Deyneka, Sr. and Jr.

Converted to Christ after coming to America in 1913, Peter, Sr., affectionately known as "Peter Dynamite," gravitated toward Russian émigrés in the Americas and Europe—first evangelizing them, then urging many to become missionaries themselves. He was known to speculate, "If Russia opens some day...," but then he would revert to thinking the door to evangelism would always remain closed. "He wasn't a dreamer waiting for the future," his son recalls. "He was very active in the present."

Peter, Sr. died in 1987, still thinking "if." The reality of the "open door" waited for his son, Peter, Jr., as the Soviet Union and Communism collapsed in 1990. The Christian faith, hidden but vibrant for many years, was allowed to flourish. Peter, Jr., says excitedly, "All of my past was preparation for these past seventeen months," since Russia opened.

Jeremiah 33:3, "Call to me, and I will answer you and tell you great and unsearchable things you do not know."

A strong right arm
Peter's wife, Vera, understood why her husband with ministry responsibilities had to travel so much. Usually staying home with the three children, she handwrote thousands of letters to follow up with people he had met. Their daughter, Ruth, said at her mother's funeral that for Vera, "Prayer was as normal as breathing. Her life was a beautiful sermon. She said amen last Monday morning."

The Life of Peter Deyneka, Sr.

1898	Born in Chomsk, Russia
1913	Emigrates to United States
1926	Marries Vera Demidovich
1934	Founds Russian Gospel Association (now Slavic Gospel Association)
1941	Pioneers Russian broadcasting
1942	Founds Russian Bible Institute
1987	Dies in Wheaton, Illinois

The Life of Peter Deyneka, Jr.

1931	Born in Chicago
1968	Marries Anita Marson
1976–89	Banned from Russia
1989	Enters Russia
1991	Founds Peter Deyneka Russian Ministries

RUSSIA

• Moscow

> *. . . the only theological training materials available to evangelicals during twenty years of Soviet rule.*

Peter, Jr., accepted Christ at home during grade school years. "One day when I was with my father and my mother in the kitchen, I realized I needed to make a personal commitment to Christ."

Saturday morning Russian lessons equipped the children with an accent-free pronunciation—something almost impossible to obtain later in life. Ruth became Mrs. Jack Shalanko, broadcasting in Russian on the radio station HCJB from 1954 to 1980.

The family lived very frugally. Vera looked forward to getting a "new" item of hand-me-down clothing; she was buried in one.

Before *perestroika*

Long before Russia opened, Peter, Jr., and his colleagues translated about a hundred book titles, printed them in the West, and imported them in the limited quantities that could be brought into Russia at the time.

He engaged in radio ministry at stations whose signals reached Russia—providing Russian-speaking staff for Heralding Christ Jesus' Blessings (HCJB), Far East Broadcasting Company, and Trans World Radio. On one program the host read the Bible at dictation speed; as a result, many listeners were able to copy down the entire New Testament.

Peter and others also organized several hundred thousand people to pray for Christian prisoners and to apply pressure through American congressmen to obtain their release.

Russians received Peter's pastoral training materials enthusiastically and incorporated them into extension courses—believed to be the only theological training materials available to evangelicals during twenty years of Soviet rule.

From 1976 until 1989, the Soviet government rejected all ten of Peter, Jr., and Anita's visa requests to visit the Soviet Union. "We went about five times [in two weeks]," to the Soviet embassy in Helsinki in 1988. "Finally, the last time they said to

Peter, Jr., added, "She didn't ask us if we wanted to study piano. She sat next to us [on the piano bench], and she had a strong right arm!" Yet she was a flexible person—a buffer between a father who considered sports the ultimate waste of time and a son whose pulse quickened every time he passed Wrigley Field.

us, 'We're sorry; we can't let you in. Your ideology is wrong!'"

During the thirteen years of exclusion, the Russian government denounced them frequently in publications. One mid-eighties book included a chapter entitled, "Lies in the Atmosphere." Accusing Christian radio of influencing Soviets in a negative way, it listed Peter, Jr., as a prime instigator in the atmospheric lying.

Links and ligaments

When *glasnost* (openness) and *perestroika* (restructuring) developed, the Deynekas finally received a visa in February 1989. After several visits, they moved to Moscow in January 1991.

Peter, Jr., describes his job as that of being

Peter Deyneka, Jr., in Moscow in 1992.

Peter Deyneka, Sr., with Bob Cook (left).

Peter Deyneka, Jr., with a Russian Christian.

a "catalyst, networker, initiator, encourager, and assister." He continues, "One great weakness of the evangelical church is segmenting and being exclusive and narrowly focused. God has given me a broad vision . . . involving as many varieties of Christian groups as possible, who have something needful to offer to the church."

The apostle Paul wrote several times of diverse organs in the body of Christ. Peter Dyneka, Jr., also sees the church as a body. He brings together people and organizations who haven't known of each others' existence, and helps them do together what none of them could do individually. His twenty-five years of experience and research on Russia are indispensable as a member of the executive committee of CoMission, a fellowship of seventy Christian organizations aiming to evangelize Russia by starting 120,000 Bible studies. The goal is to place one Bible study in every school in the former Soviet Union and see them grow into churches.

Peter and Anita now spend half of their time in Russia, half in the West, "*here* to meet with Christian leaders and formulate

strategy, and *there* to fulfill it." He and his team, called Peter Deyneka Russian Ministries, link Western Christians with Bible-believing churches in Russia, or with secular contacts that enable them to start a ministry in Russia. He has worked with more than 160 organizations in the short time that Russian Ministries has existed. Networking scores of Christian organizations using different methodologies, "has multiplied my life scores of times over."

While it is day

When asked how long religious freedom is likely to last in Russia Peter responded, "Openness will continue as long as true democracy continues. But if oppressive forces join hands, they will start limiting Christian freedom. If the economic situation continues to worsen, I think [antidemocratic]

> *The goal is*
> *to place one Bible study*
> *in every school and*
> *see them grow into churches.*

> "Communism and
> the Iron Curtain
> seemed so eternal that
> nobody believed
> it would ever open."

elements will start uniting, and at that point democracy will start diminishing." He is also concerned that some sectors of Russian Orthodoxy seem to be attempting to regain the dominant role they enjoyed before 1917. They want to become "the sole expression of Christianity" in Russia. "While it is yet day," says Deyneka, "our goal is the evangelization of the former Soviet Union by involving . . . Christian organizations . . . who have something positive to offer the indigenous church in Russia. So even if the door should close to Western agencies, the ministries they began would continue."

He is busy introducing as many helpful tools and methodologies to Russian Christians as possible—for evangelism, discipleship, and theological training. He intends that these tools and methodologies should then be developed and improved upon by Russians, making Western agencies dispensable in God's timing.

Deyneka is selective in his encouragement of Christian agencies. When the country first opened in September 1991, Russian Christians were euphoric. They encouraged Westerners to come en masse and assist them. So many did in fact come that there were weeks at a time when hardly any Russians spoke at joint meetings.

Deyneka stresses that "only those organizations that have something really positive to give" should go to Russia—those who "know the Russian church, culture, and circumstances."

How would his father react if he could see the "great and mighty things" happening in Russia today? Peter replies, "He would say, 'I can't believe it, but it's happening.' Communism and the Iron Curtain seemed so eternal that nobody believed it would ever open."

Peter acknowledges the threat of government leaders to shut down the Christian church in the Commonwealth of Independent States (CIS). "The only contingency plan we can have is to train as many national leaders, in the greatest possible variety of methodologies, as quickly as possible." He also wants to expand shortwave radio—to teach, encourage, and advise the indigenous leaders.

Pleas for prayer
Peter asks Christians to pray fervently. "This is a time of great confusion, of human hopelessness, and yet enormous potential for influencing the entire CIS with the gospel. . . . I feel that, if the people of the CIS would have a chance to develop spiritually in the next few years, they could be an enormous influence for God in Eastern Europe, Western Europe, and in the minority republics of the CIS."

As his father had emphasized "much prayer," so Peter Deyneka requests prayer "for wisdom to do what is most strategic" to assist the church in Russia—to strengthen the Russians to get along without outside help in days to come. Like his father, Peter, Jr., continues to rush toward the Russians.

David Fisher

Further Reading

Clendenin, Daniel B. *From the Coup to the Commonwealth.* Grand Rapids: Baker, 1992.

Hill, Kent R. *Turbulent Times for the Soviet Church.* Portland: Multnomah, 1991.

"In Russia: Something Beyond All Expectation." *Decision* (January 1993).

Network, quarterly, Peter Deyneka Russian Ministries, Box 496, Wheaton, Illinois 60189.

Yancey, Philip. *Praying with the KGB.* Portland: Multnomah, 1992.

UNCOMPROMISING SPOKESMAN
Peter Beyerhaus
1929–

Her article appeared in one of Germany's most respected church periodicals. Written by a feminist theologian, it condemned the Cross of Christ for putting women in a place of inferiority, making them feel like sinners. Most Christ-centered church services, the writer asserted, were occasions for women to suffer shame.

Dr. Peter Beyerhaus, theology professor at a secular German university, criticized her view publicly in a lecture. When she responded with a counterattack, he wrote her a long personal letter in which he said, "It is hard, indeed, to accept that Christ had to die for our sin, but when I look into my own heart, I know this is the only way we can live. If we take away the cross of Christ as the cure for suffering, there is no longer any hope on which to build. It is now Lent. Every morning my wife and I read from the passion of our Lord and think about how important, how essential, it is for us. We can only hope you will see this too."

Her response was silence. Undoubtedly she was angry, thought Beyerhaus. Three months later he received a letter. She was very ill, she wrote, but wanted to continue the discussion with him. She felt he had a point.

The dignified, soft-spoken professor with his old world courtesy had again raised an authoritative voice against the encroachment of anti-Christian thought upon the church. And his voice had been heard.

It was a voice that had resounded around the world.

Peter Beyerhaus, though still a child, may have been somewhat aware of the risks his father was taking, but nothing could fully prepare him or his family for the shock when his father was arrested for speaking out against the Hitler regime. Then war intervened, distracting Pastor Siegfried Beyerhaus's persecutors. He was spared imprisonment and continued ministering to his parishioners in Berlin while bombs devastated the city. Peter, with the rest of his family, was sent to a safer place.

With the fall of Germany the war ended, but not the suffering. Food and other commodities were scarce. Peter, at age sixteen, was happy to get work at a farm near Hamburg. That satisfaction abruptly ended when an accident put him in the hospital for three months.

With plenty of time for reflection, he became convinced that God wanted him in His service. What service? Peter didn't know, but a first logical step seemed to be to study theology for a pastoral ministry. Three years later, a scholarship for Uppsala University in Sweden redirected the decision.

Mission to Africa

While working toward his doctorate, Beyerhaus was greatly influenced by two people: his major professor, Bengt Sundkler, who had been a missionary in South Africa, and an attractive young Swedish woman named Ingegärd, a missionary aspirant. He married the young woman and followed the example of the professor, heading for South Africa with his wife to do mission work.

The years in Transvaal and Natal, South Africa, were some of the most enjoyable times in their lives. Both Peter and his wife fell in love with the black people and found a ministry that was both fulfilling and challenging as they moved around evangelizing,

> *God's people wanted to worship Him, but they also wanted to hang on to their pagan practices.*

planting churches, working with young people, building up believers. Later, Peter taught in a seminary.

One of the major problems in the black church, he soon discovered, was syncretism. God's people wanted to worship Him, but they also wanted to hang on to their pagan practices. Like his father, Peter (now Dr. Beyerhaus) was not one to pussyfoot around an issue. Defining the problem clearly, he urged the church to face it head-on.

Back to Germany

The year 1965 brought a tug-of-war in the form of an invitation to teach at Tübingen University in Germany. As a scholar and gifted teacher, Beyerhaus naturally felt a pull toward the prestigious academic position. On the other hand, he liked his work in Natal, where he combined lecturing with practical training for his students. And he had the satisfaction of being needed. But was he needed in Germany instead?

God seemed to be indicating he should go, but he was still hesitant. Then his eldest daughter, Karolina, became ill and could not be treated in Natal, and he realized this was confirmation. He must return to Germany.

As professor at Tübingen University and director of its Institute of Missiology and Ecumenical Theology, Beyerhaus and his family settled into the picturesque university town nestled among the forested hills of southern Germany. His was an enviable position, but he still wondered why God had recalled him from South Africa.

The year 1969 was one of student uprising worldwide, and Tübingen had its share of violence. On one occasion student activists interrupted a church service, forcing the bishop to step down from the pulpit and answer political questions. The turmoil led Beyerhaus to wonder how young theological students could survive and grow in such a hostile climate. His answer was to help establish the Albrecht Bengel House, a dormitory/lecture hall where Christian stu-

Dr. Peter Beyerhaus.

dents could get theological help and spiritual encouragement.

Concerned, however, that his students might become isolated in their own little academic world, Beyerhaus developed the practice that he had had in South Africa of taking students out with him to preach evangelistically, often going to the university hospital. Periodically he would also gather them for a retreat in the Black Forest to focus on personal Bible study and prayer.

International concerns

Soon Beyerhaus's ministry expanded beyond the university campus, as he saw that the World Council of Churches (WCC) was slipping away from its biblical moorings. The first stirrings had come in 1961 when Orthodox churches from the Soviet Union were admitted and brought with them their political agenda. The General Assembly in

The Life of Peter Beyerhaus

1929	Born in Germany
1955	Marries Ingegärd Kalen
1956	Receives Doctor of Theology degree from Uppsala University in Sweden
1957–65	Serves with Berlin Mission Society in Transvaal and Natal in South Africa
1966	Chair of Missiology and Ecumenical Theology at Tübingen University in Germany
1972	Elected president of the Theological Convention of Confessing Fellowships in Germany
1973	Special theological consultant at Eighth World Missionary Conference at Bangkok
1974	Featured speaker at the International Congress on World Evangelization in Lausanne
1975, 1983	Observer at Fifth and Sixth Assemblies of the World Council of Churches
1989	Becomes honorary rector of Korntal Graduate School for Mission

GERMANY

• Tübingen

Uppsala, Sweden, in 1968 confirmed the direction by redefining world mission in humanistic rather than redemptive terms.

In 1970 Beyerhaus drafted a critical assessment of what was happening. The document, called the Frankfurt Declaration, was sent to Christian groups and publications. Picked up by the media, it appeared in newspapers and magazines around the world.

Beyerhaus began receiving invitations to address churches, missions, and theological institutions in many parts of the world. In 1973 he was invited by Billy Graham to Atlanta for a consultation about the direction the WCC was taking. He raised his voice in favor of establishing an evangelical organization rooted in biblical principles of mission. When the International Congress on World Evangelization was held in Lausanne, Switzerland, in 1974, Beyerhaus was asked to serve as a member of the planning committee.

In the years that followed, Beyerhaus assessed subsequent WCC assemblies and became known as a forthright evangelical spokesman on ecumenical matters. In 1980 he was even invited by the pope to a private audience to discuss ecumenical concerns.

Standing for truth

Meanwhile, he carried on his duties at the university—no easy task in an atmosphere of rampant liberalism where theologians tended to consider the evangelical view as simplistic and unworthy of serious consideration. Going against the tide can be a lonely, painful struggle. Beyerhaus was often derided as a fundamentalist, reactionary, or die-hard. Even now that he has attained world stature, at meetings of theologians he still senses an inner distance that is difficult to overcome.

In 1988 his faculty met to decide upon the recipient of the prestigious Lucas Prize for outstanding scholarship and contribution to the furtherance of peace.

"What about the Dalai Lama?" suggested someone.

A lively discussion followed, ending with the majority expressing support for the choice.

"How can you do such a thing?" protested Beyerhaus. "The Dalai Lama may promote peace, but I find it totally inap-

> *A man with a mission to keep the church on course and growing healthily.*

propriate for us as a Christian theological faculty to honor a person who is worshiped as a divine being and tries to win Christian converts to Buddhism."

The Tübingen faculty turned a deaf ear. Beyerhaus protested in a public letter published in newspapers and gave a lecture warning about the danger of compromising their Christian heritage. His colleagues took offense personally.

On the day the Dalai Lama was honored at the university, Beyerhaus and a colleague who stood with him gathered a group of students and friends in his home for a prayer meeting. The event did not pass unnoticed. A few days later Beyerhaus was formally censured at a faculty meeting with the disciplinary action recorded in the minutes.

"That was one of the most trying experiences of my life," admits Beyerhaus. "Having to stand alone against the whole faculty—people whom I knew and liked."

Yet when the reprimand was delivered in written form, he responded in his usual dignified, courteous way: "Gentlemen, I consider this an honor. I intend to frame it and hang it over the desk in my study. But as for you, what you have done does not honor you."

They had no reply.

"You know, once you get through it," commented Beyerhaus later, "you feel free, independent, almost happy that the Lord has given you occasion to stand for truth and to share some of His shame."

Not long after this event, a woman colleague had a birthday. In Germany it is customary for friends to drop by unannounced to congratulate a person on his or her birthday and enjoy a lavish assortment of cakes. The colleague was astonished when Beyer-

haus and his wife walked in to congratulate her. As a result of his overture, when Beyerhaus celebrated his sixtieth birthday six months later, most of his colleagues came and old relationships were restored.

"I have learned," said Beyerhaus thoughtfully, "how important it is when conflicts come, to view the other person as a human being, even as a Christian brother for whom Christ died and for whom we must struggle to win him back."

That is Dr. Peter Beyerhaus. A man who will speak up uncompromisingly and yet be concerned for the individuals involved. A man with a mission to keep the church on course and growing healthily.

Approaching the age of mandatory retirement, Dr. Beyerhaus wonders aloud, "Who will take my place? Who will give future pastors of Germany the help they need? Who will help to raise the alarm for a drifting church?"

Who indeed?

Elaine Rhoton

Further Reading

Beyerhaus, Peter. *The Responsible Church and Foreign Missions.* Grand Rapids: Eerdmans, 1964.

——. *Missions: Which Way? Humanization or Redemption.* Grand Rapids: Zondervan, 1976.

——. *Shaken Foundations: Theological Foundations for Mission.* Grand Rapids: Zondervan, 1972.

——. *Bangkok '73: The Beginning or End of World Mission?* Grand Rapids: Zondervan, 1974.

——. *Theology as Instrument of Liberation.* Capetown: International Christian Network, Capetown, 1988.

——. *God's Kingdom and the Utopian Error.* Wheaton, Ill.: Crossway, 1992.

A CHALLENGE TO STUDENTS

Nelson C. "Bud" Hinkson

1934–1992

In his lifetime Bud Hinkson challenged hundreds of thousands of university students in America, Europe, Asia, and Africa to give their lives to serve Christ on the foreign field—a privilege he displayed alluringly in the manifest joy of his own experience. Among his own flock, Bud stimulated co-laborers to undertake for Christ and His kingdom more than they would otherwise have ventured. In the progress of his own missionary travels he established, under God, numerous indigenous ministries of evangelism and discipleship across Europe and Africa. For twenty years Bud willingly worked in secrecy (and hence without the awareness of the support front) in that rank of missionaries who operated in the Communist lands closed to the gospel, where any publicity might terminate efforts or endanger contacts. Here his focus was not simply ministering to believers but also evangelism. In the midst of the challenge of pioneer missions he was a faithful husband and father. The many thousands of letters Bud wrote from the foreign field were greatly valued around the world for their spiritual radiance and deep encouragement. For all his remarkable accomplishments in the cause of Christ, it was his vibrant spirit we shall miss most.

One cold winter's night, in a cabin in the Oregon Cascades, where lived a woodsman and his wife, a terrible accident occurred. Their son, Buddy, not yet two, fell against an axe, cutting a deep gash into his forehead. As the father sped for help, the sobbing mother held her son and prayed: "God, save his life, and I will dedicate him to You." She then fell into a dream and saw children from all countries of the world coming to her son's side. They spoke and sang together. When she awoke she felt her dream was God's answer—that Buddy would live and somehow be a blessing to many nations.

Memory harvest

As Bud grew, a godly grandmother helped to lay the first foundations of Scripture memory. This remained a lifelong discipline, which after many years had produced a "memory harvest" including eleven books of the Bible, and Psalm 119. Once he addressed a hall of collegians, reciting to them from memory 2 Timothy. Few present have forgotten that challenge.

It was not until his own college days and ensuing years of military service that the grace of God in Christ became his own experience. As with so many before him it was through the study of Romans that he grasped his full forgiveness and freedom from the labor of earning God's favor. Later he found that the words of C. T. Studd well transcribed the grateful sentiment of his own heart: "If Christ be God and died for me, no sacrifice is too great for me to make for Him."

Upon his return from the army Bud was

> *"If Christ be God*
> *and died for me,*
> *no sacrifice is too great for me*
> *to make for Him."*

Nelson C. "Bud" Hinkson (1934–1992).

challenged by Bill Bright, director of the then fledgling Campus Crusade for Christ, to reach university students. It was to be a lifelong attachment. In this context he acquired another lifelong attachment—Shirley Milligan, Crusade's National Women's Representative. Bud's ready memory came to his aid in this courtship, for a study Shirley had undertaken entitled, "The Man, If I Marry," included a lengthy list of the required biblical qualities. On one hearing Bud memorized this catalogue of traits, and whenever he exemplified one in her presence he would smile winningly and call out the appropriate number. Haunted, Shirley would repair to her list and find it true. Upon his displaying them all, they were married. From here Bud's ministry was shared, for Shirley was companion in all labors and party to most adventures. Common also was their assumption that consecration to Christ's commission to make disciples in all the world would eventually take them to its "uttermost parts."

The University Ambassador Team
It was while giving direction to Campus Crusade's West Coast work that Bud became gripped by Christ's sending of the seventy in Luke 10. He believed it was with sad frequency that missionaries went out to the field alone, lacking the encouragement and stimulus of camaraderie in the gospel. Were not two better than one? How could unbelievers see the body of Christ at work apart from a team presence? Thus the vision of the University Ambassador Team was born—seventy companions laboring together in the cause of the gospel on the foreign field. But which foreign field? A bishop of the Church of England, on visit to America, heard of the team and extended an invitation to make the universities of England the chosen field. Sensing in this God's call, the Hinksons boarded the boat for Britain, Bud's own family team having expanded to four through a son and daughter—Jon and Joi.

In England the watchword was "Win, Build, Send," and God blessed with lasting fruit. Among the harvest were many foreign students, and it was through their eagerness to be witnesses in their homelands that Campus Crusade ministries were raised up in numerous African states. So significant were these opportunities that Bud traveled one entire year in Africa, but it was not there that his energies would be focused, for his and Shirley's hearts were increasingly drawn to the lands of Eastern Europe and the Soviet Union.

Behind the Iron Curtain
In the summer of 1973 Bud, Shirley, Jon, and Joi loaded a truck and headed for Vienna with their two sheltie dogs. Confirmation that God was opening doors came in His miraculous parting of several bureaucratic seas, for they had left their passports in a desk packed inaccessibly in the van.

The Life of Nelson C. "Bud" Hinkson

1934	Born in Eugene, Oregon, March 4
1935	Committed to Christ by his mother
1952–56	At University of Oregon makes decision for Christ
1957	Law school
1957–58	United States Army, Germany
1959	Joins Campus Crusade for Christ ministry
1961	Marries Shirley Milligan
1964	Speaks at Presidential Prayer Breakfast to National Student Body Presidents
1966	Vision of University Ambassador Team—Luke 10
1967	Evangelistic blitz at University of California, Berkeley, with University Ambassador Team
1972	Recruits leadership for Africa
1973	Called by God to Eastern Europe and Soviet Union
1974–92	Sees God open the Soviet Union and every country (Poland, East Germany, Hungary, Yugoslavia, Czechoslovakia, Romania, Bulgaria, Albania) in Eastern Europe
1990	Speaks at Academy of Science Club in Soviet Union
1991	First Institute of Biblical Studies in Soviet Union
1992	Teaches Biblical Bible Study Method to more than four hundred students in Russia
1992	Dies in Germany, August 10

RUSSIA

Vienna ●

At the time the Communist governments of Eastern Europe and the Soviet Union were determined to keep their borders closed to the influence of the gospel. But Bud was a visionary prompted by God's unshakable promises. He didn't look at the obstacles—they would paralyze. He never asked, "Is it possible?" but simply, "How will we do it?" This faith honored God and so God honored this faith by granting remarkable access. His faith was often creative. Once on the Romanian border with kids, dogs and all, a guard discovered Shirley's Bible and therefore determined to deny them entry. Shirley still protests at how Bud managed to wrest sympathy from that zealous soldier: "You are right. My wife is a religious fanatic. You can't imagine what it's like to live with her. Please don't send us back. I desperately need this vacation." With a look of pity the guard raised the gate.

Bud's ministry in the East involved the whole family. Jon and Joi were taken out of school for each trip, and together they were very much a team, each with his and her part tapered to capacity. "When I was still very young," Jon recalls, "Dad would call me up with him to respond to questions. If he thought I could handle the query he would say, 'I'd like my son to answer that.'" Once when Bud called Joi up it was to promise her in marriage to any man who could penetrate Albania with the gospel. Happily a fine man, Roy Christians, took up the challenge. Good to his word, they are now married. It is not unknown in frontier missions for men to neglect their families for the ministry. Bud included his family. Perhaps it is due in part to this that his children remain in the ministry to this day.

Opportunities and adversaries

A new day has lately dawned in these lands once so closed to the gospel. To reflect upon what God has brought about is to be staggered: "I am accomplishing a work in your days," says the Lord, "which you would never believe though someone should describe it to you." Could Bud have imagined while teaching the Scriptures in the secrecy of a secluded Czechoslovakian

Cults multiplied their legions; spiritism cast its nets.

> *The Scriptures both*
> *energized him and*
> *directed those energies.*

hayloft that he would receive in his lifetime an official invitation to deliver five lectures on Christianity at the Soviet Academy of Science Club, or address the philosophy faculty at the University of Tirana in Albania? But how sweet for the hard-working farmer to receive such a share of the crop.

The very magnitude of God's harvest called for greater efforts, as did Satan's counterattacks. A wide door for effective service had opened, and there were many adversaries. With the crumbling walls came a rushing flood. Cults multiplied their legions; spiritism cast its nets; every wind of doctrine blew with gale force among the new believers— uprooting, confusing, twisting. In this crisis Bud believed the critical need was for Christians to be established in the Word of God, and to this end he focused what would be his final energies on inspiring and instructing God's people in the study of their Bibles. On his last trip to Russia it was this he passionately taught to a gathering of some four hundred students from across the former Soviet Union.

"Death, where is thy sting?"

There stands a simple cross by the roadside a few hundred yards from the family home in Starnberg, Germany, for it was here God called His servant Bud to his home above. He was racing along on his bicycle, as was his delight to do, when God summoned him. Only hours before, he had been praying and planning how God's Word might dwell richly in those among whom Christ had called him to labor. He had written out his plan for the coming years, crossing out "five" and writing "eight." No doubt Bud was surprised at his sudden summons. But he was not unprepared, for he had fought the good fight; he had finished his course.

In a cemetery in the woods there gathered from many lands many of those whose lives Bud had touched. They sang joyfully and blessed God for how He had been greatly magnified throughout Bud's life. Then they parted to press on in that same race he had finished.

The spirit of a man

Bud's was an invincible optimism, for he reckoned on eternal realities, and in their light he seemed to march in a constant pageant of triumph. He was never idle; rather he labored more energetically than most. Since Bernard there was no greater recruiter, for Bud was so obviously beside himself with the love of being a missionary that people were magnetically drawn to join him. Most significantly, Bud was dedicated to the Bible as his comprehensive missionary equipment. The Scriptures both energized him and directed those energies. In pioneer missions one cannot often draw from a wealth of experience, nor necessarily find vindication in manifest fruit. Bud understood that it is God's Word which must shape the missionary's efforts and impart confidence, that in so running, he does not run in vain.

Jon Hinkson

GIVING WINGS TO OTHERS

Josef Tson

1934–

"Scientific atheism" in Romanian schools weakened Josef Tson's faith, temporarily. Later his belief grew while he attended an atheistic university and found antidotes for each intellectual poison his professors served up.

During Nicolae Ceausescu's reign of terror, Tson pastored the 1,400-member Second Baptist Church in Oradea [oh-RAD-ee-ah], Romania—the largest Baptist church in Europe. Refusing to compromise his witness as pastor and seminary professor, he incurred the wrath of the secret police. Josef was told that he was going to be shot, but his life was miraculously spared and he left the country in 1981.

Nine years later, Ceausescu was gone and Pastor Tson was back in the country, brandishing sixty Christian books translated during his exile.

Josef Tson learned early that the mind can undermine faith. As a fourteen year old in 1948, he stopped going to church. His teacher had convinced him that scientists had proven there was no God and that only the uneducated believed in Him.

In 1950 he met some Christian intellectuals. Their existence was proof to him that the Communists had lied. He was baptized in June 1951.

A fellow student at Cluj [klooj] University warned Josef that the Communists would indoctrinate them and destroy their faith. For four years, several students met secretly every week to find facts that would keep the atheistic worldview from penetrating and polluting their minds.

No Christian books were available to them, and no Christian leaders were knowl-

edgeable enough to help. "It was a desperate but successful thing, that we stayed Christians." Four years in a Marxist school actually strengthened his faith. Many students became Christians through the efforts of the Christian group.

What atheism could not do, liberal theology did. In Josef's second year at the Baptist seminary in Bucharest, there was no one to help refute the higher criticism he was studying. He recalls, "The encounter destroyed my faith." He left seminary and the church and taught school for ten years—"all that time searching wildly, reading like mad, trying to find my way in the spiritual world." Richard Wurmbrand and Simon Cure [Kooray] helped him back to the faith.

Theology at Oxford

By a miraculous turn of events young Josef was able to go to Austria, then to Oxford University in England. He discovered that, "Theologically, Oxford is whatever you look for." When assigning a weekly essay, his professors provided bibliographies of liberal, conservative, and middle-of-the-road books. "You choose your own [approach] and prepare to defend it. For three years I was able in every subject to defend an evangelical position at the highest academic level." He received his M.A. with honors in 1972.

"Sufferology"

Josef's friends advised him against returning to Romania, knowing he could face suffering and even martyrdom. Certain that the Lord wanted him back, he spent much time formulating a biblical doctrine of suffering—he called it "sufferology"—and it revolutionized his thinking.

Most Western theologians look at suffering as primarily building the character of the

*Richard Wurmbrand and
Simon Cure helped him back
to the faith.*

sufferer. Tson discovered the Bible teaches that when God calls a Christian to suffer, it is to spread the good news, to build up the church, to advance the triumph of the truth.

Christ suffered once for all for atonement; that kind of suffering is complete. "But He is still suffering for building the Body [of Christ]. He suffers in the body" in the sense that Paul said, "I fill up the sufferings of Christ." Tson elaborates, "Whenever you do something—good or bad—to one of His little ones, you are doing it to Him. He is in the ones who accept to be sufferers for the gospel—who let Christ suffer through them."

Tson now understood that suffering is an instrument in God's economy. "I came to define my cross as any voluntary involvement in the spread of the gospel and in the building up of the body of Christ." This realization revolutionized his life.

When he went back to Romania in 1972, he was determined to preach the whole counsel of God and write without any inhibition. A fellow pastor cautioned him to be more careful for his own safety.

Tson answered, "This is the sermon the Lord gives me for this Sunday. My job is only to deliver the message. If He wants me to preach next Sunday, . . . His business is to keep me alive—if He so wishes!"

"A lioness"

Elisabeth was the girl next door and the pastor's daughter. Her father pioneered the preaching of the gospel in the central Transylvania area of Romania. He was severely persecuted in the 1920s and 1930s by the Orthodox church. Later the Nazis court-martialed him and threatened to kill him.

Elisabeth grew up in this heroic atmosphere of her father resolutely standing for Christ. Her husband, Josef, observes, "When I was called to do the same type of thing in the 1970s, she was the tougher of the two. . . . Whenever I was hesitating, she would sense it and come like a lioness and say, 'You go on and preach and die for it.' That helped me in several crucial moments when I had to make life-or-death decisions."

Josef Tson preaching in Romania.

"To die is gain"

In an interrogation session, the Minister of the Interior, the head of Ceausescu's secret police, threatened Tson. "You're going to be shot. But first I want you tortured so you will curse all that you hold sacred and holy." The official offered to reduce Josef's sentence to life imprisonment if he would confess that his papers had been written at the command of his "masters in the West."

With a smile, Tson answered, "What you offer me is spiritual suicide. I would much rather accept a physical death. . . . I don't see any reason to save my own life. Go on, shoot me."

Another time he told an officer, "Your supreme weapon is killing. My supreme weapon is dying. . . . You know that my sermons on tape have spread all over the country. If you kill me, those sermons will be sprinkled with my blood. Everyone will know I died for my preaching. And everyone

The Life of Josef Tson

1934	Born in Girbovita, Romania
1955	Graduates from University of Cluj
1959	Marries Elisabeth Cosman
1972	M.A. with honors, Oxford University, England Begins teaching at Bucharest Baptist Seminary
1973	Fired from seminary
1974–81	Pastors Baptist churches in Ploesti and Oradea
1974, 1977	Arrested
1981	Exiled from Romania Becomes president, Romanian Missionary Society
1983	Begins radio ministry
1985	Awarded doctorate of divinity degree, Gordon-Conwell Theological Seminary
1990	Relocates back to Romania
1991	Becomes chancellor, Oradea Bible Institute
1993	Establishes Christian radio stations in Romania

Josef Tson with his wife, Elisabeth, and daughter Dorothy.

who has a tape will pick it up and say, 'I'd better listen again to what this man preached, because he really meant it; he sealed it with his life.'

"So, sir, my sermons will speak ten times louder than before. I will actually rejoice in this supreme victory if you kill me."

His interrogator sent him home.

Heading West

With no seminary available to train pastors, in 1977 Pastor Tson asked Christians in Vienna to provide materials for a Biblical Education by Extension (BEE) program, a variation of Theological Education by Extension (TEE).

But he discovered it would not work successfully without Christian books as resources. Very few existed in Romania. Consequently in January 1981, he felt challenged to leave his homeland in order to translate a number of books. He resigned his church and announced that he expected to devote the rest of his life to producing theological books.

When he asked for permission to emigrate, the secret police were at first very happy. But Tson knew the government was beginning to audit church finances "with the purpose of clamping down on many activities, and also smearing the pastor." He couldn't let this practice go unchallenged, so he researched the issue from theological and legal standpoints. "I came up with a paper that demonstrated that what the state did was illegal, and what the pastors did was legal."

He distributed the paper and returned home to find a letter saying the police had refused his passport application. But when authorities found out about the paper, they angrily told Tson to leave the country and not return.

"I just took it that the Lord wanted me to come and do the books." When Tson arrived in Wheaton, Illinois, Peter Deyneka, Jr., helped him set up an office. Josef wanted to translate seventy books; sixty were completed by the time Romania reopened.

Shortly after Tson arrived in America, Radio Free Europe (RFE) approached him. He began with a ten-minute weekly program, expanding it later to fifty minutes. When he visited Romania, people recognized his voice before he mentioned his

> *The first station went on the air in Suceava in June 1993.*

name. Even high officials told him they listened. He continues on RFE and has added programs on Trans World Radio in Monte Carlo and local stations within Romania.

Back to Romania

Returning to Romania in 1990, Tson considered running for parliament. But as he thought more deeply about this, he concluded that he could make the greatest long-term impact by adopting a three-pronged strategy:

1. Training people for ministry. Tson and his colleagues now have 316 full-time students in their seminary, plus more than a hundred others studying by extension.

2. Continuing to translate and publish books.

3. Fostering radio broadcasts. Whereas the first two tasks mean taking time to produce a harvest of new converts, the radio can produce results more rapidly. Tson notes: "The immediate [results] are from reaching the home by radio." When Romania decided to license FM stations, Tson brought together various evangelical denominations to incorporate a radio

organization, The Voice of the Gospel, and applied for FM licenses in major Romanian cities. Station HCJB provides transmitters and studios, with the Romanian Missionary Society helping it with the provision of the operating funds. The first station went on the air in Suceava [soo-CHAH-vah] in June 1993. A station was scheduled for Bucharest in September 1993, with others to follow.

Thrills

"The most amazing thing in Romania was in January 1991. A few months after we started our school of theology, I was asked to go to Bucharest and talk with a government official. He told me they decided to reintroduce religion in the state schools, but they were without trained teachers. Could we add to our school of theology a Christian teacher-training college—to train teachers who would go into the public schools to teach the Christian religion?"

An even more amazing opportunity occurred while Tson was visiting Russia in February 1993. Obninsk is Russia's atomic research city, with 2,600 Ph.D.s staffing the highest institutions of learning. One postgraduate Institute of Modern Knowledge decided to start a faculty of theology. After Tson visited them, their leaders came to Oradea. "They wanted to produce people

Baptismal candidates outside Josef Tson's church.

> ## "They wanted to produce people who have a Christian worldview."

who have a Christian worldview, who would go into the university and teach Christianity for scholars—and to teach how Christianity should guide our thinking."

Tson replied that such a curriculum should be set up the way the faculty of Marxism-Leninism had been arranged, "where we were taught the Marxist worldview . . . and how it applies to history, to chemistry, to biology and politics and so on. Why don't we then create a faculty of Christian worldview?" The Russians who proposed the possibility are trying to convince their Minister of Education to accredit the concept.

Threats

Regarding threats to evangelical witness, Tson comments, "Eastern Europe never had a Reformation. Reformation was always done by university professors. The problem with the evangelicals is that they went to the village and to the outskirts of the city. They made little churches of uneducated people—ghettos who are afraid of culture.

"If we don't succeed to lift up the gospel to the level of the university, we'll never do the Reformation there. You can spread a little bit further—with little, isolated evangelical groups—but never impact the nation. So my vision is to lift the gospel to the academic position, and then influence the whole country and create a proper Reformation."

The dominant church considers Baptists and other evangelicals dangerous and takes every opportunity to hinder them. "But the problem for them is that Romania wants to get into the Common Market, and the Common Market demands democracy and freedom of minorities. So they have no chance to impose a new state-Orthodox dictatorship or discrimination."

Requests for prayer

"At this stage, our biggest need is to build a campus for a Christian university in Romania. We have the land, all the approvals, young people who want to study and young Romanians who can teach there."

This would be the first Christian university in Europe—East or West.

He also requests wisdom in knowing how to bring the right people to the faculty, "to anchor it in such a way . . . that it will stay an evangelical school, built on the inerrancy of Scripture."

Putting wings on people

What burning ambition drives this man? Tson says he envisions God as a Creator and Redeemer. God always lifts up, heals and remakes things and lives beautiful. "When I contemplate God like that, I love what I see, and I want to be like that," he says. "I want to create, I want to bring harmony and symmetry. I want to lift up, to redeem, to give a new challenge. My message is, 'Fall in love with this kind of God. Be like Him.' That's the basic call that God gives us—to be what He is, to be like our Father... It's not enough to have knowledge; you have to really love your God, and with all your being desire to be what you see in Him." He continues, "My passion and my call in life are to raise others to do the job of the kingdom—to take young people and put wings on them, and help them fly." Since starting this aspect of his ministry in the early 1970s, "I can see now very, very many young people who tell that they are what they are today, because in the 1970s I told them, 'Go for higher education, learn English, get prepared for the Lord to use you at the highest level.' Now they are people who never stopped. In that area I see the achievement of my life."

Tson finds his wings in Philippians 2:5–8: "Your attitude should be the same as that of Christ Jesus: Who, being in very nature God, did not consider equality with God something to be grasped, but made himself nothing, taking the very nature of a servant, being made in human likeness. And being found in appearance as a man, he humbled himself and became obedient to death—even death on a cross!"

Tson comments, "Developing the mind of Christ means voluntarily taking the place of a slave—being totally at God's disposal to

> ## "My passion is to take young people and put wings on them, and help them fly."

do whatever He wants with your life."

When tired or discouraged, the realization of his union with Christ keeps Josef Tson going. "I know that He united Himself with me, made me part of Him, and I am a branch of the Vine. I am tired, broken, many times a failure; but He never lets me down. So that's my strength."

David Fisher

Further Reading

Elliott, Mark. "Hit and Run Evangelism Wrong Move in Former Communist World." *News Network International World Perspectives.* (February 28, 1992).

Mojzes, Paul, ed. *Religious Liberty in Eastern Europe and the U.S.S.R.* New York: Columbia Univ., Eastern European Monographs, 1992.

Romania for Jesus Christ. Romanian Missionary Society Quarterly. P.O. Box 527, Wheaton, Illinois 60189–0527.

Tson, Josef. *Partners in Suffering.* Ann Arbor: The Center for Pastoral Renewal, 1990.

THE WORLD IS HIS PARISH

Sammy Tippit

1947–

Sammy Tippit made the mistake of dating a deacon's daughter. One Sunday night in 1965, just after Tippit had graduated from high school, his girlfriend's father wouldn't let them go out unless they went to church first. Sammy did, despite the laughter and derision of his partying friends. There Sammy heard the gospel and received Christ. Immediately he felt that God was calling him to preach.

Sammy Tippit's birth in Baton Rouge, Louisiana, came almost simultaneous to the birth of Billy Graham's public ministry in the late 1940s. Tippit would become an international evangelist in his own right, more recognized overseas than in the United States, where he headquartered his ministry in San Antonio, Texas.

A brilliant student and United Nations-honored orator as a high schooler, Sammy Tippit felt called to the ministry upon his conversion during the summer before his freshman year of college. From a humble beginning boldly sharing his faith on the streets and in the bars in his hometown, he went on to preach on every inhabited continent, specializing in the hard, out-of-the-way places.

He was arrested and stood trial in Chicago in the early 1970s, and was later arrested and deported from both the Soviet Union and Romania. He went on to hold the first ever outdoor soccer stadium crusades in both Romania and the former Soviet Republic of Moldavia, and he remains a powerful preacher and beloved evangelist in the many countries where he has ministered.

College dropout

He had already been recognized at the United Nations as the outstanding high school speaker in North America. Now all he needed was knowledge. He was discipled by his pastor, and quickly he began to visit in a nursing home and preach in the bars and nightclubs of his hometown, Baton Rouge, Louisiana.

In college Tippit was restless, still driven to witness and preach on the streets during the week and at various churches on the weekends. He married Debara Ann (Tex) Sirman in June 1968 and dropped out of college during his senior year, "unable to sit in class while the world was dying." It was a major decision, for his late father's last request was that Sammy finish college, and friends told him he would never speak in large churches or gain any ministerial reputation without a degree.

The first day on their own, Sammy and Tex saw all their belongings stolen. Now they were really living by faith; Sammy continued to witness and preach with nothing but the clothes on his back. When a friend invited him to a regional evangelism conference, Tippit, unshaven and in his only set of clothes, felt compelled to speak from the floor about his burden for kids and street people and how the church must begin ministering to them. From that brief moment came dozens of invitations to speak in churches.

Provision for restlessness

He and Tex remained faithful to their call, and Sammy developed the philosophy of ministry that remains his hallmark. "Somehow I knew that if God had put that restlessness in my heart, He would take care of Tex and me. My reputation wasn't as important to me as it had once been. I would be just as

> He dropped out of college during his senior year, "unable to sit in class while the world was dying."

Crowds gather around Sammy Tippit and Peter Duealescu in Timisoara.

happy to share Christ with one person in the middle of nowhere as to preach from the most well-known pulpit in the world."

From youth crusades all over the country to walks from Louisiana to Washington, D.C. (pushing a wheelbarrow full of Bibles), or carrying a cross to the 1972 Democratic National Convention, Tippit threw himself into ministry. He was called one of the original Jesus People, though he never identified himself that way. Living on faith, preaching Christ, and witnessing on the streets became the trademark of his fledgling ministry, which he called God's Love In Action.

Another uniqueness of Tippit's ministry was that he decided early never to ask for money. He sent out a newsletter to a small mailing list of friends and prayer partners, but he never solicited funds. He believed that income was a harbinger of God's blessing on his plans. "If the money came in, God wanted us to go. If it didn't, then He didn't."

Even in those earliest days of his ministry, Tippit felt a distinct call to Eastern Europe. He didn't understand it and had no idea how he would ever get there or what he would do when he arrived, but he harbored that inclination for years.

Witness by fasting

Settling his street ministry in Chicago in the early 1970s, Tippit and an associate were arrested for witnessing in front of nightclubs and ostensibly hurting their businesses. Sammy felt led to fast and pray in the famed Daley Civic Center Plaza for twenty-five days before his trial, which was handled gratis by a Christian attorney. The case drew worldwide interest and the charges were dropped, but many came to Christ during that period. The day of the trial, September 29, 1971, Sammy and Tex's first child, Dave, was born.

One of the great thrills of Sammy's life came nearly twenty years later when a woman at the Lausanne II Conference in Manila, Philippines, informed him that she had come to Christ through his ministry in Chicago. She had been a dancer at a nightclub, had read one of his tracts, and went to hear him speak. There she had received Christ, and now she and her husband were missionaries.

When Tippit was finally able to make his first visit to Europe in 1971, he developed a love for the people that has centered much of his ministry there ever since. He learned of the Communist Youth World Fest to be held in East Berlin in 1973, and his consuming passion became to infiltrate that meeting of 100,000 Communist young people. He and two friends preached, witnessed, and passed out tracts there, seeing two hundred receive Christ as Savior.

Later, as he was following up with some of the converts, he heard a girl add a phrase to her prayer that became another catch phrase in his ministry. She prayed that God would give her the courage to live for Him, "no matter what the cost."

Deported

In the spring of 1974 Tippit's resolve to live for Christ no matter what the cost was put to the test when he and an associate were arrested in Leningrad (Petersburg) for witnessing to Soviet college students. They were put under house arrest in their hotel, interrogated for hours, and forced to sign a confession to their crime of "spreading the disease of religion." In their confessions, however, they wrote their testimonies and explained how the reader could receive Christ.

Finally they demanded to see the American consulate. Eventually they were deported to Helsinki, Finland. Sammy had no idea how long that black mark might remain on his record and keep him from coming back to preach in the Soviet Union.

Soon Sammy began feeling that his ministry was outgrowing his maturity, so he sought a place to minister where he could settle in and grow. He accepted a three-year pastorate of an English-speaking church in Hahn, West Germany, where the congregation was made up largely of American military personnel.

The domestic front

The church, and Tippit, grew by leaps and bounds. Sammy accepted speaking engagements throughout Europe and discipled many men in his church, seeing their families grow in Christ, too. He also learned many hard lessons, the most important one from his wife, Tex.

One evening she mustered the courage to tell him that she had been harboring resentment toward him for how he had treated her. They were planning a trip to Romania, where a great revival had taken place, and

Sammy Tippit addresses an evangelistic rally.

she felt the need to get her feelings sorted out before they went.

She told Sammy that with his driving personality and his debating skills she had never been able to win an argument. He was always right, and when he wasn't he convinced himself he was and wore her down. Also, she had been on the front lines of ministry prior to the birth of Dave and, later, their daughter, Renee. Now she merely waited in the wings for him to return and report what the Lord was doing.

Sammy was devastated and broken. He

> *He learned many hard lessons, the most important one from his wife, Tex.*

asked the elders for time off, and he and Tex got away where they could work out the problem. Sammy saw that she had been right. Without being aware of it or meaning to, he had not treated Tex the way he should have. "I began to see in a new way my self-centeredness, pride, and impurities." Sammy asked for and received her forgiveness and the Lord's, and he pledged himself to be a more loving, giving husband.

With their relationship rejuvenated and Sammy's ministry flourishing, they visited Romania for the first time. Sammy developed such a loving relationship with the people there that he became a favorite and continued to preach there for years.

The Life of Sammy Tippit

1947	Born in Baton Rouge, Louisiana
1965	Commits his life to Christ
1968	Marries Debara Ann Sirman, June
Early 1970s	Begins street ministry
1971	Arrested in Chicago for preaching
1973	Preaches outside the Communist Youth World Fest in East Berlin
1974	Arrested in Leningrad for witnessing to Soviet college students
1988	"Kicked out" of Romania for witnessing
1990	Leads first soccer stadium crusade in Romania Preaches at first crusades in Moldavia
1992	Preaches to thousands in outdoor stadiums in Siberia
1993	Leads first public evangelism in Mongolia

• Leningrad **RUSSIA**
(Petersburg)

More international crusades

He accepted a couple of pastorates in the United States and eventually settled in San Antonio, but he quickly grew restless, sensing God's call to continue to preach internationally. As he battled his fears of subjecting his family to such danger and uncertainty, he ran into his old friend Arthur Blessitt, another outspoken and gifted evangelist.

Blessitt challenged him to follow God's call again. Other seemingly coincidental meetings confirmed in Sammy's heart that he must release his family to God's protection, being careful and prudent but also involving them in the traveling and the ministry to the hard places.

When he finally left the pastorate and returned to full-time international evangelism in 1986, he saw his ministry explode. He has since held crusades in India, South America, Africa, the former Soviet Union, Romania, Mongolia, Albania. In July 1988, the Romanian government blacklisted the evangelist and kicked him out of the country. But in 1990, after the revolution and the ouster of Nicolae Ceaucescu, Sammy returned to Romania and conducted the first soccer stadium crusade in that nation's history. Hundreds responded to his preaching. He also returned to the Soviet Union without incident and preached in great outdoor meetings there; at one meeting about 2,500 responded to the invitation to receive Christ as Savior.

Sammy Tippit continues to preach all over the world. He says, "The burden God has given me for lost souls is so great that I can't begin to do a thing about it. I can preach everywhere I have the time and resources to go, and there will still be millions who haven't heard the gospel."

Jerry Jenkins

Further Reading

Tippit, Sammy. *Fire in Your Heart*. Chicago: Moody, 1987.

——. *Fit for Battle*. Chicago: Moody, 1994.

Tippit, Sammy, with Jerry B. Jenkins. *No Matter What the Cost*. Nashville: Nelson, 1993.

——. *Sammy Tippit: God's Love in Action*. Nashville: Broadman, 1973.

——. *You, Me, He*. Wheaton: Victor, 1978.

International

George Fisk

1905–1977

George Fisk may not be a household name in the annals of missions history. But as the father of missionary aviation he ranks as one of the most important facilitators of the spread of the gospel in the twentieth century. His dream of reaching the lost in Borneo in a more effective way ultimately was the stimulus for the birth of six major mission aviation programs, most of which still exist and literally cover the globe with planes in the service of world missions.

Sitting on a rock, exhausted after a morning of carrying boats around an unnavigable section of a Borneo river in 1932, George Fisk looked back down river to assess his team's progress. He was dismayed to see that only a few hundred yards away was the campsite they had left that morning! As he and the porters were preparing lunch, he observed two hornbills gliding along easily, high above the jungle gorge that hemmed in the party of the porters.

Struck by the sight of these large-beaked birds, Fisk exclaimed to his companions, "Look! I'll do that!"

"You'll do what?" the startled porters asked, staring at the soaring birds.

"I'll fly the gospel here, over the rapids, over the jungle, over the mountains," Fisk declared. He then explained what "mechanical birds" were. In just a few moments Fisk and the partners were on their knees beside the racing rapids praying for an airplane. It mattered little to Fisk that these nationals didn't understand what they were praying for. He had been given a vision that was to revolutionize the spread of the gospel. He would become a pilot so that he could fly above the dangerous rapids and meandering river straight to those who so badly needed to hear the gospel.

George F. Fisk was born into a godly family in Binghamton, New York, September 17, 1905. His father had wanted to be a missionary in India, but circumstances prevented him from realizing his dream. He prayed that if he had children, they would be missionaries. George, one of three boys, would be an answer to his father's prayer.

Destination Borneo

At the age of eight, George attended a circus. When he returned home, the excited boy related all he had seen to his parents. He had been particularly fascinated by the "Wild Man of Borneo."

"Are there any missionaries in Borneo telling the story of Jesus to the natives?" he asked. His mother replied that there were none. This planted a resolve in George's mind and heart that he would be the one to take the gospel to them.

Fisk pursued missions and medical studies in college. While there, he formed a Borneo prayer group. The resolve he had as an eight year old remained very much alive. Following graduation, he approached the missionary board of a Presbyterian denomination and asked them to send him to Borneo. They had no work in that country and urged him to go where they had an established mission. But Fisk felt strongly that God had specifically called him to Borneo. He next approached the Christian and Missionary Alliance (C&MA), but again received a negative reply. Not discouraged, he boldly went to each of the board members. One of them suggested he write to Dr. R. A. Jaffrey, a C&MA missionary in China. Jaffrey had expressed an interest in establishing a work in the South Sea islands. The reply Fisk received was encouraging:

for several years a number of Christians in China had been praying for someone to go to the South Sea region. Jaffrey convinced the C&MA board that Fisk represented an answer to prayer, and he was soon accepted to work in Borneo.

Help from the hornbill
In 1929, Fisk sailed for Borneo. After learning the "Low Malay" language, he set out for the "wild men" for whom he had prayed for years. "When I reached the natives," he said, "I felt like Joshua entering the Promised Land." His excitement propelled him from the boat to the first man he saw. He grabbed his hand and shook it, claiming him for Christ. In a short time the man, and many neighbors had become followers of Christ. Fisk was committed to telling the story of Jesus to the unreached, and he pushed two hundred miles further into the interior of Borneo along the Kajan River. Supplies and several men were lost to the dangerous rapids on these trips. It was on one of these arduous journeys that the sight of the hornbills precipitated the revolution in his mind concerning missionary travel.

Fisk corresponded with Jaffrey, now his field director, about his idea. Jaffrey was supportive. On his first furlough back in the United States, Fisk set about obtaining his pilot's license and "soloed" in 1935. Planning for an airplane to fly on a mission field was no easy logistical task. Despite many obstacles, and showing the resolve that had taken him to Borneo in the first place, Fisk taught the natives to "read" the river and the sky. By their observations he was able to accumulate weather and river data, which he used to determine the best landing sites and times of day and year to fly. Finally, on June 29, 1938, the board granted Fisk's proposal to bring an airplane to Borneo, and evangelical missionary aviation became a reality.

Research as to the best type of aircraft to buy involved R. G. LeTourneau, a Christian machinery inventor and industrialist. He recommended a Waco airplane like his own and offered to provide a portion of the cost.

> *Fisk felt strongly that God had specifically called him to Borneo.*

The Life of George Fisk

1905	Born in Binghamton, New York, September 17
1913	Senses God's call to Borneo
1929	Sails to Borneo with wife, Anna
1932	Conceives airplane aid for missionaries when viewing hornbills during jungle journey
1935	Receives pilot's license
1939	Aircraft purchase approved
1941	Leaves Borneo on the eve of World War II
1943	Meets with three United States Navy pilots to plan Christian Airmen's Missionary Fellowship
1977	Death in North Carolina

BORNEO

AUSTRALIA

The C&MA board, however, wanted a Dutch plane, since it might be easier to get the plane serviced by mechanics in the Dutch East Indies. The Beechcraft SE 17B was selected, and they prepared to convert it into a floatplane when a surprise problem emerged. Learning of the plane's destination, Walter Beech, founder of Beechcraft, was furious. "Borneo?! What idiot sold a Beechcraft to another idiot in Borneo?!" He didn't want one of his planes in the hands of an amateur in the jungles.

The sale went through, contingent upon Beech's insistence that a pilot-mechanic of

Mr. and Mrs. George Fisk in 1927.

his own choosing would qualify whoever would be doing the flying. The floats were installed, and the plane tested. Then it was disassembled, crated, and shipped to Borneo, where it was reassembled with the help of Dutch navy personnel. Fisk's dream had been realized.

Missionary flight school

While in the United States, Fisk often spoke of his plan to operate an aircraft in support of his work. One evening in Buffalo, New York, a pastor was present who had set his sights on serving as a missionary to Brazil's upper Amazon. After hearing Fisk's enthusiastic and practical presentation, Paul Robinson began his pursuit of flight training. He first soloed a few days before the United States entered World War II. But by the time the war was over, Robinson was considered too old to enter missions. Armed with statistics on the huge amounts of time and money planes could save, he approached the board of trustees of his alma mater, Moody Bible Institute, to convince its members to begin a program to train missions students to fly and care for airplanes. The plan was approved, and the Missionary Technical Course (later called Moody Aviation) began.

Fisk's vision had already helped launch a program to train missionary pilots.

The entry of the United States into war temporarily ended Fisk's own missionary activity as well. He returned to the States in November 1941 on the last boat to leave the area prior to the attack on Pearl Harbor.

Missionary Aviation Fellowship

Fisk traveled to meetings, speaking of his experiences in Borneo. In 1943, James Truxton, a navy patrol bomber pilot, visited Providence Bible Institute to hear Fisk speak to the student body about flying as a means to support mission work. After the meeting, Truxton expressed a desire to use his military training to serve the Lord and arranged to meet Fisk in a Brooklyn restaurant at a later date. Truxton brought two other navy pilots, James Byers and Clarence Sodeberg, to the meeting. The four men formulated a plan to establish an organization of military pilots interested in missionary aviation with the intent of providing pilots and planes for missions. Christian Airmen's Missionary Fellowship was born in that restaurant and the three navy pilots were its first members. Fisk decided to remain in an advisory capacity as he intended to reestablsh the Borneo

A Missionary
Aviation
Fellowship
plane in Zulu-
land in 1961.

aviation mission.

Truxton gathered an interested group of aviators, and upon his discharge from the navy, formally established CAMF (later to be called Missionary Aviation Fellowship). Jim Byers was with CAMF less than a year and then went to Brazil under a Presbyterian denomination to establish an aviation program there. Clarence Sodeberg was sent by CAMF to Liberia to fly at the request of Sudan Interior Mission. His efforts resulted in the creation of SIMAIR, an aviation program supported by SIM.

CAMF was asked by Wycliffe Bible Translators to send a plane and pilot to Mexico to support their jungle camp. Differences in philosophy of aircraft operations and local government cooperation prompted Wycliffe to establish their own program, called Jungle Aviation and Radio Service (JAARS).

Fisk's persistence in pursuing the dream God had given him resulted in the creation of six mission aviation programs. In addition to his own work with the mission aviation program of the C&MA, Fisk was instrumental in the formation of CAMF and inspiring the men who started MAF, SIMAIR, Presbyterian mission aviation efforts in Brazil, and JAARS. He also inspired Paul Robinson who started Moody Aviation, which trains and supplies over half the missionary pilots, mechanics, and radio technicians in the world today.

What George Fisk didn't realize when he saw the hornbills soaring over the Borneo jungle gorge in 1932 was that God would use his vision for one plane for his own missionary efforts to spark the vision in many others regarding the great value of planes in the spreading of the gospel of Jesus Christ.

John and Steve Wells

Further Reading

Albus, Harry. "He Flew the Gospel to the Headhunters," *Sunday Magazine,* December 1945.

Lawson, Edward. "The Gospel Goes by Air." *Flying and Popular Aviation,* November 1940.

Robinson, Paul F., and James Vincent. *A Vision with Wings: The Story of Missionary Aviation.* Chicago: Moody, 1992.

Roddy, Lee. *On Wings of Love—Stories from Mission Aviation Fellowship.* Nashville: Nelson, 1981.

Wells, John R. The John Wells Collection, Archives of the Billy Graham Center, Wheaton, Illinois.

Opposite: Dr.
Billy Graham.

EVANGELIST TO THE WORLD

Billy Graham

1918–

In the middle of the twentieth century, at the time when the Los Angeles Crusade made Billy Graham a national figure in America, Christianity outside North America seemed to be heading for virtual oblivion as a force in human affairs.

In Western Europe, where Christianity had flourished for more than a thousand years, the main churches were shrinking in numbers and influence, while Eastern Europe suffered under oppressive atheist regimes. In Asia and Africa, Christianity had expanded rapidly in the previous century through European and American missionary endeavor, but the thrust was faltering amid tensions between colonialism and national movements, and between missionary societies and the churches they had brought into being. Moreover the vision of the evangelization of the world was fading as many questioned the historic truths of the faith and put a higher priority on social amelioration.

Yet by the end of the twentieth century Christianity had recovered its vigor. Communism had collapsed throughout Eastern Europe and the former Soviet Union. Evangelization had again become a top priority, balanced by social awareness. Although many personalities and organizations had played a part in this change, one man stands out: Billy Graham.

In the last week of February 1954 the thirty-five-year-old American evangelist Billy Graham and his wife and team were crossing the Atlantic by sea to begin the Greater London crusade.

Graham was already famous in his own country. Since the tent mission at Los Angeles in 1949, which had made the gospel newsworthy again, he had conducted crusades up and down America. Their blend of warmth and reverence had revived the churches and given a new thrust for evangelism.

He was still almost unknown outside America. Seven years earlier he had conducted small missions in Britain with little impact on the nation. The coming crusade at Harringay Arena could be different.

A day short of Southampton a steward knocked on Graham's door and handed him a radio news sheet. To his astonishment, Graham read that a member of Parliament would try to stop him from entering England as a political adventurer in disguise. The British press were in an uproar, baying for Graham's blood. The trouble was traced to some words in a leaked, uncorrected proof, which had been misunderstood. Graham could only commit his cause to God in prayer.

The matter was corrected quickly, and it made Graham front page news and launched the crusade as a national event. Three months later, when the final meetings took place in London's largest outdoor stadiums, with the Archbishop of Canterbury taking part, Harringay had become an honored name in Britain's religious history

> *The British press were in an uproar, baying for Graham's blood.*

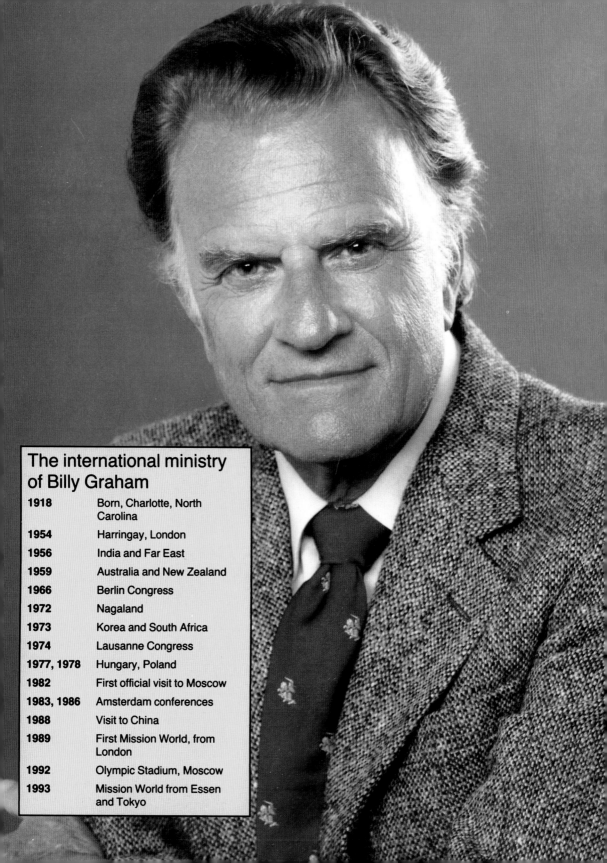

The international ministry of Billy Graham

1918	Born, Charlotte, North Carolina
1954	Harringay, London
1956	India and Far East
1959	Australia and New Zealand
1966	Berlin Congress
1972	Nagaland
1973	Korea and South Africa
1974	Lausanne Congress
1977, 1978	Hungary, Poland
1982	First official visit to Moscow
1983, 1986	Amsterdam conferences
1988	Visit to China
1989	First Mission World, from London
1992	Olympic Stadium, Moscow
1993	Mission World from Essen and Tokyo

Opposite: In 1973 Billy Graham conducted a crusade to a fully integrated audience at the Wanderers Stadium, Johannesburg, after refusing for twenty-two years to conduct segregated crusades in South Africa.

and a turning point in Billy Graham's life.

The crusade's impact did not spring from superb organization but from the dedication of thousands of Christians and of the Graham team, and because Billy Graham was a man of strict integrity and sweetness of character, with a passion for souls and a willingness to use the unfolding technology of the age. He preached the eternal gospel, the historic truth of the cross, and the bodily resurrection of Christ with a conviction that contrasted with the uncertainties of the British churches, which were emerging from decades of liberal compromise. Above all he had long been a man of prayer who knew that no soul could be won for Christ except by the Holy Spirit.

Beyond America's borders

Harringay was the start of a lifelong international ministry. It opened doors throughout the world. Graham was listened to with respect, that very year of 1954, on the continent of Europe. The next year he held a crusade in Scotland, which moved the country. It was followed by a return to Wembley Stadium, London, in the rain. At Windsor, Graham preached before the queen and the royal family. The queen mother had already summed up the effect of Harringay, when in a letter written at her command she spoke of "the spiritual rekindling you have brought to numberless Englishmen and women whose faith has been made to glow anew by your addresses."

In 1956 Graham went to India. The great crowd who listened in the open air in Kerala, South India, was an unforgettable sight and a foretaste of even greater crowds in later years in the Orient. After India, Graham went on for short stops in Asian countries where opportunities for longer missions would follow. Building on that first tour that brought together the growing churches of the East, missionaries and nationals worked together in Asia to prepare and to follow up, reaping a harvest of encouragement where Christians were in a minority, and the people were spiritually hungry.

In Australia, as in Britain, the Billy Graham crusades of the 1950s were the spiritual birthplace of many hundreds who grew to be Christian leaders in the last quarter of the century. These crusades were not brief sparks but the centerpieces of careful preparation and follow-up. Graham worked with the churches, trusting God to strengthen and refresh them as they renewed their dedication and vision.

Evangelism conferences

Graham soon began to bring church leaders together from all parts of the world. A small conference at Montreux, Switzerland, in 1960 led to the World Congress on Evangelism in Berlin in 1966, and regional congresses that followed in each continent. Then, in 1974, he convened the Lausanne Congress on World Evangelization, in Lausanne, Switzerland, which proved to be a watershed in the history of the Christian church.

At Lausanne, the division between missionary-sending and missionary-receiving nations disappeared. Whites were outnumbered; skin color and national origins were insignificant as all planned to reach out in a spirit of love.

Lausanne could never have happened without Billy Graham: his vision, his contacts with leaders everywhere, and his integrity brought in the money to finance the coming of several thousand participants. Eminent theologians and bishops were glad to set aside time, energy, and thought at his request; they trusted and loved him, and worked together to produce the document known as the Lausanne Covenant.

The participants returned home to carry forward the evangelization of the world for Christ, in fresh loyalty to the truths of Scripture and the historic facts of the faith. They were also aware of the profound consequences for the strategies and growth of the Christian church in the last quarter of the century. Yet in one respect Lausanne disappointed Graham: he had originally intended to encourage the foot-soldiers of the faith, the humble evangelists who pushed bicycles through jungles or endured the steamy heat of cities to proclaim the faith. Instead, Lausanne in the will of God had become a

> *These crusades were not brief sparks but the centerpieces of careful preparation and follow-up.*

vital planning session for the generals and staff officers. Nine years later (1983), therefore, Graham and his team organized a conference of itinerant evangelists at Amsterdam, which was repeated in 1986 because so many were unable to attend the earlier meeting.

The Amsterdam conferences were happy occasions for training and fellowship, without the tensions that had been inevitable as Lausanne struggled with mighty issues. Many of the participants had never seen more than a few hundred Christians together: now they could pray and sing and learn with thousands. From Amsterdam Graham sent a surge of encouragement across the world and strengthened a new generation of evangelists.

But Graham was far more than an international evangelist. He was a world Christian statesman. He moved freely among secular statesmen; heads of state and prime ministers received him, and he always sought to give his personal testimony and to uplift Christ, whatever his host's religion or lack of it. Graham discussed freely the problems of local Christians, especially in a non-Christian or Communist country, for he knew that their own leaders were not always able to do so.

To India's hills

His statesmanship was particularly evident in his ability to enter a situation of conflict, whether in the state or among the churches, and contribute strongly toward reconciliation. Thus, in 1972 he was given permission to enter Nagaland, a remote Indian state normally closed to foreigners, to hold a crusade to celebrate the centenary of the strong church that had arisen among the tribes who once had been headhunters.

A desire within Nagaland for independence from India had created civil strife and diverted many Christians from their earlier zeal for evangelism, but the Christian leaders had negotiated a cease-fire for the period of the crusade. A few days before the planned start, Naga hostilities killed a lieutenant and three sepoys. The Indian government did not cancel Graham's permission. Some of his advisers urged cancellation because hostile forces might kill him to gain worldwide attention, or the Indian government might exploit him. The Nagas begged

> *This Kohima crusade proved to be a decisive factor in bringing peace to Nagaland.*

him to come: "Oh, Dr. Graham," exclaimed one, "you will set the Christians back for years if you don't go."

He went; and none present could forget the colorful sight of one hundred thousand Nagas packed into the football ground, or the sound of Graham's words being simultaneously translated, a second after every phrase he spoke, into twenty languages or dialects by interpreters with megaphones or bullhorns, each tribal group sitting together, conscious only of Graham speaking, as it were, in its own tongue.

This Kohima crusade proved to be a decisive factor in bringing peace to Nagaland, although it was not until three years later that the Shillong Agreement virtually ended the rebellion.

Agent of reconciliation

Six months after Nagaland, Graham came into a much wider place of conflict: South Africa. He had refused to conduct a crusade unless conditions of apartheid were lifted, yet he had indirectly influenced South Africa already. Michael Cassidy, founder of African Enterprise, which had become a strong agent for evangelism and reconciliation among races, had been brought to Christ at Cambridge University through an undergraduate converted at Harringay, had been strengthened in his faith when Graham conducted a mission at Cambridge, and had dedicated his life to African evangelism during Graham's New York crusade.

In 1973 Cassidy persuaded the South African government to allow an interracial congress of evangelism at Durban, which Graham addressed, and two integrated stadium rallies at Durban and Johannesburg. They were permitted because Graham was the preacher. Only he could have brought black and white together in meetings of that size in the South Africa of 1973. When Graham gave the invitation a flood tide of people of all races mingled as they moved forward down the aisles: the fear that lay at the root of apartheid was lost at the foot of the cross.

"The sight of black and white South

Dr. Graham addresses the largest Christian gathering in the history of Calcutta, India, in a tent specially designed for the crusade.

Africa together," recalled a black bishop a year later, "singing and praying to the one God, was a foretaste of what future generations in this land are certain to enjoy if we today will be faithful." And when nineteen years later Nelson Mandela (himself helped by Billy Graham telecasts in prison) and President F. W. de Klerk began dismantling apartheid and preparing for a multiracial South African government, the 1973 Graham crusade could be seen as a major landmark on the long road they had come.

By November 1978, when Graham passed his sixtieth birthday, he had preached in most countries of the free world, including Korea, where more than one million gathered on the final afternoon: Korean church leaders regard the Billy Graham crusade of May 1973 as the time when "the Korean church came of age."

Behind the Iron Curtain
By the 1970s Graham had also begun to penetrate the large segment of the world that was then under Communist rule, with religion seriously constricted or oppressed. In 1977 he had preached in Hungary, a pioneering venture where he had to tread warily, for no other doors would open in Eastern Europe at that time if he failed. Graham's diplomacy with atheist officials, and with bishops who had put loyalty to the state before loyalty to Christ, and his clear preaching of the gospel made Hungary a gate to Eastern Europe. Not only was he asked back to Hungary, but the following year, 1978, he was able to make an extensive preaching tour of Poland, a predominantly Roman Catholic country, ruled at that

The Catholics threw open their cathedrals for the "Evangelization of Billy Graham."

time by a small minority of atheists, their power deriving from the might of the Soviet Union. The Catholics threw open their cathedrals for the "Evangelization of Billy Graham," and the great mission services were not only helpful to church relations but strengthened the faith of the Poles, who in a few years would take the first steps that led to the overthrow of the Communist regime. Later he made preaching tours in East Germany, Czechoslovakia, and Romania, all then under Communist regimes.

In 1982 Graham was able to make an official visit to Moscow. Twenty-three years earlier, in 1959, Graham had gone to Moscow as a tourist and had prayed that one day he would preach the gospel in a stadium, which would have been illegal then and for more than another thirty years. In 1982 his acceptance of an invitation from the Orthodox patriarch to speak at a conference "For Saving the Sacred Gift of Life from Nuclear Catastrophe" was controversial. Graham recognized the political pitfalls, but also that this might be the only opportunity to push ajar the door to ministry in the Soviet Union. He was strongly criticized (and misquoted) in the Western press and hindered by minor errors of judgment; yet his conviction was honored that he must work patiently rather than secure a short-term benefit. Little by little the door opened wider. On each visit to the Soviet Union he was able to preach to more people and to press more strongly on Soviet officials the cause of human rights and religious freedom.

With the collapse of Communism in 1991, Graham's dream of 1959 was fulfilled when he preached to fifty thousand Russians in Moscow's Olympic Stadium in October 1992. He heard the ex-Red Army choir sing religious songs and watched, profoundly moved, as thousands came quietly forward in spiritual hunger.

Graham had already been to China. His visit with his wife, who was born to missionary parents, had encouraged the rapidly rising number of Christians, but hope of a wide-ranging preaching mission had to be deferred after the 1989 massacre in Tianammen Square and the repression that followed.

As he neared his seventy-fifth birthday in 1993 the superb technology of Mission

> *Lausanne could never have happened without Billy Graham.*

World, developed by Graham's team, had carried his words to wider audiences than ever before by satellite television and video to arenas and halls, where preparations had been made as if Graham would be present in the flesh. By 1993 Mission World had been effective in Africa, East Asia, South America, and in Europe from the Atlantic to the Urals.

Billy Graham was now suffering from Parkinson's disease. But as the preparations for the Tokyo crusade in January 1994, with Mission World, neared their climax, he remained true to his calling. "My job is to be faithful, to proclaim the gospel wherever I am," he said at Sandringham, England, after preaching before the queen and members of the royal family. "It is always a time of tremendous soul searching, and great privilege, with a sense of humility and unworthiness, to preach the gospel at any time."

John Pollock

Further Reading

Frady, Marshall. *Billy Graham: A Parable of American Righteousness*. Boston: Little, Brown, 1979.

High, Stanley. *Billy Graham: The Personal Story of the Man, His Message, and His Mission*. New York: McGraw-Hill, 1956.

Martin, William. *A Prophet with Honor: The Billy Graham Story*. New York: William Morrow, 1991.

Mitchell, Curtis. *The All-Britain Crusade of 1967*. Minneapolis: World Wide, 1968.

Pollock, John. *Billy Graham, Evangelist to the World: An Authorized Biography of the Decisive Years*. San Francisco: Harper & Row, 1979.

Terrell, Bob. *Billy Graham in Hungary*. Minneapolis: World Wide, 1978.

A FAMILY OF CHRIST'S AMBASSADORS
The Howard Family

Philip and Katherine Howard were married June 14, 1922, and sailed for Belgium in July to work with the Belgian Gospel Mission. Philip had recently graduated from the University of Pennsylvania in 1921, Phi Beta Kappa. They lived in Brussels five years, working on a small paper, doing children's work, teaching in the Bible institute, and speaking at mission posts. Two of their children were born there.

After their first furlough, the Howards planned to return to Belgium, but Charles G. Trumbull, Philip's uncle and the editor of *The Sunday School Times*, prevailed on Philip to become his associate editor in 1927. Their decision to leave the mission was an intense spiritual struggle. However, the Howards never lost their missionary vision. Later on, Philip became a trustee and then president of the Belgian Gospel Mission. He was also a member of the Philadelphia council of the China Inland Mission (now the Overseas Missionary Fellowship) and served on the North American council of the North Africa Mission (now Arab World Ministries).

The Howards also visited Belgium in 1950, and in 1955 traveled to Latin America to visit two of their missionary children, Elisabeth and David.

A spiritual heritage

As with most effective Christian families, the Howards traced their spiritual heritage to their parents. Philip wrote in *The Sunday School Times* in 1962, "Father and Mother trained me from my earliest years to pray and love the Lord. I look back with profound

> *The Howards traced their spiritual heritage to their parents.*

Although Philip E. Howard, Jr., served as the distinguished editor of The Sunday School Times *for twenty years (1941–60), he is also greatly remembered as a father. For when it comes to rearing children firmly committed to Christian outreach, few families can match the record of Philip E. Howard's family. Philip and Katherine Howard had six children: Philip G., Elisabeth, David, Virginia, Thomas, and James. Four of the six are or have been missionaries, one is a pastor, and one a seminary professor. This was not a mere fluke. The Howards' family life fostered the children's interest in Christian ministry.*

The Henry Clay Trumbull family in 1900. Trumbull was the uncle of Philip Howard, Sr.

Philip E.
Howard, Sr.,
and Annie
Trumbull
Howard at
Keswick, N.J.,
in the 1930s.

> ### "His daily time with God began at 5:30 every morning."

God's help, to be a foreign missionary."

Shortly after completing his Bible school training in 1922, he met Katherine Gillingham, whom he described as "a lovely Christian girl." After their return from Belgium in 1927, they lived first in the Germantown section of Philadelphia and later moved across the Delaware River to Moorestown, New Jersey, where they became members of the Bible Protestant Church. They lived in Moorestown twenty-seven years before moving to Vero Beach, Florida, in 1963.

Personal discipline

Toward the end of his life (he died Christmas Day, 1963), Philip wrote his testimony for the readers whom he had served for thirty-six years: "As I look back over the years, my heart is overwhelmed with a sense of the goodness and mercy of God. He has guided, protected, and supplied all our needs. The one thing above all others that has kept us steady has been the habit of daily, private, Bible study and prayer, in addition to family prayers. ... Having sought to walk with God for nearly fifty years, I can say heartily that the happiest life is the Christian life, and the happiest kind of Christian life is one devoted entirely to God's service." He had survived two serious brain surgeries in 1955 and 1960. He continued to write his weekly "For Family Worship" column in *The Sunday School Times* until his death.

David describes his father's personal devotional life this way:

"His daily time with God began at 5:30 every morning. He set out everything, his Bible, pencil and paper, the night before. He prayed for us four times a day, early in the morning, after breakfast with us, after supper, and at bedtime. The personal discipline of our father and mother was so evident that all of us simply fell in with it."

Given to God

The crucial question remains for today's Christian families: How did the editor of a weekly Christian paper somehow become a missionary patriarch? One thing is clear:

thanksgiving for our lovely Christian home. We became accustomed in childhood to family prayers, Sunday school, church, and the visits in our home of missionaries from many parts of the world, other Christian workers, and interesting people from all walks of life."

David Howard recalls that at his grandfather's funeral in 1946, several Christian leaders remarked that Philip E. Howard, Sr., was the most Christlike man they had ever met. The grandchildren absorbed this godly man's influence through family visits every Sunday.

Philip, Jr., gave his heart to Christ when he was twelve. He wrote, "Several years later, in 1916, I attended a Christian conference and yielded my life to the Lord, to be used in any service He might have for me. ... In the spring of 1918 I determined, with

The Howard family in 1951: (seated) Dave, his wife, Phyllis, Elisabeth, sister-in-law Margaret with Katharine Jane (daughter of Philip G. Howard), Jim; (back row) Tom, Ginny, Katharine Gillingham Howard, Philip E. Howard Jr., Philip G. Howard.

Philip and Katherine never set out to force missionary careers on their children. In fact, it was at their son Philip's graduation from Bible school, during a prayer for more missionaries, that God spoke to Katherine about giving her children to Him for missionary service. She struggled with such a costly commitment, but then began to pray for this, and God answered. All of them entered God's work, four of them as missionaries.

Eldest son Philip G. and his wife, Margaret, went to northwest Canada with the Northern Canada Evangelical Mission where they had to cut down trees and build their own log cabin, without benefit of chain saws. They hauled water every day and were cut off from the outside world for six months at a time. Philip was a pioneer missionary, starting from ground zero. He learned the language, put it into writing, and taught the people to read. He became an expert on Northwest Territories languages and now teaches language training for the government.

Elisabeth went to Ecuador as a missionary and later married Jim Elliot, who was martyred by Auca Indians in 1956. After his death, she resumed her missionary career for a short time, focusing on linguistics. Since then she has become a prolific writer and conference speaker. Her syndicated radio program is broadcast on some two hundred stations.

David served with the Latin America Mission, from 1953 to 1968—five years in Costa Rica and ten years in Colombia. He then joined InterVarsity Christian Fellowship and directed the 1973 and 1976 Urbana student missionary conventions. He also directed the Consultation on World Evangelization at Pattaya, Thailand, in 1980. He served as international director of the World Evangelical Fellowship, 1982–92. He is now associated with the David C. Cook Foundation, Elgin, Illinois.

Virginia Sohn was a missionary for twenty-three years in the Philippines with the Association of Baptists for World Evangelization, specializing in linguistics. She translated the New Testament into the Cuyonon dialect. She now lives in Massachusetts.

Thomas worked for the missions department of InterVarsity Christian Fellowship for a short time and also for *The Sunday School Times*. Interestingly, however, none of Philip's children ever had the desire to succeed their father in the editor's chair. After earning his Ph.D. degree in literature

> *"All she had to do was look toward the switch, and we got in line."*

at New York University, Thomas launched his teaching career and now is a professor at St. John's Seminary in Boston.

James, the youngest, is a full-time pastor of a Christian and Missionary Alliance church in Cody, Wyoming. He served a rural church in Oak Hills, Minnesota, for many years. By avocation he is an artist.

The human factors

Apart from what Philip called God's goodness and mercy, what human factors came into play in this remarkable family?

As noted above, the tight spiritual discipline of Philip and Katherine had a profound influence in their children. Their discipline included not only their private devotions but also the discipline of their children in godliness. The key was consistency. "We always knew right and wrong," David recalls. Spankings were included, from Philip's hand as well as from Katherine's little switch over the door. "All she had to do was look toward the switch, and we got in line," David says. Of course, not all discipline was like that. Sometimes the children were sent to their rooms or "grounded" for periods of time.

When she was seventy-nine years old, Katherine Howard wrote in *Moody Monthly*:

Training must come before teaching. Before parents can train their children properly, they must first discipline themselves. An orderly home and orderly habits can be accomplished only by agreeing together on these things. . . . My husband insisted on a leisurely breakfast and family prayers. This is impossible unless the children cooperate. And they don't cooperate unless they are disciplined from their earliest days. This discipline lays the groundwork for teaching (quoted in *The Shaping of a Christian Family*, p. xii).

However, discipline and order were blended with what today is called quality family time. In her book *The Shaping of a Christian Family* Elisabeth recalls:

My father's recreation nearly always included his children. We could count on his

Howard Family Tree

Philip E. Howard, Jr. (1898–1963)

Katherine Gillingham Howard (1899–1987)

Philip G. Howard (b. 1923), missionary to northwest Canada.
   Two children, a daughter (pastor's wife), a son (pastor).

Elisabeth Elliot Gren (b. 1926), former missionary to Ecuador.
   One child, a daughter (pastor's wife).

David (b. 1928), former missionary to Costa Rica and Colombia.
   Four children, a son (seminary professor), a son (pilot), a daughter (pastor's wife), and a son (computer analyst).

Virginia Sohn (b. 1934), former missionary to the Philippines.
   Three children, a son (pilot), a son (violinist), and a daughter (homemaker).

Thomas (b. 1935), college and seminary professor.
   Two children, a daughter (nurse), a son (recent college graduate).

James (b. 1940), a pastor in Wyoming.
   Four children, a son (teacher), a daughter (nurse), a daughter (homemaker), a son (college student).

doing something with us on Saturday afternoons. . . Daddy took us to the zoo, the Planetarium, the Franklin Institute, long rides to the New Jersey Pines or the shore where he taught us to love silence and the smell of pine woods and salt marshes. Wherever we went he watched for birds. . . He knew how to play with small children. He would let two of us ride on his size twelve feet, hugging his calves, or get down on all fours and ride us around the dining room table (pp. 90–93).

Remarkably, the children remember their father's standard practice of apologizing to them and asking their forgiveness before he went to bed, if he had been angry with them during the day.

Family devotions were foundational to the children's spiritual development. They read Scripture together and sang hymns. When the new InterVarsity *Hymnal* was

The Howard siblings in June 1993: (front row, left-right) Elisabeth, Philip, Virginia; (back row, left-right) James, Thomas, and David.

first published, they went through it in entirety, singing the hymns page by page. Philip prayed for all his children by name, and then the family recited the Lord's Prayer together. Evening devotions consisted of reading from *Daily Light* and prayer.

Exposure to missions

How did missionary service enter the Howard family? Pretty much the same way it had entered the parents' family, by hospitality to missionaries and constant exposure to missions. They did not push missionary careers on their children, but told them it was their responsibility to find God's will for their lives.

Gradually, over the years, each child found God's will, quite apart from strong church or parachurch influences. They attended Bible conferences at Keswick, New Jersey, every summer where their father spoke. But many decisions simply grew out of times alone, especially during family vacations in New Hampshire. These vacations were crucial to building family solidarity and gave the children many wholesome activities, such as bird watching and fishing, which some have pursued in their adult lives.

Perhaps the best summary explanation of the success of the Howards was written by Elisabeth Elliot Gren in 1991, in *The Shaping of a Christian Family*:

What of the six Howard children? I speak for all when I say that we thank God for the home we grew up in. We loved our parents, and we knew they loved us. We respected them, and the principles they taught us certainly helped to shape the six homes we established when we married, as different as our spouses and our homes have been. I speak for myself when I say that I both bewildered and grieved my parents, no doubt far more often than I know, but their prayers followed me (surely they follow me still), and only Eternity will show how great is the debt I owe them (p. xix).

Far-reaching influence

Philip Howard's influence for world missions and influence extended far beyond his immediate family. Proof of that came in a letter from a missionary in Africa, who wrote to the family after his death:

Never mind who I am; just a nobody, one of thousands who found strength to meet impossible demands of a hard world through the Word of God; led through the Bible by [The Sunday School Times] which revealed your father's undaunted spirit, the

> *Philip Howard consistently called for commitment to Christ's lordship as the basis for missionary service.*

Christ who spoke through him. . . . In reading we heard not an editor but our Christ Jesus who spoke. And he was always more than ready to help individuals as his Lord did on earth (*The Shaping of a Christian Family*, pp. 211–12).

As both a speaker and writer, Philip Howard consistently called for commitment to Christ's lordship as the basis for missionary service. Jim Reapsome, when a college student, heard Howard speak on one of his favorite texts: "And he died for all, that those who live should no longer live for themselves but for Him who died for them and was raised again" (2 Corinthians 5:15). For the first time Reapsome recognized that Christ owned him; Christ had died for Reapsome, and consequently he could not go on living as he pleased. It was a significant step toward full-time Christian service.

Fourteen years later Reapsome succeeded Howard as editor of *The Sunday School Times*. As Reapsome thumbed through the paper, then in its 102nd year, he sensed that it was infused with world missions. Elisabeth Elliot's journals from Ecuador, following the martyrdom of her husband, Jim, and four other men, gave gripping testimony to God's faithfulness and to the price that sometimes must be paid to advance the gospel among pagan tribes. Reapsome also observed Howard's consistent personal discipline, his dedication to careful editorial work (in the job interview, Howard asked if Reapsome enjoyed grammar!), and his sheer delight in not only his family, but also in music, literature, and nature.

Often appearing outwardly stern, Philip Howard had a quiet sense of humor, which his children picked up also. They were and are committed to doing God's will, but their family proves so splendidly that obedience to God and enjoying life are not antithetical.

James Reapsome

COMMITTED TO EXCELLENCE

Ted Engstrom

1916–

Born in Cleveland, Ohio, in 1916, Engstrom had a strong will and independence that were not immediately submitted to the values of his godly, Christian family. His wild and carefree lifestyle might well have led to disaster. But during his college years at Taylor University he came to know Jesus Christ.

Conversion

Engstrom's new birth occurred on April 1, 1935. He well remembers that day: *There are no two conversions alike. I know that. Some just quietly and sweetly and wonderfully come to an experience. Others really don't remember when they began their Christian walk in life. Others are dynamic and dramatic. When I was converted, bells rang, lightning flashed, thunder roared. I got outside and the sky was never bluer.*

It was a cataclysmic experience with me. I can never, ever deny my conversion experience! It was transforming, revolutionizing. I knew what happened when I said yes to God and He met my heart's need in that college chapel service.

His parents' faith had set a profound example for him as a youngster. The prayers of loved ones had protected him and led toward the Savior. Now Ted Engstrom's personal encounter with Jesus Christ launched his own dynamic and unique ministry.

Ever the entrepreneur, Ted had started his own printing company even before completing high school. He moved his printing press to a downstairs room at Taylor University when he began classes there, and before long he was earning his way through school with the help of his printing skills. His first full-time job, apart from a brief stint at semi-pro baseball, was at Higley Publishing Company in Indiana.

The man looks up, smiles, and studies his visitor with clear and intelligent eyes. He is large in stature, and although his face is craggy it is remarkably youthful considering his seventy-plus years. He begins to speak, answering questions quickly, concisely, and directly. Before long, an overwhelming and unmistakable characteristic emerges from Ted Engstrom's conversation: energy.

Although he is best known as a high-level executive and management consultant, a few moments of dialogue with Engstrom disclose a much deeper stream of consciousness. And a glance at his writings (his high level of energy is reflected in the fact that he has written more than forty books) reveals far more than management skills. Engstrom's observations regarding human behavior, personal motivation, and Christian-based psychology deserve both our careful attention and respect.

For many people, however, the name of Ted Engstrom is synonymous with World Vision. From 1963 until 1984, he served as either executive vice president or president of that highly respected humanitarian organization. Today, he is World Vision's president emeritus.

> *"I can never, ever deny my conversion experience! It was transforming, revolutionizing."*

The Life of Ted Engstrom

1916	Born in Cleveland
1935	Born again at Taylor University
1940	Becomes editorial director at Zondervan; later appointed general manager
1948	Attends World Congress on Evangelism in Switzerland
1950	World Vision organized by Bob Pierce and Frank Phillips
1951	Becomes executive director of Youth for Christ; later appointed president
1963	Becomes executive vice president of World Vision; later appointed president
1984	Named president emeritus of World Vision
1989	Appointed chairman of the Evangelical Council for Financia Accountability

He has long rehearsed the fine art of commitment.

never even thought of 'world evangelism' before. It had never entered my mind."

But enter his mind it did, and by the end of 1951 he had resigned from Zondervan and was serving as executive director, then president, of Youth for Christ International, a position he held for a dozen years. Youth for Christ touched a place in Ted Engstrom's heart. He commented at the time, "My high school years were wasted, absolutely wasted, and that is one reason I am so interested in YFC and the Bible clubs. Had there been a YFC Club in our school, I feel I would have come out for the Lord."

One particular friendship was born during those Youth for Christ years that was to become pivotal in Engstrom's life. "I first met Bob Pierce at a Youth for Christ Conference in Medicine Lake, Minnesota, at the second annual conference of YFC. I was taken to him immediately, and we began what would become a long friendship. I was next with him at the great World Congress on Evangelism in Beatenberg, Switzerland, in 1948. During that time he was carrying on missionary activities and evangelism in China. It was also the time when he wrote in his Bible, 'Let my heart be broken with the things that break the heart of God,' which became his life's slogan.

"Bob and Dr. Frank C. Phillips then organized World Vision officially as an incorporated body in 1950. During those early years I was very close to Bob Pierce. I was a frequent guest in his home, and I often spoke on his Mutual Network radio broadcast in California. Bob also came to our home in Wheaton, Illinois, on numerous occasions. We would talk, pray, laugh, and enjoy each other to the point where our friendship fast became one of supreme importance to both of us."

Before long, Engstrom found himself deeply involved in a far better-known publishing house. In 1940, he and his bride, Dorothy, moved to Grand Rapids, Michigan, where he took over the responsibilities of editorial director and, ultimately, general manager of the Zondervan Publishing House. Zondervan has since become one of the largest religious publishing firms in the world. Ted continued to work with Zondervan as a freelance writer and part-time editor even during his wartime army duties. Then, in 1951, he focused his immense communications abilities on a different front—evangelism.

Youth for Christ
Three years before, in 1948, Engstrom had attended the World Congress on Evangelism in Beatenburg, Switzerland. It was sponsored by Youth for Christ (YFC). There he had encountered such powerhouses of world ministry as Oswald J. Smith, Billy Graham, Bob Pierce, Bob Evans, and Merv Rosell. Most personally significant, however, was another encounter between Ted Engstrom and Jesus Christ. During his time in Switzerland, he felt a call from God to dedicate himself to international ministry and was amazed at the new direction. "I'd

World Vision
The fellowship these two visionary men enjoyed eventually led Bob Pierce to seek Ted Engstrom's assistance in the management of World Vision. Engstrom's decision to move to World Vision in Southern California amounted to a bittersweet turning point in the lives of both men.

Bob Pierce's legendary gifts as a humanitarian pioneer did not necessarily include management and financial capabilities. By the time Ted Engstrom came alongside Pierce at World Vision, the fiscal situation was disastrous. And the efforts to resolve those urgent monetary problems unfortunately brought temporary estrangement and cooling to Pierce and Engstrom's close friendship.

The struggle to ensure World Vision's survival was perhaps the most challenging and heartbreaking period in Ted Engstrom's career. The emotional roller-coaster ride, the personality clashes with various individuals, the constant pressure from both creditors and overseas commitments—all these caused Ted to struggle with an uncharacteristic temptation to quit. He longed to resign and move on. But friends and family supported him through the strife, and he carried on, although at times reluctantly.

> *He has not simply*
> *spoken of prayer;*
> *he has prayed.*

Out of the crucible of those very painful and challenging years came many of Engstrom's most priceless management lessons, wisdom he has shared with thousands of men and women across the globe. World Vision continues to thrive as a world-class paragon of humanitarian aid and development endeavors. And ultimately the broken relationship between Bob Pierce and Ted Engstrom was mended, specifically due to the determination of two Christian men to make things right.

Today Ted Engstrom is rapidly approaching his eighth decade on this earth with all the energy and productivity of a young man. He has long rehearsed the fine art of commitment. He has grown through his mistakes and has transparently shared them with others. He has crystallized his principles and made them available to anyone who will listen.

But most significant of all, Ted Engstrom has taken his personal, inner faith in Jesus Christ and has put it to work in the world. He has not simply spoken of prayer; he has prayed. He has not just given lip service to forgiveness; he has given and received for-

Ted Engstrom, president emeritus of World Vision.

giveness. He has not only challenged others toward excellence in thought, word, and deed; he has, first of all, required excellence of himself.

Ted Engstrom's life continues to be well-spent, and his fully energetic daily schedule demonstrates the convictions of his own words: "Time is immensely valuable and utterly irretrievable. Undoubtedly time is the most valuable commodity we have. . . .

"The clocks we buy, the watches we wear, all run at exactly the same rate. No one has any more time—or less time—than you. Even our Lord: he who left eternity to enter time, he who was the Creator, becoming the creature, lived a very short span of time as we would measure it—thirty-three and a half years. And yet in spite of that recognized preciousness and the vast potentiality related to time, there's nothing we squander quite so thoughtlessly as time.

"As the wise and pragmatic Sir Walter Scott once wrote: 'Dost thou love life, then do not squander time, for that's the stuff life's made of.'"

Ted Engstrom has certainly not "squandered" his own lifetime. Instead, he has invested his decades with great care and wisdom. And, for the good of all of us, he has gathered and collected his best gifts over the years and has generously shared them with the world.

Lela Gilbert

[Engstrom's statements are originally quoted in his biography by Bob Owen, Ted Engstrom: Man with a Vision *(Wheaton, Ill.: Tyndale, 1984).]*

Further Reading

Owen, Bob. *Ted Engstrom: Man with a Vision.* Wheaton, Ill.: Tyndale, 1984.

TRANS WORLD RADIO

Paul E. Freed

1918–

The time had come in 1931 for the world to begin hearing the gospel by shortwave radio. For in that year HCJB Quito, Ecuador, went on the air after much careful planning by Clarence W. Jones and Reuben Larson.

Then in 1948 the Far East Broadcasting Company began its initial broadcast in Manila, the Philippines. God had chosen several faithful servants to lead this embryonic ministry with its purpose of reaching the Far East. Robert Bowman and John Broger, with the help of some needed financing from William J. Roberts pooled $1,000 to get this new ministry on the air.

Radio Monte Carlo

Paul E. Freed was the man God would use to round out the world coverage of the earth with Christ's message. It all started when this North Carolina Youth for Christ director traveled to Spain and received a burden to reach Spaniards with the saving gospel. His interpreter suggested to him that Tangier, Morocco, would be an ideal location for such a radio station.

Traveling across the country in their tired old car, Paul and Betty Jane and their two small children raised more than $100,000. This sum was sufficient to launch programming. On February 22, 1954, the Voice of Tangier began broadcasting the gospel on the air, utilizing a small, used 2,500-watt transmitter.

After only five years, however, notice was

Probably as important as anything else God used to create TWR was Paul Freed's spiritual upbringing by a godly mother and father.

Missionary, or international, Christian radio has been around for more than sixty years, since 1931. And Paul E. Freed of Trans World Radio (TWR) is the man who had many of the innovative ideas that transformed this medium into such an effective means for communicating the gospel of Jesus Christ throughout the world.

Freed fully developed the concept of high power AM, also known overseas as medium wave, in addition to the utilization of shortwave. He also implemented the idea of leasing blocks of air time on government and private radio stations worldwide and highlighted the value of owning stations outright. For decades the concept of buying blocks of air time has been especially successful in Monte Carlo and other locations.

Freed also initiated the concept of cooperating broadcasters. These are program producers from the United States and overseas who want their organizations' broadcasts translated, reproduced by nationals, and aired on the Trans World Radio transmitters worldwide. Today, more than two hundred such organizations are active Cooperating Broadcasters.

He also proposed the idea of enlisting national partners in various countries of the world. Germany was first with the development of Evangeliums-Rundfunk (ERF), with Norway, Finland, France, India, and Hong Kong not far behind. Dozens of nations have witnessed the emergence of their own fully involved National Partners.

served that all radio in Morocco would be nationalized. For Paul, this was, of course, disconcerting news. His mother urged him to consider seriously Monte Carlo as a replacement location. She was a woman of prayer and had learned well to discern the will of God.

Adolf Hitler had chosen Monte Carlo, after conquering the continent, as the place from which to broadcast his Third Reich Nazi message. Hitler built a bomb-proof radio building for his transmitting site in Monte Carlo. Though the German dictator never was to broadcast from that facility, through miraculous intervention Radio Monte Carlo, which was in possession of the building, was willing to discuss entering into a contract with the newly named Trans World Radio.

Many huge obstacles had to be overcome, including mountainous financial burdens. But they were conquered through God's grace. On October 16, 1960, the new gospel witness began emanating from the very building Hitler had constructed for his projected propaganda campaigns.

Now, the message of Jesus was on the air to men and women and boys and girls throughout a large part of the world, including seven of the time zones in the USSR. In

The Life of Paul E. Freed

1918	Born in Detroit, Michigan, August 29
1940	Graduates from Wheaton College
1954	Begins broadcasting the Voice of Tangier in Morocco
1960	Receives Ph.D. from New York University; forms Trans World Radio (TWR); begins transmitting from Radio Monte Carlo
1964	Second TWR station located in Bonaire, a city in the Caribbean
1974	TWR station begins broadcasting in southern Africa
1978	TWR station begins broadcasting in Sri Lanka
1981	TWR station begins broadcasting in Uruguay
1985	TWR, FEBC (Far Eastern Broadcasting Company), and HCJB announce "Project: The World by 2000"
1990–93	TWR utilizes radio stations in Albania and in countries of the CIS
1993	Retires as president of TWR; TWR has eight transmitters broadcasting in ninety-one languages

Dr. Paul E. Freed in the antenna field, Monte Carlo, 1971.

the ensuing years the witness has gone out *every* day. Some say this station and its gospel message constituted a major factor in destroying the Communist stronghold in Russia.

500,000 watts

The second TWR station was located in Bonaire, Netherlands Antilles, in the Caribbean, once again utilizing superpower AM transmitters that could reach Central and South America. The power of 500,000 watts was enormous, but so was the task of telling the world of redemption through Christ. These stations were ten to twelve times more powerful than the highest rated radio station licensed in the United States. God was at work opening doors.

In later years stations were built or added in Manzini, Swaziland, in Africa, in Sri Lanka to reach India by medium wave and other locations by shortwave. Also, powerful 100,000-watt shortwave transmitters were beamed to cover China in four of its languages. The combined transmitters' time is nearly thirty hours per day to China. Montevideo, Uraguay, was added to cover at close range the huge population of Buenos Aires and Montevideo with 50,000 watts-AM.

Since the dropping of the Iron Curtain and the fall of the Berlin Wall, Trans World has built five recording studios in the Commonwealth of Independent States and has started using the transmitters of Radio Tirana in Albania and the state-owned transmitter of Radio Moscow in Irkutsk, Russia. Who, five years ago, would have believed these miracles could happen? Today nine transmitting locations broadcast the gospel each day in 104 languages.

Radio Tirana

Only two years ago, Radio Tirana (Albania) was the most powerful Communist ideological station in all of Europe. Transmitters with a combined power of a million watts sent out the message of the only self-declared atheist society in the world. Though Albania had only four million people, it was by far the most rigidly Marxist regime on earth. God was declared nonexistent by the government. Under the iron rule of dictator Hoxha, the powerful station was built to proclaim the "God is dead" philosophy. Hoxha thought he had excellent ideas to share with the "softer" Communist nations. In 1990 a revolution

> *Powerful 100,000-watt shortwave transmitters were beamed to cover China in four of its languages.*

Dr. Freed in Africa in 1984.

swept across Eastern Europe, Communism was overthrown, and freedom of religion was restored in the nations of the region, including Albania.

When Paul Freed saw Radio Tirana, he couldn't believe his eyes. No cost had been spared to send the signal by an array of five sets of towers to Europe and by an array of eight towers to Russia. Now all of this equipment was set to send forth the glorious gospel of Jesus Christ. After the signing of contracts in Tirana, Freed marveled at how God had used the wrath of men to praise Him. "You intended to harm me, but God intended it for good to accomplish what is now being done, the saving of many lives" (Genesis 50:20). This is no doubt one of the most outstanding faith events in the life of Paul Freed.

On a trip to Southern China I asked our guide what he would like to do more than anything else in the world. He replied, "I'd like to visit the United States." I was shocked to hear his explanation of his heart's desire. He indicated that through shortwave radio Chinese people know a good deal about the outside world. Because of the radio signals they did not believe the ranting of their leaders who were so critical of the Western world. I told him of my association with a religious broadcasting company, upon which he asked, "Are you with Trans World Radio?" I was shocked to hear him name and know of the ministry of TWR. He then said, "I'm not very religious and so don't listen to your programs very much, but I should tell you that millions of our Chinese people do listen." His astounding declaration caused me to think back to the humble beginnings of such a worldwide witness.

> Thru the Bible *is translated and recorded by nationals in nearly forty languages worldwide.*

The seeds of the ministry

What were the seeds that created such a powerhouse for God? Dr. J. Vernon McGee, while pastoring the Church of the Open Door, Los Angeles, began his Bible teaching radio broadcast, *Thru the Bible*. He was concerned with reaching English-speaking people in the United States. In the mid-seventies McGee attended a Trans World Radio Conference in Monte Carlo. There Freed poured out his soul concerning the needs of the world. McGee told me that upon hearing Freed, he had a total change in his thinking, and he began taking the world to his heart. Today, *Thru the Bible* is translated and recorded by nationals in nearly forty languages worldwide.

Paul Freed, even when a student at Wheaton College, showed entrepreneurial skills by making belts, having others make belts, and selling them through a nationwide chain of stores. God was preparing Paul for a large work.

He received his Ph.D. from New York University in mass communications. This degree was another rung in the ladder of preparation for worldwide negotiation work with world communications and governmental leaders. It also enabled him to understand the communication peculiarities of the nations and regions of the world.

Probably as important as anything else God used to create TWR was Paul Freed's spiritual upbringing by a godly mother and father. Father Ralph Freed had been a very successful businessman in Michigan when he heard the call of God on his life.

Ralph Freed moved his family to the mission field, where son Paul grew to adolescence in the Middle East. Paul remembers his bicycle ride to and from school in Jerusalem from Bethlehem. Those days of example by a resolute father and deeply spiritual, praying mother laid early foundation stones for the establishment and development of the radio outreach of Trans World Radio.

Paul's wife, Betty Jane, and the family of five children were deeply involved in prayer, encouragement, and maintaining equilibrium in this forceful and visionary entrepreneur. God also assembled dedicated and patient staff members early on to undertake the day-to-day labor. Running radio stations day-in and day-out was hard, yet routine, work. Paul was given men and women to carry this load, some of whom are still working today, forty years later. Today that staff numbers more than one thousand, including national Christians in dozens of nations.

One day Theodore Epp, founder of Back to the Bible, was commenting on Rev. 3:8: "I have placed before you an open door that no one can shut. I know that you have little strength, yet you have kept my word and have not denied my name." Epp felt deeply that radio, both domestic and foreign, was that door that no person could close. Through the years Paul Freed has also believed this. In consequence, he has given himself body and soul to see that the world would be covered by radio with the glorious message of our Lord Jesus Christ.

E. Brandt Gustavson

A MINISTRY OF RECONCILIATION

Festo Kivengere

1920–1988

In his traditional African way, Bishop Festo Kivengere expressed his faith in word and deed, as he both proclaimed the gospel and demonstrated his witness through tangible acts of compassion. During his lifetime he conducted hundreds of evangelistic missions throughout Africa and the world.

In the early 1970s Festo teamed up with South African Michael Cassidy, beginning the African Enterprise (AE) ministry in Uganda, Tanzania, and Kenya. Working with teams of African nationals, Festo embarked on a distinctly African-born, African-led ministry of telling the gospel through practical African parables. In 1976 Festo, Cassidy, and the AE teams organized the Pan-African Christian Leadership Assembly (PACLA), a conference that brought together eight hundred Christian leaders from forty-seven African nations to address the challenges and needs of a mushrooming African church.

Yet it was in his own native Uganda where he had the greatest impact as a leader and elder statesman of the church. Festo spoke out against the atrocities committed under Ugandan dictators Amin and Obote, while struggling to accept the gospel message of "love your enemies."

He was able to reconcile the two. His ministry of love and reconciliation in the midst of tribulation brought credibility to the church in Uganda and around the world. Festo's message was a powerful force worldwide for bringing thousands to a knowledge of the Savior.

Telephones, mail service, and motor vehicles were rare to nonexistent throughout the East African bush of the 1930s, but news—especially good news—still traveled fast.

Strange things were happening to people in Uganda and throughout East Africa, and the news spread quickly—mouth to mouth, village to village. Ordinary people created quite a stir. Two women who had been bitter enemies were now friends. A man who had stolen a cow from his neighbor returned it and asked forgiveness. School children returned stolen books. Even religious people who went to church repented of wrongdoing.

Night after night this "new breed" of Christians met, singing and praying for hours on end. The East African Revival captured hearts and had people singing praises all hours of the day as the Holy Spirit moved in amazing ways.

The path to conversion

It was 1939, and the flames of revival had begun to spread across Rwanda and neighboring Uganda, in east-central Africa. But the heart of nineteen-year-old Festo Kivengere was hardened with agnosticism. This happy-face bunch angered Festo, and their zeal and craziness were more than he could bear. Their religion belonged in the church, not out in the streets and marketplaces.

Festo had just landed his first teaching job at the local missions school in Rukungiri, his hometown. As a staff member, he was required to attend church. But Festo hated church and God. With his friends and relatives all around committing their lives to Christ, Festo felt like it was impossible to escape.

Then one day Festo was drinking hard at

> *By the time
> Festo reached home
> the Holy Spirit had captured
> his heart.*

his uncle's house. As he wobbled home on his bicycle, he met up with a friend.

"Festo! Three hours ago Jesus became a living reality to me," the man said. "I know my sins are forgiven. I want you to forgive me, friend," and he named three specific things for which he wanted forgiveness.

"His joy overwhelmed me," said Festo. "His words, and the way he said them, shook me to the core. I felt like a shadow, having seen in my friend the reality I had missed. I cycled home utterly miserable and empty."

By the time Festo reached home the Holy Spirit had captured his heart. Festo knelt by the bedside and committed his life to following Jesus.

The struggle for reconciliation

All over East Africa in the years and months that followed, the good news of the gospel spread quickly. Men and women began new lives, loving others in a radical new way. They saw in Jesus Christ a revolutionary love, and the sacrifice, the reality of the cross moved them deeply. It was a love that illuminated the darkest of hearts. This was the gospel that Festo now began to live, preach, and teach. And its simple message drew thousands to Christ.

Immediately after receiving Christ Festo began to display this new revolutionary love, seeking forgiveness for wrongs he had done. For years Festo hated a white missionary who lived some fifty miles away. But Festo felt the Holy Spirit prompting him to reconcile with this man, despite the distance. The Spirit's words seemed clear:

"Take your bicycle on the weekend and go to see this man. Now that you are liberated, he is your brother."

"My brother? An Englishman?" Festo nearly fell over.

"Yes, your brother. You have hated your brother."

"What shall I do when I see him? You know him, Lord."

"Yes, I know him. Tell him that you love him."

The trip to Kabale was long and arduous, but Festo hoped the man would not be at home.

"He was there and suddenly I was standing in his proper English living room telling him what Christ had done for me, that I was free, and saw him now as my brother."

"I'm sorry," Festo said. "For the past five years I have hated you and talked against you. I must have made your life terribly difficult. Please forgive me."

When Festo left that day the two had become brothers. But this was only the beginning of Festo's message of the love that tears down barriers. Later this was a central focus of Festo's ministry to the emerging nations of Africa, and particularly Uganda.

But before God could use His chosen servant, He needed to show Festo many more times how costly this reconciling love could be. So God set about to transform Festo's life with His costly love.

Festo Kivengere (1920–1988).

Festo
Kivengere.

Peace in the home

One day Festo used words that hurt his wife, Mera, deeply. A cold wall began to rise between them as Festo thought about how Mera had provoked him. Worse yet, Sunday morning came, and Festo was scheduled to preach.

That morning he struggled with the Lord over reconciling with Mera. Festo actually left the house before he listened to the Holy Spirit. Then he walked back in the door.

"I'm sorry," Festo said to Mera. "I caused the quarreling. I was critical and made the Lord sad. I made you a stranger. Please forgive me."

Mera shrugged her shoulders. She thought he was apologizing so that he could preach well.

The Lord told Festo, "Do it again. Let it go deeper. You are not broken enough. You are expecting to be forgiven quickly."

"Only Jesus always forgives you quickly," said Festo. "Let other people take their time so the Holy Spirit can speak further. And when forgiveness comes, it is sweet."

Festo again asked his wife's forgiveness with deep sincerity. Mera finally forgave Festo, but on the way to church the Holy Spirit told Festo to tell the people what had

The Life of Festo Kivengere	
1920	Born in Uganda, Africa
1939	Conversion
1950–1970s	Ministry of evangelism in Uganda; links with African Enterprise
1977	Ugandan dictator Idi Amin becomes openly hostile to the Christian church; Festo escapes into exile
1988	Dies of leukemia

happened. That was hard, but he obeyed. God used Festo that day to minister to scores of broken people, and the sweet spirit of repentance moved throughout the congregation.

In the fifties, sixties, and seventies this message of God's reconciling love proved critical to an Africa emerging from the throes of colonialism. Newly independent African nations were thrust into enormous change and social upheaval, leading to wars and violence. In the middle of it all was

> ## "I had to ask for forgiveness from the Lord, and for grace to love President Amin more."

Festo Kivengere. He had given his life to declaring the gospel with its costly message of reconciling love.

Brutal dictator

Without a doubt Festo's greatest challenge in sharing God's message of reconciliation came during the rule of Idi Amin Dada, dictator of Uganda, 1971–79. During the 1970s Festo's ministry had expanded internationally. Festo received numerous invitations to preach all over Africa, and in Europe, North America, and the Middle East. At this same time Festo teamed up with Michael Cassidy and African Enterprise (AE), and founded the East African ministry of AE, teaching and preaching the gospel throughout East Africa.

Yet with the activity and excitement this brought, Festo's own home country of Uganda was caught in the turmoil of Idi Amin's cruel regime. In the first few years of his reign, Amin had expelled more than fifty thousand Asians, and a number of top officials simply disappeared. Uganda's military was granted blanket power to arrest and execute anyone seen as a threat. Tens of thousands were tortured and killed.

By 1977 Amin, a Muslim, had become openly hostile to the church, particularly Festo's own Anglican Church of Uganda. Within the first few months of that year, Amin and his henchmen made headlines worldwide when they targeted and murdered Festo's friend and colleague, Anglican Archbishop Janani Luwum. A few days later rumors flew that Festo was next on Amin's hit list.

With few options, Festo and Mera felt God directing them to leave their beloved Uganda. Into the dark night Festo and Mera escaped, climbing the mountains that stood on the border with neighboring Rwanda.

For the next few years Festo and Mera lived as refugees in exile. Festo became an international evangelist and spokesperson for the suffering and persecuted church in Uganda. But Festo's heart was again troubled. How could he lead such a far-reaching ministry of reconciliation when his own heart was hard and bitter toward Amin?

Festo wrote, "I had to face my own attitude towards President Amin and his agents. The Holy Spirit showed me that I was getting hard in my spirit, and that my hardness and bitterness toward those who were persecuting us could bring spiritual loss. This would take away my ability to communicate the love of God, which is the essence of my ministry and testimony. So I had to ask for forgiveness from the Lord, and for grace to love President Amin more."

Out of this struggle with reconciling his attitude toward Amin, Festo wrote the book *I Love Idi Amin*.

Bishop Festo Kivengere lived a life of costly reconciliation. Festo knew that true peace comes only as "a gift from the grace of God. It always comes when hearts are exposed to the love of Christ. But this always costs something. For the love of Christ was demonstrated through suffering, and those who experience that love can never put it into practice without some cost."

Festo Kivengere died of leukemia in 1988. His ministry of reconciliation through Christ continues through the African Enterprise ministry teams.

Jay Russell

Further Reading

Coomes, Anne. *Festo Kivengere*. Eastbourne, England: Monarch,1990.

—— with Dorothy Smoker. *I Love Idi Amin*. Old Tappan, N.J.: Revell, 1977.

——. *Love Unlimited*. Glendale, Calif.: Regal, 1975.

—— with Dorothy Smoker. *Revolutionary Love*. Nairobi, Kenya: Evangel House, 1981.

——. *When God Moves*. 1976. Wheaton, Ill.: Tyndale, 1973.

——. *The Spirit Is Moving*. London: Africa Christian Press, 1979.

Cassidy, Michael, and Gottfried Seai-Mensah. *Together in One Place: The Story of the PACLA*. Kisumu, Kenya: Evangel, 1978.

A TORCH BEARER

Hyung-Ja Lee

Opposite: Dr.
Hyung-Ja Lee.

In the mid-1970s a woman knelt in her living room with her sister and a friend and began praying. She was facing a series of critical problems: major family squabbles, her husband's hopeless business dilemma, and a constitutional crisis gripping the national government. The small prayer meeting began in her living room and attracted other women. Soon the group outgrew the living room and bedrooms of her home. The group had to move to a larger house for its prayer meetings. Married couples joined the group, followed by pastors and their wives, retired military officers and their wives, cadets of three branches of the armed services, directors of social service organizations, artists, doctors, professors, evangelists, orphans, hairdressers, and others.

Each group was organized and called a "torch." "Artists Torch," "Couples Torch," or "Pastors Torch" grew to the present twenty groups, twelve in Seoul and eight around the country in major cities.

Today, Torch ministries include prayer meetings, Bible studies, evangelism, discipleship training, missions, education, quality Christian music, a soccer team, retreats, revival meetings, conferences, lectures, research, library, scholarship fund, bookstore, publications, and other Christian outreaches. A few thousand Christians from all denominations come together weekly for spiritual renewal. The Torch movement is now officially named the Korean Center for World Missions (KCWM) but also uses the names Torch Mission Center, or Torch Center. It has become a significant spiritual movement in seventeen years.

On October 30, 1991, KCWM built new facilities on a hillside in south Seoul and occupied the premises. The board is chaired by Dr. Soon-Young Choi, a successful Christian businessman, chairman of the Shin Dong Ah Group, a business conglomerate, and owner of the renowned 63 Building, the tallest landmark in Seoul, Korea. He serves as an elder of the Hallelujah Christian Church. Dr. Hyung-Ja Lee, his wife, is president and founder of Torch Missions. She is the woman who started that first prayer meeting in her living room. Torch ministries is entirely funded and operated with tithes from businesses owned by Dr. Choi. It is an evangelical organization.

The bursting sunbeam

Hyung-Ja Lee was born to Christian parents, the eldest daughter in the family of four daughters and a son. Her scholar father was a gentle professor and dean of the College of Law at Ewha Women's University in Seoul. Her mother was a nurturing woman, very resourceful in caring for her family even during the war days. Her family attended a Methodist church near the university, where many of the professors and staff families worshiped.

When Hyung-Ja was a six-year-old kindergartner, she had an unusual experience. As she was entering her classroom one morning, brilliant sunlight, so bright and clean, was pouring in through the window. It showered upon her face and filled her sight. To the eyes of a young child the sunbeam was so absolutely beautiful that she stood overwhelmed by its beauty and was totally lost in it. Many years later she recalled the childhood experience. "I was momentarily so enraptured by the shining light that I felt I was in a world of fantasy, as

> *The small prayer meeting
> began in her living room and
> attracted other women.*

Spontaneously, the crowd stood to its feet and joined the choir in song. Many in the audience had tears in their eyes and hands extended in the air. The Korean Torch choir was singing "How Great Thou Art!" in Russian during a morning session of the Christ for the Nations Congress. Held during May and June of 1992, in Riga, Latvia, the conference was attended by 1,200 Christian leaders from the fifteen former Soviet Republics and other countries.

A month later, the Hallelujah Soccer Team, another facet of Torch ministries, played in Moscow, St. Petersburg, and Vladamir in Central Asia. Wherever they are playing, even in a Muslim country, sports announcers keep saying "Hallelujah" on the air to identify the team. Before a game, the players on their knees form the shape of a cross. Then the team rises and plays the game. At half time, they pass out gospel tracts and speak with people.

The Torch Center, a large complex of buildings located in Seoul, Korea, is the home of Torch ministries. On Sundays the main sanctuary of the center turns into a church. The Hallelujah Christian Church meets here. Two morning services and one evening service are held, each filling the 3,500-seat sanctuary. An English service and a Japanese service are also held in the other halls. The education building is packed with two thousand young people.

On the outside wall of the main sanctuary, the grand mosaic of the Good Shepherd greets visitors. The artwork is carefully crafted with six million pieces of glass. The mosaic stands sixty-three feet tall and forty-two feet wide. Its inscription welcomes visitors with these words: "Come and See."

And indeed, in 1995 the Torch Center will welcome the Global Consultation on World Evangelization II, part of the A.D. 2000 and Beyond Movement. More than 4,500 delegates from 150 nations around the world are expected to attend.

Behind this remarkable center for Christian witness stands a dedicated Christian couple.

I was being drawn deeply into it." It was a mysterious spiritual experience for the child. As an adult, she remembers it vividly. She cannot forget it. She felt she was in the presence of God in the bright light.

Hyung-Ja Lee grew up just like any other child. She went to school and attended church regularly with her family. She learned to pray and sing praises to the Lord. Since her junior high school was a mission school, it had daily chapels, and she faithfully attended them. One of her greatest joys was the weekly Bible study with Dr. Helen Kim, president of Ehwa's Women's University. She admired Dr. Kim greatly for her godly life, noble character, and dedicated service, and she often wished she could be like her. Hyung-Ja saw the image of Jesus in Helen Kim. During her senior high days her own personal relationship with the Lord was growing. Her diary was filled with written prayers to God.

In junior high school Hyung-Ja became interested in art. In senior high school, her interest was so intense that she wouldn't miss any art exhibition held in the city. She loved art dearly and chose to study oriental painting in college.

Hyung-Ja Lee and Torch Ministries

1968	Hyung-Ja marries businessman Soon-Young Choi
1977	Hyung-Ja begins daily prayer meetings in April Korean Center for World Missions officially organized
1980	Hallelujah Soccer teams formed Digging begins for construction of the 63 Building
1985	Construction of the 63 building is completed
1991	Korean Center for World Missions build new facilities in south Seoul
1995	Global Consultation on World Evangelization II to be held at Torch Center

She felt warm all over, and a bright light appeared before her eyes.

Personal crisis

However, during the second year of college a crisis overtook her life. She was on her way to visit Dr. Denman, a missionary, who used to hold two annual revivals for the university. While stepping down from a bus, her whole world suddenly turned into darkness. She was hit by another bus and thrown up into the air. She fell to the pavement incurring massive head injuries and internal bleeding. In the emergency room she was in a coma, and doctors covered her face with a white sheet. However, after forty-five minutes, by the grace of God she regained consciousness. It took her six months to recover from these injuries.

Upon discharge from the hospital Hyung-Ja poured herself into painting again and was chosen as the youngest promising artist. She dreamed of going to France to do further studies in art. Her plan was set in motion. However, since the accident she did not feel as well as she used to, and she became easily tired. Her father prodded her to think about marriage. By family arrangement she met Soon-Young Choi, a businessman and a thirty-two-year-old bachelor. She married him after her graduation from college.

At the end of four years of happily wedded life, her mother-in-law was diagnosed with cancer. In spite of a marathon of prayer and worship lasting one hundred days by the whole family, Hyung-Ja's mother-in-law passed away. Within a month one of her dearest artist friends died. Soon after that, her grandmother also passed away. Reeling from these three deaths, Hyung-Ja fell into a depression and was confused about life.

Business troubles

Furthermore, one of her husband's businesses, a bread company, was experiencing major difficulties. In the midst of these severe trials, Hyung-Ja came to realize that she had not been seeking the Lord as much as she should. She decided to have dawn prayers at 4 A.M. every morning. "Why haven't I been more fully trusting the Lord in all things?" While she was asking this question in prayer, she felt warm all over, and a bright light appeared before her eyes, a light similar to the one she had seen in kindergarten. At that moment, all of her fears, worries, and anxieties were wonderfully lifted from her. Her trust in God was strengthened. When she prayed with greater confidence in the Lord, she began to receive definite answers from Him.

The answers came in detail regarding how her husband was to run her business. She would tell him about the Lord's instruction, and her husband was amazed how much understanding of his business dealings her counsel showed. The couple gave over all of their impossible problems to the Lord and prayed together at 4 A.M. every day for hours. As they went on with their prayers, fresh confidence from the Lord came upon them that the complicated business problems would be resolved, and they were.

Dr. Choi started morning devotions for the employees of all his businesses. He also began tithing to the Lord the profits of his companies. At the same time Hyung-Ja Lee began the prayer meetings with a few of her friends in her living room. Mr. Choi would call her at home from his office to pray for certain issues, and she would pray. The Lord revealed to her His answer for each situation. She would call her husband back and

relay the message to him. He, in turn, obeyed precisely what she had indicated. Problems were invariably solved one by one. The husband and wife worked together as a prayer team. His companies began to flourish.

"Light the torch!"

While on her knees during a predawn prayer in 1977, an indescribable force suddenly overpowered Hyung-Ja. She fell on the floor. A voice was heard: "Light the torch! From one mountain to another, from one branch to another!" This was her call to a new avenue of ministry. The Torch movement was begun. That year, the Korean Center for World Missions was officially organized and registered with the government.

At first the Torch Center was involved with the training of future spiritual leaders and the creation of Christian mass communications. The Asian Center for Theological Studies and Missions, the Far Eastern Broadcasting Company, and the Asia Broadcasting Company have been supported by the Torch Center. Then, a scholarship fund was established to assist thirty Korean Ph.D. students, studying in some field of theology abroad. Already fifteen of them have returned home and hold professorships in leading universities and seminaries. A careful selection is made considering their denomination, their area of interest, and their leadership qualities. In this way the whole Korean church community may evenly benefit from evangelical leadership in the future.

The Center also awards scholarships to thirty ministerial M.Div. students from various theological seminaries and to two hundred high schoolers. Research stipends are made available to Korean professors who wish to integrate their specialties and Christian worldviews.

> *Christian movies and literature have been made available to the armed forces for evangelism purposes.*

The Korean Center in Seoul.

Pastors' conferences are held periodically under Torch Center leadership to assist further development of ministers, who are sometimes also sent abroad for further studies. Christian movies and literature have been made available to the armed forces for evangelism purposes. The National Fast and Prayer Movement was initiated by the Torch ministries, calling for national repentance. The Hallelujah Soccer Team was formed, and it still wins at least two or three national championships a year. The team regularly travels abroad for evangelistic purposes.

The miracle of the 63 Building

The 63 Building is famous in Korea. Offices, shops, and restaurants fill its floors. Tourists make their way to the observation floor at the top, where a panoramic view of Seoul may be enjoyed.

The renowned 63 Building was something the Lord brought about in a miraculous way. During a predawn prayer time the

> *He began to gather necessary information about skyscrapers whenever he traveled abroad.*

Lord showed Hyung-Ja Lee a vision of a building. She and her husband looked for a lot on which to build and unexpectedly found one on Yeouido Island. A plan for a building was drawn up, and prayers were continually offered for the Lord's guidance in the matter. Initially a twenty-story building was projected. But as Hyung-Ja Lee prayed, there was no peace in her heart that this was God's plan for the building. She kept asking the Lord how many floors were to be built. She asked the Lord specifically, "Do you want us to build twenty-five, thirty, or even forty floors?" The number of floors kept going up. She got scared. No definite answer came from the Lord. "Is it fifty, fifty-one, fifty-two, fifty-three?" No answer. Then she came to fifty-nine and finally sixty. At that moment the Lord stopped her and said, "Now you build a sixty-story building."

When her husband came home that evening, Hyung-Ja told him what the Lord had said to her. Angrily he said, "You are out of your mind! What do we do with such a building? It can't be done." She fired back to him, "What if it is the will of God? But do as you will." She said nothing more about it. Elder Choi is a man who does not act on

Dr. Hyung-Ja Lee.

> *Shaped like a pair of praying hands, the 63 Building is a symbol of spiritual triumph through faith in God.*

who, upon hearing his request, flatly told him no without a moment's hesitation. Discouraged, Dr. Choi came home and told his wife that the building project was impossible. She was undaunted. The Lord had already spoken! Encouraged by her unshakable belief, elder Choi also began to act on faith by digging the foundation for a sixty-three-story building, waiting for the Lord to work the rest out. He kept on digging deeper and deeper. The couple believed in the leading of the Lord. At least the foundation was being prepared.

One day tragedy struck the nation. President Park was felled by an assassin. A change of government followed, and under the new government the building law was changed. Permission was granted for the building. It took three and a half years to complete the mammoth building, sixty stories above the ground and three stories underground, altogether sixty-three.

A few years later the law was changed back again to the original ruling. Now such a tall building is not permitted in Korea. There will be only one 63 Building. The structure is a landmark in Seoul. Shaped like a pair of praying hands, it is a symbol of spiritual triumph through faith in God.

One couple trusted the Lord with all their hearts, and He has directed their paths. The Torch movement they have lit burns brightly in Korea with the wonderful gospel of Jesus Christ. More and more, its sparks are spreading to other parts of the world as well.

David Kim

anything unless he is thoroughly convinced by God that what he is about to do is what the Lord wants him to do. He was troubled because he had also prayed but had no answer from the Lord on his own, while his wife had an answer and she was sure of it. He finally decided to accept her admonition as from the Lord. He began to gather necessary information about skyscrapers whenever he traveled abroad. About this time his business, Korea Life Insurance Company, began to experience rapid growth. The building plans got underway.

Overcoming obstacles

There was a major obstacle, however. No building higher than twenty stories was permitted by law on Yeoido Island. Dr. Choi asked for an audience with President Park

MISSIONARY STRATEGIST

Ralph Winter

1924–

Probably no one in the latter part of the twentieth century has done more to change the way evangelicals "do missions" than Ralph D. Winter. His goal, and the goal of the United States Center for World Mission in Pasadena, California (which he founded in 1976), is "a church in every people group by the year 2000." And he has the statistics to show that it can be done. As a result of Winter's ideas, many missions organizations no longer think in terms of sending missionaries to foreign countries; instead, they think of reaching distinct people groups.

Nevertheless, Winter has his critics. In his September 7, 1984, Christianity Today *article, "Ralph Winter: An Unlikely Revolutionary," Tim Stafford mentions "one prominent Christian leader" who observed that ideas come out of Winter's mind a mile a minute: "Ninety-nine out of 100 will not work. One is a good one." The leader spoke of the United States Center for World Mission as a mess. "There's no sense of order." Other critics resent the fact that many churches, influenced by Winter's idea of people groups, will no longer support organizations that send missions to foreign countries. But these are minor cavils compared to the prospect of being able to evangelize all of the people of the world instead of the current possibility of only 14 percent. Change is always painful, but if it means a greater penetration of the gospel into groups that otherwise would never be reached, then change we must.*

Ralph Winter was born in Highland Park, California, just a few miles from the home he moved to in Pasadena two years later, the same one he and his wife, Roberta, live in today. "We have had the same phone number . . . [for] sixty-six years," he notes.

His childhood years gave only the faintest hint of his later creativity. He did start school a bit early, but because he was short and small he was not a leader during his public school years in South Pasadena.

In 1937, at the age of twelve, a "chalk-talk evangelist" at the Highland Park Presbyterian Church spoke during the Sunday school hour, and Ralph accepted Christ. While Winter was in high school, however, gas rationing forced his family to begin attending the closer Lake Avenue Congregational Church, where his interest in missions was stimulated by the Christian Endeavor Society meetings. While in high school he also recalls the time he shot out two streetlights; he felt so guilty he paid the cities of Pasadena and South Pasadena back for the cost. At about this time a Sunday school teacher challenged him to read the Bible, and he did so, beginning with Matthew's gospel.

Lake Avenue also contributed enormously to his life through the people he met—Dan Fuller, son of the famous radio evangelist of "The Old Fashioned Revival Hour" and a close friend in high school; Dawson Trotman, who lived and opened his Navigators headquarters only a few blocks from the Winters; later, Arthur Glasser, a navy chaplain, Navigator, and eventually influential missions leader; and above all the loving leadership of pastor James Henry Hutchins, a graduate of Moody Bible Institute (MBI), among other institutions.

The contrast presented by Ole Hallesby in

Ralph Winter
in 1956.

his book *The Christian Life* between *doing* the right things and *wanting* to do the right things helped Ralph see the difference between getting up early to read the Bible as a duty and getting up because you want to commune with God.

Memory verses

The youth-led programs of Christian Endeavor and the emphasis on Bible memory verses impacted him as well. Winter participated in the formation of the third set of verses for the Navigator "Topical Memory System" and memorized about five hundred verses. The bookstore of BIOLA (the Bible Institute of Los Angeles), now Biola University, and a visit by Harold John Ockenga of Park Street Church in Boston fertilized his passion for church history.

"Perhaps," Winter says, "it was my father's example as a civil engineer that led both my older brother, Paul, and myself on graduation from high school to enter the

> *Winter participated in the formation of the third set of verses for the Navigator "Topical Memory System."*

California Institute of Technology, located only a few miles from our home." He turned seventeen the day after Pearl Harbor, so he was able to complete one year at Cal Tech before enlisting in the navy in June 1943. The navy needed engineers, so those who enlisted knew they would be sent back to Cal Tech to complete their degrees before becoming "CBs" or "Sea Bees" (short for "Construction Battalion"). To enable the men to complete their program more quickly, class work was accelerated by the cancellation of all summer vacations. A call for pilots in the fall of 1944 led Winter to volunteer for the Naval Air Corps and to complete two semesters of study in one so that he graduated shortly after he turned twenty. (Fifteen three-hour final exams in two weeks almost killed him!) Within days he was flown to the Naval Air Corps pilot training program at Terminal Island, south of Los Angeles, then to St. Mary's Pre-Flight School outside Oakland for ground school.

Before he finished the program, however, World War II had ended, both in Europe and in the Pacific, and the need for pilots all but evaporated. Winter opted for "inactive duty" and hungered for college or Bible school courses. James Hutchins suggested that Winter accompany him to Westmont

College in Santa Barbara, where he was hired to teach remedial math to incoming freshmen and a course in topographical surveying. It was chapel speakers at Westmont who convinced him to become a full-time Christian worker.

Study of revivals

A campus revival in early 1946 sparked by Harold Voelkel, a missionary to Korea, led to Winter's study of revivals, especially during the following year (1947–48) at the newly opened Fuller Theological Seminary, where in conscious imitation of the "Holy Club" started by John and Charles Wesley he met with a small group to present papers on revivals through the centuries. During the summer of 1946, too, Winter joined a youth caravan to Mexico sponsored by Robert Boyd Munger's First Presbyterian Church, Berkeley; it left a deeply positive impression of missions in his mind that eventually came to fruition in his own lifelong involvement in missions.

Before going to Fuller, Winter went to Princeton Theological Seminary with Dan Fuller. There they met Bill Bright, later to be the leader of Campus Crusade for Christ; after one year all three decided to head home to attend the new Fuller Seminary. During his year at Princeton, however, Winter met Christy Wilson, then a staff worker for InterVarsity Christian Fellowship, and set up a retreat for Princeton students to bring Eugene Nida and Bruce Metzger to speak about language and missions. During that year he read *English Men of Science* and was struck by the fact that four of the five scientists were devout Christians, though at Cal Tech nothing had been said about their Christian faith.

Recruiting volunteers

Christy Wilson organized the first of what became the triennial InterVarsity International Student Missionary Conventions now tied to the University of Illinois campus in Urbana, though the first one was held in Toronto. Winter hitchhiked there so that he could save the $30 round-trip cost of a car pool; he had only 27¢ on him for the return hike. At the conference he attended a seminar by Clyde Taylor of the National Association of Evangelicals. In their magazine, *United Evangelical Action* (now called

> *He met with a small group to present papers on revivals through the centuries.*

Action), Winter found a news item concerning the need for thirty-one English teachers for Afghanistan. On his way back to California at the end of the school year, Winter recruited a number of volunteers for Afghanistan, as he was to do later on a much larger scale for missions in general.

During the summer of 1948 Winter decided to attend the Summer Institute of Linguistics (SIL) in Norman, Oklahoma, an arm of the Wycliffe Bible Translators. He also decided to adopt a lifestyle of "plain, economical living," insisting to his pastor's discomfort that things like neckties wasted at least a billion dollars that could be used to help the poor of the world. At SIL he was first introduced to anthropology; not only would it become his passion in further graduate study, but he also persuaded his younger brother, David, now president of Westmont College, to go into anthropology.

Afghanistan was still very much on Winter's mind and in his heart. After a term at Prairie Bible Institute in Three Hills, Alberta, Canada, he spent a winter and spring helping to collect lab and engineering equipment to be sent to a new school being founded in Afghanistan, the Afghan Institute of Technology.

Intense courtship

That summer another momentous event occurred in Winter's life. While speaking to the nurses' chapel at the Los Angeles County Hospital, he met Roberta Helm, the woman who was to become his wife. That fall he left for Columbia University and switched to Cornell not long after, but his heart was still back in L.A. After ninety letters and ninety thousand words of "intense courtship," he and Roberta were married in the summer of 1952. That summer while he taught at SIL, Roberta took courses. The Winters then headed back to Cornell where, by taking no summer break, he was able to finish his Ph.D. in structural linguistics, with minors in statistics and cultural anthropology, by the fall of 1953. The first of their four daughters was born that year.

Winter then decided to return to Princeton

Latourette Library on the campus of the U.S. Center for World Mission; (inset) staff enjoy a meal in the cafeteria.

> *In 1967 he helped found the TEE (Theological Education by Extension) program.*

to finish his seminary training, commenting that religious leaders in most cultures were highly influential. It would complete ten years of graduate study.

In 1957, with two more daughters in the family, Ralph and Roberta were sent by the Presbyterian Board of Foreign Missions to Costa Rica for language study, then to a mission post in the mountains of Guatemala to work with a dozen congregations of the Mam Indians, who according to Roberta was "one of the poorest groups of people in this hemisphere."

Simple lifestyle

The simple lifestyle Winter had advocated did not seem so simple to these people when a truck came over the narrow trail into the mountain valley bringing barrels, mattresses, and even a gas-powered wringer washer they owned. The Indians stared in unbelief. Never had they seen anyone with so many things. The Winters learned that what was a simple lifestyle in the United States could still seem extravagant to most of the people of the world.

Roberta soon sensed that Ralph was the kind of creative leader who needed her full-time assistance, so she enlisted a maid to do the housework for her family, now including a fourth daughter, so she could work with her husband on innovative adult education programs and Spanish textbooks, in addition to teaching nursing.

Winter's mind was always creating new strategies for doing more effective missionary work. In Guatemala he organized a nationwide adult education program, helped to start the evangelical Universidad Mariano Galvez, and assisted in forming a rural economic development program. Most important, in 1967 he helped found the TEE (Theological Education by Extension) program that more than a thousand schools around the world now use to train almost 100,000 local church leaders without taking them away from their homes for seminary training.

After a decade as missionaries, the Winters, near the end of their second term, were invited to join missionary leaders Donald McGavran and Alan Tippett as a professor in the School of World Mission at Fuller Theological Seminary. Ralph's parents, having decided to retire to an apartment, gave the new professor and his family their home and all its furniture.

New agencies

During those years Winter's restless creativity continued to bear fruit. He organized the American Society of Missiology in 1972, became its first secretary, and later took over as its president. While articles and books poured from his pen, he nevertheless continued to organize a number of new agencies for the completion of the Great Commission of Christ. In 1969 he helped found the William Carey Library to publish missionary books other publishers would not touch because they had too small a sales potential. Between 1970 and 1976 he helped to form the United Presbyterian Center for Mission Studies, Presbyterians United for Mission Advance, the Summer Institute of International Studies, the Association for Church Missions Committees, the Missions Summer Overseas Seminar, the United Presbyterian Order for World Evangelization, and the Episcopal Church Mission Community.

After ten years of seminary teaching Winter still did not feel, however, he was doing what was most needed to promote world evangelization. His teaching and research had led him to conclusions he presented to the 1974 International Congress on World Evangelization in Lausanne, Switzerland. Statistics had made clear to him that, as currently practiced, evangelical missionary strategy was bypassing 84 percent of the world's population, some 2.4 billion people. A new strategy was needed, and Winter was clearly God's man for the job. Thus began a new phase in Winter's career.

The Life of Ralph Winter

1924	Born on December 8 in the Los Angeles suburb of Highland Park
1937	Accepts Christ at Highland Park Presbyterian Church
1939	The Winters begin attending Lake Avenue Church in Pasadena
1943	Enlists in the navy
1945	Graduates from the California Institute of Technology with a degree in civil engineering
1969	Helps found the William Carey Library
1952	Marries Roberta Helm
1953	Completes his Ph.D. at Cornell University in structural linguistics; first of four daughters born
1955	Graduates from Princeton Seminary
1956–66	Presbyterian missionary to the Mayan Indians of Guatemala
1966–76	Serves as a professor in the Fuller School of World Mission
1967	Helps found the Theological Education by Extension program
1972	Organizes the American Society of Missiology
1976	Founds the United States Center for World Mission in Pasadena
1990	Mortgage on United States Center for World Mission burned
1990–	President of William Carey International University

> *"A church for every people by the year 2000."*

On November 1, 1976, he took a leave of absence from his position at Fuller to found what he called the United States Center for World Mission. The old campus of the Pasadena Christian College was for sale, so he and a handful of other missionaries rented part of it. Then they took the big step of making a huge down payment so they could get title to the campus. They did not use mass mailings to obtain funds. Rather, fervent prayer meetings, word of mouth, and large checks arriving at the last minute kept them from bankruptcy and enabled them to amass more than $6 million.

By 1979 another turning point came in the life of the new organization. Aware that John R. Mott's phrase, "the evangelization of the world in this generation," had symbolized the missionary activity of a previous generation, three generations of missionaries met at the United States Center to create an equally memorable watchword. The motto "A church for every people by the year 2000" has marked the Center ever since. Today almost three hundred workers from more than sixty agencies work together to reach what is seemingly an impossible goal.

Vision for 2000

But Ralph Winter is a man with enough vision to believe that the goal is within reach. "It is actually a small job when you think of it," he says. "There are perhaps 2.5 million Bible-believing congregations around the world. And there are, I estimate, about 17,000 mission fields to be approached. That's about 150 congregations per mission field. It doesn't seem impossible to form churches in each of those mission fields by the year 2000."

Roberta agrees with her husband's remarks. "What would happen to this world if more evangelical Christians were to realize that God blessed them with money in order to make them a blessing, not to pamper them. What an immense amount of money would be released for highly strategic causes."

Will there be a church within every people group by that year? The Winters believe there will be. And they have statistics to show that it can be done. The Winters are clearly the strategists the church needs today to fulfill Christ's goal of total penetration of the world for God's kingdom.

[This article is based on autobiographical material from Ralph Winter and the article written by Leslie R. Keylock, "Meet Ralph D. Winter," that appeared in the September 1986 issue of Moody Monthly.]

Further Reading

Keylock, Leslie R. "Meet Ralph D. Winter," *Moody Monthly* (September 1986).

Stafford, Tim. "Ralph Winter: An Unlikely Revolutionary." *Christianity Today* (7 September 1984): 14–18.

Winter, Roberta. *I Will Do a New Thing: The U. S. Center for World Mission . . . and Beyond.* Pasadena: William Carey Library, 1987.

WHERE THERE'S A WILL

Josh McDowell

1939–

Josh McDowell has probably spoken to more high school and college students than anyone else in history. Over the years, he has talked to more than seven million young people in eighty-four countries, including seven hundred university and college campuses.

To students, Josh speaks on the topics of "Maximum Sex" and "Why Wait?" He gives young people positive reasons to abstain from sexual involvement until marriage. He explains about God's guidelines, given to protect us and provide for us.

Josh is also known in the area of apologetics—the historical evidence for the accuracy of the Bible and the resurrection of Jesus Christ. His book, Evidence That Demands a Verdict, *is a classic in the field of apologetics. Josh's* More Than a Carpenter *has been translated into more than thirty languages and distributed in more than forty countries.*

In recent years, God has used Josh's books in the former Soviet Union. Through Josh's background as the child of an alcoholic and as a former skeptic, God has provided a unique credibility for him in these countries where atheism and alcoholism are so prevalent.

Think, Josh, think!" snapped the teacher. "You're doing it wrong. Think! Do it with your right hand!" Mrs. Duel, Josslin (Josh) McDowell's second grade teacher, smacked the table each time he reached for a block with his left hand. For several years in grade school, Josh's teachers tried to get him to use his right hand, even though he was naturally left-handed. The frustration he experienced caused him to develop a stutter, for which he was also scolded.

At home, Josh could recite his pieces without flaw, but when he was in front of the classroom, his stomach would twist into knots, and he couldn't recite without stuttering. His teachers never would have guessed that someday, this nervous little boy would travel the world speaking to millions of people about Jesus Christ.

Josh was a determined young man, and he soon learned that if he worked hard, he could compensate for his difficulties and make good grades. Josh had a brilliant mind, and he knew that if he really wanted something, he could find a way to get it. His attitude was, *Where there's a will, there's a way.* By working hard, Josh made excellent grades.

Alcoholic father

Josh loved his mother with all of his heart. She was a sweet, heavy-set woman, who taught him to respect God and the church, although Josh didn't believe that religion "worked." Josh's father, Wilmot McDowell, had a strong work ethic, and he taught Josh to be a hard worker. But Wilmot McDowell was also an alcoholic. He often embarrassed Josh when he came home knocking things over and crashing into things with his truck. Josh hated the way his father treated his mother—especially when he was drunk. Josh would find his mother crying in the barn, bruised and beaten by his father after an angry tirade.

Over the years, Josh's hatred for his father grew. Often, Josh would drag his father into the barn and tie him up. He would tie the rope around his neck and attach it to his feet, so that if he struggled to get free, he would strangle himself.

Josh McDowell at a "WHY WAIT?" teen rally at Greenville, South Carolina.

One evening, Josh found his mother crying. She told him she couldn't take it any more. The abuse from Josh's father was breaking her heart. She told Josh she just wanted to live to see him graduate from high school the next month. She asked Josh to promise her that he would never be an alcoholic, that he wouldn't swear, and that he'd be the kind of son of whom she would be proud. Josh promised.

Four months later, Josh's mother died.

The next fall, Josh entered Kellogg College in Battle Creek. Even though he had graduated tenth in his high school class, he struggled to adjust to college life.

His English teacher and counselor, Mrs. Hampton, took him aside one day. She had noticed that he was having trouble, and she shared with Josh what she thought the problem was.

Josh had grown up speaking with poor grammar and pronunciation habits. He was accustomed to using double negatives and incorrect grammar. In the farming community of Union City, Michigan, no one cared whether or not he spoke correctly. Mrs. Hampton was gentle and not condescending. She encouraged Josh to work on improving his habits, and she offered to help him.

Mrs. Hampton believed in Josh. "You have something most students here don't have, Josh. Determination—a lot of drive." *Where there's a will, there's a way.*

> *Josh would find his mother crying in the barn, bruised and beaten by his father after an angry tirade.*

The challenge

During the rest of his time at Kellogg College, Josh's determination paid off. He became involved with many activities, was voted class president, and decided to pursue law as a career choice. He had a "master plan" for his life—to go into politics and eventually become the governor of Michigan.

The Life of Josh McDowell	
1939	Born August 17 in Union City, Michigan
1957	Graduates from Union City High; mother dies four months later
1958	Believes and trusts in Jesus Christ
1961	Graduates from Wheaton College
1962	Seminary student at Talbot
1964	Joins staff of Campus Crusade for Christ
1968	Lectures on pro-Marxist campuses throughout Latin America
1971	Marries Dorothy Ann Youd
1972	*Evidence That Demands a Verdict* is published
1985	"Why Wait?" campaign begins
1988	"Teen Sex Survey in the Evangelical Church" research study released
1989	"Why Wait?" Campaign to Great Britain Josh and Petra team up for "Why Wait?" youth rallies First Russia Outreach
1990	Josh McDowell Ministry Radio Program launched Romania Outreach begins soon after fall of Ceaucescu
1991	Mission Leningrad with Finnish evangelist, Kalevi Lehtinen Mission to Russia '91
1992	Operation Carelift '92 Mission to Russia '92
1993	Operation Carelift '93 Operation PowerLink—"See You at the Party!" Mission to Russia '93

His social involvement made Josh well-known on campus. He knew almost everyone. But one group of students intrigued him. Josh watched them closely over several months. Eventually, he became frustrated. He could see that their lives were different from his own. But he couldn't discern the factor that made them different.

Finally, Josh directly asked one of the young women in the group, "Why are your lives so different from the other leaders on campus? What's changed your lives?"

The pretty girl answered simply, "Jesus Christ."

"Oh, for heaven's sake, don't give me that garbage!" Josh snarled back at her. Then he regretted his harshness. "I'm sorry . . . it's just that, well, I believe religion *is* a bunch of garbage. I'm fed up with church, the Bible, and with religion."

"Excuse me," said the girl, "But I didn't say 'religion.' I said 'Jesus Christ.' The *person* of Jesus Christ." The group challenged Josh intellectually to examine the claims of Christianity and the person of Jesus Christ.

Josh didn't understand. He had always figured that you parked your brain at the door when you went into church. He couldn't see the connection between faith and intellect. Josh was convinced that Christianity and other religions were all basically the same.

Because they had appealed to his lawyer's mentality, Josh accepted the challenge and went full speed ahead, determined to win the battle. He decided that the resurrection of Jesus Christ was the key point to refute. However, through his studies an amazing thing happened. Josh soon discovered compelling historical evidence for the reliability of the New Testament and the Resurrection.

In fact, Josh was astounded to discover 119 separate events or situations that he had to explain before he could honestly and intellectually reject Jesus Christ. As his studies began to show him, the resurrection of Jesus Christ was one of the best-established facts of history.

Now Josh had an even bigger problem. He was intellectually convinced of the truth of Christianity, but he was in the midst of a major struggle with his will.

After a sleepless night, unable to get Jesus off his mind, Josh asked Jesus to come into his life and forgive his sins. In the months

> *As his studies began to show him, the resurrection of Jesus Christ was one of the best-established facts of history.*

following that decision, Josh noticed himself changing. The biggest change was his relationship with his father. Josh's burning hatred for his father turned into love, solely by the power of God at work in his life.

Later, when Wilmot McDowell witnessed the miraculous change in his son, Josh told his father he loved him and revealed the reason for the change. "Son," said the elder McDowell, "If God can do in my life what He's done in yours, then I think He can handle my drinking problem. Will you help me?"

Josh was overcome with emotion. He explained to his father how to ask God for forgiveness and pray a prayer of trust in Christ. Josh will tell you that he has never seen such a dramatic conversion in anyone's life before or since. His father's countenance changed right before his eyes.

Wilmot McDowell not only never drank alcohol again after that day, but the town drunk was transformed into the town evangelist. He told everyone he met about what Jesus had done in his life. Soon, everyone in Union City knew of the changed life of Wilmot McDowell.

A changed life

As a Christian, Josh's goals in life changed. He set aside his plan to be governor of Michigan and, instead, transferred to Wheaton College to finish his degree. While there, he began traveling on weekends to speak at churches and evangelistic meetings. Josh realized that he would spend his life telling people about the love and forgiveness of Jesus Christ.

During his senior year at Wheaton, Josh and two friends had the opportunity to meet with Bill Bright, president of Campus Crusade for Christ. At a student coffee shop, Bright told the young men about three kinds of people in the world: natural man, spiritual man, and carnal man. He explained that the spiritual man places Christ in the driver's seat of his life and allows God's

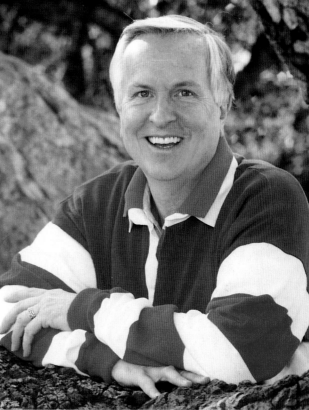

Josh McDowell.

Holy Spirit to control his life, resulting in the fruit of the Spirit being reflected in his life. Before Bright left that day, all three of the men had prayed with him and asked the Holy Spirit to take control of their lives.

After graduating from Wheaton, Josh entered Talbot Theological Seminary. While a student there, he began a speaking ministry called "Focus of Youth." On a card above his desk he put the verse "For I am not ashamed of the gospel of Christ: for it is the power of God unto salvation" (Romans 1:16). This verse is still one of Josh's life verses.

Campus Crusade for Christ

In 1964, Josh joined the staff of Campus Crusade for Christ and was assigned to be the Canadian director. He worked at the University of British Columbia and remained there for four years in this administrative role. Though he felt called to Campus Crusade, he wasn't getting opportunities to speak. What was wrong? Always before his motto—*Where there's a will, there's a way*—had worked. Didn't God want him to use his speaking ability?

Then Josh was asked to teach at Campus Crusade's Institute of Biblical Studies. Filled with excitement, he decided to teach on the book of Romans. He studied and prepared for almost six months.

One week before he was scheduled to leave, Bright called Josh. He desperately needed Josh to come to Arrowhead Springs, Campus Crusade for Christ's headquarters, and help administrate at the hotel during summer staff training. Josh's chance to teach would be lost. He was silent. "Josh, I need you," said Bright.

"OK, I'll be there." Frustrated, Josh packed his bag and drove to Arrowhead.

Josh supervised thirty staff people and organized the facilities for the almost 1,700 people who were expected to come from all over the world. Unfortunately, because of the complicated task, inexperienced staff, and recurring breakdowns of hotel equipment, even the best-laid plans resulted in chaos.

The final blow came when a horrible case of dysentery broke out. In a few days, almost everyone was ill. Every rest room had a waiting line, and the facilities were overworked to the point of breakdown.

The majority of the staff were either sick, helping prepare meals, or doing other chores. So, with a bucket, mop, and toilet plunger in hand, Josh attended to all of the rest rooms. Even though he was sick, too, he had no time to think about it. Every toilet in the hotel and other buildings had to be scrubbed twice a day. Josh worked more than twenty hours a day to maintain the facilities.

This was *not* what Josh felt God had called him to do. He was ready to resign. But then, suddenly, he realized that he had brought his bitter attitude with him from Canada. As he recalled the picture in Scripture of Jesus washing the disciples' feet, which he had read in his devotions that very morning, Josh repented. The thought came to him, *If Jesus can wash their feet, why can't I scrub their floors and clean their toilets?*

That evening, Josh prayed for God's grace to be a true servant of Christ. He realized that before he would ever become a leader, he needed to learn how to be a follower.

> *Josh realized that he would spend his life telling people about the love and forgiveness of Jesus Christ.*

Shortly after this, Josh was assigned to go to Argentina, which led to traveling and speaking in Latin America, lecturing on pro-Marxist campuses. Speaking in Latin America, in areas full of revolutionaries, was excellent training for lecturing and thinking on his feet. He became adept at debating Marxist philosophy, even in Spanish.

This practice led to lectures on North American university campuses. Josh first used the speaking tactics he had developed in Latin America at the University of California at San Diego. Often, in addition to delivering a scheduled lecture in the evening and speaking on free-speech platforms, Josh would address classes on topics that related to Christianity.

Now, as Josh traveled and saw God giving him so many opportunities to proclaim the gospel in university settings, he added four words to his motto: *Where there's a will, there's a way, if it's God's will.* In the years that followed, Josh began publishing books and recording his talks on tape. All of his previous experiences had perfectly prepared him for what God wanted him to do.

Recent years

The two main areas of focus for Josh's ministry have been apologetics and relationships. Students have always responded well to his "Maximum Sex" talk, where he outlines God's plan for sexual relationships. In 1986, the "WHY WAIT?" campaign was launched. Through this major thrust, Josh has sought to spread the message of the positive reasons that young people should save themselves for marriage. In 1989, Josh teamed up with the contemporary Christian music group Petra and toured the nation, giving the "WHY WAIT?" message to teens, parents, and pastors.

In the past few years, God has opened opportunities for Josh to travel and speak in the former Soviet Union. Some time ago, his books were translated, printed, and distributed in the Soviet Union. Now, his words

> *"Where there's a will,*
> *there's a way,*
> *if it's God's will."*

have preceded him into this atheist culture, and he has a platform there. Atheists are skeptical about Christianity, and alcoholism is a huge problem. But because Josh was a skeptic and his father was an alcoholic, he can relate to the Soviet people, and they feel an affinity with him.

Through three "Mission to Russia" trips, Josh has taken hundreds of lay Christians to Russia. The groups pass out Josh's books on the streets of the cities. People crowd around to receive them. Although some remain skeptical, the majority accept the free books with smiles and gestures of thanks.

Josh has also taken humanitarian aid to Russia through "Operation Carelift." God has provided ways for Josh to provide humanitarian aid in the form of food, clothing, shoes, boots, socks, medicine, and vitamins. As Josh has been obedient to do whatever was possible in providing for these great needs, God has used these efforts to provide ways for the gospel message to be disbursed as well. With every physical item received by a Russian hand is a copy of *More Than a Carpenter* and the gospel of John.

Josh has been a traveling representative for Campus Crusade for Christ for thirty-one years. He and Dottie, his wife of twenty-two years, live in California with their four children.

Little did Josh know, as he scrubbed toilets at Arrowhead Springs, what God had in store for his life and his ministry. Those on Josh's support staff know that many projects can seem impossible at the start. But then they will often hear Josh say, "Where there's a will, there's a way, *if it's God's will.*"

Martha Millhouse

Further Reading

McDowell, Josh. *Evidence That Demands a Verdict.* Vols. 1 & 2. San Bernadino: Here's Life, 1972, 1979 (I), 1975, 1981 (II).

——. *More Than a Carpenter.* Wheaton: Tyndale House, 1977.

——. *The Secret of Loving.* Wheaton: Tyndale House, 1985.

Musser, Joe. *A Skeptic's Quest.* San Bernadino: Here's Life, 1984.

REMARKABLE EVANGELIST

Ravi Zacharias

1946–

Ravi Zacharias was born in 1946 in Madras, India, just six miles from where the apostle Thomas is said to have been martyred. His forebears were Hindu priests in the temples of south India. They were members of the highest caste, the Brahmans, and within that structure, the priests were of the most important stratum, the Nambudiri. When four generations ago a German missionary introduced an ancestor to Christ, the family changed its name to *Zacharias*, a popular biblical name among German Christians.

Zacharias's own immediate family, however, shared no real interest in the Christian faith of their ancestors. His father and grandfather were educated in England, and his mother taught physiology. Although his father died in 1979, he is still remembered in India today as a prominent deputy secretary of domestic relations.

The Zacharias children—two girls and three boys, Ravi being the middle son—were often described as natural born leaders. Ravi played cricket and tennis competitively and engaged in mischief and practical jokes with equal passion.

Refreshments and a bomb

During these years, the ministry of Youth for Christ was very active in India. When National Coordinator Fred David heard Ravi's sister Shyamala sing, he immediately invited her to participate in the activities of a new club organized by YFC called TAMI (Teens and Twenties Are Most Important). She attended the meeting and upon hearing a speaker ask, "How many of you want peace with God?" she came forward to answer the call.

Invited to come back the following week to share her testimony, Shyamala was able to persuade Ravi to accompany her. She lured him somewhat by telling him refreshments were going to be served following the program. Being unfamiliar with Christian vernacular, Ravi remembered being alarmed at the song, "There Is a Bomb in Gilead," only to discover later that the musician was singing about a soothing *balm*. The speaker that evening was Sam Wolgemuth, the president of YFC International. Ravi was touched by the message and began to attend the weekly meetings.

The Word of God began to take root in Ravi's heart. Many questions, however, remained for him unanswered. He was an intense and reflective young man, who, as one childhood friend recalled, "thought deeply about life." Then at seventeen, a friend of his died. He witnessed the Hindu cremation ceremony. Weighted with despair, he approached the Hindu priest after the service. "Can you help me with where this person is now?" he asked.

Ravi remembered the priest giving some abstract answer and then throwing his arms into the air, saying, "It's a question you're going to be asking all your life, young man, and I'm not sure you'll ever find a satisfactory answer."

The promise of life

At that time, Ravi was studying in medical school. The priest's response, coupled with the pressure from his family's position in society to succeed, burdened him greatly. He soon found himself in a hospital bed recovering from an attempt to take his own life.

While Ravi was in the hospital, YFC director Fred David brought him a Bible. His mother, though herself unfamiliar with

> *The Word of God began to take root in Ravi's heart.*

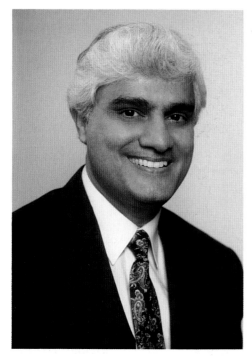

The International Conference for Itinerant Evangelists, known as Amsterdam '86, drew more than ten thousand individuals from 173 countries, the largest gathering of nations outside the U.N. Before Dr. Ravi Zacharias addressed the crowd, chairman Billy Graham introduced him as "one of the most articulate young evangelists of our time." Six years later he would speak to an audience of six: six generals at the Academy of Natural Sciences and Center for Geopolitical Strategy, the "Pentagon" of Russia.

Even when Ravi was a lad, the Lord had been uniquely shaping him "for such a time as this." Born into an influential Indian family—his father was the deputy secretary of India's Home Ministry—the young Zacharias visited the homes of the United States ambassadors as well as those of Prime Ministers Gandhi and Nehru.

Yet while his privileged upbringing would prepare him well to speak in prestigious settings, nothing eased the young man's anguish over the finality of death and the questions of life which remained unanswered. Behind the dogma of Eastern philosophy lay the acute sense of despair. The song he heard on Radio Ceylon as a teenager intensified this struggle:

From the canyons of the mind, we wander on and stumble blind,
Wade through the often tangled maze of starless nights and sunless days,
Hoping for some kind of clue, a road to lead us to the truth.
But who will answer?

And as the music faded, the rejoinder echoed in his ear: "Who will answer? Who will answer? Who will answer?"

the gospel, read to him as he was unable even to hold the book in his hands. She read him the book of John: "Because I live, you also will live" (John 14:19). A few hours later, Ravi committed his life to Christ. Little did he know how God would use this emotional and intellectual struggle to minister to thousands around the world.

The Lord's hand was undoubtedly upon Ravi. Just a few weeks later, he and a friend found a worn English book in his family's garbage can. The volume was W. H. Griffith Thomas's commentary on Romans. And two years later, having never preached a sermon, Ravi won a national preaching competition and traveled across India with the India Teen Team. (He was entered in the contest by a friend and given his topic fifteen minutes before he was to speak!)

To Canada and South Vietnam
Upon completion of his studies from college in New Delhi, Zacharias moved to Toronto, Ontario, where his family soon joined him. While pursuing a career working in hotel management, he continued to preach in the United States and Canada. In 1968 he entered Ontario Bible College.

Dr. L. L. King, then vice president of the Christian and Missionary Alliance (C&MA),

The Life of Ravi Zacharias

1946	Born in Madras, India
1963	Conversion to Christ
1964	Begins his college studies in New Delhi
1965	First preaching engagement; wins "Asian Youth Preacher Award"
1966	Family moves to Toronto, Ontario
1971	Preaches in South Vietnam, Singapore, and Hong Kong for four months; meetings trigger revival in South Vietnam
1972	Graduates from Ontario Bible College Marries Margaret Reynolds
1974	Travels and preaches in Cambodia for six weeks before the fall of Phnom Penh
1976	Graduates from Trinity Evangelical Divinity School
1980	Awarded Doctorate of Divinity from Houghton College
1981–83	Professor of Evangelism and Contemporary Thought at Alliance Theological Seminary
1983	Invited by Billy Graham to speak at Amsterdam '83, the International Conference for Itinerant Evangelists
1984	Ravi Zacharias International Ministries incorporated Inception of radio program, "Let My People Think"
1985	Delivers a major message at Houston '85, the National Convocation on Evangelizing Ethnic America
1986	Addresses ten thousand evangelists at Amsterdam '86
1990	Awarded Doctorate of Laws from Asbury College Visiting scholar at Cambridge University where he writes *A Shattered Visage*
1992	Speaks to military leaders in Russia Keynote speaker at Harvard University's *Veritas Forum*
1993	Addresses congressional leaders in Bogota, Colombia Plenary speaker at Urbana '93

> *He ministered to American and Vietnamese soldiers and in churches and tribal villages.*

remembered that even at the age of twenty-four, Ravi was a "remarkable evangelist." Dr. King arranged for his licensing as a C&MA minister. And in 1971, at the urging of the daughter of Jonathan Goforth, famed missionary to China, Ravi journeyed to South Vietnam.

As Zacharias recalled, his preaching engagements there "sealed my call into the ministry." At twenty-five, he and his seventeen-year-old interpreter, Hien, traveled by motorbike and sometimes helicopter gunship with military personnel. Preaching two to five sermons a day, sometimes only a short distance from the demilitarized zone, he ministered to American and Vietnamese soldiers and in churches and tribal villages. Longtime C&MA missionary and interpreter Helen Evans related that at the end of one service, numerous students encircled Ravi and her on the platform and fell on their knees in prayer.

The meetings in South Vietnam sparked a revival among students at a seminary, and an estimated four thousand people gave their lives to Christ. A journalist in a 1973 missions magazine reported: "Although the revival movement did not begin until several weeks after Ravi's visit, those with whom I spoke trace the revival back to his ministry. Deep repentance for sin, restoration of broken fellowship, renewal of desire to reach people for Christ swept through the student body."

In 1974, while a seminary student, Ravi traveled in Cambodia, a country with only a few believers at that time. When he finished preaching in one service, no one moved, so Ravi asked his interpreter to dismiss all except those who wished to commit their lives to Christ. The interpreter repeated this message twice and still no one moved; the entire audience of several hundred people was converted.

Answering the real questions

The years between Zacharias's travels in Cambodia and the inception of Ravi Zacharias International Ministries in 1984 were filled with many difficult days on the road. During this time the Lord cultivated in

> "This was the strongest witness for Christ I have seen in this half century."

him a unique vision and burden. His studies in theology and philosophy, and particularly the writings of C. S. Lewis, G. K. Chesterton, and Malcolm Muggeridge, prepared him to speak with skeptics. And the emotional turmoil he experienced as a young man made him sensitive to the gnawing questions of the heart which must be addressed in the preaching of the gospel.

Just as God had, unknown to Ravi, opened the door for his first preaching engagement, so too He answered a specific prayer in a remarkable manner. It was 1983. He was a professor at Alliance Theological Seminary, but he sensed that the Lord wanted to expand his ministry to reach the opinion makers of society, university students and others who had genuine questions about the Christian faith.

"I just felt that somehow the questions people were asking were really not being answered," he recalled, "and that we were being very negligent in our evangelism in ignoring these questions." The challenge, he realized, would bring extraordinary financial demands.

After much prayer and reflection, Ravi believed that with a specific financial sum, the ministry could be established. At the close of a meeting in Ohio, he asked the audience to pray for him and his wife, Margie, as they had some difficult decisions to make in the days ahead, but he did not share any other details. A few hours later as Margie and Ravi were leaving, a stranger approached them. "I do not know how this may help," he said, "but the Lord has told me to give this to you." He handed Ravi a check for the exact amount needed.

Worldwide ministry

Since then Ravi has spoken in nearly fifty countries, to business and political leaders in Peru, South Africa, Colombia, and Russia, and at such universities as Princeton, Harvard, and Ramkamhaeng University in Bangkok. Zacharias's radio program, "Let My People Think," is heard weekly on Moody stations across the United States and on Trans World Radio and HCJB all over

Ravi Zacharias addresses an evangelistic rally.

the world. Ravi Zacharias International Ministries is headquartered in Atlanta, Georgia, with offices in Toronto and India as well.

After Ravi's lectureship at Harvard University, a professor who had been there for fifty years said, "This was the strongest witness for Christ I have seen in this half century." And what was Ravi's response? "The gospel is very simple, but people's lives and the situations of life are very complicated. . . . The burden I feel most is to clear the intellectual hurdles in the minds of the resistant and to regain the moral focus so that the Cross can be seen for what it is."

Danielle DuRant

Further Reading

Plowman, Edward. "Ravi Zacharias: Encouraging Thinkers to think about God." *National & International Religion Report* (November 29, 1993): 1–4.

Niklaus, Robert L. "Amsterdam 86: Speaking in the Superlative." *The Alliance Witness* (November 5, 1986): 12–13.

Zacharias, Ravi K. *A Shattered Visage: The Real Face of Atheism* (Grand Rapids: Baker, 1990).

BUSINESS DEVELOPMENT FOR THE POOR

Opportunity International

After Moscow and St. Petersburg, Nizhni Novgorod is the third largest city in Russia. Yet few people recognize the town's name, even though Nobel Peace Prize winner Andrei Sakharov lived here for years and the city once served as a major defense center of the mighty Soviet Union. Known then as Gorki, it was an isolated city closed to all travel and communication to protect its military secrets. Now, after the collapse in 1990 of the Soviet Union and Communism, Nizhni Novgorod has become an open city—open to democracy, free enterprise, and the gospel of Jesus Christ. And the gospel is getting a hearing by these Russian people in a most amazing way—jobs.

The Soviet Union's defense industry employed seven of every ten Gorki workers, but defense orders disappeared with Communism's demise. One thousand workers lost jobs every week in 1992, and though citizens gladly welcomed the shift to private enterprise, the road to a successful economy has been rocky. Helping clear the path and lift these Russians from poverty is Opportunity International, a development agency that brings Christ's love to the poor with new jobs.

Eric Thurman on an Opportunity International assignment.

Opportunity is developing jobs by providing business loans to the very poor of Novgorod—those displaced by the military collapse, single mothers struggling to support families, and pensioners forced into early retirement whose fixed incomes have been undercut by rampant inflation. Opportunity will help people start small bakeries, sewing shops, street vending, and other businesses, as well as working with a local agency that offers social services, such as soup kitchens and distribution centers for used clothing.

Opportunity assists people that many banks ignore as unrewarding, especially the desperately poor. And more than one billion people are classified as very poor, with insufficient income to buy even the basics of life or to recover after a political or natural catastrophe. Opportunity issues loans to these people—more than $31.5 million in the past sixteen years. The result is that physical needs are met and recipients are awakened to spiritual needs.

Seventeen countries

Opportunity is now in seventeen countries. Its approach wins applause from hundreds of Third World churches. As Opportunity President Eric Thurman explains, "Ask the church leader in the Third World country, 'What can we do as outsiders that will do the most for your ministry?' and he will say, 'Please, help my people, help my community develop income.'" Thurman cites examples in country after country where Opportunity, by providing individuals with mini-loans (average amount: $1,000) and business training and development, have strengthened churches, brought the poor to Christ, and fulfilled Christ's call to love the poor and helpless through acts of kindness.

In Jamaica, Opportunity leaders trained pastors to do welding and raise chickens, giving them income to support their churches and their families.

In Bali, Indonesia, an island with less than 1 percent Christian population, the Balinese Christians provide 90 percent of church funds, a dramatic turnaround from 1978, when the struggling Christian community

> *A development agency that brings Christ's love to the poor with new jobs.*

At first glance, business enterprise and evangelism seem to mix as easily as oil and water. But one missions agency has found that meeting economic and physical needs is an effective way to make the poor aware of their spiritual needs. In a variation on the tent-making theme—using a skill to help a country and then present the gospel from a position of respect—Opportunity International earns a platform to preach by creating jobs in the Third World.

Working with national churches and partner Christian agencies in each country, Opportunity provides loans to help the poor start businesses, leads seminars to train the new business owners, and teaches spiritual principles to help the businesses grow.

"Job development is one of the hottest tools for evangelism," says Opportunity President Eric Thurman. He notes that in Asia three of every four who receive loans for new jobs are non-Christians and often are receptive to the gospel. The results show Opportunity's compassion for the poor and downcast, their zeal for the spiritual health of recipients, and the people's gratitude.

Opportunity
- *Loans more than 40 percent of all funds to women*
- *Strengthens churches by helping pastors work with community agencies and Christians start jobs*
- *Has received 95 percent repayment of loans since the program began*
- *Created or maintained almost forty-five thousand jobs in 1992*

Meanwhile, the gospel goes forth with the business loans and training in an innovative program to evangelize men and women in developing countries.

received 90 percent of its funds from the West. Opportunity was a key contributor to the change. Working with the Protestant church and using local pastors as "point men" who received training to screen applicants, the ministers recommended hundreds of men and women in villages throughout Bali to receive the loans. Hindus as well as Christians were chosen.

Loan repayment was an amazing 100 percent in the first eight years. Grateful recipients used their skills to raise pigs, grow orchids, and start fish farms, among other businesses. The pastors earned respect and authority, the churches became self-supporting, and interested Hindus attended business classes to learn biblical principles of money management and care of employees. For many, it was their first positive exposure to the Christian message. And despite rejection from family and friends, many have become Christians.

Zimbabwe

In Harare, Zimbabwe, a young woman received a loan to start a business that promised to pull her from poverty. Though pleased, she couldn't understand why she got the money. "Why do you provide loans to poor people when no one else will?" she asked.

The staff of Zambuko Trust, Opportunity's partner agency in Zimbabwe, told her that Jesus Christ motivated their actions. The woman responded by asking, "How can I become a Christian?" Soon she bowed her head with the staff to accept Christ as her Savior.

Her conversion did not influence the loan application. Of course, the staff was delighted that she had received eternal life, something of much greater value than money for business. Like all borrowers, she will receive the loan if she has "a good business idea and a reputation for being an honest and trustworthy person," says the Zambuko executive director.

Bulgaria

Most recently, Opportunity is about to channel several hundred thousand dollars to Bulgaria, a fledgling democracy, which remains threatened by the long shadows of Communism and atheism. The loans and

The History of Opportunity International

1971	Opportunity founded as the Institute for International Development Inc. by Alfred Whittaker
1977	Begins direct investment in micro-enterprises
1979	Moves from direct investment to developing autonomous local Christian agencies to carry out lending and training
1981	Launches work in Asia (Indonesia and the Philippines)
1985	Lending surpasses $1 million per year
1988	IIDI becomes Opportunity International
1989	Lending exceeds $4 million per year
1991	Creates Women's Opportunity Funds to help the Third World's poorest people—women
1992	Enters Bulgaria to begin a new phase in post-Communist Eastern Europe
1993	Receives $550,000 initial grant from USAID to expand operations in Russia

training in starting and managing a small business will help restore many Bulgarians to work and create spin-off jobs as well. All this, done in the name of Christ, will make the recipients, those they employ, and their family and friends, both grateful and open to the Christian message.

Criticism

In spite of such success, Opportunity has critics. The gospel should be presented directly to each loan recipient, some say; others assert that the focus should be souls saved, not jobs salvaged or created. One pastor in suburban Chicago told Thurman, "I appreciate what you're doing, but I could never ask our church to support your work. I think the Red Cross are good people, but I wouldn't put them in our church budget. We support missions and missionaries, not social agencies."

An Opportunity
International
project in Asia.

Thurman acknowledges that Opportunity is not the typical missions agency, but it uses two strategies for mission development that other agencies are adopting: (1) indiginization—putting local people and churches in charge in order to grow economically and spiritually; and (2) a form of tent-making that allows the gospel into closed countries—setting up microbanks that help people to start businesses and poor economies to grow. As a result, local governments continue to welcome Opportunity's help. The agency, which desires to declare the love of God through kind deeds, can enter where evangelists otherwise could not go. And in their suitcases the representatives of Opportunity International carry the gospel message.

Evangelism and enterprise

"Job development is one of the hottest tools for evangelism," Thurman declares. "We help the country's own agency to evangelize. They can define what is culturally correct." Opportunity does this by organizing "partner agencies" in each country. In 1992 there were forty partners in seventeen countries. Each agency is composed entirely of Christian business and community leaders. They screen applicants, study marketplace conditions, and offer business development training to borrowers, many of whom are non-

Christians. The borrowers repay the loans, usually within two years, and the funds remain in the country, channeled to other needy and gifted individuals, who need only money and training to get started.

Evangelism and enterprise work well together according to Thurman. Helping the poor find jobs is biblical. He cites Jesus' words in Matthew 11:28. "What did Jesus say?" Thurman asks. "He was calling 'all you who labor and are heavy laden.' He was talking about survival, employment, and the key issues of life. He implied that the poor are more likely to connect His claims."

Thurman continues: "The good news of the gospel is not just getting converts but helping the poor—those who are broken and desperately hurting—to find an entire new life in Christ. That's the Father's heart. The church needs a global vision."

Thurman says he agrees with the vision of Prison Fellowship president Charles Colson that Christians "must be the people of God," helping people now. "The entry point where the gospel becomes real is in the world right now," Thurman says. "The parents who can't feed their kids don't have space in their heart, their mind, their soul, to entertain the claims of Christ. Meet those needs for food, and people start paying attention [to the gospel]."

Personal sacrifice

Thurman was so convinced that by creating jobs Opportunity could present the gospel more effectively and strengthen small Christian communities, he left his own job as president of a TV production company to become Opportunity's chief executive officer. His salary dropped 50 percent as he said good-bye to twenty years in TV and radio journalism, including stints as a radio reporter and manager at a CBS-owned radio station and as president of the TV production company that prepared material for such corporate heavyweights as IBM and Montgomery Ward.

But for Thurman, his own personal sacrifice has been amply rewarded. "There are a series of changes happening globally in the church. I feel I'm on the cusp of change. It's exhilarating; it's where I want to be."

Visionary

The enthusiastic Thurman, who uses words like *global, gargantuan,* and *values-filled* to describe the vision of Opportunity, accepted his position after almost one year of driving a family camper cross-country with his wife, Penny, and their two children. He wanted to know his children better, so he turned over operations of the TV production company to the co-owner and hit the road with his family.

Eric Thurman the visionary is like Opportunity's first president, Alfred Whittaker. Both men gave up lucrative careers to answer God's call. Whittaker had served as president of Bristol Meyers and later Mennen, but during his visits overseas he saw a need to make people less dependent economically and more fulfilled spiritually. He teamed with Ross Clemenger, a Canadian missionary to Columbia, to found the Institute for International Development Inc. (IIDI), an agency motivated by "the example of Christ in His concern with meeting the needs of the poor." Beginning in Columbia, the two men and their supporters sought to "increase the income of the majority through the creation of job opportunities."

Today IIDI has become Opportunity International and has attracted the attention and support of agencies ranging from the United States Agency for International Development (USAID), foundations, and corporations to churches and individuals.

Ongoing challenges

The challenges before Opportunity remain immense: to bring business enterprise and evangelism to the poor and oppressed regions of the world. Thurman and his staff hope to set partner agencies deep behind the former Iron Curtain, helping Albania and Romania as well as Bulgaria. In early 1994 they opened an agency in Soweto, an all-black enclave near Johannesburg, South Africa.

Meanwhile, from Nizhni Novgorod, Russia, to Nagpur, India, new jobs continue to be a unique way to communicate the gospel. In Nagpur, loan recipients receive not only money and training but prayer. "Part of the deal when our people come to meet with you," Nagpur agency director P. Y. Singh tells borrowers, "is that we will pray that God will prosper the business and give you wisdom to know what you need to do."

The impact on recipients has been notable. Most businesses are outdoors in the villages. Opportunity's consultations often "turn into street meetings," Thurman says. "The neighbors see the consultant. They listen to the discussion, ask questions of the consultant and vendor about the product and sales. And they observe the counselor as he prays and helps their neighbor. As a result, many become interested in Christianity. Many have become believers. The gospel is communicated; it is culturally connected."

James Vincent

Further Reading

Gray, Helen T. "Beyond the Quick Fix Is Opportunity International." *Kansas City Star* (July 11, 1992): E-10.

"Income-Generating Projects for Poverty Alleviation." *Transformation Newsletter* (April–June 1990): 12–14.

"The Oxford Declaration on Christian Faith and Economics." *Transformation Newsletter* (April–June 1990): 10–14.

Samuel, Vinay, and Chris Sugden, eds. *The Church in Response to Human Need.* Grand Rapids: Eerdmans, 1987.

The Challenge

TOWARD 2000
The Great Commission

Therefore go and make disciples of all nations, baptizing them in the name of the Father and of the Son and of the Holy Spirit, and teaching them to obey everything I have commanded you. And surely I am with you always, to the very end of the age. (Matthew 28:19–20).

If we gaze at a Michelin world map, we are bedazzled by a welter of colors outlining the 195 political nations of our globe. But if we allow our mental eyes to make a transition from flat paper surfaces to peer into the international faces of the some 5,506 million people of our world, we see myriads of babies, children, youth, and adults—truly red and yellow, black and white, with browns and all other shades worked in-between, each one precious in God's sight.

Then this picture fades, and another emerges in our mind's eye: the nearly six thousand identified unreached people groups of our world and the 4,564 language groups without Scripture in their mother tongue.

The image shifts again, and we begin to perceive other diverse spiritual dimensions of our world: the massive Muslim, Hindu, and Buddhist religious blocks in the heart of the 10/40 Window. (Often called the "resistant belt," this window is a rectangle stretching from West Africa to East Asia, from 10° north latitude to 40° north of the Equator where the majority of the world's Muslims, Hindus, and Buddhists reside. It is in this geographical block we find the least evangelized countries, peoples, and cities, the heart of Islam, Hinduism, and Buddhism, and in which the remaining task requires a new analysis and distribution of our total Christian resources.) We observe the pain of planet earth as God's creation groans and people created in His image destroy and are destroyed.

But our gaze finally turns toward the glorious images of Psalm 96, where the Old Testament writer exults in God's love and passion for the world:

Sing to the Lord a new song; sing to the Lord, all the earth. Sing to the Lord, praise his name; proclaim his salvation day after day. Declare his glory among the nations, his marvelous deeds among all peoples (vv. 1–3).

Looking into the future we see that majestic parade of the nations—far greater than any Olympic opening ceremony—which the great apostle John personally witnessed in Revelation 7:9–10:

After this I looked and there before me was a great multitude that no one could count, from every nation, tribe, people and language, standing before the throne and in front of the Lamb. . . And they cried out in a loud voice: "Salvation belongs to our God, who sits on the throne, and to the Lamb."

We are humbled and awed by this splendid sight.

Even now, we know that the Gwandará people of Nigeria will be present at that parade. Who are they? Their story illustrates what this book has been about, what God has done and is doing today in our world, and the role that each of us has the opportunity of playing in God's kingdom enterprise.[1] This northern Nigerian agricultural people group, numbering close to ten thousand, had existed for most of its history untouched by the gospel. Then teams of dedicated European and North American missionaries on two different occasions attempted to penetrate this spirit-worshiping people group with the good news—but to no avail. They withdrew without seeing tangible evidence of God's breakthrough. It seemed so fruitless, the Gwandará so unreceptive.

Nonetheless, about ten years ago yet a

An American missionary practices music with Christians in Ivory Coast, West Africa.

third missionary team of ambassadors for Christ accepted the challenge to proclaim Christ among this unreached people group. Christian missionaries moved into the new territory with their families and received permission from the local elders and leaders to live on and to cultivate the land. The new team already spoke Hausa; so the main barriers they faced were not linguistic but cultural and spiritual.

Gradually trust developed, and over time the missionaries realized that in "deep Hausa" this people group was called not the "Gwandará" but the "Gwandará-wara." What was the difference? The term "Gwandará-wara" speaks of "a people who prefer to dance." Where did this name come from? As the missionaries spoke with the old storytellers, they learned that early in the nineteenth century Muslim armies had invaded Nigeria from further north, forcing conversions at sword point. A few people groups such as the Gwandará-wara had rejected Islam because they disliked the rules and legalism of the new religion and they preferred the freedom of their spirit-worship; they would rather dance than choose Islam. And that is how they got their unique name.

The missionaries returned to their homes and discussed the situation: "How does this new information shape our communication? What could be a new way to present the gospel of Jesus to these people who so love to dance?" Instead of stamping out indigenous cultural patterns, they yearned to speak of a gospel of grace and liberty, communicating it in ways that the people would understand. One of their methods was unique: they would dance the Word of God to the Gwandará-wara people. Appropriate rhythms and movements began to unveil the Creator and His creation story of redemption; they moved on through the story of the nation Israel into the life, ministry, death, resurrection, and ascension of our Lord Christ. The Holy Spirit used the Gospels and the book of Acts to break through with supernatural power, and the first converts turned to Jesus Christ.

Today the church of Jesus Christ is established among the Gwandará-wara. But who were these creative missionaries who prior to finding the cultural key to the Gwandará-wara had been equipped in their own cross-cultural training program? They were not white-skinned North Americans nor Europeans. They were some of the 888 African cross-cultural missionaries of the Evangelical Missionary Society. This is the mission agency of the Evangelical Church of West Africa, one of the largest Christian denominations in all of Africa with more than two million attenders.

And where did the ECWA church come from—with its 3,265 churches and congregations, thirteen vernacular Bible schools, and five Bible colleges and seminaries; with its publications program; with its powerful rural, educational, and medical ministry; with its scores of highly trained and gifted Nigerian leaders? God's glory chose to bless a foreign mission agency to establish His church in Nigeria. The ECWA church and its EMS flow out of Sudan Interior Mission's one hundred years of faithful ministry there. Some of the EMS missionaries themselves are first-generation believers in Christ, imbued with a passion to take Christ to the unreached people groups of their own country. The hardships and faithfulness of earlier Western missionary efforts are now paying remarkably rich spiritual dividends. More than ever, indigenous missionaries are now presenting the gospel cross-culturally in very effective ways. This represents an exciting

development in the efforts of Christians worldwide to fulfill the Great Commission.

We do not want to sound a triumphalistic note. But the planting of the Gwandará- wara church is symbolic of the breakthroughs in evangelization that have taken place within the last twenty years throughout the world. Indeed the story of God's sovereign work to bring glory to His name in our planet is nothing less than stunning. For today there are millions of ambassadors for Christ, from every walk of life who are presenting the gospel on street corners, in office buildings, in huts, almost anywhere. They work in the mixed contexts of wealth or poverty, of freedom or persecution, of low or high tech, and certainly in that of personal relationships. Our God is still sending His spokespersons throughout the world, and He is still the God of the miraculous. From the perspective of the global church of Christ, the nineteenth century is often called the "Great Century of Missions." The twentieth century could be called the "Transition from Colonial to Post-Colonial Missions," and the twentyfirst century may become the "Great Age of the Globalized Christian Church."

Translating the Bible into a new tongue in Papua New Guinea.

A Billy Graham Crusade in northern New Jersey, USA, September 1991.

Peering into the next millennium is a popular pursuit among both secularists and religious commentators. In our own reading of the world and its future, we want to give the priority to a biblical agenda as well as reflect upon the agenda that comes from our hurting world. Patrick Johnstone, author of *Operation World,* aptly comments about the discrepancy that sometimes exists between these agendas:

The visual media have served to erode the faith of believers in God's present sovereignty in the world. Television cameramen, like vultures, swoop on the wars, famines, disasters and tragedies of this world. The beautiful, wholesome and good is less camera-worthy, so what God does and what God's servants are achieving are rarely noticed.

The view from a heavenly vantage point is very different. There is a titanic struggle going on in the heavenlies between the forces of the Lord Jesus and the hosts of darkness and the effects in our world are dramatic. Yet the victory has already been won on the Cross. There are many evidences . . . here are some of global significance. The

unprecedented harvest being won. We are living in the time of the largest ingathering of peoples into the kingdom of God that the world has even seen.[2]

This will also be our perspective. First, as global Christians we will survey the condition of our planet. Second, we will develop a perspective on the Christian church. Third, we will scan some of the major challenges facing the evangelical church today. We will conclude with a personal call to each one of us to consider what might be our own involvement in fulfilling the Great Commission and with a call to pray with confidence in our loving heavenly Father for our brothers and sisters in Christ worldwide as they are "ambassadors for Christ."

A survey of global issues

Students of history understand the varied components that help explain why certain things happen the way they do: climate, geography, natural disasters; individuals, peoples, and cultures; population growth; violence and wars; political, economic, and religious competition. But the Christian also discerns the specific variable of God's supernatural power at work. He or she keenly detects the presence and power of evil supernaturalism but is conscious that the battle is not equally balanced between good and evil. Our sovereign God is the Lord of the entire universe and of all human history. He is ultimately in control of "His story." We should never forget this.

As citizens of a world approaching the historical hinge of the next millennium, we would like to consider four selected major realities that affect our planet as well as our understanding of our Christian global role.

First, we are observing the emergence of a new geopolitical lineup. Many citizens of the United States grew up with the classic map that places North America smack in the center of the world. This "Mercator projection" was originally designed to magnify the northern latitudes—particularly Europe—and minimize the southern ones. And patriotic American map makers put the United States in the center even if this meant dividing Asia. But the power centers have shifted radically, with three major geopolitical players now emerging. By the turn of the century it is possible that the Pacific Rim nations will dominate the economic picture, if not the political-cultural one. Led by Japan and Korea, in cooperation with the smaller and rapidly industrializing Asian nations and with giant China as the wild card, this Pacific Rim coalition will exercise enormous influence. From a Christian perspective we also see God at work, for in some of these very same nations—Korea, China, Singapore—the church is vibrant, growing, and mission minded.

The second major competing world power team will be North America led by the United States. North America must compete in a new world of globalized economic networks that require greater industrial agility and governmental creativity.

The third block will be Europe, led economically by Germany and France (although the prognosis for a unified region is doubtful).

What about the church in these last two regions, North America and Europe, with their rich heritages and fabulous human and material resources? Sadly, the church suffers from the ravages of modernity and spiritual atrophy. Professor Martin Marty calls Europe and North America together the great "spiritual iceberg." We need to pray for God to send a humbling revival of supernatural power to melt the spiritual indifference of the "West" and to renew the church with the power of the Holy Spirit.

And what about the rest of the world? The "poor South" will probably—with significant exceptions—become more unstable, more dependent upon the wealthier "North," and even more marginalized as it continues to provide raw materials yet lacks control of technology, networks, electronics, and the information industry. While economic development will characterize a few stronger nations, many other nations of Africa, Latin America, and Asia will be characterized by the development of underdevelopment.

Second, we are experiencing striking population growth. About 78 percent of the world's population lives in the "less-developed" areas: most of Asia, all of Africa, Latin America, the Middle East, and the Caribbean. This means that only 22 percent of the world's people live in the "more developed areas": Europe, the United States, Canada, Australia, New Zealand, and most of the former USSR. What's more, the "less developed" areas will double their population in only thirty-five years, while the latter will take—if ever—162 years to double.[1]

The implications of this growth factor are staggering from both a secular and Christian perspective. Urbanization, industrialization, violence, voluntary and involuntary immigrations, changing economic foundations, modernity, and secularization all affect the lives of people. Violence displaces millions, some brutally stripped from their families, cultures, and communities. For many our world is not a pleasant place to live. There are some 305 world-class cities of more than one million inhabitants, many of them filled with urban poor and inaccessible to traditional Christian missions.

Third, ours is a world of bankrupted economic ideologies and violent neotribalization. It is hard to comprehend the significance of the 1989 collapse of the Berlin Wall, symbol of the death of Marxism in Eastern Europe and the USSR; its death knell is not yet heard in China. Semi-free enterprise structures now appear in varied permutations, but all economic systems ultimately are secular and do not respond warmly to Christian values. Moving, at times violently, into the more recent vacuum of nonviable political and economic systems are the newer strongmen of Serbia, Croatia, Russia, Bulgaria, Somalia, Zaire, Iraq, Libya, and Peru. At the same time our world has seen in the last decade a surprising transition toward some model of democracy (Western and Asian), market economy, and modernization, in Latin America and in some Asian nations. Africa has not yet made this transition.

Tribalization rips apart the tender fabric of nations such as Yugoslavia, Somalia, Zaire, Kenya, India, Indonesia, South Africa, and many republics of the old USSR. The tragic reality is that most of today's political conflicts also have religious roots. Think of the spiritual competition in places such as Bosnia, Serbia, Croatia, India, Egypt, South Africa, Ireland, Mexico, the Ukraine, Iran, Israel/Palestine, Armenia and Nagorno-Karabakh, Nigeria, Chad, Ethiopia, and the Sudan. Not since the Holocaust have we heard of "ethnic cleansing" as has taken place in the former Yugoslavia.

Fourth, we are witnessing a striking seesaw ambivalence between secularizing modernism and competing spiritualities. Modernism, with its emphasis on international technology, the capitalist economy, centralized states, mass media, and globalization, encircles both individuals and the world. According to Os Guinness,[4] modernism cuts off transcendence, chokes off the sense of totality and the integration of faith, closes off tradition, and corrupts truth into shallow sentiment. This is an international development few of us understand fully and for which few are prepared to offer innovative Christian responses.

On the other side of this seesaw we observe a global revival of world religions coupled with varieties of personal explorations into the supernatural. Islam has renewed its missionary zeal and program, financing it with endless petro-dollars. Muslim leaders have selected Britain as their beachhead. Every week in Britain one new Koranic school or mosque is opened. The rate is similar in France and Germany. Surprisingly, Hinduism and even Buddhism have developed contemporary missionary dimensions. These three major Eastern religions take advantage of the European and North American freedoms to express and propagate religious faith, but they do not reciprocate in their countries of origin or stronghold.

When you travel through the West—Europe and North America—you discover that particular mixture of spiritualism and secularism known as the "New Age." Clearly, while Christianity expands rapidly, our Christian message is not the only religious one in the world's ideological marketplace competing for the hearts and allegiances of the peoples of our world.

Patrick Johnstone gives us a survey of the global religious statistics. There is surprising news in these statistics regarding the spread of the Christian faith.

Minarets in Cairo, Egypt. Islam is increasing in missionary zeal.

Summary of the World Religions

	Percentage	Millions	Annual Growth
Muslim	19.6 %	1,035	2.9%
Hindu	13.5 %	716	2.0%
Buddhist/Eastern	11.6 %	613	2.1%
Christian	32.8 %	1,734	2.3%
Protestant	10.3 %	543	3.3%
Evangelical	5.7 %	314	5.4%
Roman Catholic	16.8 %	892	1.3%
Orthodox	4.1 %	215	3.3%
Other	1.6 %	84	—
Animist/traditional	2.7 %	144	0.2%
Jews	0.25%	13	−1.3%
Other religions	2.8 %	145	—
Non-religions	18.3 %	969	4.5%

A perspective on the Christian church

This report of the advancing gospel is astonishing. Jesus prophesied that even the Satanic strongholds would not withstand the advance of the kingdom of God. We can look at the status of the Christian churches from a variety of perspectives. Numbers are relatively easy to count and compare; the diverse Christin "families" have their own identity. Spiritual movements are more difficult to detect and evaluate; measures that determne internal personal spirituality are even more elusive. But let us examine four striking characteristics that lead evangelicals into praise and intercession.

First, Christianity is truly globalized. This reflects a massive epicenter shift for the church of Christ. The old Western paradigm saw the center of Christianity somewhere on an axis between northern Europe and North America. But the new global picture shows the stunning movement of the Spirit of God throughout the world.

Let's think back over the last nearly two hundred years, since the year 1800, or the general starting point of this book's story line. Let's arbitrarily divide the world into "North" (Europe, North America, Australia, and New Zealand) and "South" (Asia, Latin America, Africa, most of the South Pacific, the Caribbean, and Middle East). Where has the church been in percentages throughout these years? Patrick Johnstone again helps us:

The growth in Eurasia, Asia, and Africa has been such that the centre of gravity of Christianity moved away from the West in the early '70's. Evangelical growth has been more dramatic. The post-war surge of evangelical mission thrusts has borne much fruit. In the West there has been a slow, but steady growth in contrast to the decline of the Church in general. In the so-called mission fields it has been a different story. Evangelicals in the West grew from 57.7 million in 1960 to 95.9 million in 1990 with an average annual gropwth of 1.7 percent. In the rest of the world, the 1960 total of Evangelicals of 29 million grew to 208 million in 1990, an average annual growth of 6.8 percent.[2]

EPICENTER SHIFT OF THE WORLD'S CHRISTIANS

	1800	1900	1960	1980	1993	2000
NORTH	99%	91%	68%	50%	38%	23%?
SOUTH	1%	9%	32%	50%	62%	77%?

This incredible story should cause us to leap with joy in our sovereign God who so greatly used Europe, Australia, New Zealand, and North America as the base to send this Western force to the world.

But now the church is truly global, with a massive mission base to send and support an equally large missionary force. We in the West are now world partners with Africans, Asians, Latins, and islanders in the universal task of world evangelization and stengthening of the churches. The harvest fields now include Europe and the United States. Praise God for the new harvest forces! Of some

The Global Protestant Cross-Cultural Harvest Force

"Non-West"

Africa	12,829
Asia	23,681
Latin America	4,482
Caribbean	262
Eurasia	351?
Middle East	277
S. Pacific	967

West

North America	64,378
Europe	19,564
Australia/New Zealand	5,244

127,803 evangelical missionaries, 85,325 are from the West and 42,478 are from the "non-West." As you note the distribution remember that the "non-West" force grows more rapidly than the one in the West.

Second, Christian growth is accelerated in some areas but painfully slow, if advancing at all, in others. The African continent is turning to Christianity, and it is a historic first to witness such a shift of basic spiritual allegiance. Johnstone says, "In 1900 African Christians were eight million (2.5 million Protestants) and 10% of the population (2.5 million people). In 1990 this had risen to 275 million and 57% of the population (275 million people) and is likely to reach 396 million and 61% by 2000." The African evangelical growth has gone from 1.9 percent of Africans in 1900 to 13.2 percent in 1990. Though this is but a sevenfold growth in percentages, it is a thirtyfold growth in numbers.

Worldwide Protestant growth is 3.5 percent per year. However, yearly evangelical growth is much more rapid at 5.4 percent; and the surprising Pentecostal annual growth of 8.1 percent shows where the real advance takes place. The most remarkable Pentecostal increase is seen in Latin America, where 75 percent of evangelicals are charismatic and where 40 percent of the world's ninety-three million Pentecostals live. Why such Pentecostal growth? Because they empower a witnessing laity, because of their concept of the Holy Spirit, because of their organization, and because of their vibrant worship.

Latin America, then, is also reporting an usually rapid advance. In 1900 there were an estimated 250,000 Latin evangelicals, in 1960 6.7 million, in 1980 21 million, in 1990 46 million, and the projection for 2000 passes 80 million believers. Currently Latin American evangelicals number somewhere around 11.1 percent of the population, with a continental annual growth rate of 8.8 percent.

Reports from China simply boggle the imagination. With 1,179 million people, it is the world population giant. What has God done in China? When the Communists took over about 1950, it was estimated that China had less than one million Christians. I well remember during my days as a student at Moody Bible Institute that we would pray for "the disappeared church of China." China proves that the Holy Spirit knows no closed doors to His power. In the context of violent persecution, terrible poverty, and unprecedented restrictions Christians persevered and the church grew. One seasoned "China watcher" based in Hong Kong has estimated some 25–30 million Christians, others suggest a figure close to 50 million. Patrick Johnstone offers a higher figure of 58 million Chinese Protestants and some 8.7 million Catholics, totaling 66.7 million Christians for the entire nation.[5] Will China ever open up to the West? Possibly in the next century, but pray God that evangelicals do not invade China with the same "Lone Ranger" mentality with which they have moved into Russia!

Our East Asian scenario of growth moves across Indonesia, the Philippines, Singapore, and Korea. In Korea you find the world's largest churches of Pentecostals, Presbyterians, and Methodists. Johnstone affirms that "Asian evangelicals probably surpassed the number in North America in about 1987 and in the entire Western world in 1991."

But not all the regions report exciting statistics. The other story speaks of stagnation, of decades of tough slogging, seed sowing, and watering, and a limited harvest so far. Asia alone has eighty-nine world-class cities of more than one million people, most of them unevangelized. India has 897 million people and only seventeen million evangelicals. The Hindu block has only been marginally touched by the gospel. The least evangelized countries of Asia also include

Afghanistan, Bangladesh, Bhutan, Cambodia, and Mongolia.

And what about the cradle of the Christian faith, the Middle East, with so much lifeless orthodoxy? The seat of Islamic power, this is one of the most gospel-resistant areas of the world. At the same time we must interpret the peace movement in that area from a missiological perspective. How will these changes facilitate the movement of the gospel? Africa north of the Sahara is Muslim and violently opposed to the gospel. In Latin America certain countries like Ecuador, Paraguay, Mexico, and Uruguay are resistant to the gospel, stark contrasts to harvest lands such as Brazil, Chile, and Guatemala.

Nor should we ignore the nearly six thousand unreached people groups. The majority of these groups are found in the less evangelized regions. The church will be established in those areas primarily by long-term missionary teams who must invest ten to thirty years to learn the language, understand the culture, and love the people as they communicate the gospel by the power of the Spirit.

A similar challenge faces us in regard to the world-class cities. We praise God for movements such as "AD 2000 and Beyond," which motivate, mobilize, and network intercession and action for world evangelization with a particular focus on the 10/40 Window.

Third, this growth has come with a high price tag. In many regions of the world the advance of the gospel has come not in the context of prestige, nor economic power, nor public official acceptance of Christians. Quite the contrary. In spite of persecution that in some cases has decimated Christian families, churches, and entire communities, the growth continues. For example, the stories that reach us from the Sudan are heartbreaking. The harassment and persecution of believers in the Middle East is hard for North Americans to understand. At the same time it was Iraq's invasion of Kuwait that amazingly opened the Kurds to the gospel for the first time in history! Using the broadest possible definition for "Christian" (from nominal to biblically committed), statistician David Barrett reports that just in 1992 there were 308,000 Christian martyrs, and estimates that in 1993, 150,000 Christians will die for their faith.[6]

Fourth, the Christian churches are challenged to a biblical, holistic ministry. In the providence of God most evangelicals have moved beyond the false dichotomy between "gospel" and "social responsibility." The Great Commission and the Great Commandment are partners. Demonstrating compassion through relief and development projects has served as a bridge for the gospel to be proclaimed in power and truth. Today churches exist among formerly unreached Muslim communities in Ethiopia simply because Christians in the name of Christ dug wells and established credibility for the gospel.

Bryant L. Myers in "The Changing Shape of World Mission"[7] pictorially presents the human reality behind the stark statistics of our hurting planet: a world of contrasting income, the status of the world's poor and why they cannot catch up, the inadequate conditions of water and health, the fact of more people and less arable land, child mortality and the plague of abortion, the exploding urban poor, the insidious advance of the structures of sin, and those particularly sinned against—the refugees, homeless, children and women in servitude, youth without a real future, illiterates (so many women), and other distressing facts.

Challenges to the Christian church

First, all churches throughout the world face the tension between vitality and atrophy. The clear evidence of evangelical vitality is seen today in those countries formerly thought of as the "mission fields." If you travel across North America and Europe, Asia, Africa, Latin America, the Pacific, Caribbean, and the Middle East, the overall impression you receive is that Western churches struggle with nominalism, declining denominations, and spiritual lassitude. So many churches have succumbed to the seduction of the spirit of the age. The West is so rich, perhaps too rich, in human and material resources. It is more on the cutting edge of the advancing church that we see hearty vitality and accompanying maturity to stabilize the growth.

Encouraging news for Christians is the rapid growth of a vast international network of informal and formal prayer movements. Spearheaded by both women and men these networks focus on two major requests. One is for repentance and revival of the church, particularly in North America and Europe. The other is for world evangelization, particularly for the unreached peoples of the world that live in that massive unevangelized block of the 10/40 Window.

Granted, not all is good news in church growth, and we must seriously question the reliability of some numerical reports. Let us be accurate in our counting, checking and counter-checking our sources and data. Moreover we should keep in mind two major questions in our assessments: what is the spiritual quality of the church we are attempting to analyze, and what is the nature of true church growth? A church may boast a huge membership and be spiritually impoverished, whereas a small church may be playing a vital role in Christ's kingdom. The challenge before the Western church is to seek godly humility and renewed spiritual vitality. The challenge before the non-Western church is to continue to grow, avoid the dangers of success, reduce the number of divisions, and transform numerical growth into spiritual maturity.

Second, the church around the world faces the challenge of biblical creativity in life, theology, and witness. In every region there are particular theological battles to wage. Some in particular, however, seem to cross boundaries. Our world is increasingly pluralistic, accepting all religions as equally valid and intolerant of any that would proclaim absolute truth. Biblical Christians are accused of intolerance and bigotry because we affirm the centrality and authority of the inspired Word of God and because we claim the uniqueness of Jesus Christ as the only Savior of mankind.

Internationally, as the church establishes itself in new countries and cultures, it must come to grips with its own biblio-theological integrity and cultural relevance. We have thought of healthy churches as those that are self-governing, self-supporting, self-reproducing. But we should add a newer healthy trait: self-theologizing—or "doing theology." This refers to the challenge of evangelical contextualization, rooted in Scripture and sensitive to differing worldviews and cultures. Systematic theologians from the West have established the major "theological categories." But Asian, African, and Latin American theologians discern other categories in Scripture. These godly evangelical thinkers who are faithful to the Word must be trusted as they apply Scripture to their own context.

Then, what must a local church look like? Sadly, visits around the world demonstrate how we continue to export our denominations with our particular ecclesiology and even our architecture. We can foresee, by God's grace, large numbers of converts to Christ from the Muslim, Hindu, Buddhist, and secular worlds. What will their new contextualized assemblies of believers look like? And in North America and Europe, where fresh contextualization must take place, what will the new churches look like?

Leadership is a third issue facing the global church. Men and women emerge into church leadership through varied routes. The traditional paths in the West tend to track through educational institutions as college and seminary graduates often become the key leaders. This is not generally true in the rest of the world, and increasingly in all the globe we will see more and more creative and committed leaders among ambassadors for Christ emerging from non-traditional routes. What's more, different cultures produce leadership with different styles, different problem-solving processes, different attitudes toward administrative structures and long-range planning.

Bible translators David Payne and Sanule Ashenico Campa in Lima, Peru.

The West has tended to call the leadership shots for the past hundred years. But as the global evangelical church has matured, it has produced its own competent and well-equipped leaders. Can the West generate international servant leaders who are able to work alongside and under non-Western colleagues? Will the West relinquish absolute control of the international and national agenda and purse strings? And will the non-West refrain from criticizing the West and assume mature responsibility for the agenda and develop its own set of material and human resources?

How will leaders be trained in the future? The World Evangelical Fellowship Theological Commission estimates that there are some thirty-five hundred evangelical theological institutions worldwide. But these alone cannot equip the vast numbers of new leaders desperately needed by the churches. New programs and centers must be developed, adding to the already creative resident and distant educational alternatives operating today on all educational levels—from preliterate to postgraduate. Moreover, laypersons from all walks of life need to be encouraged in their witness to their neighbors and friends.

And will the global evangelical leadership be godly and holy? An international plague has struck high-profile Christian leaders in every region. Pride, disregard of accountability, divisive spirit, the drive for power, a sense of invincibility, rationalizing of sin, all these are sabotaging our leaders, both male and female. How many more times must we bow our heads in tears, shamed and broken by the moral fall of yet another one of our respected leaders?

Finally, the global evangelical churches face the challenge of transition, partnership, and unity. Transition refers in part to the transfer of leadership from the older men and women to the younger ones. But this transition also speaks of the leadership shift from one of Western dominance and non-Western dependence to a new spirit of interdependence: not independence, which breeds non-Christian autonomy, but rather interdependence, which recognizes the varied gifts and resources in the global body of Christ.

Partnership has emerged as another vital challenge facing the church. In the past the West has controlled the agenda by virtue of the strength of its heritage, its powerful leaders, its human and material resources. The "younger churches" of Asia, Latin America, and Africa must not be seen as just cheap labor for the global harvest. These regions have tremendously gifted leaders and vital organizations that are making a significant impact right now. What will it take to foster genuine and practical partnership at all levels of ministry and structure?

Then there is the touchy subject of evangelical unity. We have had too much fractured infighting in the body of Christ. But just as in biblical Israel God placed the peoples into tribes and families, so today we are placed in spiritual families, each making our distinct contribution. Yet we must demonstrate that evangelicals are already spiritually united around foundational biblical beliefs and mission commitments. But today as never before biblical Christians have a responsibility and opportunity to demonstrate tangible unity. Does this call for a new power structure that will weaken Scripture and control churches and organizations worldwide? Absolutely not. Existing international networks and alliances, such as the World Evangelical Fellowship, are poised to provide an open international forum and network for biblical fellowship. They are also available to offer a unified front where needed to advance the gospel and to defend the rights of Christians when they are harassed and persecuted.

A final word

In the stories of this book, we trust that you have sensed the power of the dynamic Triune God at work through history. You have read the biographies of men and women who have lived in integrity, sought holiness, prayed, and whose ministry God has tangibly blessed. Some of their names are new to you, reflecting the epicenter change of the worldwide church of Jesus Christ.

We trust this book about ambassadors for Christ will have moved you to rejoice. But we also hope that it has prompted you to think about what your own role is in fulfilling Christ's Great Commission. None of us is without gifts to use in this divine cause. Although many of the persons described in this book were or are missionaries, others came from diverse walks of life. We are all "ambassadors for Christ," regardless what our occupation may be. If we are believers, the Great Commission is *our* commission. As Jesus was moved by compassion when He looked upon the multitudes, may the Holy Spirit so work in our lives that we will be moved by compassion to tell others about the Savior.

And may we also pray. Prayer always precedes an outpouring of the Spirit of God. If our own circumstances do now allow us to leave our homes, let alone go to foreign fields, we can still play a major role in fulfilling the Great Commission as prayer warriors. And those of us who may be more active ambassadors for Christ should be people who do not simply talk about prayer but actually pray.

The church of Jesus Christ will accomplish much more on its knees in the fulfillment of the Great Commission than we often suppose. Spiritual battles are won there. Many non-Western Christians bathe an area in prayer years before they send a first missionary into the region.

We are involved in a cosmic struggle. On the one hand, God's supernatural power is being poured out, and, on the other, the Satanic forces are releasing their entire battery of evil supernaturalism. Most of the battle takes place in the invisible spheres, but enough of it is seen on planet earth for us to believe in a powerful God whose forces are in combat with the evil one. It is not a war of equal forces. Christ will triumph, but there will be casualties on the battleground of our globe. We worship the unique Lord of history as we see His supernatural power being poured out in the multiple gifts of the Spirit.

Is history on the brink of being wrapped up? Will Christ return soon? We hope so! The historical and contemporary pieces of the cosmic chessboard seem to be in place for the divine checkmate and the glorious ensuing events surrounding the coming of our Lord. But even as we live in expectancy, we will also plan for the next hundred years;

for only the Father knows the times and the seasons.

Our Michelin map again attracts our attention. It has triggered a kaleidoscope of images and thoughts that represent the realities of today's swiftly changing world. How glad we are as believers that there is an unchanging, faithful, sovereign God who holds all the world in His hands. Jesus is building His church, and we are witnessing before our very eyes the preparation of the Bride for her Bridegroom. Let us rejoice even as we pray and persevere, for our destiny approaches when we will forever worship the Lamb, who alone is worthy of our praise for ever and ever and ever. Amen!

William Taylor

Notes

1. Personal conversations with ECWA leader Panya Baba, and SIM Int. executives.

2. Patrick Johnstone, *Operation World* (Grand Rapids: Zondervan, 1993).

3. *1993 World Population Data Sheet* of the Population Reference Bureau, Inc. 1875 Connecticut Avenue, NW, Suite 520, Washington, D.C. 20009.

4. Os Guinness, "The Impact of Modernization," *Proclaim Christ Until He Comes* (Minneapolis: World Wide Publications, 1989), 283–88.

5. "Counting China's Christians," *Christianity Today,* 21 June 1993, 60.

6. David Barrett, "Annual Statistical Table on Global Mission, 1992," *International Bulletin of Missionary Research* (January 1992), 26–27; "Annual Statistical Table on Global Mission, 1993," *International Bulletin of Missionary Research* (January 1993), 22–23.

7. Bryant L. Myers, "The Changing Shape of World Mission," *1993–95 Mission Handbook,* MARC (1993), 1–37.

INDEX

Picture Acknowledgments

Ruth Graham Dienert: pp. 68, 71
Ebenezer Pictures/Susanna Burton: p. 240
Mary Evans Picture Library: pp. 43, 47, 53
David Fisher: pp. 267, 268, 269
Harold Fuller: pp. 221, 222, 231
Guy Gardner: p. 95
Joe Gibbs Organization: p. 83
Billy Graham Center, Wheaton: pp. 181, 182, 183, 280
Billy Graham Evangelistic Association: pp. 283, 285, 287, 339
Steve Green Ministries: p. 115
Elisabeth Elliot Gren: pp. 289, 290, 291, 293
Foreign Mission Board of the Southern Baptist Convention: pp. 153, 155
Manfred Grohe: p. 259
Carl F. H. Henry: p. 76
Jon Hinkson: pp. 263, 265
David M. Howard: p. 135
IVP, Leicester: pp. 225, 227
Dr Sang-Bok David Kim: pp. 309, 311, 312, 313
Cliffe Knechtle: pp. 97, 99
Olive Liefeld: pp. 128, 131
Josh McDowell Ministry: pp. 321, 323
Tom Maharias: pp. 101, 103
The Mansell Collection: pp. 27, 39
NASA: p. 93
NNI/Chris Woehr: p. 139
Dr. Dieumème Noelliste: p. 145
OM Publishing: p. 129
OM Ships: pp. 25, 241
Opportunity International: pp. 330, 333
John Perkins: p. 81
Jim & Carol Pluedemann: pp. 217, 219
Prison Fellowship: p. 75
Jay Russell: pp. 305, 306
Russian Ministries: pp. 255, 256
Edith Schaeffer: pp. 248, 251, 252
Mrs M. Thompson: pp. 201, 203
Lasse Thorseth: p. 197
Tiger Design Ltd: p. 341
Sammy Tippitt Ministries: pp. 273, 274/5
Trans World Radio: pp. 300, 301, 302
Joshua Tsutada: pp. 10, 12
U.S. Center for World Mission: pp. 315, 317
Vereinigte Evangelische Mission Bildarchiv: pp. 147, 149
Willow Creek Community Church: pp. 107, 109
World Vision: p. 297
Wycliffe Bible Translators Inc.: pp. 119, 120, 121, 123, 126, 337, 338, 345
Ravi Zacharias: pp. 327, 329
Zefa: title page

Illustrations

Shirley Bellwood: pp. 57, 151, 166, 193, 237
Donald Harley: p. 129
Mark Peppé: p. 34

Every effort has been made to trace copyright holders and to attribute copyright correctly. The editors and publishers wish to apologize for any errors or omissions.